1 MONTH OF
FREE
READING

at

www.ForgottenBooks.com

By purchasing this book you are eligible for one month membership to ForgottenBooks.com, giving you unlimited access to our entire collection of over 1,000,000 titles via our web site and mobile apps.

To claim your free month visit:

www.forgottenbooks.com/free524217

ISBN 978-0-666-19132-8
PIBN 10524217

THE

LAW OF LIENS

IN

PENNSYLVANIA.

BY

WILLIAM TRICKETT.

IN TWO VOLUMES.

VOL. II.

———•———

JERSEY CITY, N. J.:
FREDERICK D. LINN & CO.,
Law Publishers and Booksellers.
1882.

Y, PRINTER
N, N. J.

CONTENTS OF VOLUME II

CHAPTER XVIII.

LIEN OF WAGES.

CHAPTER XIX.

LIEN OF DECEDENT'S DEBTS.

CHAPTER XX.

TESTAMENTARY LIENS.

CHAPTER XXI.

LIEN OF RECOGNIZANCES IN THE ORPHANS' COURT.

CHAPTER XXII.

LIEN OF RECOGNIZANCES OF SHERIFFS AND CORONERS.

CHAPTER XXIII.

LIEN OF TRANSCRIPTS FROM ORPHANS' COURT.

CHAPTER XXIV.

LIEN OF AWARDS OF ARBITRATORS.

CHAPTER XXV.

STATUTORY DOWER.

CHAPTER XXVI.

LIEN OF REPORT OF COUNTY AUDITORS.

CHAPTER XXVII.

LIEN OF DEBTS DUE THE STATE.

CHAPTER XXVIII.

LIEN OF TAX COLLECTOR'S ARREARS.

CHAPTER XXIX.

LIEN OF GROUND RENT LANDLORD.

CHAPTER XXX.

LESSOR'S LIEN UPON THE LEASEHOLD.

CHAPTER XXXI.

LIEN OF SURPLUS BONDS.

CHAPTER XXXII.

LIEN FOR PURCHASE MONEY.

CHAPTER XXXIII.

LIENS ARISING FROM PARTITION OF LANDS.

CHAPTER XXXIV.

LIEN OF TAXES.

CHAPTER XXXV.

MUNICIPAL LIENS.

CHAPTER XXXVI.

LIEN OF BAILEE.

CHAPTER XXXVII.

LIEN OF CORPORATIONS ON CAPITAL STOCK.

CHAPTER XXXVIII.

LIEN ON BANK DEPOSITS.

CHAPTER XXXIX.

LIEN OF UNITED STATES ON DISTILLERY.

CHAPTER XL.

LIEN OF COLLATERAL INHERITANCE TAX.

CHAPTER XLI.

LIEN IN ESCHEAT.

CHAPTER XLII.

SUBROGATION OF LIENS.

CHAPTER XLIII.

DIVESTITURE OF LIENS.

CHAPTER XVIII.,

LIEN OF WAGES.

Railroads and Public Improvement Companies.

§ 472. The resolution of the general assembly adopted 21st January, 1843, [P. L. 367,] declared it unlawful for any incorporated railroad or other public internal improvement company to assign, mortgage, convey or transfer[1] any real or personal property of the company without the written consent of any contractors, laborers and workmen employed in the construction or repair of such improvements, so as to defeat, postpone, endanger or delay these creditors, and rendered null and void any such mortgage, conveyance, etc., made in contravention of this resolution. . The act of April 4th, 1862, [P. L., 235,][2] provides that if such company shall divest itself of its real or personal property, contrary to the provisions of this resolution, the contractor, laborer or workman may obtain judgment against the company, and then issue a *sci. fa.* thereon, with notice to any person or incorporated company claiming to hold or own the said property.

§ 473. The lien of the contractor is superior to that of a subsequent mortgage, though he fail to recover judgment for his debt until after the mortgage is executed.[3] And if such mortgage is executed without his consent, and under it

---

[1] A lease of a railroad is such conveyance or transfer. Penna. and Delaware R. R. Co. v. Leuffer, 84 Pa. St. 168.

[2] This act does not widen the classes preferred by the act of 1843, but simply extends their remedies.

[3] Shamokin Valley, etc., R. R. Co. v. Malone, 85 Pa. St. 25; Pittsb , C. and St. Louis Railway Co. v. Marshall, 85 Pa. St. 187; Fox v. Seal, 22 Wall. 424; Tyrone and Clearfield R. R. Co. v. Jones, 79 Pa. St. 60; Woods v. Pittsb., etc., Railway Co., 11 W. N. C. 130.

the property and franchises of the corporation are sold, and the purchasers become incorporated under a new name, the contractor, not being able to obtain a judgment against the extinct corporation, may, by a bill in equity, obtain a decree that the mortgage was void as to him, that the new company shall pay his debt, and that, in default of payment, the property and franchises of the old corporation vested in them shall be sold, and the proceeds applied to his debt.[1] An assignment of stock subscriptions, made before the debt due the contractor arises, is valid, without his consent.[2] When, with the assent of a contractor, a railroad company agrees to pay a part of the money due him, to a sub-contractor, the sub-contractor is, in respect to this claim, not within the protection of the resolution of 21st January, 1843.[3] One who contracts to furnish 5,000 railroad ties, is not a contractor in the sense of the act of 1843. If he were, every man who furnished a pound of spikes to the railroad would have a lien.[4]

Acts of 7th April, 1849, 22d April, 1854, and 30th March, 1859.

§ 474. The act of 30th March, 1859, [P. L. 318,] makes a first lien upon collieries, and the property in or about the same, in the counties of Schuylkill, Northumberland, Somerset, Carbon, Washington and Dauphin, the wages for a period not exceeding six months, and for an amount not greater than $100, due to miners, mechanics, laborers or clerks employed about the mining of coal, whether by the

---

[1] Shamokin Valley, etc., R. R Co. v. Malone, 85 Pa. St 25; Woods v. Pittsb., etc., Railway Co., 11 W. N. C. 130.

[2] McBroom & Wood's Appeal, 44 Pa. St. 92. If, to a bill in equity on the mortgage, the contractor is made a party, but fails to appear and make proof of the superiority of his claim, a decree that the mortgage is a first lien will be conclusive on him. Woods v. Pittsb., etc., Railway Co., 11 W N C. 130.

[3] McBroom & Wood's Appeal, 44 Pa. St. 92 Sub-contractors, and laborers employed by sub-contractors, are not protected by the acts of 21st January, 1843, and 4th April, 1862. Hopkins' Appeal, 38 Leg. Int. 12

[4] Bell's Appeal, 38 Leg. Int. 12.

owners of the soil or by lessees of coal mines, by individuals or by corporations. This lien prevails against liens not of record prior to the passage of the act; against all mortgages or other liens on coal leases, or coal-mining rights, and the machinery and fixtures appurtenant thereto, executed after the passage of the act, and against the landlord's claim for rent beyond that of one full month and any fraction of a month, accruing immediately prior to the levy in execution, or otherwise, of the property. The act of April 22d, 1854, [P. L. 480,] directs that when an assignment for the benefit of creditors is made by any person or corporation, whether of real or personal property, the wages of miners, mechanics and laborers employed by such person or corporation shall, to an amount not exceeding $100, be paid before debts due other creditors. In case of the dissolution, failure or insolvency of the corporations provided for by the act of April 7th, 1849, [P. L. 563,] and by subsequent acts, this act provides that all debts due to operatives or laborers for services performed, for any period, shall first be paid from the assets.

The Act of 2d April, 1849.

§ 475. The act of April 2d, 1849, [P. L. 337,] applicable only to the counties of Schuylkill, Berks, Washington, Centre, Somerset, Westmoreland and Carbon, gives a preference to the extent of $50, to the wages of miners, mechanics and laborers, employed about the mining of coal, about forges, furnaces, rolling mills, nail factories, machine shops or foundries, when their employer, whether a person or a chartered company, shall make an assignment of real or personal property on account of inability to pay his debts. Also, when a levy is made on the property of the employer, under executions, landlords' warrants, attachments and writs of a similar nature, and the miner, laborer or mechanic gives notice of his claim before the actual sale, such claim, to the extent of $50, must be paid as landlords' claims for rent are payable.

The Act of 9th April, 1872.

§ 476. The act of April 9th, 1872, [P. L. 47,] provides that any miner, mechanic, laborer or clerk, to whom, for labor and services rendered, moneys are due by any person or chartered company, whether owners, lessees, contractors or under-owners, of any works, mines, manufactory or other business, where such clerks, miners or mechanics are employed, shall have a lien on the interest of his employer in such works, mines, etc., or other property connected therewith in carrying on said business, (in case such works, mines, etc., shall be transferred by execution or otherwise,) for wages earned at so much *per diem* or otherwise, within six months next preceding such transfer and sale, and not exceeding in amount $200.[1] Excepted from the operation of this act were contracts existing, or liens of record vested, prior to its passage.[2]

§ 477. In all cases of execution, landlords' warrants, attachments or other writs of a similar nature, against any person or chartered company engaged as aforesaid, such miner, laborer, mechanic or clerk must give notice of his claim, in writing, to the officer executing the writ, at any time before the actual sale of the property levied on. Such officer must then pay to such miner, etc., out of the proceeds of the sale, the amount each is legally entitled to receive, not exceeding $200. When such person or chartered company engaged as aforesaid, shall become insolvent, or make an assignment for the benefit of creditors, or execution shall be issued against them, the lien of the laborer, etc., shall extend to all the property of said person or chartered company.

[1] The provision requiring the filing of the claim in the prothonotary's office was repealed by the act of May 8th, 1874, [P. L. 120.]

[2] Mode's Estate, 76 Pa. St. 502. A., in 1871, lent money to B, to assist him in manufacturing glass, B. contracting that A. should have a lien on the products till paid. After another creditor had issued execution against B., A. issued one, and B.'s property at the manufactory was sold. Held, that since B.'s laborers could not claim for wages against A., they could not against the execution prior to A.'s.

Supplemental Acts.

§ 478. This lien of laborers, etc., is superior to all other liens except mortgages or judgments entered before such labor was performed. The act of May 8th, 1874, [P. L. 120,] declares that coal-lease mortgages shall be postponed to the lien of wages mentioned in the act of 1872. By the act of April 20th, 1876, [P. L. 43,] any persons entitled to the lien of the act of 1872, may, after the expiration of thirty days from any voluntary assignment for the benefit of creditors made by their employers, enforce the collection of their claims, just as if no such assignment had been made. If the assignee has sold the property assigned, he may be compelled to file his account notwithstanding that the year for the filing thereof allowed by law has not yet elapsed.[1] The act of 12th June, 1878, [P. L. 207,] prefers the workmen, etc., mentioned in the act of April 9th, 1872, to landlords, in all claims for rent of mines, manufactories or other real estate held under lease, where the lessee is the party employing miners, mechanics, laborers or other clerks, provided that these workmen shall give notice of the nature and amount of their claims to the landlord or his bailiff before the actual sale of the property levied on.

Act of 12th June, 1879.

§ 479. The act of 12th June, 1879, [P. L. 176,] entitles any laborer to whom moneys are due from any person or persons, for work done in or about the cutting, peeling, skidding, hauling and driving of saw logs, for a period not exceeding six months prior to the death of such person, or to an assignment made by him for the benefit of creditors, or to a sale of said saw logs on execution process against such person, to be first paid out of the proceeds of any executor's, assignee's, sheriff's or other officer's sale of said saw logs, as the property of said person, to an amount not exceeding for any one laborer, $200. The laborer must, by

---

[1] De Leon's Estate, 3 W. N. C. 76

himself or agent, give notice in writing of the amount of his claim before the said sale.   If the work has been done by said laborers, for contractors, and not for the owner of the saw logs, the owner may pay directly to the laborers any moneys due to them for such work, and such payments shall be a good charge against the contractor, in favor of the owner, in a settlement of their accounts.

For Whom the Lien Exists.

§ 480. In the act of 1872, the word laborer and the associated words, clerk, miner, mechanic, do not embrace a skilled florist, employed at $10 per week to tend flowers, and do work necessary to their culture in a floral establishment,[1] nor a clerk in a grocery store,[2] or in a drug store,[3] nor a cook[4] or other servant in a hotel,[5] nor a farm laborer.[6] A. agreed to deliver at B.'s saw mill, timber cut on a certain tract for the price of $2.50 per thousand feet, and hired teams and drivers who did the work, A. not being present at the tract when any of the work was done. A. had no lien ; the act of 1872 means to favor those who work with their own hands, not mere contractors, who cause the work to be done by others.[7] The lien exists in favor of employes in a paper mill;[8] of one who is employed to make boxes at so much apiece;[9] of a machinist engaged in the manufacture of sewing machines;[10] of a night watchman, employed by an enameling company at $12 per week;[11] of employes of a

[1] Pfaender v. Hoffman, 4 W. N. C. 171.

[2] Fell v. Duffy, 6 W. N. C. 44. But a book-keeper in a store was decided to be such a laborer, in Askam v. Wright, 1 W. N. C. 156.

[3] Reichard v. Duryer, 10 W. N. C. 189.

[4] Sullivan's Appeal, 77 Pa. St. 107 ; Allen's Appeal, 81½ Pa. St. 302.

[5] Allen v. Fehl, 33 Leg. Int. 366 ; Allen's Appeal, 81½ Pa. St. 302.

[6] Solm's Estate, 34 Leg. Int. 169 ; Brindle v. Lichtenberger, C. P. of Cumberland, 1880.

[7] Wentroth's Appeal, 82 Pa. St. 469.

[8] Dunn v. Megarge, 6 W. N. C. 204.

[9] O'Brien v. Hamilton, 35 Leg. Int. 68.

[10] Graham v. Machine Co., 35 Leg. Int. 70.

[11] Schnapp's Appeal, 2 W. N. C. 149.

merchant tailor,[1] engaged in sewing and making up suits and garments for customers, in a rear room on the premises of their employer.[2] Laborers cannot, by any contract with their employer, relinquish or impair the lien conferred on them by this act.[3]

§ 481. Under the act of April 2d, 1849, when the proprietor of a rolling mill in Berks county employed men to puddle iron at so much per ton, who each called in the assistance of one or two "helpers," whom they engaged to pay, these helpers had each a lien to the amount of $50, if they had not been paid by their immediate employer, and the latter had also a lien to the extent of $50, provided that that sum, together with what was paid to his employes, did not exceed the contract price of his work. If the helpers had been paid by their immediate employer, he had a lien to the extent of $50 only for what was due him under his contract.[4]

§ 482. The act of April 4th, 1862, gives a lien to those who gain their livelihood by manual toil. A civil engineer, who makes diagrams and plans, marks lines and grades on a railroad, directing and superintending the work on the ground, is not a workman or laborer within its meaning.[5]

The Wages.

§ 483. Under the act of 1872, the wages must be earned by labor rendered within six months before the sale in execution. Hence, when a mortgage was made on the machinery of a paper mill more than six months before its sale in execution, this was sufficient to establish its priority to the claims of laborers, against the proceeds of the machinery.[6] If the sale in execution takes place January 25th, 1875, the labor for which a claim may be made must have been rendered not earlier than July 25th, 1874. That a part of the labor was rendered after that date will not preserve a lien for the

[1] Teets v. Teets, 6 Luz. L. Reg. 19.
[2] Allison v. Johnson, 92 Pa. St. 314.
[3] Nesmith's Appeal, 6 Leg. Gaz. 117.

[4] Seider's Appeal, 46 Pa. St. 57.
[5] Penna. and Delaware R. R. Co. v. Leuffer, 84 Pa. St. 168.
[6] Dunn v. Megarge, 6 W. N. C. 204.

part rendered before it.[1] Wages earned between the levy in execution and the sale, are entitled to the lien, as against the execution. The execution creditor must urge the sheriff to speedy sale.[2] A judgment was confessed January 24th, 1861, by the proprietor of a rolling mill, for wages then due down to January 1st, and an execution immediately issued. Another execution issued against the same defendant on the same day, but at a later hour. The workmen had a lien under the act of 1849, as against this second execution, for the wages of labor rendered between January 1st and January 24th.[3] Though the wages earned within six months prior to the sale, are greater than $200, no more than this amount can, under the act of 1872, be allowed as a lien.[4] Under the act of 1849, $50 is the maximum.[5] The mode in which compensation for labor is to be made, does not affect the laborer's right of lien. He may, under the act of 1872, be paid by the time in which he works, or by the amount of work done, e. g., when he is employed to cut and haul wood at $2.50 per thousand feet,[6] to make boxes at so much apiece.[7] So, also, under the act of 1849; e. g., to puddle iron at so much per ton.[8]

---

[1] Schnapp's Appeal, 2 W. N. C. 149.

[2] Askam v. Wright, 1 W. N. C. 156; McCuttle v. Fitzgerald, 2 W. N. C. 396. In Nogle v. Cumberland Ore Bank Co., these decisions were followed by the C. P. of Cumberland county. Wages of miners, earned between July 23d, 1880, the date of the levy, and August 18th, 1880, the day of sale, were preferred. In Schrader v. Burr, 10 Phila. 620, and Kindig v. Atkinson, 34 Leg. Int. 196, Judge Pershing decided the contrary, as did Judge Butler in Graham v. Machine Co., 35 Leg. Int. 70. In Schrader v. Burr, a fi. fa. was levied on the printing establishment of the Standard newspaper, and a rule to set it aside was, after considerable delay, discharged. The purchaser at the sale declining to comply with his bid, a second sale was necessary. Meanwhile the paper continued to be issued. The printers were denied a preference, in distribution of the proceeds, for their wages between the levy and sale. See, also, Schwartz v. Banks, 34 Leg. Int. 250.

[3] Seider's Appeal, 46 Pa. St. 57.

[4] O'Brien v. Hamilton, 35 Leg. Int. 68; Schnapp's Appeal, 2 W. N. C. 149.

[5] Seider's Appeal, 46 Pa. St. 57.

[6] Wentroth's Appeal, 82 Pa. St. 469.

[7] O'Brien v. Hamilton, 35 Leg. Int. 68.

[8] Seider's Appeal, 46 Pa. St. 57.

Assignment of Claim.

§ 484. The assignee of a workman's claim for wages is entitled to his lien.[1] When A., a store-keeper, agrees to furnish. goods to miners for a month, and takes from them an assignment of their wages in advance, for an amount sufficient to cover the value of the goods so to be furnished, A. has the miners' preferential rights, in the distribution of the proceeds of the sale in execution of the mining lease and fixtures.[2] If the arrangement is that their employer shall, at each monthly pay-day, deduct from their wages the amount due from them to A. for their purchases, A. and his assignee have the lien for wages which the miners themselves could have asserted.[2] But an acceptance by A. of orders drawn on him by their employer, in their favor, in part payment of their wages, does not give him their rights as miners, he not taking an assignment of their claims.[2] A master puddler who pays his "helpers," extinguishes their claim for wages, and is not, therefore, subrogated to it;[3] and when A. is employed to make boxes at so much apiece, and employs two assistants, who saw the lumber, and whom he pays, A.'s claim, under the act of 1872, is limited to the $200, if so much is due him under his contract.[4]

The Notice of Claim.

§ 485. The claimant of wages must, under the act of 1872, give notice in writing of his claim, to the officer executing the writ, at any time before actual sale. This is necessary even when the execution on which the sale takes place is on a judgment confessed by the owner of a coal lease and mining right, to a trustee for the wages due his miners. The record of the amicable action in which the judgment was confessed, is not such notice.[5] The written notice must state all the

[1] Nogle v. Cumberland Ore Bank Co., C. P. of Cumberland County, 1880.

[2] Phila. Trust Co.'s Appeal, 2 W. N. C. 593.

[3] Seider's Appeal, 46 Pa. St. 57.

[4] O'Brien v. Hamilton, 35 Leg. Int. 68.

[5] Stichter v. Malley, 9 W. N. C. 28.

facts which show that the claimant has a lien under the statute; the business of the employer, that the claim is made against the property taken in execution, the amount claimed, the particulars of the service.[1] A list containing the names of persons, with amounts set opposite to them, handed to the sheriff, with a verbal statement that the names were those of laborers entitled to a lien to the amounts attached to them, and a promise to draw up a formal statement in writing before the sale, is not sufficient, the written notice, though drawn up and sent to the sheriff, not reaching him until after the sale had taken place.[2] A paper simply stating that A. is indebted to B. for labor, to the amount of $28.60, unsigned by the claimant, is insufficient.[3] A notice to a constable that, " I have a claim for labor against said A. to the amount of $20, and that I shall claim the same out of the proceeds of the sale," is inadequate, because it does not indicate A.'s business, or that the chattels seized in execution were property in and about the site of business, or used in carrying it on, or in connection therewith, or what the kind of labor was, or when it was rendered.[4] A paper headed "Labor claims against Samuel Atkinson, October and November, 1876," contained a list of names, with amounts opposite to each, and concluded with "A. B., sheriff, pay out of proceeds of sheriff's sale." It was signed by an attorney. Such paper was insufficient.[5] And so was one drawn up in the form of a bill, charging the company defendant in the execution with wages due from May 1st to August 31st, at $5 per day, to which was annexed a notice to the sheriff thus: "I notify you that the above bill is due me from the company." It omitted to show, beside the amount claimed, and the time of the performance of the

[1] Allison v. Johnson, 92 Pa. St. 314; Fulton v. Howard, 22 Pittsb. L. J. 74; Peiffer's Estate, 6 Luz. L. Reg. 101.

[2] McMillen v. First National Bank of Corry, 1 W. N. C. 55.

[3] Halifax Bank v. Christman Bro., 2 Pearson 247.

[4] Allison v. Johnson, 92 Pa. St. 313.

[5] Kindig v. Atkinson, 34 Leg. Int. 196, per Pershing, J.

labor, the nature of the labor; it did not assert that the wages due were claimed as a lien, nor did it make any reference to the process in the sheriff's hands.[1] A notice after the sale, cannot supplement any deficiencies in the notice given before sale.[2]

On what Wages are a Lien.

§ 486. Under the act of 1849, the wages of miners bind all the personal property of the employer, whether used in his business or not,[3] and the lien extends to real estate as well as to personalty.[4] When A. and B., as partners, are lessees of a coal mine and contract debts to miners, these debts cannot be paid out of the proceeds of the sale of A.'s interest in the partnership, under a judgment against him for his individual debt.[5] Under the act of 1872, both personal and real property, if used in the business, are subject to the lien of wages,[6] e. g., the machinery and fixtures of a paper mill,[7] a grocer's store wagon,[8] saw mill fixtures,[9] contents of a florist's greenhouse, flowers in pots, tools used in gardening,[10] stock of goods in a trimming mill,[11] stock and fixtures in a store,[12] glassware in a manufactory,[13] tools of a sewing machine company,[14] household and hotel furniture,[15] cloths, trimmings, buttons, thread, sewing machines, etc., of a tailor's establishment.[16] Wages due by a firm of A. and B., cannot be claimed out of the proceeds of the sale of A.'s

[1] Graham v. Machine Co., 35 Leg. Int. 70. A claim for "labor performed and furnished" was said not sufficiently to describe the nature of the labor. See Bennett's Estate, 7 Luz. L. Reg. 2, for a more liberal rule.

[2] Allison v. Johnson, 92 Pa. St. 313.

[3] Reed's Appeal, 18 Pa. St. 235; Vastine's Appeal, 38 Pa. St. 164.

[4] Wade's Appeal, 29 Pa. St. 328.

[5] Beatty's Appeal, 3 Grant 215.

[6] Taylor v. Rowley, 2 W. N. C. 140.

[7] Dunn v. Megarge, 6 W. N. C. 204.

[8] Fell v. Duffy, 6 W. N. C. 44.

[9] Wentroth's Appeal, 82 Pa. St. 469.

[10] Pfaender v. Hoffman, 4 W. N. C. 171.

[11] McCuttle v. Fitzgerald, 2 W. N. C. 396.

[12] Askam v. Wright, 1 W. N. C. 156; De Leon's Estate, 3 W. N. C. 76.

[13] Mode's Appeal, 76 Pa. St. 502.

[14] Graham v. Machine Co., 35 Leg. Int. 70.

[15] Sullivan's Appeal, 77 Pa. St. 107.

[16] Allison v. Johnson, 92 Pa. St. 314.

interest in the partnership property, on a judgment for his individual debt. These wages are a, lien, not on A.'s interest, but on the corpus of the partnership property, which, notwithstanding the execution against A., remains subject to the firm debts.[1]

Against what the Lien Prevails.

§ 487. By the act of 1849, the lien for wages is inferior to liens of record, *e. g.*, judgments existing at the date of a sheriff's sale.[2] When a lease is made reserving the right of re-entry for arrears of rent to the lessor, the lessor's claim for rent from the proceeds of the sale of the leasehold is superior to that of laborers for wages.[3] As to the proceeds of the chattels found on the demised premises, the lessor's claim for one year's rent is superior to the claim for wages, the lease having been made before the act of 1849 was passed;[4] but inferior, if the lease was made afterwards.[5] The lien of wages is superior to that of the execution which realizes the proceeds.[6] But the lien conferred on laborers by the act of 1872, prevails against all liens except mortgages and judgments existing before the labor is performed. Of labor performed after a mortgage or judgment, the lien of the wages is inferior to that of the mortgage or judgment, though the laborer began to work before such mortgage was executed or judgment recovered, and continued uninterruptedly in the service of his employer afterwards. A. being in the employ of B. before the 25th July, 1874, continued therein for six months after that date, without intermission. On August 8th, 1874, a judgment was recovered against B., under which a sale took place January 25th, 1875. A. had a preference for the wages accruing only between 25th July and the 8th August, 1874.[7] A chattel mortgage executed more than six

[1] King *v.* King, 2 W. N. C. 201 ; Ward's Appeal, 81½ Pa. St. 270.

[2] Wade's Appeal, 29 Pa. St. 328.

[3] Wood's Appeal, 30 Pa. St. 274.

[4] *Ibid.*

[5] Reed's Appeal, 18 Pa. St. 235.

[6] Vastine's Appeal, 38 Pa. St. 164.

[7] Schnapp's Appeal, 2 W. N. C. 149.

months before the sale in execution of the machinery mortgaged, being prior in time to all wages for which a lien
exists by the act of 1872, is superior in lien.[1]   When a
lease exists before the wages are earned, rent becoming due,
whether after[2] or before[3] the labor was performed, is an
inferior lien to that of the wages.

[1] Dunn *v.* Megarge, 6 W. N. C.
204.

[2] O'Brien *v.* Hamilton, 35 Leg. Int.
68; Nogle *v.* Cumberland Ore Bank

Co., C. P. of Cumberland County,
1880.

[3] Ege *v.* Marsh, No. 1, August
Term, 1880, C. P. of Cumberland
County, in Equity.

CHAPTER XIX.,

LIEN OF DECEDENTS' DEBTS.

Source of the Lien.

§ 488. The fourteenth of the principles agreed upon in England as laws for the province of Pennsylvania, on the 5th of May, 1682, was that "all lands and goods shall be liable to pay debts, except where there is legal issue, and then all the goods and one-third of the land only."[1] The act of 1700[2] and that of 1705,[3] are the first statutory recognition of the liability of lands of the living for the payment of their debts. The "act for the better settling of intestates' estates," passed in the year 1705,[4] provided that if any person should die intestate, being owner of lands or tenements within this province, it should be lawful for his administrator to sell such part of said lands for defraying his just debts, as the orphans' court of the county where such estate lay, should think fit to allow, order and direct, from time to time. This act simply regulated the mode in which a decedent's lands should be made to pay his debts. In an early case,[5] Yeates, J., said that "the general opinion from the first settlement of this government has been, that the lands of an ancestor, though aliened *bona fide* by the heir, are still subject to the

---

[1] Charter to William Penn, etc., published 1879, under the direction of John B. Linn, Secretary of State for Pennsylvania, p. 100.

[2] Recorded A., vol. I., p. 37; 1 Dall. Laws, p. 12.

[3] Recorded A., vol. I., p. 199; 1 Dall. Laws, p. 67.

[4] Recorded A., vol. I., p. 163.

[5] Morris v. Smith, 1 Y. 238. In Penn v. Hamilton, 2 W. 53, Gibson,

C. J., says that the "lien of the creditors on a decedent's land springs exclusively from the intestate laws, which make his estate a fund for the payment of his debts." In Hannum v. Spear, 1 Y. 553, the lien of a decedent's debts is shown to spring from the agreement made in England in 1682, and frequently recognized in provincial legislation. See, also Graff v. Smith's Adm., 1 Dall. 501.

payment of his debts, and at this day it would be highly dangerous to impeach it. In the course of my practice I have known some cases of this kind, both before and since the revolution, acquiesced in, although attended with circumstances of apparently considerable hardship."

§ 489. Under these early laws, and the general understanding to which they gave rise, all the debts of a person, existing at the time of his death, in whatever form, whether secured by mortgage, judgment, recognizance, bond or other form of security, and whether evidenced in writing or not, became a lien upon his lands the instant that he died. Comparatively late legislation, beginning with the act of 19th April, 1794, section two, [3 Dall. L. 521,] expressly recognizes this as the law, as do the act of April 4th, 1797, [4 Dall. L. 155,] supplementary to that of 1794, and the act of 24th February, 1834, section twenty-four, [P. L. 1833–4, p. 73.]

Duration of the Lien.

§ 490. As the law stood through the seventeenth, and nearly the whole of the eighteenth century, there was no limitation to the time during which these debts of a decedent continued to bind his lands. In a case already cited, decided in 1793,[1] Shippen, J., remarked that the increase of population and of business in the state might "show the necessity of legislative interference in order to limit the time of the lands remaining liable, but cannot be a reason for a court of justice to overturn a construction which has prevailed for near a century past in Pennsylvania." Chief Justice McKean, in the same case, adopts the opinion of an eminent jurist, written before the revolution, "that until payment of the just debts of an intestate, no descent or distribution can give the children an indefeasible right in the

---

[1] Morris v. Smith, 1 Y. 238. In this case, the devisee had sold the land devised, and subsequently, on a judgment recovered against the decedent's executor, the land was sold by the sheriff, whose vendee's title was held superior to that of the devisee's vendee. At what time after the testator's death the sheriff's sale took place, does not appear.

lands of the intestate; but they, and all purchasers under them, take the lands under the act,[1] subject to the payment of the intestate's just debts, and the practice has gone accordingly."[2]

§ 491. The act of 19th April, 1794, section two, [3 Dall. L. 521,] recognized the indefiniteness of the lien of decedents' debts, and at the same time introduced a limitation to it. After reciting that "inconveniences may arise from the debts of deceased persons remaining a lien on their lands and tenements for an indefinite period of time after their decease, whereby *bona fide* purchasers may be injured and titles become insecure," it enacted that no debts, unless secured by mortgage, judgment, recognizance or other record, should remain a lien on said lands or tenements longer than seven years after the decease of the debtor, unless a demand should be made therefor, or an action for the recovery thereof commenced and duly prosecuted against his executor or administrator, within the said period of seven years, or a copy or particular written statement of any bond, covenant, debt or demand, where the same is not payable within the period of seven years, should be filed within the said period in the office of the prothonotary of the county where the lands lie. An act supplementary to this, passed April 4th, 1797, [4 Dall. L. 155,] re-enacts this clause without essential modification.[3]

§ 492. The twenty-fourth section of the act of 24th February, 1834, [P. L. 1833–4, p. 73,] enacts that no debts of a decedent, unless secured by mortgage or judgment, shall remain a lien on his lands after his death longer than five

---

[1] Act for the better settling of intestates' estates, of the year 1705, 4 Anne.

[2] In Trevor's Adm. *v.* Ellenberger's Exr , 2 P. & W. 94, Rogers, J., says, "before the act of 1797, the debts of a deceased person remained a lien for an indefinite length of time." See, also, Bruch *v.* Lantz, 2 R. 391;

Konigmaker *v.* Brown, 14 Pa. St. 269; Bredin *v.* Agnew, 8 Pa. St 233; Payne *v.* Craft, 7 W. & S. 458; Steel *v.* Henry, 9 W. 523; Wallace's Appeal, 5 Pa. St 103; Penn *v.* Hamilton, 2 W. 53; Campbell *v.* Fleming, 63 Pa. St. 242; McMurray's Adm. *v.* Hopper, 43 Pa. St. 468.

[3] Section 4.

years,[1] unless an action for the recovery thereof be commenced and duly prosecuted against his heirs, executors or
administrators within 'that period, or unless a copy or particular written statement of any bond, covenant, debt or
demand, where the same is not payable within that period,
shall be filed within that period in the office of the prothonotary of the county where the real estate to be charged
is situate.   When such statement or copy is filed, the bond,
covenant, debt and demand shall continue a lien for only
five years after they severally shall become due.[2]

Lien of Mortgage.

§ 493. Under this legislation, the lien of a mortgage
executed by a decedent in his life-time, continues until
actual payment, or until there is an unrebutted presumption
of payment by the lapse of twenty years from its execution,
or from the occurrence of any fact which shows its non-payment at the time of such occurrence.   As against heirs or
devisees, even an unrecorded mortgage of a decedent continues an indefinite lien.   A mortgage was executed June
22d, 1869, but was not recorded until June 5th, 1875.   The
mortgagor died May 29th, 1870, more than five years before
the recording.   On a *sci. fa.* issued on the mortgage, February 24th, 1876, the heirs being still in possession of the
premises, a judgment was recovered against them.[3]   On a
mortgage executed in 1794, by A., who died in 1798, a *sci.*

---

[1] The five years run from the
debtor's death, not from the grant
of letters of administration. Hence,
when D. died August 10th, 1854, an
order of the orphans' court for sale
of his land to pay debts, made August 22d, 1859, was too late, though
letters of administration were not
issued until August 31st, 1854. Demmy's Appeal, 43 Pa. St. 155.

[2] By its terms, this act was to go
into operation on the 1st October,
1834. It did not apply to estates of

persons who died before that date.
Hence, when a person died July
18th, 1832, the seven years' limitation
of the act of 1797 applied. Benner
v. Phillips, 9 W. & S. 13.   When a
debtor died June 1st, 1828, and judgment was recovered against his executors in 1833, the lien of the debt
continued for twelve years from the
death. Keenan *v.* Gibson, 9 Pa. St.
249.

[3] McLaughlin *v.* Ihmsen, 85 Pa. St.
364.

fa. issued against his administrator in 1829, and, on a judgment recovered thereon, a sale took place. The sheriff's vendee acquired a good title, though the mortgage was defectively recorded as against the heirs of A.[1]

Lien of Judgments.

§ 494. A judgment recovered in his life-time against a decedent, remains a lien for the same time as does a mortgage, upon such of the decedent's lands as were at any time bound by it, so long as such land continues in the possession of the heir or devisee as against such heir or devisee.[2] A judgment was recovered to December Term, 1854, against A., who died in December, 1865, leaving a will by which he devised his land to B., whom he also appointed executor. To a *sci. fa.* to revive this judgment issued May 27th, 1872, against B., as executor and devisee, he continuing to own the devised land, the lapse of eighteen years from the rendition of the judgment, and of more than six years since A.'s death, was no defence.[3] A judgment recovered in 1808, against A., was a lien on a house owned by him. He died in 1814, leaving several children as heirs. The judgment was revived by *sci. fa.* against his administrator, in 1827, and in 1828 the house was sold by the sheriff under the revived judgment, to B. B.'s title was held valid in an ejectment against him, brought by one who bought the house from the heirs in 1853.[4] An award of arbitrators was rendered against A., October 30th, 1819. A. died December 20th, 1826, seized of real estate owned by him when the award was rendered and which vested in his heirs. To April Term, 1834, a *sci. fa.* was issued against A.'s administrator and the heirs, who continued to own the

[1] Tryon *v.* Munson, 77 Pa. St. 250.
[2] Shearer *v.* Brinley. 76 Pa St. 300. In Bindley's Appeal, 69 Pa. St 295, a sale by an administrator under an order of the orphans' court, granted more than five years after decedent's death, was valid, because, among the debts, was a judgment recovered in the decedent s life-time, though not revived.

[3] Baxter *v.* Allen & Needles, 77 Pa. St. 468. Here the judgment was not a lien at the decedent's death.
[4] Fetterman *v.* Murphy, 4 W. 424.

land, to revive the lien of the award. Judgment was given against the defendants.[1] In 1833, a judgment was recovered which bound the defendant's lands, who died, subsequently, the same year, devising the lands to his wife and children. On a *sci. fa.* to revive this judgment, issued in 1844, the plaintiff obtained judgment against the executors and the devisees.[2] Against A., who owned land, judgments were recovered December 3d, 1825. A. died February 25th, 1829, devising a part of his land, and, as to another part, intestate. In June, 1848, a *sci. fa.* issued to revive these judgments against the administrator and the heirs and devisees. Judgments of revival were recovered.[3]

When Judgment was never a Lien.

§ 495. In the first three cases just cited, the judgment, though a lien on land at its entry, had ceased to be such at the death of the defendant, on account of its non-revival. When the judgment recovered against the defendant is never a lien upon his land in his life-time, such judgment is like an ordinary debt, as to the length of its lien after his death. In 1834, judgment was entered against B., who purchased lands in 1839, of which he died seized in 1840. In 1846, a *sci. fa.* to revive this judgment issued against his administrator, widow and heirs, and no recovery was permitted. It was said that the judgments whose liens are excepted from the limitation of the twenty-fourth section of the act of 24th February, 1834, are only such as are liens on the decedent's land at the time of his death.[4] As a judgment is not a lien upon after-acquired property, so, if,

[1] Brobst *v.* Bright. 8 W 124.
[2] Wells *v.* Baird, 3 Pa. St. 351.
[3] Konigmaker *v.* Brown, 14 Pa. St. 269. In Miner *v.* Warner, 2 Grant 448 a grantee in a deed, designed to defraud creditors. holds the place of a devisee or heir, as respects the creditor to be defrauded. A judgment recovered against the grantor,

and not revived within five years of its recovery, nor within five years of his death. could be revived subsequently as against the fraudulent grantee.

[4] Moorehead *v.* McKinney, 9 Pa. St. 265. The lands in this case were not bound by the judgment, because acquired after its entry.

by agreement between the parties, it is to be a lien on only
a specified tract, it will not encumber other tracts. As to
these other tracts, such a judgment will continue a lien after
the death of the defendant, for only five years, unless within
that time it be revived by *scire facias*. A., selling land to
B., March 30th, 1838, took from B. a confession of judgment for the purchase money, with stipulation that the lien
should attach only to the purchased land. B. died in 1840
or 1841. In 1841, a *scire facias* was issued, served on the
administrator alone, and on April 5th, 1845, judgment was
recovered. On this judgment, another *sci. fa.* issued to
June Term, 1845, and a judgment was obtained on it,
December 22d, 1847. In July, 1851, another *sci. fa.* was
issued, and for the first time served on the widow and heirs
as well as the administrator. Since the land to which the
lien of the original judgment had been restricted, had been
sold, judgment was given for the defendant. The first two
judgments on *sci. fa.* simply prolonged the judgment, with
its restricted lien, the heirs and widow not having been
parties. The lien of the judgment, as a debt, had ceased at
the end of five years from B.'s death.[1]

Judgments Liens at Death of Decedent.

§ 496. As against a *bona fide* purchaser, mortgagee or
judgment creditor of a decedent, all judgments which are, at
the time of the defendant's death, liens on his land, not only
continue to bind such lands during the period of five years
from his death, although they be not revived by *scire facias*
within that time, but they preserve the rank which they
had at the time of his death. After the expiration of five
years from the defendant's death, if they have not been
revived in that period, they cease to be a lien on the decedent's land, as against a *bona fide* purchaser, mortgagee or
other judgment creditor.[2] *A fortiori* is this the case, if such

---

[1] McMurray's Adm. *v.* Hopper, 43
Pa. St. 468.

[2] Section 25 of the act of 24th February, 1834, [P. L. 77.]

judgments were not a lien on the decedent's lands at the time of his death.[1]

Debts Not of Record.

§ 497. As to all other debts than those in mortgage, or in judgments which either are liens on land at decedent's death or have ceased to be such by failure to revive, the limitation of the twenty-fourth section of the act of 1834 applies. These debts are divided by the act into two classes : those which will not be payable within five years from the death of the testator, and those which will be payable within that period.[2]

Debts Not Payable Within Five Years.

§ 498. The act requires a copy or a particular written statement of any bond, covenant, debt or demand, when the same is not payable in five years from the debtor's death, to be filed in the prothonotary's office of the county where the real estate is situate. A. executed a bond to B., for the payment to B., as trustee for C., of a certain sum on C.'s attaining his majority. A year afterwards, and eighteen years before C.'s majority, A. died, devising his land to his three sons. Two months after C.'s majority, he entered a copy of the bond in the prothonotary's office. One of the sons having sold his land to his brother, recovered judgment on the bond for the purchase money, under which the land was sold by the sheriff. C. was not permitted to claim out of the proceeds against the judgment. The provision in the act of April 4th, 1797, that if a creditor was in his minority when the debtor died, he should have four years after reaching his majority within which to prosecute his claim,[3] did not apply to a case where the debt was payable to a trustee of the minor.[4]

---

[1] As we have seen, in Moorehead v. McKinney, 9 Pa. St. 265, and McMurray's Adm. v Hopper, 43 Pa. St. 468, a judgment not a lien upon land at the decedent's death, ceases as to that land to be a lien at the expiration of five years from his death, if not revived in that time, even as against heirs and devisees.

[2] McMurray's Adm. v. Hopper, 43 Pa St. 468.

[3] The act of 1834 omits this provision for minors, femes covert, persons non compotes mentis, in prison, or beyond the limits of the United States.

[4] Klinker's Appeal, 1 Wh 57.

§ 499. If the administrator is a creditor of the intestate, on bonds becoming due after the statutory limitation, he can file a copy of his claim in the prothonotary's office within that period. Failing to do this, he cannot, when that time has elapsed, file an account, and take credit therein for the debts due him, with a view to obtaining an order of the orphans' court for the sale-of the decedent's land.[1] If a judgment has been confessed, payable at a future day, and the defendant die more than five years before its maturity, the provision for filing a copy of the claim in the prothonotary's office is not applicable, A *scire facias* must issue on the judgment within five years of defendant's death, with proper service on the necessary parties. Otherwise the lien will be lost on land, as to the heirs and devisees.[2] If a surety in an administration bond die, and his estate be not fixed for any default of the administrator within five years of his death, a copy of such bond must be filed in the prothonotary's office within that period, in order to protract its lien beyond.[3] So, a recognizance in the orphans' court, not being a lien on lands of the surety, becomes a lien on them as a debt, at his death, but only for five years, unless a copy be filed in the prothonotary's office.[4]

Debts Payable Within Five Years of the Debtor's Death.

§ 500. For such debts, an action must be commenced and duly prosecuted within five years. If the debt has been reduced to judgment before the debtor's death, a *scire facias* to revive it, is the form of action for the purpose of prolonging the lien of the debt which it represents as to real estate which the judgment *qua* judgment never bound in the defendant's life-time.[5] In other cases, the form of action must be suited to the nature of the debt. When an action

---

[1] Clauser's Estate, 1 W. & S. 208.

[2] McMurray's Adm. *v.* Hopper, 43 Pa. St. 468.

[3] Commonwealth *v.* Severn, 3 W. N. C. 303.

[4] Commonwealth *v.* Clark, 2 Luz. L. Obs. 379.

[5] McMurray's Adm. *v.* Hopper, 43 Pa. St. 468; Moorehead *v.* McKinney, 9 Pa. St. 265.

has been begun in the life-time of the debtor, and, pending it, he dies, the substitution of the administrator may be considered as the commencement of a new action, within the equitable construction of the statute.[1] This substitution can take place, though twelve years have elapsed from the commencement of the action, and though the decedent had not appeared, nor had any steps been taken other than the service of the summons.[2]

Proving Claim Before Auditor.

§ 501. Proving a claim before an auditor, in the distribution of the personal estate, within five years, is not commencing an action such as the act of 1834 requires. A. died April 1st, 1869. In 1870 a creditor proved a claim before an auditor who was distributing the personalty. On April 27th, 1871, the executor petitioned the orphans' court for an order to sell the real estate; the order was issued October 28th, 1871, which, on appeal to the supreme court, was affirmed, and on January 26th, 1874, the record was returned to the orphans' court. On February 21st, 1874, the guardian of a minor heir obtained a stay of the order to sell, which stay was revoked June 20th, 1874. An appeal from this revocation to the supreme court was *non-prossed* on January 6th, 1876. A sale under the order, made in May, 1876, was void. The claim proved before the auditor had lost its lien.[3] So, when a part of the decedent's real estate is, within five years after his death, sold by order of the orphans' court for the payment of debts, and a creditor proves his claim before an auditor appointed to distribute its proceeds, and obtains a dividend therefrom, this will not preserve the lien of the debt so that, when another part of the estate is sold beyond the five years, it may receive a dividend from the proceeds.[4] An action and recovery of a

---

[1] Breden v. Agnew, 8 Pa. St. 233; Pry's Appeal, 8 W. 253.

[2] Thouron v. Farmers' and Mechanics' Bank, 4 Pittsb. L. J. 676.

[3] Craig's Appeal, 5 W. N. C. 243.

[4] Bindley's Appeal, 69 Pa. St. 295.

judgment had before a justice, are not sufficient to preserve
the lien. The transcript of the judgment must be filed
within the five years.[1] A. died in 1816. A judgment was
recovered before a justice for a debt due by him, in 1820, a
transcript of which was filed with the prothonotary of the
county April 8th, 1820, and the lien was kept alive.[2]

Orphans' Court Sale.

§ 502. An application for an order of the orphans' court
for the sale of decedent's land for the payment of debts,
in response to which the order is granted, and land is
sold within five years from the death of the decedent, is
not an action such as will preserve the lien of the debt as
to other land not embraced in this order of sale.[3] And if
an order of the orphans' court for the sale of land of the
decedent for the payment of his debts, is granted within two
years of his death, but, owing to a stay by the court, (subsequently revoked,) and to an appeal to the supreme court,
(subsequently *non-prossed*,) it is not executed by a sale
until seven years after the decedent's death, the sale will be
set aside on petition of the purchaser in which the devisee
concurs.[4] Presenting a claim to an administrator, and
payment of it by him, are not a substitute for an action. A.
dying in 1827, the executor filed an account in November,
1829, showing a balance in his favor, which account was
confirmed. In 1832, a second account was filed, showing a
large balance in his favor, including the previous one, which
was confirmed November, 1833. On the 19th March, 1839, a

---

[1] Wilkinson's Estate, 7 Luz. L. Reg.
12.

[2] Trevor's Adm. v. Ellenberger's
Exr., 2 P. & W. 94. See, also, Duncan v. Clark, 7 W. 217, where the
decedent died 27th December, 1819,
and a judgment before a justice was
obtained in November, 1825, and
filed about that time in the prothonotary's office. Sanders v. Wagonseller, 19 Pa. St. 248; Sample v. Barr,

25 Pa. St. 457; Simmonds' Estate, 19
Pa. St. 439; McClure v. Smith, 2 M.
255.

[3] Bindley's Appeal, 69 Pa. St. 296.
It is uncertain, from the report of
this case, whether the land sold under an order granted before the lapse
of five years, was all to which that
order was applicable.

[4] Craig's Appeal, 5 W. N. C. 243.

third account was filed, showing a still larger balance due the accountant, including the previous balance. This balance, on exception, was reduced to less than one-half of the balance in the first account. An order of the orphans' court made in 1843, on the petition of the executor, for the sale of A.'s land for the payment of this balance, which represented debts of A. paid by the executor in excess of the personalty, was erroneous.[1] D. died August 10th, 1854. His administrator on October 12th, 1857, filed his final account showing a balance due him, which was confirmed by the court. This balance was made up partly of debts for which actions had been brought, as well as for others for which there had been no action commenced. On August 22d, 1859, on the administrator's petition, an order was made by the orphans' court for sale of the decedent's land for the payment of this balance. The sale, which took place 24th September, was valid only because of the debts embraced in the balance, whose lien had been continued by suit.[2]

When within the Five Years the Action must be Brought.

§ 503. The act of 24th February, 1834, requires that within the period of five years after his decease, an action for the recovery of the decedent's debts, shall be "commenced and duly prosecuted." At any point of time within this period, though not until immediately before its expiration,[3] the action may be begun. A. dying September 30th, 1862, an action begun against his executor, June 29th, 1867, was in time.[4] So, in the following cases: Action begun March 4th, 1868, the debtor having died 29th March, 1863,[5] and one begun June 4th, 1857, the debtor having died July

---

[1] McCurdy's Appeal, 5 W. & S. 397.

[2] Demmy's Appeal, 43 Pa. St. 155; Loomis' Appeal, 29 Pa. St. 237.

[3] Trevor's Adm. v. Ellenberger's Exr., 2 P. & W. 94

[4] Eyster's Appeal, 65 Pa. St. 473. Here judgment was taken by default, August 6th, 1867, within the five years.

[5] Campbell v. Fleming, 63 Pa. St. 242. The action here was defeated because nearly ten years had elapsed since the debt was contracted.

20th, 1856;[1] death of debtor in 1816, judgment in action against his administrator in 1820;[2] death 16th April, 1813, action commenced to November Term, 1819;[3] death January 29th, 1801, action brought to April Term, 1802;[4] death 26th February, 1838, action brought and judgment confessed March 15th, 1838;[5] death 26th February, 1838, action brought February 4th, 1843;[6] death June 9th, 1839, action May 17th, 1844;[7] death December, 1794, action 19th September, 1801;[8] death December, 1839, judgment in action against the administrator January, 1840;[9] death July 29th, 1828, action commenced December 24th, 1833;[10] death July 18th, 1832, action commenced March 1st, 1839;[11] death January 8th, 1835, suit to April Term, 1837, and judgment on 12th April, 1839;[12] death June 1st, 1817, judgment obtained against the administrators October 6th, 1819;[13] death 12th June, 1867, suit brought against the

[1] Corrigan's Estate, 82 Pa. St. 495. Judgment was recovered, 23d February, 1859.

[2] Trevor's Adm. v. Ellenberger's Exr., 2 P. & W. 94.

[3] Payne v. Craft, 7 W. & S. 458. The judgment was obtained 10th March, 1821. This was under the act of 1797, which made seven years the limit within which the action must be brought.

[4] Maus v. Hummel, 11 Pa. St. 228. The judgment was obtained August 15th, 1810.

[5] Schwartz's Estate, 14 Pa. St. 42.

[6] Ibid. This was a second action brought within five years, debt on a previous judgment recovered against the executor. Regarded as an "independent action brought within five years from the death of the testator," it was "competent proprio vigore to prolong the lien of the original debt."

[7] Kitteras' Estate, 17 Pa. St. 416.

[6] Buehler's Exr. v. Buffington, 43 Pa. St. 278. This was under the seven years' limitation. The lien was lost, however, because the action was by A. against three administrators, one of whom was his wife; service was had on her alone, and no attempt was made within seven years to bring in the others.

[9] Atherton v. Atherton, 2 Pa. St. 112. The levy on the lands was, in this case, set aside, because the terretenants had not been called in by scire facias to show cause, etc.

[10] Warden v. Eichbaum, 14 Pa. St. 121. This was under the seven years' limitation. Judgment was recovered December 13th, 1834, and a sale in execution, November 23d, 1835, was valid.

[11] Benner v. Phillips, 9 W. & S. 18.

[12] Sherman v. Farmers' Bank, 5 W & S. 373.

[13] Steel v. Henry, 9 W. 523.

administrator 25th January, 1871, and judgment recovered 4th April, 1873, on appeal from an award of arbitrators, filed 15th May, 1871.[1]

Prosecution of Action.

§ 504. The action when commenced must be " duly prosecuted." No definition of due prosecution has been attempted in the decisions of the courts. Since the action need not be commenced until the period of five years is about to expire,[2] it is manifest no steps need be taken in it towards procuring a judgment within that time.[3] A. died before January 29th, 1801. To April Term, 1802, an amicable action was entered between a creditor and A.'s administrator, which was permitted to slumber on the record until August 15th, 1810, when a judgment was confessed. The lien of the debt was continued, nevertheless, five years beyond the seven to which the act of 1797 restricted the lien of decedent's debts unless revived by action.[4] A fortiori the judgment itself need not be recovered within the first period of limitation.[5] Thus, A. dying June 9th, 1839, action was commenced against his administrator May 17th, 1844, and judgment was recovered not before the 16th January, 1846.[6] B. died April 16th, 1813; an action was begun to November Term, 1819, and judgment was obtained March 10th, 1821.[7] Kennedy, J., says, when " the suit is commenced within the seven years, but judgment cannot be had in it until afterward, the pending of the suit would seem to be sufficient to keep the lien alive."[8] The action must be concluded by a judgment within ten years from the date of the debtor's decease, and sufficiently early before the expiration of that period to permit a *scire facias* to issue upon it for the purpose of its

---

[1] Hope *v.* Marshall, 38 Leg. Int. 308.

[2] Maus *v.* Hummel, 11 Pa. St. 228 ; Trevor's Adm. *v.* Ellenberger's Exr., 2 P. & W. 94.

[3] Maus *v.* Hummel, 11 Pa. St. 228.

[4] *Ibid.*

[5] *Ibid.*

[6] Kitteras' Estate, 17 Pa. St. 416.

[7] Payne *v.* Craft, 7 W. & S. 458.

[8] Duncan *v.* Clark, 7 W. 225. This case was under the act of 1797.

revival. This results from the principle, to be considered hereafter, that in order to continue the lien of a decedent's debt beyond ten years, it is needful to revive within that time the judgment which shall be obtained in an action begun within five years of his death.

§ 505. If an action is abandoned before a valid judgment is obtained, the lien which it would have continued expires. A. brought an action in November, 1801, against B. and C., executrixes of D., who died in December, 1794. Service was had on B. alone, who was the wife of the plaintiff, and who confessed judgment in December, 1801. This judgment was a nullity, but implied, as the law then stood, an abandonment of the action as to the other executrix. In September Term, 1803, a *scire facias* issued on this judgment to both the executrixes. C. appeared, but before a judgment was obtained other administrators were appointed in her stead. A judgment was then obtained by A., on January 13th, 1808. The issue of the *sci. fa.* was too late, and the lien was lost.[1]

Necessary Parties to the Action.

§ 506. The twenty-fourth section of the act of 24th February, 1834, requires the action to be commenced and duly prosecuted against the decedent's "heirs, executors or administrators." The thirty-fourth section of that act[2] requires that in all actions against the executor or administrator of a decedent, whose real estate the plaintiffs intend to charge with their debts, the widow and heirs or devisees, and the guardians of such as are minors, be made parties. As to the interest in decedent's land of such widow, heir or devisee as shall not be made a party, or shall not be served with

---

[1] Buehler's Heirs *v.* Buffington, 43 Pa. St. 278.

[2] Prior to this act, lands of a decedent could be taken in execution on judgments recovered against his administrator or executor, though no notice was ever given to the widow heirs or devisees, to show that the debt did not exist. Payne *v.* Craft, 7 W. & S. 458; Maus *v.* Hummel, 11 Pa. St. 228.

notice of the summons, the judgment recovered in the action cannot be levied upon or paid out of it. An action against either the heirs or the executors or the administrators within five years of the decedent's death, will be sufficient to preserve the lien. It is never necessary to make the widow or devisees parties to this action, and when the action is against the executors or administrators, it is not requisite that the heirs should be joined.[1] To join others to the personal representatives in the primary action would require anomalous pleadings to adapt it to the purpose. The creditor should, therefore, proceed to judgment against the executor or administrator alone. The widow and heirs or devisees may be subsequently made parties to a *scire facias* issued thereon, with a view to execution.[2]

§ 507. If there are two executors, and a writ issues against both, but is served on only one of them, the return as to the other being "*nihil*," and a judgment generally against the defendants by default for want of an appearance is entered, the lien of the debt will be carried beyond the five years, when a *scire facias* issues on this judgment within that time, and is directed to and served upon the widow and heirs, one of whom is the executor not served in the original action, and purchaser of the land under a sale made by the executors in virtue of a testamentary power.[3] When there were

---

[1] Murphy's Appeal, 8 W. & S 165. The widow and heirs may be joined in the original action. Kitteras' Estate, 17 Pa. St. 416; death, June 9th, 1839; action to which they were parties, May 17th, 1844 See Walthaur's Heirs v. Gossar, 32 Pa. St. 259; Soles v. Hickman, 29 Pa. St. 342.

[2] Atherton v. Atherton, 2 Pa. St. 112; Benner v. Phillips, 9 W. & S. 13; Moore v. Skelton, 14 Pa. St. 359; Emerick v. White, 34 Leg. Int. 115; Schwartz's Estate, 14 Pa. St. 42,

Steele v. Lineberger, 59 Pa. St. 308; McMurray's Adm. v. Hopper, 43 Pa. St 468; Bredin v. Agnew, 8 Pa. St. 233; Kitteras' Estate, 17 Pa. St. 416; Sanders v. Wagonseller, 19 Pa. St. 248; McKerrahan v. Crawford's Exr., 59 Pa. St 360; Keenan v. Gibson, 8 Pa. St. 249; Walthaur's Heirs v. Gossar, 32 Pa. St. 259; Stewart v. Montgomery, 23 Pa. St. 410; Hope v. Marshall, 38 Leg. Int. 308; Stadelman v. Penna. Co., 6 W. N. C. 134.

[3] Eyster's Appeal, 65 Pa. St. 473.

two executrixes, one of whom was the wife of the plaintiff, and the writ was served on the wife only, and judgment was taken against her only, in 1801, the law then existing being that taking judgment against one was an abandonment of the suit against the other defendant, it was necessary to begin another action within seven years from decedent's death, in order to preserve the lien of his debts, since the plaintiff's judgment against his wife was a nullity. If, then, a *scire facias* on this judgment, to which the other executrix appeared, did not issue until more than seven years from the decedent's death, the lien of the debt was lost.[1]

Result of Not Bringing Action in Five Years.

§ 508. The language of the act of 1797 and of 1834, is peremptory. Failure to bring the action in five years from decedent's death, extinguishes the lien of the debt. A. died January 24th, 1816. To November Term, 1824, an action on a bond executed by him was begun, and a judgment obtained on November 8th, 1824. The lien of the bond upon the lands of his heir was lost.[2] A., executor of a will which bestowed a legacy, promised to pay it, thus making himself personally liable for it. He died in 1810. Not till 1826 was an action brought for the purpose of enforcing his liability. Its lien was then gone as to the lands of A. in possession of his son as heir.[3] B., dying in 1819, an action was brought against his administrators in 1835. The lien was lost as to the interest of the heirs in the land of B.[4] A. died 14th March, 1819. Suit was brought in January, 1828, against his administrator, on a debt due by him in his life-

[1] Buehler's Heirs v. Buffington, 43 Pa. St. 278.

[2] Kerper v. Hoch, 1 W. 9, as against the judgment creditors of the heir.

[3] Quigley v. Beatty, 4 W. 13.

[4] Commonwealth v. Pool, 6 W. 32. It appears that for the effecting of a partition of B.'s lands, they had been sold before the seven years' limitation had expired. The money which represented them retained the property of land, however, as to lien of B.'s debts. These ceased to bind it, at the end of that period, if no action therefor had been brought.

time. Its lien was gone[1] S. died January 8th, 1835. Action against his administrator was brought May 16th, 1842. On land of S. sold in execution in 1842, the debt had lost its lien and was not entitled to share in the proceeds.[2] N. died in November, 1836. Action was brought in April, 1842, against his administrators, who were also his sole heirs, and who had filed no account. A levy upon real estate of N. under the judgment recovered, was set aside.[3] When an action on a note was brought and a judgment obtained eleven years after the debtor's death, and, on a judgment obtained in his life-time for another debt, his land was then sold, the note was not payable out of the proceeds.[4] An order of the orphans' court, made fifteen years after the death of a decedent, to his administrator, to sell his lands for the payment of his debts for which no action had ever been brought, was erroneous.[5] If, by the consumption, for the payment of debts, of the fund from which a demonstrative legacy is to be paid, the legatee is subrogated to the lien of debts paid, as against the land embraced in a residuary devise, still, after five years from the testator's death, the lien as to the devisee is lost, if no action within that time for the debts has been brought.[6]

Time to which the Lien is Extended by Action.

§ 509. Like its predecessors (the acts of 1794 and 1797), the act of 24th February, 1834, simply limited the lien of decedents' debts to five years, unless an action was brought within that time. It did not say that if such action was brought, the lien should be extended- for only a limited period beyond. Judicial decision has, however, determined that the effect of such action would be merely to prolong the lien for an additional period of five years, that is, to the

---

[1] Seitzinger v. Fisher, 1 W. & S. 293, as to decedent's heirs. Bailey v. Bowman, 6 W. & S. 118.

[2] Shorman v. Farmers' Bank, 5 W. & S. 373.

[3] Pray v. Brock, 1 Cl. 354.

[4] McClure v. Smith, 2 M. 225.

[5] McCurdy's Appeal, 5 W. & S. 397.

[6] Mellon's Appeal, 46 Pa. St. 165.

end of ten years from the decedent's death.[1] A. died in
March, 1804. To November Term, 1806, amicable actions
were begun against his executors, and judgment was entered
January 8th, 1807. An amicable *sci. fa.* and confession
of judgment were entered to revive this judgment, on December 29th, 1812. To revive the last judgment, a *sci. fa.* issued
to November Term, 1821. On the 9th of October, 1826,
the devisee of a tract of land under A.'s will, sold it to B.,
and on the 26th November, 1828, judgment was entered on
the *sci. fa.* of November Term, 1821. The lien of the debt was
lost by the failure to revive the last judgment in five years.[2]
Against the administrator of A., who died in 1810, an action
was brought in 1812, and a judgment recovered in 1816.
A sale on this judgment in 1833, of land then in the
possession of A.'s heirs, conveyed no title, though a *fi. fa.*
had issued on the judgment in 1818, on which other lands
of A. were sold, and the *fi. fa.* issued in 1828, on which the
sale of 1833 took place.[3] A. died before January 29th,
1801. In 1802, an amicable action was entered against his
administrator, in which, on August 15th, 1810, judgment
was confessed. To the August Term of 1810, a *fi. fa.* issued
which was levied on certain lands of A., and they were sold.
To November Term, 1813, a *fi. fa.* issued and was levied on
the remaining land of A., which was sold in 1814. No title
was acquired by the vendee as against the heir of A.[4]

---

[1] Loomis' Appeal, 29 Pa. St. 237.
That the executor files an account
over twelve years from the decedent's death, in which he claims a
balance due him for debts paid, but
which were not continued liens, by
reviving the judgments therefor, will
not entitle him to payment out of
the realty.

[2] Penn *v.* Hamilton, 2 W. 53. The
same would have been the case if
the devisee had not aliened the land.

[3] Greenough *v.* Patton, 7 W. 336.
An order of the orphans' court for
the sale of the decedent's land, made
twenty years after his death, for
debts which had been kept alive
only twelve years, was erroneous:
Pry's Appeal, 8 W. 253.

[4] Maus *v.* Hummel, 11 Pa. St. 228.
The heir's title was sold in 1828, and
the purchaser of 1814 failed to recover against the heir's vendee, in
ejectment.

§ 510. The action brought within five years, will, if not abandoned, continue the lien for ten years from the decedent's death,[1] however soon after his death it may be begun, or a judgment therein may be recovered. If, when the judgment is recovered within the five years of the debtor's decease, the lien of the debt should be held to continue for five years from the date of the judgment only, the vigilant creditor would be in a worse condition than the negligent one.[2] The lien of debts continued for five years after the first statutory limitation, in the following cases: Death 27th December, 1819, judgment November Term, 1825;[3] death June. 1st, 1817, judgment October 6th, 1819;[4] death July 20th, 1856, suit brought June 4th, 1857, and judgment obtained February 23d, 1859;[5] death in 1816, judgment in 1820;[6] death February 26th, 1838, judgment March 15th, 1838;[7] death May 6th, 1824, judgment recovered August 11th, 1830;[8] death before 19th March, 1804, judgment January 8th, 1807.[9]

Abandonment of Action.

§ 511. If an action is duly begun within five years after the debtor's death, and continues into the succeeding period of five years, but is then abandoned, the lien of the debt ceases. A. died before December 9th, 1794, appointing his three daughters executrixes of his will. The husband of one of them brought an action against them September 19th, 1801, which was served on his wife alone, from whom, on the 29th of December, 1801, he accepted a confession of judgment. This was an abandonment of the action as to the

---

[1] Shearer v. Brinley, 76 Pa. St. 300.

[2] Duncan v. Clark, 7 W. 224.

[3] Duncan v. Clark, 7 W. 224. Under the act of 1797, when the first statutory term was seven years.

[4] Steel v. Henry, 9 W. 523.

[5] Corrigan's Estate, 82 Pa. St. 495.

[6] Trevor's Adm. v. Ellenberger's Exr , 2 P. & W. 94.

[7] Schwartz's Estate, 14 Pa. St. 42.

[8] McLaughlin v. Kain, 45 Pa. St. 113; McLaughlin v. McCumber, 36 Pa. St. 14. Under act of 1797.

[9] Penn v. Hamilton, 2 W. 53.

other executrixes, and, since the judgment against his wife
alone was a nullity, the lien of his debt was lost.[1]

Continuance of the Lien Beyond Ten Years.

§ 512. As we have seen, the act of 1797, which limited the
lien of a decedent's debts, simply required an action to be
brought within seven years, in order to prolong the lien
beyond that period. It did not require any additional steps.
But, upon a principle of analogy, the courts applied to the
judgment recovered in such action, the requisite of the acts
of 1798 and 1827, in regard to the prolongation of liens of
judgments obtained against living persons, to the extent of
holding that where no proceedings had been had or act done
on a judgment obtained against the personal representatives
of a deceased debtor (negativing the idea of its being paid)
within five years after the seven years [of the act of 1797] from
the debtor's death had expired and the judgment had been
obtained, the lien of the debt on the real estate should be
considered extinct.[2] A. died in 1810. To January Term,
1812, an action was begun against his administrators, on
which a judgment was obtained in 1816. An execution
issued, and certain lands were sold in 1818. Nothing more
was done until 1828, when other lands were levied under an
execution then issued. This execution was void.[3]

§ 513. A debt of A., who died in April, 1813, was continued
a lien down to the 19th of June, 1833, (when his lands were
sold under the judgment recovered for it,) by the following
means: action brought to November Term, 1819; judgment
10th March, 1821; agreement filed and entered of record
August 22d, 1822, that the "judgment shall be revived
without a *sci. fa.;*" agreement filed and entered of record

---

[1] Buehler's Heirs *v.* Buffington, 43
Pa. St. 278.

[2] Payne *v.* Craft, 7 W. & S. 458. In
Steel *v.* Henry, 9 W. 523, the same
judge, Kennedy, intimates that the

act of 1827, concerning the revival
of judgments, does not apply to decedent's debts. See, also, Shearer
v. Brinley, 76 Pa. St. 300.

[3] Greenough *v.* Patton, 7 W. 336.

August 4th, 1823, "that the year and day shall not begin to run till this day;" a *sci. fa.* to April Term, 1828, judgment confessed; agreement filed and entered of record December 8th, 1831, "that the old judgment stand revived."[1] The lien of a debt of S., who died June 1st, 1817, was continued to August 10th, 1837, thus: action in which judgment against his administrators was obtained October 6th, 1819; *fi. fa.* to November Term, 1820, levied on two houses; *alias fi. fa.* to August Term, 1822, levied on the same houses; inquisition, but not condemned; *liberari facias* and *alias liberari facias* in 1824; *pluries lib. fac.* in 1827, executed; *sci. fa.* on the judgment February 28th, 1829, and judgment April 22d, 1829; *fi. fa.* to November Term, 1829, levied on same property as before; inquisition and condemnation; *vend. ex.* to April Term, 1830; sale; sale set aside on June 5th, 1830; *fi. fa.* to August Term, 1830, levied on same property; rule to set aside the levy made absolute March 22d, 1831, and judgment on the *sci. fa.* opened, that defendant might plead matters in defence; payment pleaded April 9th, 1834; judgment November 8th, 1834; rule made absolute April 5th, 1836, to set aside the *alias fi. fa.* of 1822, and all proceedings thereon; *scire facias* to April Term, 1836, to revive the judgment of April 22d, 1829; service set aside and *alias sci. fa.* issued to August Term, 1836; judgment in November Term, 1836; *fi. fa.* to April Term, 1837, levied on lot of ground; *vend. ex.* August Term, 1837.[2] A. died before April 1st, 1825, and a judgment was recovered against his administrators to April Term, 1827. A *fi. fa.* issued April 26th, 1828, inquisition on May 17th, 1828, and land condemned; on the 14th April, 1838, a *venditioni* issued, and on August 10th, 1838, the land was sold. The

---

[1] Payne *v.* Craft, 7 W. & S. 458. Acts were done in intervals of less than five years, evidencing that the debt was not paid.

[2] Steel *v.* Henry, 9 W. 523. These proceedings, it was said, would have continued the lien of a judgment under the act of 1798.

sale conveyed a valid title.[1]   Since the passage of the act of 24th February, 1834, it has been said that the lien of a decedent's debts could not be continued by issue of execution on the judgment obtained therefor, (as had often been held to be the case under the act of 1798, regulating liens *inter vivos*,) but that the only method appropriate to that purpose is a revival by *scire facias* every five years.[2]

Revival of Judgment.

§ 514. When the revival of the judgment by *scire facias* is relied upon exclusively in order to preserve the lien of the debt, the directions of the acts of 1798 and 1827 for the revival of the liens of judgments against living persons must be followed, with one notable exception. When, in the action begun against the executor or administrator, a judgment is recovered before the lapse of five years from the debtor's death, it is not necessary that the *sci. fa.* to revive it should issue within five years from its rendition. It will be in time if issued within ten years from the decedent's death. Thus it was when the death occurred in 1816, judgment was obtained April 21st, 1820, and the *sci. fa.* issued March 17th, 1826;[3] or when the death happened in March, 1804, judgment was obtained January 8th, 1807, and amicable *sci. fa.* to revive was entered January Term, 1813;[4] or when death occurred June 1st, 1817, judgment was obtained October 6th, 1819, and the *sci. fa.* issued February

---

[1] Shearer *v.* Brinley, 76 Pa. St 300.

[2] McLaughlin *v.* McCumber, 36 Pa. St. 14. Six years after A.'s death, which occurred May 6th, 1824, a judgment was recovered against his administrator. The next day a *fi fa.* issued, returned *nulla bona.* Less than a year afterward, a *testatum fi. fa.* was docketed in another county, which, four years after, was discontinued, and an *alias testatum* was docketed twelve days afterwards, and less than twelve years from A.'s death. A.'s land was sold two months after the twelve years from his death expired. Whether the *testatum fi. fa.* could have prolonged the lien is left doubtful. The lien was lost, because the heirs had not been given a day in court within twelve years.

[3] Trevor *v.* Ellenberger, 2 P. & W. 94.

[4] Penn *v.* Hamilton, 2 W. 53.

28th, 1829;[1] or when the death took place July 20th, 1856, judgment 23d February, 1859, and *sci. fa.* 9th March, 1865.[2] If, however, the *sci. fa* is issued neither within five years of the judgment (recovered within five years of the decedent's death), nor within ten years of his death, the lien is lost. A. died 27th June, 1815, and against his administrator a judgment was recovered in an amicable action, on 31st January, 1822. The *sci. fa.* did not issue until the August Term, 1828. The lien of the debt was gone.[3]

The Lien Beyond Ten Years.

§ 515. It has been seen that a judgment recovered, however early after the decedent's death, will, *proprio vigore*, protract the lien of his debt until ten years after his death. It does not seem, however, that if the judgment should not be recovered until near the end of the period of ten years, it would carry forward the lien for a space of five years from its rendition, as would a judgment against a living person. A. dying in January, 1801, an action begun in 1802 was terminated by judgment 15th August, 1810. The lien of the debt was not thus protracted to 15th August, 1815, but ceased with the expiration of twelve years from A.'s death.[4] No judgment, therefore, rendered in the original action, within ten years, can prolong the lien beyond that period, but a *sci. fa.* must issue in every case within that time. If the original judgment in the action is recovered, and a *sci. fa.* thereon to revive it is issued, more than five years before the lapse of ten years from the debtor's death, it is question-

[1] Steel *v.* Henry, 9 W 523. This was under the seven years' period of the act of 1797.

[2] Corrigan's Estate, 82 Pa St 495

[3] Baldy *v.* Brady. 15 Pa. St 103.

[4] Maus *v.* Hummel, 11 Pa. St 228. A sale in the beginning of 1814 on this judgment conferred no title. The *fi. fa.* did not issue until after the lapse of the twelve years following the debtor's death, though a former one had issued to August Term, 1810, under which other property of the deceased was sold. In Trevor *v.* Ellenberger, 2 P. & W. 94, Rogers, J., remarks that if suit is brought immediately before the seven years expire, the lien will continue until five years after the recovery of judgment.

able whether, if no judgment is recovered on this *sci. fa.* within those ten years, a judgment could be recovered afterwards, or the *sci. fa.* would continue the lien beyond. It seems, however, that in all cases where the *sci. fa.* issues less than five years before the expiration of the period of ten years, it will prolong the lien of the debt five years from its issue. A. dying July 20th, 1856, suit was brought against his administrator in 1857, and judgment recovered 23d February, 1859. A *sci. fa.* issued March 9th, 1865. A.'s estate being sold in July, 1868, for the payment of debts, under an order of the orphans' court, this judgment was permitted to share in the proceeds.[1]

Judgment of Revival within Ten Years.

§ 516. The original judgment, we have seen, though recovered less than five years before the expiration of the period of ten years, does not carry the lien beyond ten years.[2] Whether, when, on a *sci. fa.* issued on the original judgment, either less or more than five years after the debtor's death, a judgment of revival is recovered within ten years from the death, such judgment of revival protracts the lien beyond the ten years, and to a point of time five years after the date of its rendition, does not appear.[3] It is clear that, if the *sci. fa.* issues on such judgment after the ten years, and more than five years from its rendition, the lien is lost. Thus was it when A. died in 1804; a judgment was recovered in 1807, which was revived December 29th, 1812, and a *sci. fa.* did not issue on this judgment of revival until November Term, 1821.[4] If a *sci. fa.* issues on a judgment of revival after the period

---

[1] Corrigan's Estate, 82 Pa. St. 495; Benner *v.* Phillips, 9 W. & S. 13; Sanders *v.* Wagonseller, 19 Pa. St. 248; Moore *v.* Skelton, 14 Pa. St. 359; Keenan *v.* Gibson, 9 Pa. St. 249.

[2] Maus *v.* Hummel, 11 Pa. St. 228.

[3] There was such in Penn *v.* Hamilton, 2 W. 53. In McMurray's Adm. *v.* Hopper, 43 Pa. St. 468, one judgment of revival was obtained within six years of the debtor's death. The lien was not carried farther than ten years, because the widow and heirs had not been made parties to any proceeding within that time.

[4] Penn *v.* Hamilton, 2 W. 53 (act of 1797); McCracken *v.* Roberts, 19 Pa. St. 390.

of ten years has elapsed, and a judgment is not recovered within five years, the lien perishes, unless there is some legal excuse for the inaction. So was it when a *sci. fa.* issuing to November Term, 1821, nothing was done till May 12th, 1828, when the death of one of the executors was suggested, and a judgment was recovered 22d November, 1828.[1]

The Widow, Heirs and Devisees Parties.

§ 517. The thirty-fourth section of the act of 24th February, 1834, [P. L. 73,] as we have seen, requires the widow, heir, devisee or guardian of minor heirs and devisees, to be made parties to all actions instituted with the design of charging decedent's land.[2] While it has been decided that under this act the original action may properly be brought against the personal representative of the decedent alone, this act makes it impossible to sell his real estate under the judgment recovered, and so give effect to the lien, until the widow, heirs and devisees have, according to its terms, been given a day in court to show cause why the land should not be taken in execution. If the widow, heirs and devisees have had no opportunity to show cause why the debt should not be levied of the land, an execution, even within five years from the decedent's death, will be set aside.[3] And a sale made on such an execution will confer no title on the purchaser. A. died 15th August, 1833. On a transcript of a judgment before a justice recovered against his executor, January 19th, 1835, and entered in the common pleas

---

[1] Penn *v.* Hamilton, 2 W. 53.

[2] The provisions of the act of 1834, in regard to widows, heirs and devisees, apply to estates of persons who died before that act went into operation, even where a judgment had been recovered against the administrator. Benner *v.* Phillips, 9 W. & S. 13; Keenan *v.* Gibson, 9 Pa. St. 249; Kessler's Appeal, 32 Pa. St. 390; McLaughlin *v.* McCumber, 36 Pa. St. 14. But, when the land was in actual process of execution when the act of 1834 went into operation, the widow and heirs had no right to be made parties. Thus was it, when, on a judgment against an administrator, a *fi. fa.* issued in 1828, and a *vend. ex* thereon issued in 1838, in which the sale took place. Shearer *v.* Brinley, 76 Pa. St. 300.

[3] Atherton *v* Atherton, 2 Pa. St. 112. On application of the alienee of the heir.

January 28th, 1835, a *sci. fa.* issued against the executor alone, who confessed judgment of revival 15th February 1836. On this judgment a sale took place in 1836. The sheriff's vendee acquired no valid title as against the devisees, although they were by the terms of the will to have such part of testator's land only, as "should remain after payment of debts."[1] *A fortiori* a sale on an execution issued at any later time on a judgment to which the heirs, etc., have not been made parties, will be, as to them, void.[2]

Collateral Conversion

§ 518. It does not distinctly appear whether a sale of decedent's lands by order of the orphans' court for the payment of debts made within ten years of his death, will be void, in a collateral proceeding, because the widow and heirs were not in some way permitted to appear and show cause why the debts should not be paid thereout. A refusal, however, by the orphans' court to permit the heir, on his application, to show why the land should not be sold, will, on appeal, be cause for reversing the order of the court before a sale has been consummated under it.[3] If a sale takes place, either for the payment of debts under the order of the orphans' court, or in proceedings in partition, the heirs will be at liberty to impeach the claim of the creditor who seeks to share in the distribution of the fund. Hence, when A. died February 26th, 1838, and judgment was obtained against his executrix March 15th, 1838, the right of the plaintiff therein to share in the proceeds of real estate sold in partition June, 1846, could be contested by the devisees.[4] When,

---

[1] Sample *v.* Barr, 25 Pa. St. 457; Leiper *v.* Thomson. 60 Pa. St. 177.

[2] McCracken *v.* Roberts, 19 Pa. St. 390. Here the sale was eighteen years after decedent's death. Warden *v.* Eichbaum, 14 Pa. St. 121. Debtor died July 29th, 1828, judgment recovered December 13th, 1834, sale November 23d, 1835. Soles *v.* Hickman, 29 Pa. St. 342. Judgment within five years of testator's death, and sale within six years thereof.

[3] Murphy's Appeal, 8 W. & S. 165.

[4] Schwartz's Estate, 14 Pa. St. 42. Here, however, an action of debt on the judgment had been brought, to which the heirs had been made parties. The judgment therein concluded them.

within ten years, a sale takes place of decedent's land under a mortgage executed by him, the proceeds are payable to creditors who brought suit within five years against the executor alone, the heirs and devisees making no objection.[1] K. dying June 9th, 1839, actions were begun by B. and C., respectively, against his executor, to June Term, 1843, and on May 17th, 1844. Judgment was recovered in C.'s suit 16th January, 1846. A sale of K.'s lands under a mortgage was made in the beginning of 1846. B. and C. were permitted to share the residuum after paying the mortgage.[1]

Lien as to Widow and Heirs After Ten Years.

§ 519. While making the heirs and devisees parties to an action against the executor or administrator is not necessary to preserve the lien of a debt for ten years from the decedent's death, though necessary to a sale on the execution, or to a distribution to it from the proceeds of a sale on some other proceeding than execution of the judgment against the administrator or executor, yet making them parties to an action within ten years is absolutely essential to the prolongation of the lien beyond that period. If they have not been made parties to an action,[2] or to a *sci. fa.* for the revival of a judgment recovered for the debt, within ten years, the orphans' court will not decree a sale of the lands for its payment. A. died January 23d, 1842. On July 6th, 1842, a judgment was confessed by his executor, which was amicably revived against him alone in 1845 and 1848. In 1854, the orphans' court properly refused to grant an order to sell real estate for the payment of this judgment.[3] So, when, in 1857,

---

[1] Kitteras' Estate, 17 Pa. St. 416.

[2] If, after judgment against the administrator has been recovered, an action of debt is brought within ten years of decedent's death, upon it, to which the widow and heirs are made parties, a judgment thereon against them estops them from denying the liability of the land for the debt.

Schwartz's Estate, 14 Pa. St 42. A plea by the widow and heirs that they took nothing by descent, is improper. McClurg v. Chambers, 38 Leg. Int. 348.

[3] Loomis' Appeal, 29 Pa. St. 237. That more than five years elapsed after the second judgment without steps to revive it, would have been sufficient reason.

lands of A., who died in 1832, were sold by the order of the orphans' court for the payment of debts, B. was not permitted to share in the proceeds, for a debt on which he obtained a judgment against A.'s administrator in 1833, revived against the administrator in 1839, 1844 and 1857.[1]

§ 520. If the *scire facias* to bring in the widow and heirs does not issue until after ten years from the decedent's death, the lien is gone, and no judgment can be recovered thereon against them. A., against whom was a judgment whose lien was, by agreement, restricted to certain realty, died before the 31st July, 1841. On two successive *sci. fas.* against his administrator alone, this judgment was revived before the end of 1847. This continued its lien as a debt only (not as a judgment) so far as the realty not embraced in its original lien was concerned. As a debt only, its lien was lost at the expiration of ten years from A's death, as to such realty. A *sci. fa.* served 31st July, 1851, on the heirs, was too late to perpetuate the lien thereupon.[2] W. died 1st June, 1828, and in 1833 a judgment was obtained against his executors, which was revived in 1838, on a *sci. fa.* against them alone. In 1843 a *sci. fa.* issued against both executors and devisees. It was too late.[3] If the administrator pays a judgment recovered against him in an action brought within five years of the intestate's death, but no *sci. fa.* issues thereon to the widow and heirs within ten years after that event, the administrator, on filing his account after the ten years,

[1] Kessler's Appeal, 32 Pa. St. 390.

[2] McMurray's Adm. v. Hopper, 43 Pa St. 468.

[3] Keenan v. Gibson, 9 Pa. St. 249. The reason assigned here for the loss of lien, is that the *sci. fa.* to which the devisees were parties, did not issue within five years of the judgment in the original action. In Hope v. Marshall, 38 Leg. Int. 308, A. dying 12th June, 1867, suit was commenced against his administrator 25th January, 1871, and on 15th May, 1871, an award of arbitrators against him was filed. He appealing, a trial was had 30th January, 1873, and on 4th April, 1873, judgment was rendered against him. On 26th December, 1877, a *sci. fa.* issued, by which the widow and heirs were brought in. Judgment was rendered thereon in their favor.

showing a balance due him on account of the payment of this judgment, cannot obtain an order of the orphans' court for the sale of the decedent's land.[1]

Judgment Against Heirs Within Ten Years Unnecessary.

§ 521. It is sufficient to have made the widow, heirs and devisees parties by a *sci. fa.* served on them within ten years from the decedent's death; judgment thereon may be recovered afterwards. B. died 18th July, 1832, and against his administrator a judgment was recovered in 1840. On 2d March, 1842, a *sci. fa.* issued against the administrator, the heirs and devisees, to which they appeared. The lien was preserved.[2] So, when C. died 20th July, 1856, and a judgment was recovered against his administrator 23d February, 1859, a *sci. fa.* thereon, with notice to the heirs and devisees, issued 9th March, 1865, on which no proceedings were had until 1874, when there was a trial and verdict for the heirs and devisees, but no judgment, preserved the lien to July, 1868. From the proceeds of C.'s real estate then sold for the payment of debts, by order of the orphans' court, this judgment was paid.[3] S. died in November, 1841. The transcript of a justice's judgment against his administrator was filed in the common pleas 7th December, 1843, on which a *sci. fa.* was issued and served on the heirs and *terre-tenants* 25th January, 1850. Judgment was entered against the heirs and *terre-tenants* 25th June, 1852.[4]

Necessary Parties under the Thirty-Fourth Section of the Act of 1834.

§ 522. The *terre-tenant* of the realty is a necessary party

---

[1] Loomis' Appeal, 29 Pa. St. 237.

[2] Benner *v.* Phillips, 9 W. & S. 13.

[3] Corrigan's Estate, 82 Pa. St. 495. Here, and in Sanders *v.* Wagonseller, 19 Pa. St. 248, the *sci. fa.* issued more than five years after the judgment, though within ten years after the debtor's death. In Benner *v.* Phillips, 9 W. & S. 13; Moore *v.* Skelton, 14 Pa. St. 359; Keenan *v.* Gibson, 9 Pa. St. 249, it is said the *sci. fa.* to which the heirs are parties must issue within five years after the judgment is recovered in the original action.

[4] Sanders *v.* Wagonseller, 19 Pa. St. 248.

2K

to the proceeding by which cause is shown why it should
not be taken in execution.[1] Hence, if the alienee of a
devisee is not made a party, though the devisee himself is, a
judicial sale upon the judgment recovered will be void,[2] and
a levy in execution will be set aside at the instance of the
alienee of an heir who has had no day in court to show why
the land should not be sold.[3] A conveyance in his life-time
by A., though in fraud of creditors, is valid against his heirs
and devisees. As to such land, therefore, the creditors whom
the conveyance defrauded are not bound to make the heirs
and devisees parties. Sales within ten years, of the land
fraudulently conveyed, on judgments recovered by them in
five years of A'.s death, against his administrator alone, will
be valid.[4] If the fraudulent grantee is a trustee for the wife
and children of the grantor, the same principle is applicable.[5]
When the debtor, by his will, divests the interest of his heirs
in his lands, by a peremptory direction to his executors to
sell them, and, on a judgment recovered against his executor
alone, in an action brought within five years after his death,
the lands are sold in execution before the executors have
complied with the direction of the will, the sheriff's sale is
valid.[6] The executor being the sole devisee, an action against
him alone as executor will be sufficient. On a *sci. fa.* thereon,
wherein he is cited also as devisee, neither he nor one to
whom he has aliened the land since the *sci. fa.* issued can
make any original defence.[7] Non-joinder of some of the
heirs must be pleaded in abatement,[8] and if a minor heir is

[1] Keenan v. Gibson, 9 Pa. St. 249.
[2] Soles v. Hickman, 29 Pa. St. 342.
[3] Atherton v Atherton, 2 Pa. St. 112.
[4] Smith v. Grim, 26 Pa. St. 95;
Drum v. Painter, 27 Pa. St. 148;
Shontz v. Brown, 27 Pa. St. 123. In
Sanders v. Wagonseller, 19 Pa. St.
248, a *sci. fa.* was served on the heirs
and *terre-tenants* eight years after the
decedent's death.
[5] Stephens v. Brown, 2 Miles 244.

[6] Leiper v. Thomson, 60 Pa. St. 177.
[7] Stewart v. Montgomery, 23 Pa. St.
410; McLaughlin v. McCumber, 36
Pa. St. 14.
[8] Schwartz's Estate, 14 Pa. St. 42.
When the land is converted by a sale
in partition in the orphans' court, the
court will permit the creditor to take
out of the fund only so much as represents the share of the debt which
the heirs made parties should bear.

personally summoned, other heirs cannot take advantage of it, nor can he if he appears by a guardian *ad litem*.[1] If, after judgment has been obtained on a *sci. fa.* sur judgment against an administrator, to which *sci. fa.* the widow and heirs are parties, an execution issues, and they petition the orphans' court to stay it, and to grant an order to the administrator to sell the land, and the order is made and the land sold by the administrator, they cannot set up against the innocent purchaser that they were not formally notified, or that for the minor heirs there was no appearance by guardian.[2]

Defences and Judgment.

§ 523. A judgment against one of the executors, both acting as such, in the original action against them, would not bind the other executor, or the personal estate represented by them;[3] *a fortiori* it would not bind the realty. A judgment against the executor, in the action against him alone, is, in a *sci. fa.* thereon, to which heirs are made parties, *prima facie* evidence of the debt. If it is the only evidence offered, judgment must be for the creditor.[4] But the heirs and devisees may, in the trial of the *sci. fa.*, go into a defence against the debt, on original grounds,[5] and if the judgment against the heirs is less than that previously rendered against the administrator, payment of the amount of the judgment against the heirs out of the personalty, is an extinguishment of the debt as respects the land.[6] The object of the proceeding against the heirs is simply to charge debts of their ancestor on land the title to which is derived from him. No other lands could be bound by a judgment against them,

---

[1] Schwartz's Estate, 14 Pa. St. 42. In this case the creditor was one of the heirs, a married woman.

[2] Simmonds' Estate, 19 Pa. St 439.

[3] Hall *v.* Boyd, 6 Pa. St. 267.

[4] Moore *v.* Skelton, 14 Pa. St. 359; Steele *v.* Lineberger, 59 Pa. St. 308.

[5] Steele *v* Lineberger, 59 Pa. St. .308; Benner *v.* Phillips, 9 W. & S 13; Shontz *v.* Brown, 27 Pa. St. 123.

[6] Walthaur's Heirs *v.* Gossar, 32 Pa St. 259. The judgment against the administrator is conclusive as to the personalty.

e. g., lands conveyed in the life-time of the ancestor to one who would be his heir at his death.[1] Hence, on the trial of a *scire facias* against widow and heirs, it is not error in a court to refuse to allow them to amend and plead that they took nothing by descent.[2] They cannot set up want of title in the decedent.[3] That the administrator has not settled an account, and it does not, therefore, certainly appear whether the personalty will not be sufficient to pay the debts, is no reason why judgment should not be rendered against the heirs.[4] But, if the account has been settled, and it appears that, but for a misappropriation of assets, the debts could have been paid from the personalty, this will make a good defence for the heirs.[5] So will the fact that, under an order of the orphans' court, lands of the heirs have already been sold, the proceeds of which are ample to pay debts.[6] But it would seem that if the executor is the sole devisee, it would be no defence to him, on a *sci. fa.* against him in both capacities, based on a judgment against him as executor, that the personalty had been misappropriated.[7] The judgment may be against the administrator and for the heir.[8] No judgment can be entered against the heir or devisee for want of an affidavit of defence.

Who are Protected by Limitation of the Lien.

§ 524. The lien of a decedent's debts upon his lands expires, unless kept alive according to the statutes, as against the heirs or devisees themselves;[10] as against pur

[1] Shontz v. Brown, 27 Pa. St 123.

[2] Coulter v Selby, 39 Pa. St. 358.

[3] Britton v. Van Syckel, 24 Leg. Int. 276.

[4] Benner v. Phillips, 9 W. & S. 13; Stewart v. Montgomery, 23 Pa. St. 410.

[5] Pry's Appeal, 8 W. 253; Kelly's Estate, 11 Phila. 100.

[6] Benner v. Phillips, 9 W. & S. 13.

[7] Stewart v. Montgomery, 23 Pa. St. 410. Comp. Pray v. Brock, 1 Cl. 354.

[8] Hemphill v. Carpenter, 6 W. 22.

[9] Stadelman v. Penna. Co., 6 W. N C. 134.

[10] Kerper v. Hoch, 1 W. 9; Penn v Hamilton, 2 W. 53; Hemphill v Carpenter, 6 W. 22; Wallace's Appeal, 5 Pa. St. 103; Clauser's Estate 1 W. & S. 208; McCurdy's Appeal 5 W. & S. 397; Keenan v. Gibson, Pa. St. 249; Seitzinger v. Fisher, W. & S. 293; Pray v. Brock, 1 Cl 354; Greenough v. Patton, 7 W. 336 Kessler's Appeal, 32 Pa. St. 390 Commonwealth v. Pool, 6 W. 32

chasers from the heirs or devisees;[1] as against lien creditors of the heirs or purchasers;[2] as against other debts of the decedent the lien of which has been duly preserved.[3]

What Exempts Debts from the Statutory Limitation.

§ 525. If an agreement is made between the heirs or devisees and the creditor, that if he will not bring suit, his debt shall continue a charge on their land, it cannot be doubted that so long as they continue owners of it, the agreement will be enforced. So, if the administrator is induced to pay the debts from his own money, by a like promise, the debts so paid will, for his benefit, preserve their liens indefinitely.[4] But a purchaser from the heir, though he had notice of this agreement before his purchase, would not be bound by it, unless, when he bought the land, he promised to pay these debts as a part of the price he was to give.[5] That the land was fraudulently conveyed away in the life-time of the debtor, does not preclude the necessity of revival of the lien, though making the widow and heirs parties at any stage is then unnecessary.[6] Nor does the fact that the heir never obtained possession of the land preclude the need of revival.[7]

Testamentary Trusts for Creditors.

§ 526. A devise of real estate to executors for the purpose of selling to pay debts, creates a trust in the executors for

Bailey v. Bowman, 6 W. & S 113; Baldy v Brady, 15 Pa. St. 103; McMurray's Adm. v Hopper, 43 Pa. St. 468; Quigley v. Beatty, 4 W. 13; Konigmaker v Brown, 14 Pa. St. 269; Hutchins v. Terradill, 21 Leg. Int. 300.

[1] Penn v. Hamilton, 2 W. 53; Wallace's Appeal, 5 Pa. St. 103; Hemphill v. Carpenter, 6 W. 22; Maus v. Hummel, 11 Pa. St. 228; Soles v. Hickman, 29 Pa. St. 342; Mellon's Appeal, 46 Pa. St. 165.

[2] Kerper v. Hoch, 1 W. 9; Klinker's Appeal, 1 Wh. 56.

[3] Kitteras' Estate, 17 Pa. St. 416; Shorman v. Farmers' Bank, 5 W. & S. 373; Trevor's Adm. v. Ellenberger's Exr., 2 P. & W. 94.

[4] For thirty-three years. Wallace's Appeal, 5 Pa. St. 103.

[5] Hemphill v. Carpenter, 6 W. 22.

[6] Sanders v. Wagonseller, 19 Pa. St. 248; Shorman v. Farmers' Bank, 5 W. & S. 373; Smith v. Grim, 26 Pa. St. 95; Drum v. Painter, 27 Pa. St. 148; Shontz v. Brown, 27 Pa. St. 123.

[7] Kessler's Appeal, 32 Pa. St. 390.

the benefit of creditors, and no limitation of the lien of the
debt will in such case arise, other than that furnished by a
presumption of payment from lapse of time.[1] A clause in B.'s
will contained an order to his executors to sell his real estate, in
fee-simple, and, his just debts and certain legacies being first
paid, to divide the residue of the moneys arising from the
sale, equally between his two sons.   B. dying in 1804, judgment was obtained for a debt against his executors in 1805
which was revived in 1808 and in 1814, and upon which a
testatum fi. fa. issued in 1830, on which the land was sold
by *vend. ex.* in 1837.   The title acquired by the sheriff's
vendee was good.[2]   G. devised some of his land to his
executors, directing them to sell it for the payment of
debts.   A judgment recovered against his executors August
19th, 1815, within seven years of his death, was not
revived by a *sci. fa.* until August Term, 1828.   Its lien
though lost as to land not included in the devise to the
executors, continued as to the land so devised down to
1845.[3]   So, when the executors were simply authorized to
convert the realty for the purpose of paying debts, it was
decided that the testator dying in 1817, a sheriff's sale of
his land could properly take place in 1837, on a judgment
recovered for a debt in 1819.[4]   When, however, the direction
to sell land for the payment of debts was absolute, but the
debts were described as demands to be brought in to his
executors in due and lawful time, a debt for which no valid
judgment was recovered against the administrators till 1808
the decedent having died in 1794, had ceased to be a lien.
A general direction in a will that all debts shall be paid

[1] Hall *v.* Boyd, 6 Pa. St. 267; Agnew
v. Fetterman, 4 Pa. St. 56; Bank *v.*
Donaldson, 7 W. & S. 407.

[2] Alexander *v.* McMurray, 8 W.
504   The contest was between a
sheriff's vendee under an execution
against one of the two sons. This
sale was void, since the will had

transmuted the land into personalty
as to the sons.

[3] Baldy *v.* Brady, 15 Pa. St. 103.

[4] Steel *v* Henry, 9 W 523; Sprenky
v. Lackey, 11 Pa. L. J. 219. *Contra*
Agnew *v.* Fetterman, 4 Pa. St. 56.

[5] Buehler's Heirs *v.* Buffington, 4
Pa. St. 278.

followed by a list of creditors, and then the further direction that "to pay the debts" all his personal, and, if necessary, his real property shall be sold, does not make such a trust for creditors not enumerated, as will preserve the lien of their debts beyond five years from the testator's death, if no suit is brought against the executors within that period.[1]

What are not Debts within the Limitary Acts.

§ 527. Services lawfully performed for the benefit of the decedent's estate, after his death, are not within the restrictions of the act of 24th February, 1834. If the executor or administrator pays for these, he is entitled to re-imbursement, at whatever lapse of time after the decedent's death. He may be unavoidably delayed for many years in settling his account, by litigation or other causes; may, after the lapse of five years from the decedent's death, be involved in large outlays for counsel fees, officers' fees and other expenditures. Commissions may accrue to himself, likewise, for services rendered beyond that period. For outlays thus made, or services thus rendered, the lien will exist for at least five years thereafter.[2] When, more than twelve years after the testator's death, his executor filed an account, showing a balance due him as well for expenses of administration and for compensation as executor as for debts of the testator paid by him, so much of it as was not for the debts paid was admitted to be a lien.[3] A. dying in 1828, his executor filed a first account in 1835, a second in 1841, a third in 1844, and a fourth in 1852. On exceptions to the last an auditor was appointed, who found the balance due the accountant $277.31 for his commissions. Under an order of the orphans' court, land was sold and the balance paid. The executor may exhaust the personalty in paying debts,

---

[1] Trinity Church v. Watson, 50 Pa. St. 518.

[2] Demmy's Appeal, 43 Pa. St. 155.

[3] Loomis' Appeal, 29 Pa. St. 237. An order was refused for the sale of decedent's lands to pay this balance, because the executor had been compensated by the use of these lands for a series of years.

and obtain his expenses and commissions out of the sale of the realty.[1] B. died in 1852. His executor filed an account in 1854, and then a second account, claiming credit for loss of a vessel, with whose value he had previously charged himself. This credit being allowed, a balance resulted in favor of the accountant for expenses of the administration. An order was properly made in 1877, by the orphans' court, for the sale of real estate of B. to pay this balance.[2] An administrator who pays debts of the decedent can be re-imbursed only by filing an account and having a credit for the payment allowed him. If he borrows money from another on a mortgage of the land which he has taken in partition of the decedent's estate, and uses this money in payment of some of the ancestor's debts, and this land is sold under an order of the orphans' court for the payment of other debts, the proceeds are primarily payable to these remaining debts, and not to the mortgage, the administrator never having filed an account.[3]

Subject of the Lien.

§ 528. As we have seen, the debts of a decedent are a lien upon his real estate. Ground-rents of the deceased are subject to this lien,[4] as is also an undivided one-half of land, owned by the debtor at his death; the proceeds of its sale in partition, effected after his death, must, if the personalty is insufficient, be applied to his debts.[5] If, after the death of a co-tenant, amicable partition is made *in specie*, his debts will attach to the share allotted to his heirs in severalty.[6] Lands held in trust, under an unrecorded declaration of trust, are not subject to the lien of the debts of the deceased trustee.[7] The allotment in partition, of the decedent's land to one of his heirs, does not disturb the lien of the debts upon it.[8] All

---

[1] Cobaugh's Appeal, 24 Pa. St. 143; Bowker's Estate. 6 W. N. C. 254.

[2] Johnson's Estate, 4 W. N. C 76.

[3] Blank's Appeal, 3 Grant 192.

[4] *In re* Peneveyre, 6 W. & S. 446.

[5] Kerr's Estate, 4 Phila. 182.

[6] Alexander *v.* McMurry, 8 W. 504.

[7] Thomson's Estate, 9 W. N. C. 118.

[8] Blank's Appeal, 3 Grant 192.

the lands of which the deceased debtor died seized, within the limits of the state of Pennsylvania, are bound by his debts. Hence, when A. died in Cumberland county, his debts became a charge on his lands in Perry.[1] An action begun and judgment obtained in Philadelphia against the administrator continued the lien of the debt on lands in Crawford county for twelve years.[2]

Order of Lien.

§ 529. General debts not preferred by statute, become liens of equal rank, by the death of the debtor. Hence, when, on a mortgage executed in his life-time by the decedent, the premises were sold, the proceeds, after satisfying the mortgage, were divided *pro rata* among the general debts, although actions had been begun and judgments recovered therefor at different times.[3] The twenty-first section of the act of 24th February, 1834, [P. L. 77,] directs that claims against the deceased shall be paid in the following order: (1) funeral expenses, medicine furnished and medical attendance given during the last illness of the decedent, and servants' wages, not exceeding one year; (2) rents, not exceeding one year; (3) all other debts, except those due the commonwealth; (4) debts due the commonwealth. This order applies not merely to the proceeds of personalty but also to the proceeds of realty sold for the payment of debts, and encumbered by no liens recovered in the life-time of the decedent.[4] If there are such liens, they must be paid from the proceeds of the land which they encumber, before the general debts (in whatever order the latter may be payable according to the terms of the act of 1834) shall be paid.[5]

---

[1] Bredin v. Agnew, 8 Pa. St. 233; Seitzinger v. Fisher, 1 W. & S. 293; Payne v Craft, 7 W. & S. 458; Brown v. Webb, 1 W. 411; Grant v. Hook, 13 Serg. & R. 259.

[2] McLaughlin v. McCumber, 36 Pa. St. 14.

[3] Kitteras' Estate, 17 Pa. St. 416; Blank's Appeal, 3 Grant 192; Shorman v. Farmers' Bank of Reading, 5 W. & S. 373; Trevor v. Ellenberger, 2 P. & W. 94.

[4] Ramsey's Appeal, 4 W. 71.

[5] Ramsey's Appeal, 4 W. 71; Hocker's Estate, 2 Pearson 493; Bryan's Appeal, 4 Phila. 228; Wade's Ap-

All the debts embraced within any one of these classes, including interest thereon,[1] must be paid *pro rata*, *e. g.*, funeral expenses have no precedence over medicine or medical attendance, or servants' wages.[2] Rents, the second class of claims, cannot be paid until those of the first class have been paid in full, and however the exigency under which the administrator has paid them may appeal to the feelings of a humane man, he cannot be allowed credit therefor as against creditors of the first class.[3] The widow may pay the undertaker and may furnish grave-clothes, and be re-imbursed out of the estate.[4]

Wages.

§ 530. The servants whose wages are preferred, are such as are so called in common parlance, those who make part of a man's family, and whose duty it is to assist in the economy of the household, or in matters connected therewith. They do not include a person employed in manufacturing iron, and in business incident thereto,[5] or one whose principal function is to labor on and to manage a farm and to do other outdoor work, though he may occasionally assist in conducting the affairs of the family, and discharge some menial offices.[6] A clerk or book-keeper is not such servant.[7] A barkeeper in a tavern, which is carried on in the building in which the family resides, and is intimately connected with the household economy, is a servant entitled to the preference of the act of 1834,[8] as is also one employed by a butcher principally in the market and slaughter-house, but, also, in the domestic labors of the family, when he is so required.[9] Taking a single bill from his employer payable in nine months with

---

peal, 29 Pa. St. 328. *In re* Estate of John Miller, 1 Ash. 323, is contrary.

[1] Shultz's Appeal, 11 Serg. & R. 182.

[2] Estate of S. S. Ritter, 11 Phila. 12, 32 Leg. Int. 29.

[3] Estate of S. S. Ritter, 11 Phila. 12.

[4] Francis' Estate, 75 Pa. St. 221.

[5] *Ex parte* Meason, 5 Binn. 167.

[6] McKim's Estate, 2 Cl. 224.

[7] *Ex parte* Meason, 5 Binn. 167.

[8] Boniface *v.* Scott, 3 Serg. & R. 351.

[9] Estate of John Miller, 1 Ash. 323.

interest, will deprive the servant of his preference.[1] The year's wages preferred need not be of the year immediately preceding the employer's death. A servant who 'left the house of the master eight months before his death, was entitled to a full year's wages owing to her, as a preferred claim.[2] The act of April 2d, 1849, [P. L. 337,] puts wages to the extent of $50 due to miners, mechanics and laborers employed in mining operations, in forges, furnaces, rolling mills, nail factories or machine shops, in the rank just before rents, in case their employer shall die.[3] This preference exists with respect to the proceeds of any property of the employer, whether employed in the business or not,[4] or whether real or personal.[5] The act of 9th April, 1872, [P. L. 47,] in case of the death of any person engaged as owner, lessee, contractor or under-owner of any mining, manufacturing or other business, where clerks, miners, mechanics or laborers are employed, gives to such clerks, miners, etc., a lien for wages not exceeding $200, earned within six months preceding such death, whether they are employed at so much *per diem* or otherwise. This lien operates upon all the property of the decedent, and is superior to all other liens save mortgages and judgments recovered before the performance of such labor.

Medical Attendance and Rent.

§ 531. The medical attendance for which a preference is given, must have been rendered during the last sickness. When A. receiving an injury from a fall in May, was attended by Dr. B., for some time, and so far recovered as to be able to discharge his ordinary business, receiving little or no medical attendance during a considerable interval, but afterwards called in Dr. C., and died in December, Dr. B. had no preferred

[1] Silver *v.* Williams, 17 Serg. & R. 292.

[2] Martin's Appeal, 33 Pa. St. 395.

[3] This act applies to Schuylkill, Berks, Washington, Centre, Somer-

set, Westmoreland and Carbon counties.

[4] Reed's Appeal, 18 Pa. St. 235.

[5] See the act.

claim, though the effects of the fall probably caused the patient's death. By "last illness" is meant that which is the proximate, not the remote cause of death.[1] A physician, though a brother of the deceased, has a claim against the estate, but he cannot be compensated for services dictated by the affection of a brother, and additional to the purely professional services rendered.[2] When A. grants to B. the privilege of taking coal out of a mine, B. stipulating to pay twenty-five cents per cubic yard of coal taken out, this is rent, and, on B.'s death, A. is entitled to it as a preferred claim.[3] When land is leased for a year, and the lessee dies in the middle of the year, the rent payable at the expiration of the year, according to the terms of the lease, is not due in the sense of the act of 1834, and the lessor has no preferred claim therefor.[4]

Discharge of Lien.

§ 532. A sale, fair, open and regular, of the land of the decedent, by his executor, under a power conferred by the will to sell for the payment of debts, will, if the proceeds are properly applied thereto, discharge the land from such debts as are not reached by them.[5] Under a power to sell land of the decedent, for the purpose of paying his debts generally and educating his children, a sale by the executor will discharge the debts, some of which are in judgment against the executor, and the purchaser is not bound to see to the proper application of the purchase money. Enumerating in the will some debts only of the same class will not impose on the purchaser the duty of seeing to the application of the purchase money, since this would require him to know all the debts. If, however, the debts enumerated constitute all of a preferred class, the land is discharged only when the proceeds are properly appropriated to them.[6] If the purchaser

---

[1] Reese's Estate, 2 Pearson 482.

[2] Estate of Thomas Moffett, 11 Phila. 79.

[3] Greenough's Appeal, 9 Pa. St. 18.

[4] McKim's Estate, 2 Cl. 224.

[5] Hannum v. Spear, 1 Y. 553.

[6] Grant v. Hook, 13 Serg. & R. 259.

pays in fact no money, taking the title simply for the purpose of mortgaging it, in order to raise the necessary money, this is not a good exercise of the testamentary power of sale, but the mortgagee, having no notice of the impropriety, is not affected by it. Hence, when the trustees sold to A., who paid no money, but made a mortgage for $7,000, which sum was used in paying debts, the mortgagee having no notice that A. had not paid a full consideration, the proceeds of the land, when sold under the mortgage, were first payable to the mortgagee.[1] Specific encumbrances by mortgage, recognizance or judgment are not divested by a sale under a testamentary power.[2] Hence, a judgment recovered before the testator's death is not divested by an executor's sale under such a power for the payment of debts.[3] A sale under a power to sell for the payment of legacies will not discharge the lien of debts.[4] If the assets coming to the administrator are sufficient to pay debts, the land is discharged, though they be wasted by him,[5] and on a *sci. fa.* against the administrator *d. b. n.* with the will annexed, with notice to devisees, the devisees may prove that, by an order of the orphans' court, other lands were sold for the payment of debts, yielding sufficient to satisfy them.[6] When, after judgment has been recovered against the administrator, a *sci. fa.* thereupon issues, to which the widow and heirs are made parties, and a judgment for a less amount is recovered against them, a payment from the assets of this less amount discharges the lands from the entire debt.[7] That the debtor devises lands specifically to be sold for the payment of his debts, does not discharge the remaining land from their lien, though the

---

[1] Cadbury *v.* Duval, 10 Pa. St. 265.

[2] Grant *v.* Hook, 13 Serg. & R. 259; Cadbury *v.* Duval, 10 Pa. St. 265.

[3] Fisher *v.* Kurtz, 28 Pa. St. 47. In Mitchell *v.* Mitchell, 8 Pa. St. 126, it was held that a sale under a testamentary power for the payment of debts, divested the dower of the widow.

[4] Hannum *v.* Spear, 1 Y. 553.

[5] Kelly's Estate, 11 Phila. 100; Pry's Appeal, 8 W. 253.

[6] Renner *v.* Phillips, 9 W. & S. 13.

[7] Walthaur's Heirs *v.* Gossar, 32 Pa. St. 259.

land thus appropriated to their payment does not appear insufficient. If the land not thus devised is sold judicially, the debts of the ancestor are payable from the proceeds in preference to those of the heir.[1]

[1] Evans *v.* Duncan, 4 W. 24.

CHAPTER XX.

TESTAMENTARY LIENS.

§ 533. Since it is not the policy of the law to encourage continuing or permanent liens,[1] moneys directed to be paid by a devisee are not a charge upon the devised land, unless the testator in his will clearly manifests the intention that they shall be such.[2] This intention may be shown, not only by express words, but by implications of various kinds,[3] the appreciation of which is practicable only by an examination of the classes of cases in which they have been held to exist. We shall group these cases, according to the principle by which they seem to have been determined.

Express Charge.

§ 534. The money payable by the devisee in respect of the land, may be expressly charged upon it, as when the will says the money shall " be and remain a lien " thereon ;[4] shall be "chargeable upon and yearly payable out of" it ;[5] "I hereby charge my farms   *   *   *   with the payment of the same;"[6] "I hereby charge upon my real estate   *   *   * the sum of $3,333.33⅓."[7]

[1] Mellon's Appeal, 46 Pa. St. 165.

[2] Ibid.; Cable's Appeal, 91 Pa. St. 327; Brandt's Appeal, 8 W. 198; Montgomery v. McElroy, 3 W. & S. 370.

[3] Ripple v. Ripple, 1 R. 386. That certain legacies are expressly charged is a presumption that others, not so charged, were not intended to be a lien on the land. Mellon's Appeal, 46 Pa. St 165; Montgomery v. McElroy, 3 W. & S. 370; Wright's Appeal, 2 Jones 257. But the presumption is not conclusive. McCredy's Appeal, 47 Pa. St. 442; McLanahan v. Wyant, 1 P. & W. 96; Fishburn's Appeal, 10 W. N. C. 489.

[4] Clarke's Exr. v. Wallace, 48 Pa. St. 80. Addams v. Heffernan, 9 W. 529. See, also, Snively's Appeal, 47 Pa. St. 437.

[5] St. Joseph's Hospital's Appeal, 1 W. N. C. 209.

[6] Dewart's Appeal, 70 Pa. St. 403, 43 Pa. St. 325; Schnure's Appeal, 70 Pa. St. 400. In Fishburn's Appeal, 10 W. N. C. 489, is a similar expression.

[7] McCredy's Appeal, 47 Pa. St. 442. In Steele's Appeal, 47 Pa. St. 437,

Devise, Subject to Payment of Money.

§ 535. The testator may devise his land "subject" to the payment of money; and in such a case, the money is a charge upon the land. Instances are the following: A gift of real estate, "subject however to the following reservations, to wit, It is my will and I do hereby give and bequeath unto my oldest daughter, R., the sum of $500;"[1] a devise to a son, "under and subject to the following payment, that is to say, he shall pay for the said land the sum of $30 per acre;"[2] a devise "subject, nevertheless, to the hereinafter mentioned legacies and bequests, if there should not be other or surplus funds to pay them;"[3] a devise "subject, nevertheless, to the payment of the sum of $7,000, with its interest."[4]

The Land Devised Subject to the Payment

§ 536. In some cases, not the devise, but the land devised, is declared to be subject to the payment of money. These differ in form merely, from those just considered, and the money to be paid is a lien on the land. Thus, a devise of a farm was made, "which said farm and premises hereinbefore devised, shall be subject to and chargeable with the payment of the sum of $2,500, with interest;"[5] and another, the testator "subjecting my land, nevertheless, to be liable to the several payments hereafter mentioned;"[6] and a third, followed by a legacy "to be chargeable upon the real estate devised."[7]

Devise, Provided That Payments Are Made.

§ 537. When land is devised, "provided" that the devisee pays money to certain persons, this money is made a lien

lands were "charged and chargeable" with a widow's maintenance.

[1] Wertz's Appeal, 69 Pa. St. 173.

[2] Lobach's Case, 6 W. 167.

[3] Loomis' Appeal, 22 Pa. St. 312.

[4] McClurken's Appeal, 48 Pa. St. 211. Here the charge was on a life-estate. See, also, Hodgson's Adm. v. Gemmil, 5 R 99.

[5] Newman's Appeal, 35 Pa. St. 339.

[6] McLanahan v. Wyant, 1 P. & W. 96, 2 P. & W. 279.

[7] Mellon's Appeal, 46 Pa. St. 165.

upon the real estate devised. Instances are the following: A devise to a son, " provided, however, that he shall pay over to my executors, for the benefit of the legatees hereafter mentioned, the sum of $3,500;"[1] or, " provided he pays or causes to be paid to my executors, hereafter named * * * the sum of £3,000;"[2] or, " provided he pays to my other three children £300;"[3] or, " provided he charges himself with the sum of £2,000, the price at which I value the same."[4]

Devise on Condition that Payments are made.

§ 538. A devise " on condition " that payments are made is the same as one " provided " that payments are made. The payments are charged on the land devised. Thus, when a gift of land is made to one, "upon the following conditions: "That he shall maintain my wife * * * and pay the other legatees the sums that I direct,"[5] or " upon condition that they pay to my executors * * * such sum as * * * it shall be necessary to raise * * * in order to pay the legacies,"[6] or " with the exceptions and on the conditions hereafter mentioned," a direction to the devisee to pay legacies following,[7] the land will be encumbered by the moneys directed to be paid.

Land Devised, the Source of Payment.

§ 539. When the testator directs moneys to be paid, and describes certain land as the source from or out of which they are to be derived, they are a lien upon it.[8] The following are specimens: A devise of land to a son, " yielding and paying out of the same $7,250;"[9] to a son and his heirs, "he or they paying thereout and therefor * * * the

---

[1] Downer v. Downer, 9 W. 60.

[2] Ruston v. Ruston, 2 Y. 54.

[3] Holliday v. Summerville, 3 P. & W. 533.

[4] Dobbins v. Stevens, 17 Serg. & R. 13.

[5] Craven v. Bleakney, 9 W. 19.

[6] Hanna's Appeal, 31 Pa. St. 53.

[7] Pierce v. Livingston, 80 Pa. St. 99.

[8] Cable's Appeal, 91 Pa. St. 327; Dewitt v. Eldred, 4 W. & S. 414.

[9] Hoover v. Hoover, 5 Pa. St. 351; Sheaffer's Appeal, 8 Pa. St. 38; Neal v. Torny, 4 Cl. 454; Reed v. Reed, 1 W. & S. 235.

sum of £50;"[1] a devise, following a bequest of $300 "to be paid out of my estate;"[2] a devise to a son, "he paying to the widow the interest of $1,500 above mentioned, out of the said sixty acres;"[3] he "paying thereout unto my other children hereinafter named, the several sums of money to them respectively bequeathed;"[4] a devise to one daughter, followed by a direction that another daughter "shall have her main support from" the farm;[5] a devise to trustees for A., of the rents and profits, subject to the payment of a debt owing by A., "out of the said rents, issues and profits."[6]

When the Money Remains in the Land.

§ 540. If the land is described as the depository where the money is to remain, it will be charged with the payment thereof. This may be done in several ways, as, when the testator directs that the money bequeathed "shall remain in" the land,[7] or shall "be secured in said farm;"[8] that the purchaser to whom his land shall be sold, shall "hold the amount" of certain legacies "in my plantation" till the legatees become of age;[9] that certain installments of money to be paid by the devisee "shall remain unpaid and charged" on said land.[10]

When the Duty of Paying Legacies Follows the Title.

§ 541. If the testator imposes the duty of paying money not only upon the devisee, but also upon his heirs or assigns, he indicates a purpose that the money shall be charged on the land. Examples of this are, when the devise is to sons, and they "or their heirs and assigns shall pay" $3,000;[11]

---

[1] Jessup v. Smuck, 16 Pa. St. 327; Hellman v. Hellman, 4 R. 439.

[2] Riley's Appeal, 34 Pa. St. 291.

[3] Fahs v. Fahs, 6 W. 213.

[4] Swoope's Appeal, 27 Pa. St. 58.

[5] Snyder's Appeal, 75 Pa. St. 191.

[6] McClurken's Appeal, 48 Pa. St. 211. See, also, Eleanor Newell's Will, 1 Bro. 311; Mellon's Appeal, 46 Pa. St. 165; Addams v. Heffernan, 9 W. 529; Estate of Thomas Heddleson, 8 Phila. 602; Pierce v. Livingston, 80 Pa. St 99; Commonwealth v Shelby, 13 Serg. & R. 348

[7] Strickler v. Sheaffer, 5 Pa. St. 240; Mohler's Appeal, 8 Pa. St. 26; Sheaffer's Appeal, 8 Pa. St. 38; Postlethwaite's Appeal, 68 Pa. St. 477.

[8] Baker's Appeal, 59 Pa. St. 313.

[9] Neal v. Torny, 4 Cl. 421.

[10] Addams v. Heffernan, 9 W. 529.

[11] Solliday v Gruver, 7 Pa. St. 452.

when the devise is to the testator's son, his heirs and assigns forever, "he or they paying" a designated sum.[1]

Devise of Land at a Valuation.

§ 542. When a devise is made, the devisee paying a sum either designated by the testator or to be fixed by a valuation, the money constitutes the price of the land, and remains charged upon it until payment.[2] So was it when a devise of land was made to a son, "at such valuation as shall be made thereof by six respectable bricklayers and carpenters;"[3] or, as shall be put upon it by three disinterested persons;[4] or, when several devisees of distinct tracts were directed to fix the price of each tract, or, if unable to agree, to call in three or five disinterested persons to appraise the same.[5] The testator may himself appraise the land, e. g., when he gives it to a son "at $33 per acre;"[6] or directs that the devisees "shall pay $20 per acre;"[7] or declares that his son is to have his farm "for $6,000 in gold, or its equivalent in lawful money of the United States;"[8] or gives his farm to A., with the restriction that "he is to pay for said farm $5,500;"[9] or provided that A. "charges himself with the sum of £2,000, the price at which I value the same;"[10] or that he or his heirs and assigns pay "therefor the sum of £1,000."[11] When a testator devised an undivided one-half of land to his son Henry, adding, "for which

[1] Addams v. Heffernan, 9 W. 529; Stone v. Massey, 2 Y. 363.

[2] Hackadorn's Appeal, 11 Pa. St. 86, is inconsistent with this principle, and with the later decisions which affirm it, notwithstanding the effort in Gilbert's Appeal, 85 Pa. St. 347, to save it by distinguishing it.

[3] Hart v. Homiller, 20 Pa. St. 248, 23 Pa. St. 39.

[4] Fishburn's Appeal, 10 Pa. St. 489.

[5] Commonwealth v. Shelby, 13 Serg. & R. 348.

[6] Gilbert's Appeal, 85 Pa. St. 347; Snively v. Stover, 78 Pa. St. 484.

[7] Lobach's Case, 6 W. 167; Hennershotz's Estate, 16 Pa St. 435.

[8] Baker's Appeal, 59 Pa. St. 313; Sheaffer's Appeal, 8 Pa. St. 38; Strickler v. Sheaffer, 5 Pa St. 240

[9] Grim's Appeal, 7 W. N. C. 517; Mohler's Appeal, 8 Pa. St. 26.

[10] Dobbins v. Stevens, 17 Serg. & R. 13.

[11] Addams v. Heffernan, 9 W. 529.

latter devise I will and direct that Henry shall pay in equal proportions to my two married daughters,   *   *   *   at the rate of twenty dollars per acre," the twenty dollars per acre, as in part the *consideration* of the devise, were said to be a charge on the land.[1] The mode by which the value of the land is to be ascertained may not be suggested, as when a farm is given to a daughter, "she paying two-thirds of the value thereof to her two sisters."[2]

Devise of the Rest, Residue and Remainder.

§ 543. When a residuary devise, including both realty and personalty, is described as of the rest, residue or remainder of the testator's estate, in a will which makes bequests to others than the devisee, land embraced within this residuary devise will be charged with the bequests.[3] This was so when, after giving legacies, "all the rest and residue of my estate, real and personal," was willed to testator's son,[4] or all the "rest, residue and remainder of my estate, real and personal."[5] A devise of "all the remainder,"[6] "all the residue,"[7] "all the rest,"[8] of the testator's estate, real and personal, charges pecuniary legacies on the land included therein, and so does a bequest of "the remainder of my property."[9]

[1] Etter v. Greenawalt, 11 W. N. C. 148.

[2] Gause v. Wiley, 4 Serg. & R. 509. In Drake v. Brown, 68 Pa. St. 223, the testator willed that two sons should have all his property "by paying to my three girls, each of them, $300." Shimp's Appeal, 1 W. N. C. 521, and Johnson v. Johnson, 1 W N C. 385, are devises at a price.

[3] Jane Gallagher's Appeal, 48 Pa. St 121.

[4] Nichols v. Postlethwaite, 2 Dall. 131, Hassanclever v. Tucker, 2 Binn. 525; McCredy's Appeal, 47 Pa. St. 442; Davis' Appeal, 83 Pa. St. 348.

[5] Witman v Norton, 6 Binn. 395; Conard's Appeal, 33 Pa. St. 47; English v. Harvey, 2 R. 305.

[6] Bank v. Donaldson, 7 W. & S. 407; Donaldson v. West Branch Bank, 1 Pa. St. 286.

[7] Mellon's Appeal, 46 Pa. St. 165. The specific bequest of a debt due from A. was not a charge on the land embraced in a residuary devise. See Brisben's Appeal, 70 Pa. St. 405.

[8] Postlethwaite's Appeal, 68 Pa. St. 477.

[9] Stewart's Estate, 3 W. N. C. 332.

Confusion of Land and Personalty in a General Devise.

§ 544. When land and personalty are blended together in a devise of all the estate of the testator, though the devise is not characterized as of all the rest or residue of the decedent's estate, legacies given are made a charge upon the land thus devised.[1] Examples are: when the testator declared, "to my sons * * * I give and bequeath all my real and personal estate, * * * except such part as hereafter reserved," and then made sundry legacies;[2] or, "to my nephew * * * I give and bequeath all my estate, real and personal, he paying the legacies hereinafter mentioned;"[3] or, when it was stated to be the testator's will that when his youngest child became of age his two sons "shall have all the real and personal estate at that time by paying" to each of his daughters $300.[4]

Special Cases.

§ 545. When the will manifests the intention on the part of the testator to exempt the personalty from the payment of the legacies, in whatever way this is done, the legacies will be payable from and charged upon the realty. A.'s personal estate at the time of his death was worth about $3,000, and his realty about $8,000. He devised all his land to his wife for life, and after her death to another in fee (he had no children), and bequeathed pecuniary legacies amounting to $8,004, to be paid after the decease of his wife, and gave all the residue and remainder of his personal estate, goods and chattels of whatever kind, unto his wife, whom he made sole executrix. The legacies were held to be charged on the land, in view of their excess beyond the

---

[1] Estate of Thomas Heddleson, 8 Phila. 602.

[2] McLanahan v. Wyant, 1 P. & W. 96, 2 P. & W. 279.

[3] Tower's Appropriation, 9 W. & S. 103; Wertz's Appeal, 69 Pa. St. 173.

[4] Drake v. Brown, 68 Pa. St. 223.

In Burt v. Herron, 66 Pa. St. 400, it was decided that real estate was not charged, under a will providing that all the debts of the testator and of his sons should be paid, and then devising "all my estate, real, personal and mixed," to his wife.

value of the personalty, and of the purpose of the decedent to make his widow the first object of his bounty, manifest from the circumstance that he was childless and that the legacies were payable only on her death. The personalty was described as a residue because of the debts and funeral expenses, that were to be first paid.[1] A will began thus: "Wishes in regard to the disposal of my property. * * * I estimate the value of my house in School street at $4,000. I have nearly $5,000 on interest in A.'s hands." The testatrix then bequeathed to several persons $8,000, but made no special devise of her real estate. The personal property was appraised at only $228.75. The great excess of the legacies over the personalty was evidence of an intent to charge the land with them.[2] A testator made several bequests to his son W. and his daughters. He then devised to his sons A. and B., a certain tract of land, to be equally divided between them; and to C. and D., other sons, two other tracts respectively. He then directed that if the personalty was insufficient to pay his bequests, the devisees should "make up the deficiency equal among them." This was regarded by the court as a division of his estate among his children, some of whom were to take their shares in money, the others in land, and the legacies were held to be charged on the land devised.[3] Already owning one tract of land, and having contracted to purchase another, a testator directed his executor to complete the purchase, taking the title to one-fourth to one son, A., and that to the rest to another son, B. A. was to pay £280 towards the said land, and B. was to keep and provide for the widow and two eldest daughters, during their lives. Should the executor be unable to complete the purchase, he directed that the land on which he lived should not be sold, but held by his widow and children till the youngest arrived of

---

[1] Clery's Appeal, 35 Pa. St. 54. At the widow's death, the orphans' court ordered the sale of the land for the payment of the legacies.

[2] Estate of Susan E. Monro, 9 Phila 309.

[3] Field's Appeal, 36 Pa. St. 11.

age, when it was to be sold and the proceeds divided. Meantime, B. was to work it, and pay rent for one-third of it to the testator's widow and daughters. The purchase was completed and the land on which the testator lived was sold. Since the land purchased was to be a substitute for the land sold, and the latter was charged with the support of the widow and daughters, it was held that the land purchased was bound for this support.[1]

When Lands are not Charged.

§ 546. The mere direction to a devisee to pay legacies, does not constitute them a lien on the devised land.[2] A testator declared his will to be that his sons should have a plantation. He then gave to his wife and daughters, respectively, £250, "to be paid to them by my sons in fifty-pound payments." The legacies were not a charge.[3] When a son is directed to take possession of all the testatrix's real estate soon after her death, and it is ordered that after the death of her surviving husband, "he shall pay" to her daughters $50,[4] or when a testator gives all his lands to A., and legacies to B. and C., "to be paid by" A.,[5] or which he "allows A. to pay,"[6] the legacies are not charges on the lands.

Devising Clause Qualified by Direction to Pay.

§ 547. The direction to pay legacies, though incorporated into the devising clause, or so connected as to qualify it, does not, therefore, make the sum to be paid a charge. So was it

---

[1] Ripple v Ripple, 1 R. 386.

[2] Miltenberger's Appeal, 7 Pa. St. 241; Wright's Appeal, 12 Pa. St. 256. Yet, in Knepper v. Kurtz, 58 Pa. St. 480, where the will gave the balance of his real estate to testator's son, "my son A. to pay all my debts; * * * and further, my son shall pay the rest of my children" certain amounts, it was held the land was charged with the legacies.

[3] Brandt's Appeal, 8 W. 198. The sons, by accepting the devise, became personally liable. Wright's Appeal, 12 Pa. St. 256; Dewitt v. Eldred, 4 W. & S. 414; McCullough v. Wiggins, 22 Pa. St. 288. The accepting devisee is liable personally, though the legacy is charged on the land. Etter v. Greenawalt, 11 W. N. C. 148.

[4] Harper's Estate, 2 Pearson 492.

[5] Dewitt v. Eldred, 4 W. & S. 414.

[6] McCullough v. Wiggins, 22 Pa. St. 288.

when the following phraseology was used: "I give and
bequeath unto my two sons, A. and B., all my farm after my
death, to them so long as they do live, and, after their death,
to their children. But the said A. and B. is to pay to my
four daughters as follows: To C. * * * $500, to D.
$500, to E. $500, to F. $300, to be paid in two years after
my death."[1] Other specimens are these: A devise of land
to three daughters, unless one of them, A., should be childless at testator's death, in which event it was his will that
her share should go to the other two, "them paying to A.,
in lieu thereof, the sum of $800, to be paid equal between
them;"[2] a gift of certain lands to a son, "enjoining on him
to pay to my daughter A. $400;"[3] "I will that A. is to take
the within-mentioned one hundred acres of land * * *
at my death, and pay $700 to each of my within-named
heirs."[4]

Co-existence of Devise and Legacy.

§ 548. That the same will contains both devises and
bequests, will not make the latter charges upon the former.
Thus, a will gave to the testator's son all of the land on
which he lived. In a subsequent part, the testator added,
"I bequeath to my daughter A. $300, and one bed and bed-
stead, to make her equal to what the rest have." These
bequests were not charges on the land.[5] A testator devised
a farm to two sons, besides which he had $10,000 of per-
sonalty and other real estate, which was directed to be sold,
and the proceeds blended with the personal estate. He then

---

[1] Cable's Appeal, 91 Pa. St. 327.
The orphans' court had no authority
to decree payment of these legacies
out of the devised land.

[2] Montgomery v. McElroy, 3 W. &
S. 370. Why was the $800 not treated
as the price of A.'s one-third, and so
charged on the land?

[3] Buchanan's Appeal, 72 Pa. St.
448. When a burial ground was

laid off from this land, A. was not
permitted to take the damages
awarded.

[4] Hamilton v. Porter, 63 Pa. St.
332. *Assumpsit* was sustained by a
legatee against the devisee.

[5] Okerson's Appeal, 59 Pa. St. 99.
The administrator of the devisee was
not allowed a credit for the payment
of the legacy to A.

gave legacies and an annuity of $60 to his widow for life. The personal fund was ample for both the legacies and the annuity. These were not a charge on the real estate.[1] When the intention is clearly manifest that the legacy shall be paid out of the personalty, it will not be a lien on the devised land, though there are phrases in the will which, taken alone, might indicate the contrary. Testator devised one tract to a son, and another tract to the heirs of his daughter, excepting an illegitimate son, "which shall have £400 out of my estate," this sum to remain in the hands of the executors until he should attain his majority. The remainder of the personalty was to be equally divided between his son and his son-in-law. The £400 were not a charge on the land.[2]

Bequests of Maintenance and Support.

§ 549. Instead of directing the payment of a legacy or pecuniary annuity, the testator not infrequently orders, in general terms, that certain persons shall have a support from the devised estate. He may give his widow "a good and comfortable living," or his daughter "a maintenance," out of the farm;[3] he may order his widow to be furnished with a comfortable room and sufficient maintenance during her natural life, to be furnished by the devisees and chargeable upon the devised lands;[4] or, devising a farm to one daughter, he may order that another daughter "shall have her main support" from it;[5] or, having devised all his estate, he may "reserve a living" for his widow during her life.[6] It is not

---

[1] Finney v. Reed, 1 Pearson 111.

[2] Brookhart v. Small, 7 W. & S. 229. In the Estate of John Lynch, 37 Leg. Int. 94, the testator devised all his real and personal property to his wife, for her life, adding, that if she elected to take against the will, his property should be sold, and her interest paid under the intestate law. He then bequeathed several legacies. Held, the legacies were not a charge on the real estate during her life, she accepting the provisions of the will.

[3] Craven v. Bleakney, 9 W. 19; Riley's Appeal, 34 Pa. St. 291. Comp. Wusthoff v Dracourt, 3 W. 240.

[4] Steele's Appeal, 47 Pa. St. 437.

[5] Snyder's Appeal, 75 Pa. St. 191.

[6] Hamilton v. Overseers, 12 Pa. St. 147.

necessary that the devisee provide, or the legatee accept, a
room on the premises. Either may, if there be reasonable
cause, insist that the place of abode shall be elsewhere than
on the devised land.[1] If the beneficiary declines a room on
the land, she is entitled to compensation in money, and the
amount of allowance will depend on the circumstances of
each case.[2] This compensation must be made either by the
devisee[3] or by his alienee, when the maintenance is charged
on the land,[4] and can be enforced by the orphans' court under
the authority conferred on it by the fifty-ninth section of the
act of 24th April, 1834, [P. L. 84,] in respect to legacies
charged on a decedent's lands.[5] In case the owner of land,
charged by will with the support of any person, shall fail to
yield to such person such support, the orphans' court will
appraise it in money, having regard to the station, habits and
tastes of the testator, and of the widow or other beneficiary.[6]
If the value of the testator's estate is found to be much less
than he supposed, and the child whose support he ordered is
not the main object of his solicitude, this support must abate
proportionately, and in proper circumstances, though $400
annually be found necessary to furnish it, the yearly allowance will be limited to $200.[7] The value in money of the
support, when ascertained by the orphans' court, will be a
charge on the land.[8]

The Lien.

§ 550. All interests in land, legal or equitable, may be
charged with the payment of legacies, and since a ground-
rent is an incorporeal hereditament, it may be subject to a
testamentary encumbrance. Should the ground-rent be

---

[1] Craven v. Bleakney, 9 W. 19;
Steele's Appeal, 47 Pa. St. 437.

[2] Ibid.

[3] Craven v. Bleakney, 9 W. 19.

[4] Steele's Appeal, 47 Pa. St. 437.

[5] Ibid.; Craven v Bleakney, 9
W. 19; Hamilton v. Overseers, 12

Pa. St. 147; Marcy's Estate, 22 Pa.
St. 140.

[6] Steele's Appeal, 47 Pa. St. 437.

[7] Snyder's Appeal, 75 Pa. St. 191.

[8] Steele's Appeal. 47 Pa. St. 437;
Craven v. Bleakney, 9 W. 19; Snyder's Appeal, 75 Pa. St. 191.

redeemable, and be in fact redeemed, the redemption money must be properly invested to support the annuity charged upon it, or the money may be paid to the devisee of the ground-rent on his giving proper security to the annuitant.[1] The lien of the legacy begins with the death of the testator, and prevails against all subsequent liens or alienations. If, of an annuity charged on land, later arrearages have been assigned, and two judgments have been recovered, one for the earlier and the other for the later arrearages, these judgments will share *pro rata* in the proceeds of the land charged with the annuity.[2] When one of several legatees, whose bequests are charged on land, obtains a judgment against the executor, he has no precedence to the other legatees.[3]

Lands Jointly Bound.

§ 551. When two tracts of land are devised in severalty to two persons, and legacies are charged thereon, "to be borne in equal proportions" by the devisees, each is liable for one-half of each of the legacies.[4] Certain pecuniary legacies were made a common charge on lands devised in severalty to four sons, with a proviso that the devisees should make up equally any deficiency of the assets to pay them. This made each liable for one-fourth of the legacies.[5] The interest of each of eight persons to whom land charged with a legacy is devised, is liable for only one-eighth of the legacy, and when one of them alienes an undivided one-sixteenth, the land so aliened is liable for the one-sixteenth of the legacy.[6] When land is devised to three in common, subject to the payment of legacies, and, in proceedings in partition, begun at the suit of one of them, an equal partition is amicably effected, each purpart is liable for only one-third of each of the lega-

---

[1] Conard's Appeal, 33 Pa. St. 47. The devise of an undivided one-half was subject to legacies, in Etter v. Greenawalt, 11 W. N. C. 148.

[2] Mohler's Appeal, 5 Pa. St. 418.

[3] Otty v. Ferguson, 1 R. 293.

[4] Clark's Exr. v. Wallace, 48 Pa. St. 80.

[5] Fields' Appeal, 36 Pa. St. 11; Loomis' Appeal, 22 Pa. St. 312.

[6] Newman's Appeal, 35 Pa. St. 339.

cies, and on a sheriff's sale of one of those shares only one-third of each of the legacies is payable from the proceeds.[1]

Remedies.

§ 552. When legacies are a charge on land, the legatee[2] may apply by bill or petition to the orphans' court having jurisdiction of the executor's account, which may make such decree touching the payment of the legacy out of such estate as shall be just,[3] and if the legacy is chargeable on an undivided third, the court will decree partition as a preliminary to effecting a sale of the part charged.[4] This remedy is exclusive of all others for the recovery of the legacy in respect of the devise,[5] and the orphans' court may decree that the devisee shall personally pay the legacy, or that his alienee shall personally pay such legacy,[6] or the installments of an annuity charged on the land, becoming due during his ownership.[7] The devisee, after aliening the land charged with the legacy, may be decreed by the orphans' court to pay it,[8] and after his death his administrator is the proper party against whom to proceed.[9]

---

[1] McLenahan v. McLenahan, 2 P. & W. 279; Lapsley v. Lapsley, 9 Pa. St 130.

[2] Or a trustee for the legatee. Littleton's Appeal, 93 Pa. St. 177. The executor is not the proper party. Fields' Appeal, 36 Pa. St. 11.

[3] Section 59, act 24th February, 1834, [P. L. 84.]

[4] Cassady's Estate, 9 W. N. C. 275.

[5] Reed v. Reed, 5 Pa. St. 241, n.; Strickler v. Sheaffer, 5 Pa. St. 240; Craven v. Bleakney, 9 W. 19; Downer v. Downer, 9 W. 60, 9 Pa. St. 302; Mohler's Appeal, 8 Pa. St. 26; Hart v. Homiller, 20 Pa. St. 248; Miltenberger v. Schlegel, 7 Pa. St. 24; Becker v. Kehr, 49 Pa. St. 223; Swoope's Appeal, 27 Pa. St. 58; Hoover v. Hoover, 5 Pa. St. 351; Solliday v. Gruver, 7 Pa. St. 452; Harper's Estate, 2 Pearson 492; Conard's Appeal, 33 Pa. St. 47; Pope's Estate, 4 W. N. C. 431; Steele's Appeal, 47 Pa. St. 437; Snyder's Appeal, 75 Pa. St. 191; Baker's Appeal, 59 Pa. St. 313.

[6] Fields' Appeal, 36 Pa. St. 11.

[7] Mohler's Appeal, 8 Pa. St. 26; Snyder's Appeal, 75 Pa. St. 191; Clark's Exr. v. Wallace, 48 Pa. St. 80; Sheaffer's Appeal, 8 Pa. St. 38. Yet, in Newman's Appeal, 35 Pa. St 339, Lowrie, C. J., says that the orphans' court can enforce payment of legacies charged on lands, only out of such lands. See, too, Brown v. Furer, 2 Serg. & R. 213.

[8] Steele's Appeal, 47 Pa. St. 437.

[9] Swoope's Appeal, 27 Pa. St. 58. Whether the legacy has been paid or not, may be referred by the orphans' court to the common pleas in a feigned issue.

By the acceptance of a devise, (and a recovery of the land by the devisee in an action of ejectment is proof of acceptance,[1]) the devisee becomes personally liable for the payment of the legacies charged on it,[2] although the debts which he is compelled to pay are greater than the testator supposed they were,[3] and a conveyance by the devisee to another of the land charged does not exonerate him from this liability.[4] Since the personal assets are primarily liable for legacies, even when they are charged on land, the jurisdiction of the orphans' court, as against the land or the devisee, is not exclusive of the ordinary remedies against the executor.[5] When a legacy, though directed to be paid by a devisee, is not charged on the land, the orphans' court has no jurisdiction to enforce the payment of it by the devisee.[6] The decree of the orphans' court for the payment of the legacy may be executed by the writ of *levari facias.*[7]

[1] Snyder's Appeal, 75 Pa. St. 191.

[2] Hoover v. Hoover, 5 Pa. St 451; Lobach's Case, 6 W 167, McCredy's Appeal, 47 Pa. St. 442; Ruston v. Ruston, 2 Y. 54; Swoope's Appeal, 27 Pa. St. 58; Snyder's Appeal, 75 Pa. St. 191; Steele's Appeal, 47 Pa. 487; Clark's Exr. v. Wallace, 48 Pa. St. 80; Etter v. Greenawalt, 11 W. N. C. 148. In Dewitt v. Eldred, 4 W. & S. 414, Kennedy, J., argues that charging a legacy on lands, the testator could not have intended the devisee to be personally liable; but, in Lobach's Case, 6 W. 167, he argues contrariwise.

[3] Hoover v. Hoover, 5 Pa. St. 351. Here the debts and legacies equalled the full value of the land. See, also, Ruston v. Ruston, 2 Y. 54.

[4] Steele's Appeal, 47 Pa. St. 437. Even when legacies, directed to be paid by the devisee, are not charged on the devised land, an acceptance of the devise makes him personally liable for their payment. Miltenberger v. Schlegel, 7 Pa. St. 241; Hackadorn's Appeal, 11 Pa. St. 86; Lobach's Case, 6 W. 167; Brandt's Appeal, 8 W. 198; Buchanan's Appeal, 72 Pa. St. 448; Dewitt v. Eldred, 4 W. & S 414; Wright's Appeal, 12 Pa St. 256; Hamilton v. Porter, 63 Pa. St. 332; McCullough v. Wiggins, 22 Pa. St. 288; Montgomery v. McElroy, 3 W. & S. 370.

[5] Bredin v. Gilleland, 67 Pa St. 34.

[6] Hamilton v. Porter, 63 Pa. St. 332. Here *assumpsit* was sustained against the devisee. See, also, Galloway's Appeal, 6 Pa. St 37; Harper's Estate, 2 Pearson 492.

[7] Hart v. Homiller, 23 Pa. St. 39; Pope's Estate, 4 W. N. C. 431; Newman's Appeal, 35 Pa. St. 339. The decree of the orphans' court that a legacy is a charge, is, unappealed from, conclusive. Littleton's Appeal, 93 Pa. St. 177.

Exoneration of the Land Devised.

§ 553. Unless the contrary appears from the terms of the will, the personal fund is primarily liable for legacies.[1] If this fund is sufficient, the land is discharged, although the executor may have wasted it; the legatee must see that it is properly applied.[2] The act of 23d February, 1853, [P. L. 98,] provides that when a testator has bequeathed annuities or legacies payable at a future time, or upon contingencies, and such legacies or annuities are a charge on his residuary estate, the executor, or other person interested in the estate, may petition the orphans' court having jurisdiction of the accounts of the executor, to make an order discharging and exonerating such part of the residuary estate as shall not be necessary for the full security of the said annuities or legacies. If the debts have been paid, the court may decree the setting apart, for the security of said legacies and annuities, of such part of the residuary estate, or of such real securities or investments in public stocks, as shall be sufficient to insure their payment, and may discharge all the rest of said estate. The securities so set apart must be the property of the decedent's estate at the time of the decree. Such part of that estate as has, by the administration, been devolved on others, cannot be included.[3] While the statute of limitations does not apply to an action against the executor for a legacy,[4] there is a presumption that it has been paid, after the lapse of twenty years from the time the money was demandable. Until that time expires, the burden is on the defendant to show payment; after its expiration, the legatee must rebut the presumption by evidence from which

---

[1] Bredin v. Gilleland, 67 Pa. St. 34. In Commonwealth v. Shelby, 13 Serg. & R. 348, it was said that when legacies were payable out of the entire estate, the personalty was first to be applied to them, then the undevised lands, and lastly the devised lands.

[2] Hanna's Appeal, 31 Pa. St. 53.

[3] McCready's Estate, 7 Phila. 478.

[4] Thompson v. McGaw, 2 W. 161; Doebler v. Snavely, 5 W. 225; Patterson v Nichol, 6 W. 379. The statute applies to actions against accepting devisees for legacies which they are by the will directed to pay. Etter v. Greenawalt, 11 W. N. C. 148.

non-payment may be legitimately inferred.[1] The legacy charged on land may be released, but if the legatee be the wife of the releasee, and no consideration passed for the release, it will be void, and the legacy will be payable from the proceeds of the judicial sale of the land charged, except as against such creditors as had advanced moneys to the releasee after they had actual knowledge of the release, or the constructive knowledge implied by a proper recording thereof. An improper recording will not be constructive notice.[2] A married woman may release a legacy charged on land, the husband consenting, without separate acknowledgment; and if the release is to him, as *terre-tenant* of the land, his consent will be presumed.[3]

---

[1] Bentley's Estate, 8 W. N. C. 455, 10 W. N. C. 225; Foulk *v.* Brown, 2 W. 209.

[2] Powell's Appeal, 10 W. N. C. 485.

[3] *Ibid.*

CHAPTER XXI.

LIEN OF RECOGNIZANCES IN THE ORPHANS' COURT.

Recognizances Not Liens.

§ 554. A recognizance is not, in England, a lien by the common law, but by the statute of Westminster 2, which enacted that "when debt is recovered or knowledged in the king's court, or damages awarded, it shall be from henceforth in the election of him that sueth for such debt or damages, to have writ that the sheriff *fieri faciat* of the lands and goods," etc. This statute has never been in force in Pennsylvania.[1] Recognizance of special bail is not a lien in Pennsylvania. When a judgment is recovered on it, the lien of such judgment does not relate to the recognizance. Hence, if, after recognizance, but before the judgment upon a *scire facias* thereupon, a mortgage is executed by the recognizor,[2] or a judgment is recovered against him,[3] this mortgage or judgment is the earlier lien

Special Case of Lien.

§ 555. By a common law which has grown up in this state, a recognizance entered into by a purchaser of land sold by the administrator of a decedent, under an order of the orphans' court for the payment of his debts, is a lien on the land so sold. Said Rogers, J.: "That the recognizance taken by an orphans' court to secure the purchase money is a lien on the lands, is now too well settled to admit of question. The very object of taking a recognizance is to secure a lien on the land, and it was the intention of both parties that it should be a lien."[4]

[1] Allen *v.* Reesor, 16 Serg. & R. 10, per Gibson, C. J.

[2] Patterson *v.* Sample, 4 Y. 308.

[3] Campbell *v.* Richardson, 1 Dall. 131.

[4] Ramsey's Appeal, 4 W. 71.

Recognizance in Partition in Orphans' Court.

§ 556. Very early in the history of this state, the interests of the widow and' heirs in the lands of a deceased husband and ancestor, were, in cases of partition, in which owelty became payable, secured by recognizance. In the year 1788, C. J. M'Kean deprecated the custom of taking bonds in the orphans' court for this purpose.[1] The orphans' court ought, said he, "instead of bonds, which are a mere personal security, to take recognizances, by which the lands themselves would be bound for the payment of the distributive shares." In 1819, C. J. Tilghman remarked that from the time of Walton *v.* Willis, "it may be safely asserted that these recognizances have been generally understood to be a lien," and the supreme court decided, in an action of *sci. fa.* on a recognizance entered into October 27th, 1801, to secure to the widow and children their shares of the appraised value of lands of the decedent, taken in partition by the recognizor, that the lands so taken, though sold by the recognizor in 1804 to O., and by O. to C. in 1808, remained charged with the shares of the widow and children in 1818.[2] From this time there has been no doubt that recognizances in the orphans' courts, to secure owelty in partition, are liens.[3] They are legal, not merely equitable ones, liens of record, of which a purchaser is bound to take notice.[4]

Origin of the Lien.

§ 557. When it is said that the recognizance is a lien, it is to be understood that it becomes such from its date. A

[1] Walton *v.* Willis, 1 Dall. 265.

[2] Kean *v.* Franklin, 5 Serg. & R. 147.

[3] Hartman's Appeal, 21 Pa. St. 288; Riddle & Pennock's Appeal, 37 Pa. St. 177; Allen *v.* Getz, 2 P. & W. 310; Commonwealth *v.* Hantz, 2 P. & W. 333; Ebbs *v.* Commonwealth, 11 Pa. 374; Neel's Appeal, 88 Pa. St. 94; Hillbish's Appeal, 89 Pa. St. 490;

Addams *v.* Heffernan, 9 W. 529; Gilmore *v.* Commonwealth, 17 Serg. & R. 276. In Taggart *v.* Cooper, 1 Serg. & R. 501, a recognizance was considered as a lien on land taken in partition, but partly on account of the phraseology of the recognizance. See, also, Share *v.* Anderson, 7 Serg. & R. 43.

[4] Kean *v.* Franklin, 5 Serg. & R. 147.

judgment subsequently recovered on it, would give effect to this lien, by relation to the date of the recognizance.[1]

Upon What it is a Lien.

§ 558. The recognizance binds only the land taken by the recognizor in partition,[2] not, as at one time was supposed, all the lands belonging to him at the time of its execution.[3] When an heir accepts several distinct tracts of land, severally appraised by the inquest, and enters into a single recognizance to secures the shares of the other heirs, each tract is chargeable only with its own valuation remaining unpaid.[4] It must not be inferred, however, that a recognizance given by one heir binds only the fractional shares of the other heirs in the land allotted to him; it is a lien on the entire title, including the inherited share.[5] The lands of a surety in a recognizance are not bound by it.[6] If a husband, in right of his wife, accept land at the appraisement, the recognizance into which he enters binds the shares acquired by him, but not the share of his wife. The wife retains the interest she had at the death of her ancestor. Hence, when, on her death, this interest is sold by her administrator under an order of the orphans' court for the payment of her debts, the recognizee in the husband's recognizance is not entitled to a share of the proceeds.[7] But the process of partition does not enlarge the interest of the wife in any part of the lands of her ancestor. Under the intestate act of 1794, the oldest son was entitled to two shares in his deceased father's land. A. dying leaving six children, and fewer tracts of land, some of these tracts were allotted to two of the sons, and the rest to the husband of another. The interest of the wife in

---

[1] Hillbish's Appeal, 89 Pa. St. 490.

[2] Allen v. Reesor, 16 Serg. & R. 10; Allen v. Getz, 2 P. & W. 310; Commonwealth v. McIntyre, 8 Pa. St. 295; Crawford v. Crawford, 2 W. 339.

[3] Cubbage v. Nesmith, 3 W. 314; Fisher v. Kean, 1 W. 259.

[4] Allen v. Getz, 2 P. & W. 310; Reigart v. Ellmaker, 14 Serg. & R. 121.

[5] Cubbage v. Nesmith, 3 W. 314.

[6] Allen v. Reesor, 16 Serg. & R. 10.

[7] Hoffer v. Wightman, 5 W. 205.

the two tracts not taken by her husband was converted into personalty, and in the tract taken in her right by her husband, continued only one-seventh. On the remaining six-sevenths, therefore, the husband's recognizance was a lien.[1]

Duration of its Lien.

§ 559. The lien of a recognizance is not limited by statute to any period of time. It is therefore indefinite. Still, after twenty years a presumption of payment arises in favor of later lien creditors, without rebuttal of which the lien will be lost. Evidence rebutting it, would be an admission of non-payment made by the recognizor or his attorney within the twenty years, an action pending on the recognizance, a verdict and judgment in favor of the recognizee, etc.[2] The presumption of payment arises in twenty years, even though the person interested as recognizee is a minor, having a guardian.[3]

Validity and Form of the Recognizance.

§ 560. The court in which the recognizance is made must have jurisdiction, otherwise it will be void. Hence, when a

---

[1] Kean v. Ridgway, 16 Serg. & R. 60 ; Snevely v. Wagner, 8 Pa. St. 396 , Johnson v. Matson, 1 P & W. 371 ; McCullough v. Elder, 8 Serg. & R. 181. In McMillan & Crossman's Appeal, 52 Pa. St. 434, there were three daughters of a decedent, two married. In partition, the share of the unmarried one was taken by the husbands of the other two in common. Held, each husband became owner in fee of an undivided sixth, and each wife remained owner of an undivided third. On sale by one husband and wife to the other husband, he became the owner of two-thirds, his wife being the owner of the remaining third.

[2] Ankeny v. Penrose, 18 Pa. St. 190; Allen v. Sawyer, 2 P. & W. 325. In Hillbish's Appeal, 89 Pa. St. 490, the recognizance was given in 1837 ; a judgment was recovered by a creditor against the recognizor in 1860. In 1862 the recognizor confessed a judgment in an amicable action of debt on the recognizance. The first judgment was held to be a prior lien to that of the recognizee, but whether on account of presumption of payment of the recognizance when A.'s judgment was recovered, or because of want of sufficient evidence that there had been a recognizance, (it not being found,) does not appear from the opinion of the court.

[3] Galbraith v. Galbraith, 6 W. 112.

decedent left a will, directing that his son should have a certain tract of land on giving security to the other children for their shares, and the orphans' court, on his petition, ordered an inquest, and a recognizance was taken from him to secure payment of owelty to the heirs, this recognizance was void, and a *sci. fa.* could not be sustained upon it. The orphans' court had no jurisdiction in the case.[1] A guardian of minor children may accept for them land of their ancestor, in partition, and a recognizance in their name will bind their interest.[2]

§ 561. A recognizance is defined to be an obligation of record which a man enters into before some court of record or magistrate duly authorized, with condition to do some particular act, as to appear at the assizes, to keep the peace, to pay debts, or the like.[3] The orphans' court has authority to take it to secure the shares of the widow and heirs in a decedent's land.[4] In the absence of statutory requirement, the form of the recognizance is immaterial. A short memorandum of it is enough. The omission of the sum measuring the penalty is unimportant, and the lien is not impaired, though it be not supplied until after a judgment is recovered by a creditor against the recognizor. The amount for which the recognizance is a lien may be ascertained by reference to the proceedings in partition in which it was acknowledged, and a purchaser or lien creditor is bound to make such reference.[5] A recognizance for a named sum, concluding thus: "Which sum the said R. (the principal recognizor), willeth and granteth to be levied on the said tract of land and premises, upon the condition above mentioned," is valid against the surety as a personal security.[6] If wanting in

---

[1] President of the Orphans' Court v Groff, 14 Serg. & R. 181.

[2] Kean v. Ridgway, 16 Serg. & R. 160; Eberts v. Eberts, 55 Pa. St 110; Gelbach's Appeal, 8 Serg. & R. 205; Penna. Annuity Co. v. Vansyckel, 2 Pittsb. 535.

[3] Good v. Good, 7 W. 195.

[4] Ibid.

[5] Riddle & Pennock's Appeal, 37 Pa. St. 177; Bailey v. Commonwealth, 41 Pa. St. 473.

[6] Taggart v. Cooper, 1 Serg. & R. 497.

precision, such construction must be given to the recognizance, if possible, as is consistent with the requirements of the law and the design of the parties.[1]   Though a recognizance was conditioned for the payment to the heirs of their several shares within one year from date, and nothing was said about the widow's interest, it was a lien on the lands taken by the heirs and conveyed to *bona fide* purchasers, for the principal sum of the widow's dower, on her decease, which occurred twenty-years after it was given.[2]   When the eldest heir appeared for the purpose of taking land at the valuation of the inquest, and the clerk made a minute of that fact, and of the award to him by the court, "upon his giving security in the sum of $7,000, that he shall pay, etc. B. G. and —— each *tent.* in the sum of $7,000 as security, that E. G. (the heir) shall pay," etc., and this minute was filed away, but not docketed, it was said that even if docketed, it would have been an insufficient recognizance to justify the absolute award of the land to E. G., but, before awarding it to another, it was the duty of the court to give him an opportunity to perfect it.[3]

§ 562. A recognizance may be taken before the court, or before its clerk. It need not be taken in open court. When it has been ordered to be taken, its amount fixed, and the parties named by the court, the court's ministerial officer, the clerk, can reduce it to writing in vacation.[4]   It may even purport to be taken and acknowledged before the clerk; nor is it necessary that it be copied at length upon the orphans' court docket. A minute therein that the recognizance has been filed, is sufficient to give notice to purchasers and creditors.[5] The recognizance is properly taken to the commonwealth for

[1] Stewart *v.* Moody, 4 W. 169.

[2] Bailey *v.* Commonwealth, 41 Pa. St. 473. The *terre-tenant* had paid the interest annually to the widow during her life.

[3] Gregg's Appeal, 20 Pa. St. 148.

[4] Riddle *v.* Pennock's Appeal, 37 Pa. St. 177.

[5] Hartman's Appeal, 21 Pa. St. 488. Comp. Bodine *v.* Commonwealth, 24 Pa. St. 69.

the use of the parties in interest, and the legal title to sue upon it resides in her.[1] There are cases, however, where it has been made directly to the heirs; or to some of them for themselves and in trust for the others.[2] In some counties the recognizance was formerly made in the name of the president judge of the orphans' court and his successors, and its validity sustained,[3] though the practice was not commended.[4] In such case, the *sci. fa.* was sued out properly in the name of him who was the judge at the time it issued.[5] When the docket of the orphans' court shows that "security" was offered by one of the heirs for the owelty of the other heirs, and that the court adjudged the tract of land to him, " he having entered into the usual securities to pay the other heirs according to law," that a recognizance was given will not be presumed, when neither bond, nor recognizance, nor other security can be found, as against a creditor of the heir who obtained judgment against him twenty-three years after the supposed execution of the recognizance.[6]

Number of Recognizances Taken.

§ 563. It is convenient to take a single recognizance, even when the recognizor takes several distinct tracts of land. A separate recognizance for each is unnecessary.[7] When there are several heirs, it is unnecessary for the heir who accepts any tract of land, to make a separate recognizance to secure the owelty of each of the others. In one case where such a method was pursued,[8] the recognizances were multiplied to

[1] Commonwealth v. Shuman's Adm., 18 Pa. St. 343, Eshelman v. Shuman's Adm., 13 Pa. St. 561; Kidd v. Commonwealth, 16 Pa. St. 426.

[2] Mentzer v. Menor, 8 W. 296.

[3] Kean v. Franklin, 5 Serg. & R. 147; President, etc., v. Groff, 14 Serg. & R. 181; Reigart v. Ellmaker, 6 Serg. & R. 44; Taggart v. Cooper, 1 Serg. & R. 497; Good v. Good, 7 W. 195; Commonwealth v. Shuman's Adm., 18 Pa. St. 343; Galbraith v.

Galbraith, 6 W. 112; Hubley v. Hamilton, 1 Y. 392.

[4] Commonwealth v. Shuman's Adm., 18 Pa. St. 343.

[5] Kean v. Franklin, 5 Serg. & R. 147.

[6] Hillbish's Appeal, 89 Pa. St. 490.

[7] Reigart v. Ellmaker, 14 Serg. & R. 121; Allen v. Getz, 2 P. & W. 310.

[8] Alexander v. Ramsey, 5 Serg. & R. 338.

the exorbitant number of four hundred and eighty. Indeed, it is unusual for the orphans' court to attempt to determine the shares due to each heir (in view of possible advancements, debts, etc.,) in the proceedings in partition.[1] But the act of 12th April, 1855, [P. L. 214,] requires the orphans' court clerk, when no auditor is appointed to ascertain advancements, etc., to make a calculation exhibiting the amounts due the respective parties in interest, and to record said calculation, when approved by the court, upon the docket of the court, as a part of the proceedings in the case. If, there being seven heirs, three tracts of land are adjudged to three of the heirs jointly, and partition among themselves is then made, by which one lot is taken by each of them in severalty, a several recognizance by each for the four-sevenths of the appraised value of the tract taken thus by him is valid.[2]

The Surety.

§ 564. A recognizance entered into by a principal and his sureties, in a certain sum "to be levied of their goods and chattels, lands and tenements, respectively," is joint and several,[3] and a surety is personally bound, though by its terms the sum recognized is to be levied on the lands awarded to the heir.[4]

Conclusiveness of the Recognizance.

§ 565. A recognizance in the orphans' court is in the nature of a judgment. Hence, the recognizor cannot, in an action of debt upon it, reduce its amount by showing that the appraisers of his father's land included in their valuation improvements made by himself, at his own expense, between the time of his father's death and the inquisition.[5] A recognizance to secure a sum calculated on the supposition that

---

[1] Blanchard v. Commonwealth, 6 W 309. In Shelly v Shelly, 8 W. & S 60, a case is mentioned in which there were 250 recognizances.

[2] Ebbs v. Commonwealth, 11 Pa. St. 374.

[3] Wampler v. Shissler, 1 W. & S. 365.

[4] Taggart v. Cooper, 1 Serg. & R. 497.

[5] Beatty v. Smith, 4 Y. 102.

the land taken contained two hundred acres, more or less, cannot be increased by a decree of the orphans' court five years afterwards, on discovering that the actual number of acres was forty-three more than had been believed.[1] Nor, in an action on the recognizance, will a reduction of the debt acknowledged be made, because the land embraced twenty acres less than had been supposed.[2] The inquest cannot decide how much of the appraised value of land is payable to the heirs; this must be done by the orphans' court itself. Hence, though the inquest did determine the amount payable to each heir, and the recognizance was to pay the heirs according to the inquest, it was competent for the recognizor, in an action on the recognizance, to show advancements made to the use-plaintiff. It would have been otherwise, had the court itself determined the share of the plaintiff.[3] If the recognizors are also administrators of the estate, and, after giving the recognizance, it appears that the estate is indebted to them, the orphans' court, on their petition, may decree a reduction of the recognizance three years after it was entered into.[4] So, if an inquest, in ascertaining the value of the decedent's lands, overlook the façt that they are charged with the dower of a widow of a former owner, the orphans' court may, several months after the recognizances are given, and the land awarded, order a reduction of them.[4] For the same reason, an abatement may be made in the trial on *sci. fa.* on the recognizance, as also for collateral inheritance tax due the commonwealth, and charged upon the land taken in partition.[5] The heirs, after partition in the orphans' court, may agree to a new arrangement among themselves, with the effect of discharging the recognizance.[6] A surety in the recognizance who is also *terre-tenant*, may show that the

[1] Galbraith *v* Galbraith, 6 W. 112.

[2] Nichols *v.* Rummel, 3 P. & W. 195.

[3] Blanchard *v.* Commonwealth, 6 W. 309.

[4] Dech, Adm., *v.* Gluck, 47 Pa. St. 403.

[5] Seaton *v.* Barry, 4 W. & S. 183; Goepp's Appeal, 15 Pa. St. 425.

[6] Bavington *v.* Clarke, 2 P. & W. 115.

decedent had, during the life of a first wife, married a second, by whom he had a daughter, and after the death of his first wife, three other daughters, and that though the lands were awarded to the oldest daughter, on whose recognizance he became surety, she took no title, being illegitimate.[1]

For How Much a Lien.

§ 566. When an heir accepts land at the valuation, the recognizance into which he enters is simply to secure the owelty of the other heirs, as well that which is payable immediately as that which is payable only on the death of the widow. The recognizor's own share in the principal of the widow's third, payable at her death, is merged in his estate in the land, if he continues to own it until that time.[2] If, however, the accepting heir conveys the land during the life of the widow, subject to the payment of the principal of the widow's third, at her death, the lien for the entire third will follow the land. The recognizor died during the life of the widow, and his estate was sold by order of the orphans' court for the payment of debts to A., subject to the widow's third described *in numero*. A. sold it to B., subject to the same encumbrance set forth again *in numero*. On B.'s death, the land was divided between his heirs, and, the widow of the first decedent then dying, was liable to the administrator of X., for his share in the principal of her dower.[3] After A. had accepted land, in partition, and had given a recognizance for the shares of the heirs in the widow's third after her death, the land was sold by the sheriff to B., who sold to C. C.'s title was sold by the sheriff to D., who sold to E., subject to the payment of interest on $6,186.76, to the widow during her life, and the principal sum to the heirs and legal representatives of the decedent. The other deeds were silent regarding this widow's charge. It was

---

[1] Davis *v.* Houston, 2 Y. 289.

[2] Dech *v.* Gluck, 47 Pa. St. 403; Shelly *v.* Shelly, 8 W. & S. 153; Stecker *v.* Shimer, 5 Wh. 451; Duey *v.* Clemens, 1 Pa St. 118; Reigle *v.* Seiger, 2 P. & W. 340, Erb *v.* Huston, 18 Pa. St. 369.

[3] Dech *v.* Gluck, 47 Pa. St. 403

held that E. was liable on the widow's death to pay to D. the share of A., in the principal sum.[1] The right of accepting land at the appraisement was assigned by a son of the decedent to A. the husband of a daughter of the decedent, who entered into recognizance for the payment of the principal of the widow's third at her death. In her life-time, he conveyed the land to B., expressly subject to this principal "including the said A.'s hereditary portion." B. also executed a bond stipulating to pay to A. his wife's share in the principal. B. subsequently conveyed the land to C., in the life-time of the widow, subject to the payments which B. had assumed. On the widow's death, C. was compelled to pay to A. his wife's share in the widow's third.[2] A son who took land in partition, giving a recognizance conditioned *inter alia* for the payment of one-third of the valuation at the widow's death, and who subsequently sold it by a deed, "reserving his interest at the death of the widow," was entitled, at her death, to his share of the recognizance.[3]

§ 567. When the accepting heir conveyed the land to A., under and subject to the payment "to the *other* children" of the decedent of their shares in the principal of the widow's dower, and A. conveyed it to B., "under and subject" to the payment "to the children," (*other* being omitted) of the decedent, the heir's share in the widow's dower was merged and extinguished.[4] The heir sold, giving a bond of indemnity to his grantee against all encumbrances save "the widow's third." The purchaser's interest was then sold by the sheriff, whose vendee again sold it, by a deed reciting the exact sum of the widow's third to which the land was subject. Two other successive conveyances were then made, the same clause being in the deeds. It was decided that the heir had reserved nothing for himself, and on the death of

---

[1] Erb *v.* Huston, 18 Pa. St. 369. This was an amicable action.

[2] Shelly *v.* Shelly, 8 W. & S. 153. This was *assumpsit* against C.

[3] Updegrove *v.* Updegrove, 1 Pa. St. 136 ; White *v.* Williams, 3 Phila. 460.

[4] Stecker *v.* Shimer, 5 Wh. 451.

the widow he could recover nothing from the *terre-tenant*.[1] After the heir had accepted lands of the decedent, and, during the widow's life-time, his interest was sold by the sheriff, "subject to the payment of a dower," whose exact sum was mentioned, "the interest whereof to be paid yearly unto the widow, * * * and after her death the principal to be paid to the heirs of the said deceased." An assignee of the heirs' share in this sum, could not recover anything from the *terre-tenant*, after the widow's death.[2]

Proceedings on the Recognizance.

§ 568. Effect may be given to the recognizance by a *sci. fa.*,[3] a long usage sanctioning such a writ from the common pleas, though the record on which it is based is in the orphans' court.[4] An action of debt is also an appropriate remedy.[5] *Assumpsit* may be brought against a *terre-tenant* for the principal of the widow's dower, at her death,[6] but against the recognizor himself the action must be on the recognizance.[7] Under the act of May 17th, 1866, [P. L. 1096,] "an act enlarging the powers of the orphans' court, so as to discharge liens upon real estate," the orphans' court may, on petition of the person entitled to money secured by a recog-

---

[1] Duey *v.* Clemens, 1 Pa. St. 118.

[2] Reigle *v.* Seiger, 2 P. & W. 340.

[3] Stewart *v.* Martin, 2 W. 200; Kean *v.* Franklin, 5 Serg. & R. 147; Ebbs *v.* Commonwealth, 11 Pa. St. 374; Wentzer *v.* Menor, 8 W. 296; Baily & Pott *v.* Commonwealth, 41 Pa. St. 473; Kidd *v.* Commonwealth, 16 Pa. St. 426; Nichols *v.* Rummel, 3 P. & W. 195; Ankeny *v.* Penrose, 18 Pa. St. 190; Seaton *v.* Barry, 4 W. & S. 183; Wishart *v.* Downey, 15 Pa. St. 77; Pauley *v.* Pauley, 7 W. 159. *Sci. fa.* is said to be the proper remedy on a recognizance for the appearance of the defendant at the quarter sessions, in Bodine *v.* Commonwealth, 24 Pa. St. 69. In President, etc., *v.*

Groff, 14 Serg. & R. 181, the *sci. fa.* on the recognizance in the orphans' court was sued out in the district court.

[4] Allen *v.* Reesor, 16 Serg. & R. 10.

[5] Taggart *v.* Cooper, 1 Serg. & R. 497; Good *v.* Good, 7 W. 195; Blanchard *v.* Commonwealth, 6 W. 309; Hubley *v.* Hamilton, 1 Y. 392. Stewart *v.* Moody, 4 W. 169, was a recognizance of an administrator ordered to sell real estate of the intestate for the payment of his debts.

[6] Pidcock *v.* Bye, 3 R. 183; Shelly *v.* Shelly, 8 W. & S. 153; Kline *v.* Bowman, 19 Pa. St. 24.

[7] Shelly *v.* Shelly, 8 W. & S. 153.

nizance, decree that it shall be paid, or, in default thereof
order an execution to issue to be levied on the real estate
charged.[1]

Merger by Judgment.

§ 569. A judgment in one *sci. fa.* upon the recognizance
does not so merge it that another *sci. fa.* cannot be sustained
upon it to the use of another party in interest.[2] Though
before the widow's death, an heir obtained judgment on a
sci. fa. for his share of the owelty, an assignee of the widow's
interest, not paid in her life-time, also obtained judgment
therefor, on a *sci. fa.* issued after her decease.[3] A judgment
on a *sci. fa.* to recover the annual installments due the
widow, does not bar a second *sci. fa.* to recover interest subsequently accruing and in arrear.[4]

The Parties Defendant.

§ 570. The recognizor must be made a defendant, though
he has ceased to own the land, and is insolvent.[5] If he die
after the issue of the *sci. fa.*, his personal representative
must be brought in. The action cannot proceed against the
terre-tenant alone. If the personal representative should
fail to appear, on a *sci. fa.* to call him in, judgment should
be signed against him *de bonis testatoris,* and then the *terre-
tenant* may plead and defend *pro interesse suo;* if the verdict
is against him, the judgment will be *de terris.*[6] As already
implied, the *terre-tenant* may be made a party to an action
of debt[7] or to a *sci. fa.*[8] on a recognizance, by a notice to

[1] Neel's Appeal, 88 Pa. St. 94. In
order to reach the surety, or other
property of the recognizor, *sci fa.* or
debt on the recognizance would be
necessary.

[2] Good *v* Good, 7 W. 195; Ebbs *v.*
Commonwealth, 11 Pa. St. 374; Ankeny *v.* Penrose, 18 Pa. St. 190.

[3] Good *v.* Good, 7 W. 195; Ebbs *v.*
Commonwealth, 11 Pa. St. 374.

[4] Stewart *v.* Martin, 2 W. 202.

[5] Kean *v.* Ellmaker, 7 Serg. & R. 1;
Kean *v.* Franklin, 5 Serg. & R. 147.

[6] Reigart *v* Ellmaker, 6 Serg. & R.
44. 14 Serg. & R. 121.

[7] Good *v.* Good, 7 W. 195; Nichols
v. Rummel, 3 P. & W. 195; Commonwealth *v.* Shuman's Adm., 18 Pa. St.
343; Crawford *v.* Crawford, 2 W.
339.

[8] Reigart *v.* Ellmaker, 6 Serg. & R.
44, 14 Serg. & R. 121; Mentzer *v.*

appear and defend it.   If the principal recognizor is dead, the
sci. fa. must issue to his administrator and the surviving
recognizor, with notice to the *terre-tenant.*[1]

The Parties Plaintiff.

§ 571. The commonwealth being the legal recognizee, the
action should be brought in her name, and when less than
the whole number of claimants bring it, their names should
be suggested.[2]   The action may be brought by so many of
the parties interested, as, being aggrieved, desire to bring it.[3]
It is not error, therefore, that more than one and less than
all of the use-recognizees should join in the suit.[4]   If the
heir whose owelty is secured by the recognizances dies, the
action must be instituted by his personal representative;
the interest is money, and not real estate.[5]   If the heir has
assigned his right to the money, it is not necessary that the
assignee's name should be suggested of record.[6]   The
defendant cannot show that the party for whom the *sci. fa.*
issues, has assigned his interest to another,[7] or that the
assignment was procured by fraud.[8]

Menor, 8 W. 296; Ebbs *v.* Commonwealth, 11 Pa. St 374; Baily & Pott *v.* Commonwealth. 41 Pa. St. 473.

[1] Ebbs *v.* Commonwealth, 11 Pa. St. 374.

[2] Kidd *v.* Commonwealth, 16 Pa. St. 426; Blanchard *v.* Commonwealth, 6 W. 309; Commonwealth *v* Hantz, 2 P. & W. 333; Eshelman *v.* Shuman's Adm., 13 Pa. St. 561; Commonwealth *v.* Lightner, 9 W. & S. 117. In Ankeny *v.* Penrose, 18 Pa. St 190, separate *sci. fas.* on the same day were issued at the suit of the several heirs. In Good *v.* Good, 7 W. 195, the use-plaintiff was suggested. In Shaupe *v.* Shaupe, 12 Serg. & R. 9, Gibson, J, said that an action would not be sustained on a recognizance, unless all the parties

interested were joined, if objection were taken at the trial.

[3] Commonwealth *v* Lightner, 9 W. & S 117.

[4] Kidd *v.* Commonwealth, 16 Pa. St. 426.

[5] Pauley *v.* Pauley, 7 W. 159. The right of the administrator does not depend on showing the existence of debts, to which the money must be applied.

[6] Reigart *v.* Ellmaker, 6 Serg. & R. 44.

[7] Commonwealth *v.* Lightner, 9 W. & S. 117.

[8] Blanchard *v.* Commonwealth, 6 W. 309. Yet, in Shaupe *v.* Shaupe, 12 Serg. & R. 9, it was decided that a widow's interest having been sold on execution, an action on the recognizance could not be supported in her name.

The Scire Facias.

§ 572. A *sci. fa.* which, after reciting the recognizance, commands the sheriff to make known to the defendant that he be
and appear, etc., and show cause why the moneys due "should
not be made of his lands and chattels and levied to the use
and behoof" of the plaintiff, *i. e.*, demanding an award of
execution of the amount due, is in proper form.[1] Since the
sci. fa. contains the substance of a declaration, distinct
declarations are unusual and unnecessary.[2]

Pleas, Defendants and Judgment.

§ 573. Payment, and payment with leave, is a proper
plea,[3] and under it, matters of set-off, existing at the time
the recognizance was entered into, may be shown. So, the
defendant, one of the heirs, may show that another tract of
land was sold by a trustee, and the proceeds remaining after
paying decedent's debts, were received by the plaintiff in the
sci. fa. without objection from the defendant.[4] A release of
the recognizance may be shown under this plea of payment,
with leave, etc., but when one recognizance is given by an
accepting heir to secure the owelty of other heirs in several
distinct tracts, valued separately by the inquest, a release of
one of these tracts from the lien of the recognizance, is not
a release of the other tracts in favor of a purchaser of one
of them, the consideration of the release being the payment
of the owelty charged upon the tract released, and no more,[5]
and a release of a part of one tract from the recognizance
does not discharge the remaining portion.[6] Judgment
should be, not for the penalty of the recognizance, but
for the amount actually due to the use-plaintiff.[7] Against

[1] Stewart *v.* Martin, 2 W. 200.

[2] Kean *t.* Franklin, 5 Serg. & R.
147.

[3] Commonwealth   *v.*   Shuman's
Adm., 18 Pa. St. 343; Ebbs *v.* Commonwealth, 11 Pa St. 374.

[4] Kidd *v.* Commonwealth, 16 Pa.
St. 426.

[5] Reigart *v.* Ellmaker, 14 Serg. &
R. 121; Kean *v.* Ellmaker, 7 Serg.
& R. 1.

[6] Crawford *v.* Crawford, 2 W 339.

[7] Stewart *v.* Martin, 2 W. 200; Kidd
v. Commonwealth, 16 Pa. St. 426;
Ebbs *v.* Commonwealth, 11 Pa. St.
374. Yet, in Commonwealth *v.* Haf-

the *terre-tenant*, it should be *de terris*,[1] that is, that the plaintiff have execution of the lands in his hands for as much as has been found against him.[2] Against the recognizor himself, or his legal representative, if he be dead, a personal judgment is rendered.[3] When the judgment is satisfied of record, the clerk of the court must, on a certificate thereof from the prothonotary, mark the recognizance satisfied.[4]

fey, 6 Pa. St. 348, on a recognizance in partition in the common pleas, a judgment for the penalty was affirmed by the supreme court.

[1] Kline *v.* Bowman, 19 Pa. St. 24;
Pidcock *v.* Bye, 3 Rawle 183. This was *assumpsit* against the *terre-tenant.*

[2] Kean *v.* Ellmaker, 7 Serg. & R. 1.

[3] *Ibid.*

[4] Act 3d April, 1860, [P. L. 630.]

CHAPTER XXII.

LIEN OF RECOGNIZANCES OF SHERIFFS AND CORONERS.

The Lien.

§ 574. The sixty-fourth section of the act of 15th April, 1834, [P. L. 547,] directs the sheriff and coroner, together with their sureties, to enter into a recognizance to secure the faithful performance of their respective duties. The seventy-fourth section directs that "all the real estate, within the same county, of a sheriff and coroner and their respective sureties, shall be bound by a recognizance taken in the manner aforesaid, as effectually as by a judgment to the same amount in any court of record of such county." It is by virtue of this, and previous legislation for which this is a ~ubstitute, that such recognizances become liens.[1] In so far as they bind the lands of the sureties,[2] they differ from the recognizances taken in the orphans' court in partition.[3]

Upon What Lands a Lien.

§ 575. Under the law, as it existed prior to the act of 15th April, 1834, [P. L. 547,] it was the opinion of a majority of the supreme court in 1831, that the lien of the sheriff's recognizance operated upon all the lands owned by him within the state of Pennsylvania, at the time of its execution.[4] That act makes it a lien on "all the real estate within the same county, of a sheriff and coroner, and their respective sureties." The act of April 3d, 1860, [P. L. 650,] which directs that the recognizances of sheriffs[5] "of the several

---

[1] Allen v. Reesor, 16 Serg & R. 15. In re Morris' Estate, 4 Pa. St. 162.

[2] Stuck v. Mackey, 4 W. & S. 196; McCarty v. Springer, 3 P. & W. 157; McKensey's Appropriation, 3 Pa. St. 156.

[3] Allen v. Reesor, 16 Serg. & R. 15.

[4] Snyder v. Commonwealth, 3 P. & W. 286.

[5] Coroners are not mentioned.

counties of this commonwealth shall continue to be a lien on the real estate owned by said sheriffs, respectively, at the dates of said recognizances, for the term of ten years from said dates," was intended to limit the duration of their lien, but not to broaden the geographical scope of it. The act of March 28th, 1803, [4 Sm. L. 48,] directed that "all the lands, tenements and hereditaments which such sheriffs, coroners, and their sureties, shall possess or be entitled to, in every county within this commonwealth, shall be bound by recognizance taken in manner aforesaid, as effectually as a judgment of the same amount in the court of common pleas of all the counties aforesaid, might or could now bind the same." Of this act, as well as of that of 15th April, 1834, the intent seems to be, to limit the lien of the recognizance to lands owned at the date of its execution.[1] The act of April 3d, 1860, [P. L. 650,] expressly declares that the recognizances of sheriffs "shall continue to be a lien on the real estate owned by said sheriffs, respectively, *at the dates* of said recognizances*," for the term of ten years. This act, however, has no application to Philadelphia.

Duration of the Lien.

§ 576. By an act passed March 5th, 1790, [2 Dall. L. 771,] it was declared that the recognizances of sheriffs and coroners should be "in the nature and effect of a judgment obtained in the supreme court," and should bind their lands, tenements, etc., "in the same manner as such judgments." The act of 28th March, 1803, directed that their lands, tenements, etc., in every county of the state, should be bound as

---

[1] The question is alluded to in Fricker's Appeal, 1 W. 393, but not decided. Yet, the recognizance was dated October 20th, 1817; a *sci. fa.* issued on it to November Term, 1823, on which judgment was recovered November 14th, 1827. On a sale of the land bound by the recognizance, the recognizee was preferred, in distribution of its proceeds, to a creditor whose judgment was obtained November 11th, 1822. In Stuck v. Mackey, 4 W. & S. 196, Judge Grier, in a charge which was sustained by the supreme court, declared that if land was acquired October, 1824, it was not bound by a recognizance entered into in 1820.

effectually as by "a judgment for the same amount in the court of common pleas of all the counties" aforesaid. Under these acts, the opinion was expressed in 1831, by C. J. Gibson, that the lien of the recognizance of sheriffs and coroners is indefinite in duration, and a *sci. fa.* issued September 26th, 1827, on a recognizance taken October 19th, 1812, the sheriff's term having expired in 1815, was sustained.[1] The act of 3d April, 1860, [P. L. 650,] declares that the recognizances of sheriffs (except those of Philadelphia) shall continue a lien on the real estate owned by them at the dates of their recognizances, for the term of ten years only from said dates,[2] and the act of 13th April, 1868, [P. L. 948,] makes five years from the date of the recognizance, the term within which an action thereon, against any sheriff or coroner in the city of Philadelphia, may be sustained.[3] It will be observed that the lien of the recognizances of *coroners*, outside of Philadelphia, remains indefinite in duration, as it was prior to the act of 1860.

§ 577. The bringing of an action on the recognizance of sheriffs and coroners against their sureties is restricted by the act of 28th March, 1803, [4 Sm. L. 48,] to five years from their dates, and since no such suit can be maintained on them afterwards, their lien is gone against the sureties, with the expiration of that period.[4] On a recognizance dated October 18th, 1833, suit brought against the sureties October 25th, 1838, was too late, although the recognizance was not approved by the governor, nor the sheriff's commission issued by him, until October 25th, 1833.[5] A sheriff's

---

[1] Snyder *v.* Commonwealth, 3 P. & W. 286. This was *sci. fa.* against the sheriff alone.

[2] This limit applied to recognizances already made, at the passage of the act, unless ten years had already elapsed, in which case the lien was continued one year longer.

[3] On any existing recognizances, suit could be brought within one year after the passage of the act.

[4] Smith *v.* Miller, 13 Pa. St. 339.

[5] Wilson *v.* Commonwealth, 7 W. & S. 181.

bond and his recognizance are distinct securities, and though the sureties are the same in both, an action on the bond within five years, will not keep alive the liability of the sureties on the recognizance beyond that term.[1] If the *sci. fa.* issues within five years against the sureties, there is no definite time within which it must be prosecuted to judgment. Hence, it is no defence for the personal representative of a surety, dying October 28th, 1820, that though the action was brought December 20th, 1821, no trial was had on it for seventeen years afterwards.[2]

For How Much the Recognizance is a Lien.

§ 578. The penalty of the recognizance is the measure of the liability of the recognizors thereupon, but to this extent they (the sureties, as well as the sheriff,) are liable on that instrument for the losses occasioned to others by the sheriff's default, although the sheriff himself or his sureties in the bond may have become liable for and paid an equal amount for his misfeasances. The recognizance binds the recognizors, not simply that the sheriff shall, either as sheriff or as obligor on his bond, make up any damages occasioned by his misconduct, to the extent of the penalty of the recognizance, but that they shall, *as such recognizors* make up any damages so occasioned to that extent.[3] Hence, even if the same persons were sureties both on the bond and on the recognizance, they would be liable on each instrument for its separate penalty, and a discharge of the bond by payments made thereon, either by the sheriff or themselves, to the extent of its penalty, would not discharge the recognizance.[4]

---

[1] Smith *v.* Miller, 13 Pa. St. 339. In Commonwealth *v.* Rainey, 4 W. & S. 186, it was decided that though a cautionary judgment for the penalty of the sheriff's bond had been obtained within five years, no *sci. fa.* could be issued thereon by persons aggrieved, when that term had expired.

[2] Beale *v.* Commonwealth, 7 W. 183.

[3] Commonwealth *v.* Montgomery, 31 Pa. St. 519; Commonwealth *v.* Lelar, 13 Pa. St. 22; Withrow *v.* Commonwealth, 10 Serg. & R. 231.

[4] Commonwealth *v.* Montgomery, 31 Pa. St. 519.

Liability for Escapes.

§ 579. The sheriff and his sureties are liable if, on a *capias ad respondendum*, he takes insufficient bail, and suffers the defendant to go at liberty, under the following circumstances: The plaintiff excepts to the bail in due time and form, and gives notice to the sheriff of his exceptions; the bail does not justify; other bail is not substituted; the plaintiff obtains judgment against the defendant; sues out a *capias ad satisfaciendum*, which is returned *non est inventus;* a writ then issues against the bail, who fails to surrender the defendant on or before the fourth day after the return day of the *ca. sa.;* the bail is proceeded against to judgment and execution. For so much of the debt as is not thus realized, damages may be recovered on the recognizance.[1] When, to a writ of *capias ad satisfaciendum,* the sheriff returns "served and delivered to court," this will charge him with the defendant in the first instance, and being bound from a reasonable time after the arrest to keep the defendant in jail, his subsequent appearance at large is an escape which fixes the sheriff for the debt.[2] If the sheriff permit one arrested on a *ca. sa.,* upon condition of his presenting himself every morning at the sheriff's office, to go at large during the day, until, under the insolvent laws, the prisoner is discharged, the sheriff is liable to the plaintiff for a permissive escape.[3] The insolvency of the defendant is immaterial, and for such escape the sheriff is liable for the entire debt and costs.[4] The neglect of the sheriff to commit a person convicted of fornication and bastardy until the sentence is complied with, or the discharge of such person by the sheriff, makes him liable to the mother of the prosecutrix for the amount which the defendant was sentenced to pay.[5]

[1] Commonwealth *v.* Watmough, 1 Cl. 412.

[2] Beale *v.* Commonwealth, 7 W. 183.

[3] Hopkinson *v.* Leeds, 2 W. N. C. 177.

[4] Wolverton *v.* Commonwealth, 7 Serg. & R. 273.

[5] Snyder *v.* Commonwealth, 1 P. & W. 94; Smith *v.* Commonwealth, 59 Pa. St. 320.

Levy on Stranger's Goods.

§ 580. The sheriff and his sureties are liable when, under an execution, he levies on property which belongs to another than the defendant, and sells it.[1] If the property asserted by the plaintiff in the *fi. fa.* to belong to the defendant is claimed by another, the sheriff is not bound to levy upon it if, on his demand, the plaintiff declines to indemnify him, when the claim of property is such as would raise apprehension in the mind of a reasonable and constant man.[2] Even if the plaintiff is not notified of the adverse claim, the sheriff is excused from levying when the goods are in fact the claimant's; the plaintiff in the action on the recognizance must, therefore, show that they were the property of the defendant.[3] Though the claimant fails to plead under a rule by the sheriff, and thus loses his action against that officer, in case of levy and sale of his goods, these do not cease to be his, and, in an action by the execution-plaintiff against the sheriff, the latter may show that they were in fact the claimant's.[4] But, if the property has been sold or assigned by the defendant, and such assignment is valid as to him but invalid as to the creditors, the sheriff will not be excused on that account from levying on it, and for his refusal an action lies immediately; the plaintiff need not wait till the arrival of the return day of the *fi. fa.*[5] An attachment under the act of 17th March, 1869, does not justify the seizure of goods belonging to the garnishee, whatever the result of the attachment suit may be.[6] If, to a *fi. fa.*, the sheriff make return "levied" on personal property, this return will estop him from denying that the property belonged to the defendant.[7] A refusal to make a levy may

---

[1] Carmack *v.* Commonwealth, 5 Binn. 184.

[2] Spangler *v.* Commonwealth, 16 Pa. St. 68 ; Miller *v.* Commonwealth, 5 Pa. St. 294.

[3] Shannon *v.* Commonwealth, 8 Serg. & R. 444.

[4] Commonwealth *v.* Megee, 4 Phila. 258.

[5] Shannon *v.* Commonwealth, 8 Serg. & R. 444.

[6] Rothermel *v.* Marr, 10 W. N. C. 421.

[7] Miller *v.* Commonwealth, 5 Pa. St. 294.

be justified by the sheriff's showing that all the goods of the defendant had been assigned in trust for the benefit of creditors on the day previous to the *fi. fa.* reaching his hands.[1]

Liability to Parties to Execution.

§ 581. The sheriff is *prima facie* liable for the whole amount of an execution, if he fails to make a levy,[2] or having levied, causes the lien of the writ to be postponed to that of other writs by his improper conduct,[3] or permits the property levied on to be eloined,[4] or misappropriates the moneys made by a sale[5] or received from the defendant, though after the return day, a levy having been made before the return day,[6] or abandons the levy.[7] If a surplus remains from the sale of real estate bound by a judgment, the sheriff is liable if he mistakenly pays it over to a person not entitled to it.[8] The officer, whether he be sheriff or coroner, cannot dispute the authority of the court to issue the writ, or to direct it to him for execution.[9] In making a levy and sale the sheriff must be governed by the amount endorsed on the back of the *fi. fa.;* that in the body of the writ is often merely nominal, and the endorsement contains the real demand.[10]

§ 582. A return of "levied on personal property," makes the sheriff *prima facie* liable for the debt, but this *prima facies* may be rebutted. The sheriff may show that while the writ was stayed by the court, another execution was issued, under which a levy and sale were had, and thus raise a presumption that the property levied was consumed by the

---

[1] Leeds *v.* Commonwealth, 3 W. N. C. 554.

[2] Dorrance's Adm. *v.* Commonwealth, 13 Pa. St. 160; Linton *v.* Commonwealth, 46 Pa. St. 294.

[3] Commonwealth *v.* Contner, 18 Pa. St. 439.

[4] Mitchell *v.* Commonwealth, 37 Pa. St. 187.

[5] Commonwealth *v.* Rogers, 4 Cl. 252.

[6] Beale *v.* Commonwealth, 7 W. 183; Juniata Bank *v.* Beale, 1 W. & S. 227.

[7] Commonwealth *v.* Contner, 18 Pa. St. 439.

[8] Commonwealth *v.* Lelar, 13 Pa. St. 22.

[9] Beale *v.* Commonwealth, 11 Serg. & R. 299.

[10] Commonwealth *v.* McCoy, 8 W. 153.

second execution, which the plaintiff must rebut.[1] That there were prior executions in the hands of the coroner, on which levies had been made on the property subsequently levied on by the sheriff, and which exhausted the proceeds of its sale, is a sufficient excuse to the sheriff.[2] So, it may be shown by the coroner to whom a *fi. fa.* against one of the sheriff's sureties is directed, and who returns levied on certain articles, together with the whole of the defendant's personal property, that the value of such property was less than the debt.[3]

§ 583. An intentional omission to sell under a given writ, though it does not destroy its lien, and though, on distribution of the proceeds of the sale on a later writ, the plaintiff in the first might successfully claim an appropriation to his execution, will make the sheriff and his sureties liable to such plaintiff to the amount of the proceeds of such sale that would have been applicable to his writ. He is not bound to go before the auditor who distributes the proceeds of the sale.[4] *A fortiori* will the recognizors be liable, when, by the sheriff's conduct, the lien is really postponed. A *fi. fa.* having issued against B., under which a levy was made on certain chattels, A. claimed them as his, and the sheriff applied for a rule to interplead, under which the court ordered him to surrender the goods to A. on his filing a declaration and giving a bond. A. doing neither, the sheriff, nevertheless, abandoned possession of the goods levied on. Subsequently another execution issued, under which the same goods were levied and sold. The first execution had lost its lien by the sheriff's act, and he and his sureties became liable on his recognizance for the execution.[5] But the recognizors may show that, had the writ been properly executed, it would have been paid only in part, on account of a

---

[1] Beale *v.* Commonwealth, 7 W. 183; Juniata Bank *v.* Beale, 1 W. & S. 227.

[2] Juniata Bank *v.* Beale, 1 W. & S. 227

[3] Beale *v.* Commonwealth, 11 Serg. & R. 299.

[4] Commonwealth *v.* Contner, 18 Pa. St. 439.

[5] *Ibid.*

landlord's claim for rent, which would probably have been put in,[1] notwithstanding that, after the levy and sale, the landlord entered on the demised premises and so determined his right to demand the arrears of rent.[2] It is no excuse to a sheriff, for not executing a *vend. ex.* issued after his return of *levied* to a *fi. fa.*, that he had ceased to be sheriff between the making of his return and the issue of the *vend. ex.*, an interval of one and one-half years, occasioned by a rule to show cause why the judgment should not be opened.[3]

§ 584. If the sheriff becomes liable for not levying a *fi. fa.* before the return day, and so permitting its lien to perish, he may show that there were other simultaneous executions, and that the leviable property would have paid only a percentage of these *fi. fas.;* nor is the defence impaired by the fact that the owners of these other executions, having originally joined in the action against the sheriff, have been since paid in full.[4] The defendant's promise to pay the debt in a few days, is no excuse for omitting to levy before the return day, and the issue of an *alias fi. fa.* by the plaintiff implies no condonation of the sheriff's misfeasance.[5]

Misappropriation of Proceeds of Execution.

§ 585. For an appropriation of the proceeds of a sale to a judgment not entitled to receive them, the sheriff will be liable, but the fact that, after his appropriation, the judgment has been reversed for error, will not make wrong an appropriation to liens apparently valid at the time it was made.[6] The sheriff is liable to a creditor to whom he fails to appropriate the money under a mistaken belief that he is not entitled.[7] From the failure to make a return to a *fi. fa.*, a

---

[1] Commonwealth *v.* Contner, 18 Pa. St. 439, 21 Pa. St. 266.

[2] Commonwealth *v.* Contner, 21 Pa. St. 266.

[3] Spang *v.* Commonwealth, 12 Pa. St. 358.

[4] Linton *v.* Commonwealth, 46 Pa. St. 294.

[5] Myers *v.* Commonwealth, 2 W. & S. 60; Evans *v.* Boggs, 2 W. & S. 229.

[6] Commonwealth *v.* Rogers, 4 Cl. 252.

[7] Reed *v.* Reed, 1 W. & S. 235.

presumption will arise, after several years, that the debt has been collected and misappropriated, and the sheriff must show affirmatively facts which will excuse him.[1] A return that the money has been made will be conclusive, unless on its face something appears to qualify the meaning, e. g., that the sheriff, being indebted to the defendant in the execution, agreed to pay the execution in partial satisfaction of this indebtedness. In such case, the sheriff will be liable, not as having received the money, but as not having properly executed the writ by levy and sale, and can offer such defences as would excuse him from levy or sale, or from liability in whole or in part, for the omission of either.[2] He is liable for the costs of a judgment and execution which he has made, or which he might have made from the defendant's property, but not to the plaintiff in the execution unless the latter has actually paid them to the officers. On the sheriff's receipt of the costs, he becomes directly liable to the officer entitled.[3] The same rule holds, when the judgment was for the defendant; the defendant recovers costs, only when he has previously advanced them.[4] Attorneys' fees are within the same principle.[5]

Miscellaneous Questions of Liability.

§ 586. When the law requires the sheriff to make advertisements in newspapers or by hand-bills, of audits, inquisitions, rules of the orphans' courts, etc., failure to do so will be a breach of his recognizance; neither the sheriff, however, nor his sureties are liable on that instrument to the printer for compensation for such advertising. The sheriff must be pursued personally, as he must be for his debt to his deputy, or to the livery stable keeper who supplies him with convey-

---

[1] Commonwealth v. McCoy, 8 W. 153.

[2] Juniata Bank v. Beale, 1 W. & S. 227.

[3] Beale v. Commonwealth, 7 W. 183; Commonwealth v. McCoy, 8 W. 153.

[4] Commonwealth v. McCoy, 8 W. 153.

[5] Pontius v. Commonwealth, 4 W. & S. 52; Commonwealth v. McCoy, 8 W. 153.

ance, or to the stationer.[1] When the county commissioners draw orders on the county treasurer in favor of the sheriff for "fees," which, at the time they are drawn, are in excess of the fees actually due, on his allegation that that amount would be coming to him, he his personally liable to refund the excess in *assumpsit*, but no action can be sustained on his recognizance.[2] When a writ of restitution issues, commanding the sheriff to restore a defendant to the possession of lands taken from him by an extent, he is liable for failure to restore him as against the plaintiff in the extent, or one claiming under him, or an intruder. He is not liable, however, for not turning out of possession one claiming a fee-simple paramount to the defendant in the extent.[3] A sheriff returned to a *sci. fa.* sur mortgage, *nihil habet*. Had he gone to the premises, he would have found that the defendant was dead, and his return must have been *mortuus est*, and no judgment could have been entered on the *sci. fa.* Since, however, the mortgage debt was really due, no damages were suffered for which the sheriff and his sureties in the recognizance were liable.[4] For a mere non-return of a *fi.fa.* the sheriff is not liable even for nominal damages. It must appear that *prima facie* the plaintiff has been damnified by the sheriff's inaction with respect to the *fi. fa.* He must show, therefore, that he had an interest in the execution of the writ.[5] But nominal damages can be recovered for the sheriff's neglect to make a return by a certain date, after he has been ruled to do so by the court, at the prayer of the plaintiff in the *fi. fa.*[6] For a false return to a *fi. fa.* there can be no recovery against the sheriff, without damage to the plaintiff; if the return was that the

[1] Commonwealth *v.* Swope, 45 Pa. St 535.

[2] Commonwealth *v.* Hoffman, 74 Pa. St. 105.

[3] Commonwealth *v.* Staub, 85 Pa. St. 137.

[4] Commonwealth *v.* Lyle, 1 W. N. C. 90.

[5] Commonwealth *v.* McCoy, 8 W. 153; Commonwealth *v.* Allen, 30 Pa. St. 49.

[6] Commonwealth *v.* Allen, 30 Pa. St. 49.

fi. fa. was superseded by a writ of error, when in fact no writ of error had been sued out, but the judgment had been paid before the *fi. fa.* issued, the plaintiff cannot recover even nominal damages.[1]

The Recognizance Itself.

§ 587. The form of the recognizances of sheriffs and of coroners is prescribed by the act of 15th April, 1834, [P. L. 547.] They are not under seal, and, therefore, no deeds.[2] Signing by the recognizors is not essential, though proper, as a means of securing the evidence of the identity of the recognizors, which their handwriting affords.[3] The recognizance is the oral assent of the recognizors to the engagement propounded to them by the officer, in the language prescribed in the act of 1834.[3] The sixty-eighth section of the act of April 15th, 1834, directs that the recognizance shall be taken by the recorder of deeds of the proper county, and shall be recorded in his office. Thus recorded, it becomes a "most solemn record," made by an officer sworn to perform his duties with fidelity. Hence, it cannot be shown, even by the testimony of the recorder himself, that the defendants never acknowledged or entered into the recognizance. It might, however, be competent for him to show some fraud practiced on the defendants, or a false personation of them by other persons.[4] The omission to record the recognizance does not vitiate it. The production of the original itself at the trial would be sufficient.[5] Nothing prohibits that the same persons should be sureties in both the bonds and the

[1] McCurdy *v.* Lelar, 5 Cl. 167.

[2] McMicken *v.* Commonwealth, 58 Pa. St. 213. Hence the plea of *non est factum* is bad.

[3] McMicken *v.* Commonwealth, 58 Pa. St. 213. The *dictum* of C. J. Gibson, in Brownfield *v.* Commonwealth, 13 Serg. & R. 265, that the recognizance of a sheriff is not a record, and, therefore, the plea of *nul tiel record* would be bad, is rejected.

[4] McMicken *v.* Commonwealth, 58 Pa. St. 213.

[5] Young *v.* Commonwealth, 6 Binn. 88. This was an unrecorded coroner's bond, under the act of March 28th, 1803.

recognizances of sheriff and coroners,[1] though this is not necessary.[2]

§ 588. The seventy-fourth section of the act of 15th April, 1834, requires the recorder of deeds, so soon as the sheriff or coroner shall be commissioned, to certify the recognizance taken by him to the prothonotary of the court of common pleas of the same county, and makes it the duty of the latter officer to enter the names of the recognizors upon his judgment docket in like manner as judgments are by law required to be entered. The sixty-second section of the act of 15th April, 1834, [P. L. 547,] directs that every sheriff, "before he shall be commissioned or execute any of the duties of his office, shall enter into a recognizance and become bound in a bond," etc. It does not declare a commission void, however, as did the act of 1803, for non-compliance with this requirement, and an omission to give the bond would not probably vitiate the recognizance.[3] A commission will be presumed from proof of official acts in the absence of evidence that no commission ever issued.[4]

Proceedings on the Recognizance.

§ 589. The act of 28th March, 1803, directs that persons aggrieved by the misconduct of the sheriff or the coroner, may institute actions of debt, or may cause *sci. fa.* to be issued upon his recognizance, against him and his sureties, their heirs, executors or administrators.[5] Since the sheriff

[1] Commonwealth *v.* Montgomery, 31 Pa. St. 519; Smith *v.* Miller, 13 Serg. & R. 339; *In re* Morris' Estate, 4 Pa. St. 163.

[2] *In re* Morris' Estate, 4 Pa. St. 163.

[3] Under the act of 1803, a coroner's bond was declared void, because no recognizance had been entered into. Young *v.* Commonwealth, 6 Binn. 88.

[4] Young *v.* Commonwealth, 6 Binn. 88.

[5] *Sci. fa.* was used in Wolverton *v.* Commonwealth, 7 Serg. & R. 273; Brownfield *v.* Commonwealth, 13 Serg. & R. 265; Carmack *v.* Commonwealth, 5 Binn. 184; Spangler *v.* Commonwealth, 16 Serg. & R. 68; Spang *v.* Commonwealth, 12 Pa. St. 358; Commonwealth *v.* Lelar, 13 Pa. St. 22; Snyder *v.* Reigart, 3 P. & W. 286; McCarty *v.* Springer, 3 P. & W. 157; Leeds *v.* Commonwealth, 3 W. N. C. 554; McMicken *v.* Common-

and his sureties, in their recognizance, acknowledge to owe to the commonwealth "the sum of ——, to be levied and made of your several goods and chattels," etc., the recognizance is several as well as joint, and an action can be brought against any one, whether the sheriff,[1] or his surety,[2] or against all. The same is true of the coroner and his sureties.[3]

§ 590. A *sci. fa.* which requires the sheriff to make known to the defendants to show cause why the penalty of the recognizance should not be levied and made of their goods and chattels, lands and tenements, etc., thus pursuing the language of the recognizance, is probably correct, but, if not, is amendable both in the court below and in the supreme court.[4] A *sci. fa.* dispenses with a declaration.[5] It is, indeed, a declaration, and the breaches of the recognizance should be assigned in it with as much certainty as in a declaration. Hence, it must state in what way the plaintiff was damnified, in what action or legal proceeding the sheriff violated his duty. Hence, a judgment on a *sci. fa.* was erroneous, when it did not state the amount of money the sheriff neglected to pay over, in what action, by whom and how it was recovered.[6] When the complaint is that the sheriff has not returned the writ of *fi. fa.*, and has not sold property on which he levied, nominal damages may be recovered for the mere non-return of the *fi. fa.*, but no substantial damages for the non-payment of the money to the plaintiff made by a sale of the property levied on.[7] It is not error to sue in the

wealth, 58 Pa. St. 213; Commonwealth v. Hoffman, 74 Pa. St. 105. In the following cases *debt* was employed: Beale v. Commonwealth, 7 W. 183; Commonwealth v. McCoy, 8 W. 153; Commonwealth v. Swope, 45 Pa. St. 535; Commonwealth v. Contner, 21 Pa. St. 266, 18 Pa. St. 439; Reed v. Reed, 1 W. 235.

[1] Commonwealth v. Hoffman, 74 Pa. St. 105.

[2] Brownfield v. Commonwealth, 13 Serg. & R. 265; Commonwealth v. McCoy, 8 W. 153; Juniata Bank v. Beale, 1 W. & S. 227.

[3] Beale v. Commonwealth, 11 Serg. & R. 299. One of the sureties was sued.

[4] McMicken v. Commonwealth, 58 Pa. St. 213.

[5] Beale v. Commonwealth, 7 W. 183.

[6] Withrow v. Commonwealth, 10 Serg. & R. 231.

[7] Commonwealth v. Allen, 30 Pa. St. 49.

name of the commonwealth alone, omitting the name of the person to whose use the suit is brought,[1] though it has been held error to sue on the bond of the sheriff in the name of the commonwealth, without suggesting the parties aggrieved to whose use the action was brought.[2] Suggesting the name of the party damnified by the misconduct of the sheriff is proper, notwithstanding that he has assigned his interest in the writ from whose improper execution by the sheriff he was aggrieved, before the action. The name of the assignee is unnecessary.[3] The *terre-tenants* should be called in, for the purpose of making defence.[4]

§ 591. Since the act of 28th March, 1803, gives to all parties aggrieved an action on the sheriff's recognizance as often as they shall suffer damages, it follows that each aggrieved party may bring a separate action thereon, and a judgment in one action is no merger of the recognizance.[5] A judgment in trover against the sheriff is no extinguishment of the recognizance, nor a bar to an action thereon against the sureties;[7] but neither is such judgment conclusive in favor of the plaintiff in the action on the recognizance for the same misconduct.[6] A judgment on the sheriff's bond for the penalty, satisfied out of his real estate, is no bar to an action on the recognizance against his sureties.[7]

§ 592. The judgment should not be for the penalty of the recognizance, but for the amount of the damage proven to have been suffered by the plaintiff, by the malfeasance of

---

[1] Beale v. Commonwealth, 7 W. & S. 183.

[2] Dunn v. Commonwealth, 14 Serg. & R. 431. In Shaeffer v. Jack, 14 Serg. & R. 426, a judgment for the penalty of the bond, the commonwealth being the plaintiff, was treated as a nullity, in an ejectment in which the title of the purchaser at the sheriff's sale under it, came into question.

[3] Brownfield v Commonwealth, 13 Serg. & R. 265

[4] Spang v. Commonwealth, 12 Pa. St. 358.

[5] Withrow v. Commonwealth, 10 Serg. & R 231; McMicken v. Commonwealth, 58 Pa. St. 213, Campbell v. Commonwealth, 8 Serg. & R. 414.

[6] Carmack v. Commonwealth, 5 Binn. 184.

[7] Commonwealth v. Montgomery, 31 Pa. St. 59.

the sheriff.[1] If, however, a verdict should b᛫ rendered by the jury both for the penalty and the actual damage suffered, the court may set aside the part referring to the penalty, and enter judgment for the damages.[2] A judgment on a recognizance relates, as a lien, to the date of the recognizance, or rather has no lien independent of that of the recognizance,[3] except when, for some reason, the recognizance is not a lien, e. g., the period of its lien having expired, or real property having been acquired subsequently to its execution. The judgment recovered upon it will, in such case, like any other judgment, be an independent lien.[4]

§ 593. A judgment for want of an appearance, against the sheriff, for a breach of his official duty, in an action on the recognizance, is conclusive upon the sureties,[5] and, in the trial against them, dispenses with evidence of a demand on the sheriff for the money collected by him, while a verdict for the plaintiff cures the omission of an allegation in the sci. fa. that such demand had been made.[6] The sheriff's return is equally conclusive on his sureties and the sheriff, for the reason for which a judgment against him is. Having returned that he made the money, the sureties cannot show that the money was not in fact made, but that the plaintiff in the sci. fa. requested him to falsely make the return as he did.[7] The sheriff's receipt to the defendant for the amount of an execution, cannot be contradicted by himself or sureties, by showing that no money was in fact paid, but that the sheriff agreed with the defendant, in discharge of a debt due by himself to the latter, to pay the execution.[8]

---

[1] Wolverton v. Commonwealth, 7 Serg. & R. 273 ; McMicken v. Commonwealth, 58 Pa. St. 213.

[2] McMicken v. Commonwealth, 58 Pa. St. 213. The supreme court will reverse the judgment for the penalty, if one be entered, and affirm that for the damages.

[3] In re Morris' Estate, 4 Pa. St. 162.

[4] Fricker's Appeal, 1 W. 393.

[5] Commonwealth v. Hoffman, 74 Pa. St. 105.

[6] McMicken v. Commonwealth, 58 Pa. St. 213.

[7] Brownfield v. Commonwealth, 13 Serg. & R. 265.

[8] Juniata Bank v. Beale, 1 W. & S. 227.

CHAPTER XXIII.

LIEN OF TRANSCRIPTS FROM THE ORPHANS' COURT.

The Lien.

§ 594. The twenty-ninth section of the act of 29th, March, 1832, [P. L. 197,] makes it the duty of the prothonotaries in the several counties to file and docket, whenever the same shall be furnished by any parties interested, certified transcripts or extracts of the amount appearing to be due from, or in the hands of any executor, administrator, guardian or other accountant, on the settlement of their respective accounts in the orphans' court. The transcripts or extracts so filed, shall constitute liens on the real estate of the accountant, from the time of such entry, until payment, distribution or satisfaction. Actions of debt or *scire facias* may be instituted thereon, by any person or persons interested, for the recovery of so much as may be due to them respectively.[1] This transcript need not be a copy of the whole administration or other account, while a mere copy of the figures at the foot of it, or an extract of a part of it, would be insensible. An abstract—in other words, a condensation of the substance of the account, stating the time when it was settled and confirmed, and that from it there appears to be due from the accountant a certain sum, and signed by the clerk of the orphans' court, and sealed with the seal of the said court—is sufficient.[2] If the account of a guardian of several minors, shows the balances due to each, a single

---

[1] The transcript itself is not a judgment, and could not share as such in the personalty of a decedent, under the act of 19th April, 1794. Ramsey's Appeal, 4 W. 71; Roshing v. Chandler, 3 Pa. St. 369.

[2] McCracken's Heirs v. Graham, 14 Pa. St. 209. For form of transcript, see, also, Roshing v. Chandler, 3 Pa. St. 369.

certificate of the account may be filed, exhibiting all these several balances.[1] Transcripts may be filed in all the counties in which the accountant has real estate, e. g., an extract of the account of an executor, whose testator's will was probated in Philadelphia, was filed in Montgomery county.[2] The transcript must be filed before the death of the accountant; after his death, the lien of his debts cannot be disturbed by the filing thereof.[3] A transcript of a guardian's account may be filed, though the account be not final, and will not be superseded as to lien or proceedings to obtain execution thereof, by the subsequent filing of a second account.[4] A transcript' of an executor's account confirmed *nisi* only, to which exceptions filed by a distributee of the estate are pending, cannot constitute a lien, but if, after the appointment of an auditor to consider exceptions to such account, nothing is done, and three and one-half years afterwards the distributee files a transcript, he will be presumed to have abandoned his exceptions, and the transcript will constitute a lien.[5] The transcript must be filed at the instance of a party interested,[6] e. g., a legatee;[7] a ward;[8] the heirs of a decedent, whose land has been sold by the accountant, an administrator, and who has not paid over to them the balance of the proceeds;[9] the widow and heirs, entitled, as distributees, to the balance of the personalty of the decedent;[10] a creditor of a decedent who has obtained judgment against his executor;[11] the executors to whom a co-

[1] Royer v. Myers, 15 Pa. St. 87.

[2] Hanson v. Bank of Penn Township, 7 Pa. St. 261.

[3] Rowland v. Harbaugh, 5 W. 365. Filed before his death, it will be paid as a lien out of his real estate, sold by his administrator. Ramsey's Appeal, 4 W. 71.

[4] Royer v. Myers, 15 Pa. St. 87.

[5] Roshing v. Chandler, 3 Pa. St. 369. Comp. Eaton's Appeal, 83 Pa. St. 152; Lentz v. Lamplugh, 12 Pa. St. 344.

[6] Laverty's Estate, 23 Pittsb. L. J. 81.

[7] Roshing v. Chandler, 3 Pa. St. 369; McNeal v. Holbrook, 25 Pa. St. 189.

[8] Royer v. Myers, 15 Pa. St. 87.

[9] Ramsey's Appeal, 4 W. 71.

[10] Rowland v. Harbaugh, 5 W. 365; McCracken's Heirs v. Graham, 14 Pa. St. 209.

[11] Hanson v. Bank of Penn Township, 7 Pa. St. 261.

executor, on his discharge by the orphans' court, has been ordered to pay the part of the balance in his· hands.[1] In case of appeal from the orphans' court, the lien of the transcript is good only for the amount finally decreed.[2]

The Scire Facias.

§ 595. The enforcement of the lien is accomplished by the terms of the act of 1832, by means of an action of debt or a *sci. fa.* upon the transcript, and the lien is prolonged beyond five years from the entry of the transcript only by the issue of a *sci. fa.* in the same manner as in case of judgments. Each person interested in the balance found against the accountant may issue the *sci. fa.*[3] on the same transcript.[4] The accountant, or, if he be dead, his personal representatives, as well as the *terre-tenants,* must be made parties.[5] Such *sci. fa.* is within the compulsory arbitration law, and the accountant cannot appeal from the award without paying costs.[6] The fact that about the time the *sci. fa.* issued a second account was filed, claiming credits for disbursements and allowance for services, does not oust the jurisdiction of the common pleas, which may deduct these credits from the amount of the balance as filed.[7] Nor does the filing of the transcript oust the jurisdiction of the orphans' court: *multo fortiori,* if, after a balance is found against them, but before the transcript is filed, the orphans' court discharges one of three executors on his paying the moneys in his hands to the other two, will his payment of these moneys to his co-executors be a full defence to the *sci. fa.* against him.[8] The *sci. fa.* is confined to the lands or real estate alone bound by the filing of the transcript, so that no other can be taken in execution by virtue of the judgment which may be had therein.[9]

[1] McNeal *v.* Holbrook, 25 Pa. St. 189.

[2] Section 29, act 29th March, 1832.

[3] *Ibid.*

[4] Royer *v.* Myers, 15 Pa. St. 87.

[5] Rowland *v.* Harbaugh, 5 W. 365.

[6] Royer *v.* Myers, 15 Pa. St. 87.

[7] *Ibid.*

[8] McNeal *v.* Holbrook, 25 Pa. St. 189.

[9] Rowland *v.* Harbaugh, 5 W. 365; Ramsey's Appeal, 4 W. 71.

CHAPTER XXIV.

LIEN OF AWARDS OF ARBITRATORS.

Amicable Arbitration.

§ 596. The act of 16th June, 1836, [P. L. 717,] provides for arbitration with the consent of both parties, known as amicable arbitration, and arbitration at the will of either party, and, therefore, called compulsory. There are two classes of amicable arbitrations, the first embracing controversies not in suit, and the second such controversies as are the subjects of suits pending in courts. With respect to the former of these classes, the first and second sections of the act of 16th June, 1836, provide that all persons desirous to end any controversy, suit or quarrel, except such as respect the title to real estate, may agree in writing to submit the same to the award or umpirage of any person or persons, inserting in their agreement to submit, the stipulation that the submission shall be made a rule of any court of record having jurisdiction of the subject-matter. On the production and filing of an affidavit by the witnesses to this agreement, in the court of which the same is agreed to be made a rule,[1] the agreement of submission shall be entered of record in such court, and a rule shall thereupon be made by the said court that the parties shall submit to and finally be concluded by the arbitration or umpirage which shall be made pursuant to such submission. On the award, when filed, a judgment will be entered by the prothonotary.[2]

---

[1] If the agreement is entered by the prothonotary, without the affidavit, and judgment is entered on the award, it is not void, though voidable, and will support a *sci. fa.* to revive. Wall *v.* Fife, 37 Pa. St. 394.

[2] Wall *v.* Fife, 37 Pa. St. 394 If the award finds a sum in favor of the defendant, he will be the plaintiff in a *sci. fa.* founded thereupon to revive and continue its lien.

When a Suit is Pending.

§ 597. When a suit is pending, the parties thereto may consent as aforesaid, to a rule of court for referring the matter in controversy to referees, reserving all matters of law for the decision of the court.[1] The report of the referees, setting forth the facts found by them, shall have the effect of a special verdict, and the court may proceed as upon a special verdict. Within a time limited by the rules of the several courts, the party against whom the award is, may except thereto for misbehavior of the arbitrators or umpire, for plain mistake of law or fact, and for corruption or other undue means used to procure the award. If no exceptions are filed within this time, or, being filed, the court, nevertheless, approves the award, and it is entered upon the record, it shall be taken to be as available in law as a verdict of a jury, and the party in whose favor the report shall be, whether plaintiff or defendant, shall have judgment thereon. If the exceptions to law or fact are sustained, the court shall refer the cause back to the same referees for further proceedings. The award, therefore, is not itself a judgment or a lien. Under a rule of court which provided that on the filing of such an award, the prothonotary should enter judgment *nisi*, and, after four days' notice of the filing of the award by the party wishing to enforce it, he should be entitled to judgment absolute, unless exceptions were meantime filed, an award was filed 18th February, 1854, on which judgment *nisi* was immediately entered, and, no exceptions being filed thereto, on 28th February, 1854, final judgment was entered. The judgment began to exist on this last date, and the plaintiff's lien then commenced.[2] The judgment

---

[1] The act of 6th April, 1869, [P. L. 726,] provides that in the county of Bradford, the parties to a suit may agree on a reference to a single referee, who shall find distinctly the law and the facts, and on whose award on the whole issue judgment shall be entered. This method of arbitration is, by later acts, extended to Susquehanna, Wyoming, Wayne, Luzerne, Tioga and Potter counties.

[2] Stephens' Exrs.' Appeal, 38 Pa. St. 9.

absolute must be docketed in the judgment index, otherwise
its lien will not be valid against other lien creditors, notwithstanding that the judgment *nisi* was docketed on the day it
was entered.[1] The lien of such a judgment must be revived
as that of ordinary judgments, in conformity w th the provisions of the acts of 1798 and 1827. It is lost if a *sci. fa.*
does not issue within five years from the entry of judgment
absolute.[2]

Compulsory Arbitration.

§ 598. The eighth and succeeding sections of the act of
16th June, 1836, secure to either party in any civil suit or
action the right to enter, at the prothonotary's office, a rule
of reference, calling for the selection of arbitrators on a day
certain. These arbitrators must be three or five in number.
Having heard the evidence, they must forthwith proceed to
determine the matters in controversy submitted to them, and
they shall make out their award, which shall be signed by
all or a majority of them, and shall transmit the same to the
prothonotary within seven days after they shall have agreed
upon it.[3] The prothonotary shall forthwith enter it of record
in the proper dockets. Every award so entered shall have
the effect of a judgment with respect to the party against
whom it is made, whether he be plaintiff or defendant,[4] from
the time of the entry thereof,[5] and shall be a lien upon his
real estate until reversed upon appeal, or satisfied according
to law.[6] If, however, the party in favor of whom the award
is, dissatisfied with the amount of money awarded him,

---

[1] Stephens' Exrs.' Appeal, 38 Pa.
St. 9.

[2] *Ibid.*

[3] Failure to transmit it within the
seven days, while it forfeits the pay
of the arbitrators, does not vitiate
the award. Boone *v.* Reynolds, 1
Serg. & R. 231. Hence, if the arbitrators delay to file their award, they
may be compelled by rule to do so.
Monohan *v.* Strenger, 1 Phila. 376.

[4] M'Kennan *v.* Henderson, 5 W. &
S. 370.

[5] An award for $176.26 in furni-
ture, is void; it cannot be cured by
striking out the word furniture.
Ramler *v.* Brotherline, 1 Pearson
462.

[6] Section 24, act 16th June, 1836,
[P. L. 722.] A *fi. fa.* issued before
the time for appeal has elapsed, is
merely irregular, and none but the

appeals therefrom, he repudiates its lien, and if, pending the appeal, other judgments are recovered against the defendant, they will take precedence to the award. A subsequent withdrawal of the appeal will not re-instate the award in its lost priority.[1] If, during the pendency of an appeal by the plaintiff, the defendant sells his land, the judgment subsequently recovered on the appeal, though for a larger sum than had been awarded, is not a lien even for the amount of the award.[2] An appeal by the party against whom the award is, will not discharge its lien until reversal.[3] If one of two defendants appeals, and, the other dying, a sale of his lands takes place, enough of the proceeds must be retained to satisfy the lien of the award, in case it shall be affirmed on appeal.[4] If, on the appeal, a larger judgment with costs is rendered against the defendant, this excess beyond the original award, and the interest thereon, is a lien only from the date of the judgment.[5]

Duration of Lien.

§ 599. The acts of 4th April, 1798, and 26th March, 1827, which require the revival of the lien of judgments every five years, are applicable to awards of arbitrators constituted judgments by act of assembly. After it had been decided that, when an appeal was taken from an award, the five years did not begin to run until the abandonment thereof, or the entry of judgment thereon,[6] the act of 21st April,

defendant can take exception to it on that account. Wilkinson's Appeal, 65 Pa. St. 189.

[1] Eaton's Appeal, 83 Pa. St. 152.

[2] Lentz v. Lamplugh, 12 Pa. St. 344. Withdrawal of an appeal leaves the award in force as a judgment. Phillips v. Israel, 10 Serg. & R. 391; Moore v. Hamilton, cited M'Kennan v. Henderson, 5 W. & S. 370.

[3] Christy v. Crawford, 8 W. & S. 99. Permitting the appellant to take a non-suit at the trial of the appeal,

extinguishes the award. M'Kennan v. Henderson, 5 W. & S. 370.

[4] Ramsey's Appeal, 4 W. 71.

[5] Christy v. Crawford, 8 W. & S. 99.

[6] In Dietrich's Appeal, 4 W. 208, the five years commenced to run from three months after the award was entered, when the appeal was abandoned. In Ramsey's Appeal, 4 W. 71, an award entered in 1824, on which an appeal continued to pend in 1835, was a lien during that period, without revival.

1840, [P. L. 449,] enacted that the lien of the award should cease five years after its entry, notwithstanding an appeal taken therefrom, unless it should be revived within that period, according to the provisions of the act of 26th March, 1827, relating to the revival of judgments. Awards existing at the date of the passage of the act of 21st April, 1840, were to continue liens for three years, within which time they must be revived by *sci. fa.*, or by amicable agreement to revive, filed and docketed. When the award is of a sum of money in favor of the defendant, he will be the plaintiff in the *sci. fa.*[1]

Transfer to Other Counties.

§ 600. The act of 5th May, 1876, [P. L. 110,] provides that an award of arbitrators may at any time, whether within the period for taking an appeal or afterwards, and after an appeal has been in fact taken,[2] be transferred to any other court of common pleas, by filing of record therein a certified copy of the whole record in the case. If an appeal is entered after the transfer, the plaintiff must, within twenty days thereafter, file with the transferred record, a certificate of the entry of the appeal. The prothonotary receiving the certified copy of the record or the certificate, shall file the same, and forthwith transcribe the docket entry thereof into his own docket; and thereupon such award shall continue a lien on the defendant's real estate in the county in which the same has been transferred, until reversed upon appeal, or satisfied according to law. After judgment is entered on the appeal, or the judgment is satisfied, the plaintiff must, in twenty days, file with the transferred record a certificate of said judgment or satisfaction. On the plaintiff's neglect to file the certificate of appeal, judgment or satisfaction, as

[1] M'Kennan *v.* Henderson, 5 W. & S. 370. See Wall *v.* Fife, 37 Pa. St 394.

[2] In Hallman's Appeal, 18 Pa. St. 310, it was decided that the award could not be effectively transferred, under the act of 16th April, 1840, until it had become absolute by the lapse of time for appeal, without appeal, or the abandonment of the appeal entered.

aforesaid, within the time limited, the defendant, or any other person interested, may have the transferred record stricken off.

Judgment Docket.

§ 601. The act of 29th March, 1827, requires the prothonotary to copy into the judgment docket all judgments and awards of arbitrators, immediately after and in the order in which they shall have been entered. An award not entered in this docket, is not a lien; but if, after later liens have been obtained against the party against whom the award is, the prothonotary inserts in its proper place by interlineation, the omitted award, the entry so made will be conclusive on the auditor who makes distribution of the proceeds of a judicial sale of the defendant's real estate, and the striking out of the interlineation rests in the sound discretion of the court, from the exercise of which there is no appeal to the supreme court.[1]

Legal Arbitration.

§ 602. The act of 6th April, 1870, [P. L. 948,] which extends to the counties of Erie, Elk, Crawford and Lawrence, provides for what it terms legal, as contrasted with lay, arbitration. After a rule is entered for arbitration by one of the parties, under the compulsory arbitration law, the other party may elect that it shall be a legal arbitration, by one arbitrator only, who shall have been duly admitted to practice law in the courts of record in the county in which the suit is pending. The facts must be found by this arbitrator, in the form of a special verdict, and the award filed by him in the prothonotary's office within seven days after the finding thereof. On this award judgment shall be entered *nisi*, to become absolute if no exceptions thereto or motion to set it aside, is made within twenty days after the filing thereof. The judgment *nisi* is and continues a lien until final judgment.

---

[1] Kendig's Appeal, 82 Pa. St. 68. Compulsory arbitrations do not exist in Philadelphia. Act of 1st May, 1861, [P. L. 521.]

CHAPTER XXV.

STATUTORY DOWER.

§ 603. The forty-first section of the act of 29th March, 1832, [P. L. 202,] directs that, if, on the decease of a person seized of land, partition is made thereof in the orphans' court, and the same is adjudged to an heir or heirs, the sum at which the widow's share shall be valued, shall remain charged upon the premises, the legal interest of which shall be annually paid to her during her natural life. On her death, the principal sum shall be paid to the persons thereunto legally entitled. The forty-third section of the same act provides that, when the real estate of a decedent, or any part thereof, shall be sold by order of the orphans' court, that court shall direct that the widow's share of the purchase money shall remain in the hands of the purchaser during her natural life, and that the interest thereof shall be annually paid to her during her life-time.

The Lien.

§ 604. The principal of the widow's one-third, as well as the interest annually payable to her, are charged on the premises by the forty-first section of the above act. No decree of the court is necessary to make them a charge, nor could any decree of the court exonerate the land from their lien.[1]

Hise *v.* Geiger, 7 W. & S. 273; Fisher *v.* Kean, 1 W. 259; Wynn *v.* Brooke, 5 R. 106; White *v.* Williams, 3 Phila. 460; Penna. Annuity Co. *v.* Vansyckel, 2 Pittsb. 535. Yet, in Moorhead *v.* Commonwealth, 1 Grant 214, one-third of the proceeds of the land sold in partition was invested, by order of the court, for the widow, and in Giddings' Appeal, 81½ Pa. St. 72, a sale in partition was held to have converted the widow's third into personalty, and the appointment of a sequestrator under a *fi. fa.* issued on a subsequent judgment against the widow, was vacated.

A bond, a recognizance,[1] a mortgage[2] or a judgment recovered for them,[3] is simply a cumulative security, and the taking of such security implies no waiver of the lien which the law itself creates. The lien of the widow's third, however, is confined to the land taken in partition. Hence, if the accepting heir sells it to a stranger, and sues the latter for the unpaid purchase money, the verdict and judgment cannot properly include this third. An execution upon the judgment cannot be levied on other lands of the vendee, for a sum embracing the widow's third, nor is it competent for the court, in making distribution of the proceeds of sale, to direct the amount of this third (the widow still living) to be paid to a mortgage and judgment creditor of the stranger, on his assigning his mortgage and judgment *pro tanto* as a security for it.[4] If, at the death of one who has an equitable title under articles for the purchase of land, the land is taken in proceedings in partition by the two sons, and, some years afterwards, the administrator paying the purchase money due, a deed is made to the sons, containing no reference to the proceedings in partition, or the previous equitable title of the decedent, and if the son's title is subsequently sold in execution, on judgments recovered after the deed was made to them, the sheriff's vendee, having no notice of the proceedings in partition and of the decedent's former equitable estate, takes the land divested of the widow's third; he is protected by the recording acts.[5]

§ 605. A sale of the land in partition, in pursuance of the forty-third section of the act of 29th March, 1832, leaves the one-third of the purchase money a charge on the premises, just as when they are taken by the heir.[6] Hence,

---

[1] Medlar *v.* Aulenbach, 2 P. & W. 355; Wynn *v.* Brooke, 5 R. 106; Brooks *v.* Smyser, 48 Pa. St. 86; De Haven *v.* Bartholomew, 57 Pa. St. 126.

[2] Vandever *v.* Baker, 13 Pa. St. 121.

[3] Hillbish's Appeal, 89 Pa. St 490.

[4] Fisher *v* Kean, 1 W. 259.

[5] Dickinson *v.* Beyer, 87 Pa. St 274.

[6] Hawk *v.* Geddis, 16 Serg. & R. 23, Kline *v.* Bowman, 19 Pa. St. 24. Under the act of April 2d, 1804, it

when no order was made by the orphans' court with respect to the widow's third, but bonds were executed by the purchaser to the administrator, for the payment to the widow, during her life, of the interest on one-third, and the principal at her death to the heirs, on which judgments were recovered in 1816 and 1817, but never revived, *assumpsit* was sustained after the death of the widow, in 1850, to recover from one who purchased the premises at sheriff's sale during the widow's life-time, the principal of her dower.[1] Payment to the administrator of the bond or mortgage executed to him, for the widow's third, at her death, will not discharge the lien of this third; the heirs are entitled to receive it.[2]

§ 606. The purchase money beyond the one-third which represents the widow's dower, is not made a charge by statute. The purchaser must " give good security by recognizance or otherwise, to the satisfaction of the court, for the payment thereof, with legal interest, in some reasonable time, not exceeding twelve months, as the court may direct."[3] This distinction existed before as well as since the legislation of 1832, and while security was necessary before that date for the interests of the heirs in the remaining two-thirds of the purchase money, the third which stood for the principal of the widow's dower was secured by operation of law itself.[4] If a recognizance, said to have been taken in

---

was decided in Eshelman *v.* Witmer, 2 W. 263, that the widow's share was no lien on the land, in the ownership of a *terre-tenant,* because in making the partition the orphans' court had omitted to decree that it should be a charge on the land.

[1] Kline *v.* Bowman, 19 Pa. St. 24.

[2] Hise *v.* Geiger, 7 W. & S. 273; Hillbish's Appeal, 89 Pa. St. 490. Yet, in Unangst *v.* Kraemer, 8 W. & S. 391, it is decided that payment may be properly made, either to the administrator of the decedent, or to his heirs; and in Brooks *v.* Smyser, 48 Pa. St. 86, it is said that a mortgage to an administrator to secure the widow's third may, at her death, be sued out by him, or, he being dead, by the administrator *de bonis non.*

[3] Section 37, act 29th March, 1832. Comp. sections 38 and 39.

[4] Walton *v.* Willis, 1 Dall. 265; Kean *v.* Franklin, 5 Serg. & R. 155; Medlar *v.* Aulenbach, 2 P. & W. 355.

partition to secure the interest of an heir in the principal of the widow's dower, as well as in the remaining two-thirds, cannot be found, nor satisfactory evidence that it ever existed offered, though a judgment is confessed by the accepting heir, as if on a recognizance, but is not properly revived, the lien of the principal of the widow's third will, at her death, be valid, but that of the remaining two-thirds will be invalid, as against a later judgment properly kept alive.[1]

When the Widow's Interest is Not Assigned.

§ 607. So long as the widow's interest is not assigned by proceedings in the orphans' court or in a court of equity,[2] it does not appear by any decision yet published, whether the widow's share in the annual yield of her husband's land, is a charge upon it or not. When an interest is devised to her, she takes as devisee, by purchase, and has only the remedies which any other co-tenant would have, e. g., ejectment.[3] If the testator, leaving a son and a widow, devises to the latter "one-third part of the issues and profits of my real estate, and the one-third part of the mansion house, for her use as long as she lives," an estate different from what she would acquire under the intestate law, she takes by purchase as devisee, and her remedy will be like that of any other tenant-in-common, to recover her one-third of the rents and profits.[4] But, taking by descent as widow, her

---

[1] Hillbish's Appeal, 89 Pa St. 490.

[2] Borland v. Murphy, 4 W. N. C. 472; Murphy v. Borland, 92 Pa. St. 86; Borland v. Murphy, 92 Pa. St. 91; Act of 17th March, 1845, § 3, [P. L. 160.]

[3] Thomas v. Simpson, 3 Pa. St. 69.

[4] Anna M. Zeigler's Appeal, Supreme Court. No. 117, May Term, 1874, appeal from the C. P. of Cumberland. In this case the testator, after the devise to his widow, added, " I also give and bequeath to my son

Levi, my plantation or real estate of any description, to him, his heirs and assigns forever." From 1850, the year of testator's death, to 1869, the widow continued to live in the family of the son, in the mansion house of the farm, and, in 1869, removed with him to Carlisle, where she remained with him as before. No steps were taken by the widow to have her dower assigned, nor was the will ever probated. From 1869 on, several judgments were recov-

interest, though real estate,[1] does not constitute her a tenant-in-common with the heirs.[2] She cannot, as a tenant-in-common may, sustain ejectment;[3] nor can the heir bring ejectment against her.[4] She has, at common law, no freehold in the land until the assignment of her dower.[5] The statute of Merton, in force in Pennsylvania,[6] first gave the widow damages for detention of dower. The act of 29th March, 1832, [P. L. 201,] provides a substitute for the

ered against the son, until, in 1873, the real estate was sold on a judgment recovered against the son, and from the proceeds of the sale the widow claimed the arrears of dower, as a lien superior to the judgments of her son's creditors. The auditor disallowed her claim. The common pleas denied her right to the lien, because, being devisee, she had simply the rights of a co-tenant as to the rents and profits. The opinion of the supreme court was as follows: "*Per Curiam.* We are of opinion that the interest of the appellant (the widow) was an estate in the land devised by the husband, and not a mere charge upon the land. In this view, of course, if she permitted her son to take her share of the rents, issues and profits, it became a mere personal claim against him, to be asserted by an action, but not a lien to follow the proceeds of sale. The opinion of the court below sufficiently indicates the correct ground of decision. Decree affirmed and appeal dismissed at the costs of appellant." When the husband was a co-tenant with another, and for that reason, on his decease, the orphans' court could not assign the widow's dower, she could bring an action of dower *unde nihil habet*, and recover therein the arrears of dower,

as well as have it assigned to her for the future, but the lien of the judgment for the arrears did not relate beyond its own date of rendition. Evans *v.* Evans, 1 Phila. 113.

[1] Gourley *v.* Kinley, 66 Pa. St. 270; Zeigler's Appeal, 35 Pa. St. 189; Schall's Appeal, 40 Pa. St. 177; Bachman *v.* Chrisman, 23 Pa. St. 163. Her interest can be taken in execution as real estate. Shaupe *v.* Shaupe, 12 Serg. & R. 12; Thomas *v.* Simpson, 3 Pa. St. 60. When, after dower is charged in partition on land, the second husband of the widow becomes the owner of the premises, and subsequently he dies, she surviving, her right to receive the annual installment revives, as against the alienee of her second husband. Miller *v.* Leidig, 3 W. & S. 456.

[2] Pringle *v.* Gaw, 5 Serg. & R. 536; Bratton *v.* Mitchell, 7 W. 113.

[3] *Ibid.*

[4] Seider *v.* Seider, 5 Wh. 208; Gourley *v.* Kinley, 66 Pa. St. 270.

[5] Mark *v.* Mark, 9 W. 410; Power *v.* Power, 7 W. 205. See 4 Kent Com. 61; 1 Washburn Real Property 301, *et seq.*

[6] Seaton *v.* Jamison, 7 W. 533. Comp. 4 Kent Com. 63, 70; Lyle *v.* Richards, 9 Serg. & R. 368.

method of assigning dower at common law, and it would possibly be the duty of the orphans' court to make provision in its decree for arrears of dower due the widow at the time of the assignment of dower. The principles which regulate the ascertainment of the arrears in an action of dower, might probably be adopted by the orphans' court. Now, under the statute of Merton, a *terre-tenant* who had been in possession of the premises for seven years, was decreed personally to pay the arrears of dower which had accumulated through a period of twenty years.[1] The estate of the widow in her deceased husband's lands is often styled a rent-charge.[2] There cannot well be a reason for denying to such a rent, the property of lien, as in cases of rent-service.[3] If a landlord lets land at one-third of the grain that shall be grown, the rent is definite enough to be distrained for, and be a lien on the proceeds of the sale of chattels in execution, as against the execution creditor. The widow's one-third can be as definitely ascertained without prior appraisement as can the rent just spoken of. Whether a widow's annual demand, as a dowress, are a lien before adjustment in the orphans' court, must be deemed uncertain until some authoritative adjudication.

Remedies.

§ 608. The lien of a widow's third, principal and interest, can be enforced by the orphans' court, under the act of May 17th, 1866, [P. L. 1096,] entitled "an act enlarging the powers of the orphans' court so as to discharge liens upon real estate:" the decree will be, that in default of payment, the money shall be levied out of the land.[4] Against the *terre-tenant* of land charged with the widow's third, an action

[1] Seaton v. Jamison, 7 W. 533.

[2] Thomas v. Simpson, 3 Pa. St. 60; Bishop's Appeal, 7 W. & S. 251.

[3] Ingersoll v. Sergeant, 1 Wh. 337; Bantleon v. Smith, 2 Binn. 146; Gordon v. Correy, 5 Binn. 552; Devine's Appeal, 30 Pa. St. 348; Workman v. Mifflin, 30 Pa St. 362.

[4] Neel's Appeal, 88 Pa. St. 94. Here, there being no widow, the heirs sought to enforce the lien of a recognizance.

of debt[1] or *assumpsit*[2] may be maintained, and it is not necessary to prove that he made an express promise, either to his vendor or to the heir entitled to the money charged on the land, to pay it; nor is the land, in his ownership, discharged by reason of a bond, recognizance, or other personal assumption entered into by his vendor.[3] That the *terre-tenant* has an equity that his vendor should discharge the lien, does not make it necessary to first sue the latter, or to make him a co-defendant.[4] On the death of the widow whose one-third was charged on land accepted by an heir in partition, the person thereto entitled may bring *assumpsit* against the purchaser.[5] Each heir should bring a separate action at the death of the widow for his share in the principal of her third.[6] The heir accepting land in partition is personally liable for the widow's third, principal and interest, and a personal judgment may, in *assumpsit*, be properly entered against him,[7] and it is immaterial that the heir is a minor, and that the property was accepted for him by his guardian.[8] Irregularities in the proceedings in partition are no defence for a *terre-tenant*.[9]

Payment and Discharge.

§ 609. The widow can release her right to the annual interest in one-third of the purchase money in partition, but the principal thereof must nevertheless be paid to the parties entitled.[10] The orphans' court has no authority to order the prin-

---

[1] Unangst *v.* Kraemer, 8 W. & S. 391. Debt was used in Heist *v.* Baker, 49 Pa. St. 9, against a *terre-tenant* of land charged by deed with a sum of money.

[2] De Haven *v.* Bartholomew, 57 Pa. St. 126; Kline *v.* Bowman, 19 Pa St. 24; Pidcock *v.* Bye, 3 R. 183; Penna. Annuity Co. *v.* Vansyckel, 2 Pittsb. 539. In Dickinson *v.* Beyer, 87 Pa. St. 274, the accepting heir was made defendant, and his vendee was called in as *terre-tenant*.

[3] Pidcock *v.* Bye, 3 R. 183; De Haven *v.* Bartholomew, 57 Pa. St. 126.

[4] De Haven *v.* Bartholomew, 57 Pa. St. 126, questioning Unangst *v.* Kraemer, 8 W. & S. 391.

[5] Shelly *v.* Shelly, 8 W. & S 153.

[6] Kline *v.* Bowman, 19 Pa. St. 24.

[7] Penna. Annuity Co. *v.* Vansyckel, 2 Pittsb. 535.

[8] *Ibid.*

[9] Unangst *v.* Kraemer, 8 W. & S. 391.

[10] When land is charged with a widow's third, it is not discharged by her subsequent marriage with the owner of the land. First National Bank *v.* Cockley, 2 Pearson 122.

cipal to be paid to the administratrix upon her giving security for its faithful application, and to direct her to deliver to the *terre-tenant* a deed of release and quit-claim releasing the premises from the said principal.[1] In twenty years from the death of a widow, a presumption arises that the principal of her third has been paid. She dying July 22d, 1822, if an action to recover this principal is brought July 22d, 1842, it will be necessary for the plaintiff to show facts or circumstances by which the presumption of payment may be rebutted. Non-surrender of bonds given to secure the widow's third, or payment, three or four years before the action was brought, to one of the heirs entitled, of his share in the principal, would be such facts in favor of another heir suing for his share therein.[2] The widow having died twenty-six years before the suit was brought for four-sevenths of the principal of her dower, evidence was given at the trial that the defendant admitted, seventeen or eighteen years after her death, that these four-sevenths were unpaid.[3] The statute of limitations does not apply to actions brought to recover the principal of the widow's third on her decease.[4]

---

[1] Soley's Estate, 10 W. N. C. 67.

[2] Unangst *v.* Kraemer, 8 W. & S. 391.

[3] De Haven *v.* Bartholomew, 57 Pa. St. 126.

[4] *Ibid.*

CHAPTER XXVI.

LIEN OF REPORT OF COUNTY AUDITORS.

§ 610. The forty-seventh section of the act of 15th April, 1834, [P. L. 545,] requires the auditors of each county of the state to assemble at the seat of justice thereof on the first Monday of January, in every year, and at such other times as they may find necessary. When thus convened, they "shall audit, settle and adjust the accounts of the commissioners, treasurer, sheriff and coroner of the county, and make report thereof to the court of common pleas of such county, together with a statement of the balance due from or to such commissioners, treasurer, sheriff or coroner." The officer should receive notice to appear before the auditors, and this is essential to give validity to their report. Hence, in an action by a county against one whom it had overpaid for scrip purchased by it through him, a former county commissioner, who, without a hearing, had been surcharged by the county auditors with this excess, was a competent witness, notwithstanding the auditors' report.[1] The auditors' report must be filed among the records of the court of common pleas of the county, and, from the time of being so filed, shall have the effect of a judgment against the real estate of the officer found to be indebted either to the commonwealth or to the county.[2] The

[1] Wilson v. Clarion County, 2 Pa. St. 17; Snyder County's Appeal, 3 Grant 38; Lancaster County v. Slocum, 4 Leg. Opin. 473. Yet, in Hoffman's Estate, 2 Pearson 157, it is said that though an auditor's report does not expressly say that the officer was summoned to appear, this would be presumed; the report would be prima facie valid against him, and, he acquiescing in it, would be conclusive against other lien creditors.

[2] Section 55, act of 15th April, 1834. In Mudge v. Williamsport, 78 Pa. St. 158, it was decided that the report of auditors of the city of Williamsport, finding a balance due by the city treasurer, could not be filed in the

officer or the county may, within sixty days after the filing of the report, appeal to the court of common pleas, and the court may direct an issue to be tried by a jury, upon whose verdict final judgment shall be entered. On appeal, the whole matter is taken up *de novo*, and, therefore, no injury can be done the officer by failure to give him notice to appear before the auditors.[1] By the act of 30th March, 1791, [3 Sm. L. 15,] the courts of common pleas of the several counties were directed to appoint three persons to audit county treasurers' and commissioners' accounts. These auditors were required to report the balance due to or from these officers to the next county court. The court was directed to thereupon cause such report and settlement to be filed among its records. From the time of such filing, it was to have the effect of a judgment on the lands of the officer. Under this act, the filing of the report without an order of the court authorizing it, evidenced by its records, was void. Hence, when the report was filed in vacation, and the records showed no order of the court directing it to be filed, it was not a lien on the lands of the commissioners surcharged in it.[2] Under the act of 15th April, 1834, authority from the court for the filing of the report must also be obtained.[3] When filed, the auditors who made the report have no further power over it, nor can a subsequent board of auditors re-examine the matters embraced in it for the purpose of correcting an error against the accounting officer.[4]

common pleas, and become a lien under the act of 22d March, 1870, which authorized the audit of the treasurer's accounts, and directed the auditors to make their report to the city council, and conferred on them the same authority as county auditors now have.

[1] Brown v. Commonwealth, 2 R. 39.

[2] Irish v. Commonwealth, 3 Binn. 91.

[3] Lancaster County v. Slocum, 4 Leg Opin 473. In Snyder's Appeal, 3 Grant 38, the auditors' report, finding a balance due by the county treasurer, was presented to the court and ordered to be filed; also, in Hoffman's Estate, 2 Pearson 157. See Commonwealth v. Hoffman, 74 Pa. St. 105, remarks of Pearson, J.

[4] Northampton v. Yohe, 24 Pa. St. 305. The auditors' report is conclu-

§ 611. The act of 15th April, 1834, gives the report of the auditors, when filed, "the effect of a judgment against the real estate of the officer." Since a judgment is not a lien against real estate, unless it be entered in the lien docket, that is a reasonable construction of this act which understands it to require the entry of the balance found by the auditors against the officer in the lien docket, in order to make it valid as a lien against other lien creditors. When, therefore, the auditors having found a balance against the county treasurer of $266.51, presented their report to the court of common pleas, which ordered it to be filed, and the following entry was made in the appearance docket: "Statement of receipts and expenditures of Snyder county, presented and ordered to be filed," but the entry was not indexed in the appearance docket, nor was a copy of it entered in the lien or judgment docket, later judgment creditors were permitted to take the proceeds of the sheriff's sale of the treasurer's real estate, in preference to the county.[1]

sive, unappealed from, and an action cannot be sustained against the county to recover moneys paid to it by the accounting officer, in excess of the amount with which he was fairly chargeable.

[1] Snyder County's Appeal, 3 Grant 38; Commonwealth v. Hoffman, 74 Pa. St. 105; Hoffman's Estate, 2 Pearson 157. In this last case, the auditors found a balance due by the sheriff of $2,991.97. It was filed properly in the prothonotary's office, but, because it was not entered in the lien docket, the county was postponed to later lien-creditors, in the distribution of the proceeds of the sheriff's land.

CHAPTER XXVII.

LIEN OF DEBTS DUE THE STATE.

§ 612. The act of 30th March, 1811, [5 Sm. L. 230,] directs that all accounts between the commonwealth and any person or body corporate, whether he be an officer of the revenue or any other person, who may have become possessed of public money, shall be examined and adjusted by the auditor-general according to law and equity. This provision applies whenever one retains public moneys which ought to be paid into the treasury of the state, whether it be a dividend tax, fees of office, or any other moneys whatsoever. It embraces taxes due on dividends declared by a bank,[1] tolls collected by a collector of tolls on the Pennsylvania canal,[2] or on the Columbia railroad, at Lancaster, from 1839 to 1843,[3] taxes due from the city of Philadelphia to the state,[4] taxes on the capital. stock of a coal company,[5] of a canal company,[6] and of a bridge company,[7] fees of a prothonotary, fifty per cent. of which are due by him to the commonwealth,[8] taxes collected by a county treasurer for the state,[9] a balance due by the sheriff to the commonwealth,[10] or

[1] Bank v. Commonwealth, 10 Pa. St. 442.

[2] Speck .v. Commonwealth, 3 W. & S. 324.

[3] Commonwealth v. Reitzel, 9 W. & S. 109; Forney v. Commonwealth, 10 Pa. St. 405.

[4] Philadelphia v. Commonwealth, 52 Pa. St. 451.

[5] Lehigh Crane Iron Co. v. Commonwealth, 55 Pa. St. 448.

[6] Delaware Division Canal Co. v. Commonwealth. 50 Pa. St. 399.

[7] Commonwealth v. Runk, 26 Pa. St. 235.

[8] Hutchinson v. Commonwealth, 6 Pa. St. 124; Hays v. Commonwealth, 27 Pa. St. 272; Commonwealth v. Hays, 1 Pittsb. 316; Porter v. Commonwealth, 1 P. & W. 252.

[9] Commonwealth v. Porter, 21 Pa. St. 385. In re Arnold's Estate, 46 Pa. St. 277.

[10] Commonwealth v. Fitler, 12 Serg. & R. 277.

by a brigade inspector of the Pennsylvania militia, under the act of 2d April, 1822, which required him to pay into the state treasury any surplus arising from fines and forfeitures, after discharging all expenses required to be paid by that act.[1]

The Lien.

§ 613. When, on any settlement made agreeably to the act of 1811, a balance is found to be due to the commonwealth, this balance, together with interest from the expiration of three months after the date of the settlement, "shall be deemed and adjudged to be a lien, from the date of the settlement of such account, upon all the real estate of the person or persons indebted, and on his or their securities[2] throughout this commonwealth."[3] It would seem that the transmission by the auditor-general to the prothonotaries of the respective counties, of the certified copies of the balances due the commonwealth, and the entry of record of such copies in the offices of the prothonotaries, are necessary in order to maintain the lien of such balances as against other lien creditors of the debtor.[4] Thus, when, on the 25th January, 1839, a brigade inspector in the militia settled his accounts in the office of the auditor-general, and a balance was found due by him to the state, but no copy of the account was forwarded to the prothonotary of the county wherein his lands were, the commonwealth was postponed to

[1] Spangler v. Commonwealth, 8 W. 57; Commonwealth v. Farelly, 1 P. & W. 52. In re Wilson, 4 Pa. St. 164; Commonwealth v. Aurandt, 1 R. 282.

[2] Securities means sureties. Forney v. Commonwealth, 10 Pa. St. 405.

[3] Section 12, act 30th March, 1811, [5 Sm. L. 230;] Commonwealth v. Coovert, 1 Pearson 163; Forney v. Commonwealth, 10 Pa. St. 405. The law was similar in 1796. A settlement of a public account, entered in the books of the controller-general and register-general, created a lien on all the real estate of the debtor within the state. Smith v. Nicholson, 4 Y. 6.

[4] In Commonwealth v. Coovert, 1 Pearson 163, the opinion is expressed that the lien of the state is not lost by the prothonotary's entering the balance, $455.34, instead of $18,374.60, as it was, in fact, transmitted to him.

judgment creditors, whose judgments were recovered against him subsequently to the settlement, in the distribution of the proceeds of a sheriff's sale of his real estate.[1] A like failure to transmit the copy of the balance to the prothonotary postponed the commonwealth to creditors whose judgments were recovered after the settlement, in the distribution of the proceeds of a sheriff's sale of the lands of the sureties of a county treasurer.[2] If, however, the balance found due by an officer is transmitted to the prothonotary of the proper county, and by him entered as a lien against the officer's estate, it is not necessary that it should likewise be entered against the sureties in order to bind their estates. Valid against their principal, the lien is valid *ipso facto* against them. Hence, when the balance was entered by the prothonotary as a lien against a defaulting collector of tolls, on April 11th, 1844, it was preferred to a mortgage executed on April 13th, 1844, by one of his sureties, in distributing the proceeds of the land of this surety, sold by the orphans' court after his death, for the payment of his debts.[3]

[1] *In re* Wilson, 4 Pa. St. 164.   Forney *v.* Commonwealth, 10 Pa.
[2] *In re* Arnold's Estate, 46 Pa. St.   St. 405.
277.

CHAPTER XXVIII.

LIEN OF TAX COLLECTORS' ARREARS.

§ 614. By the act of 15th April, 1834, [P. L. 514,] the commissioners of the several counties of this commonwealth are directed to cause duplicate lists of the taxable inhabitants, and of the taxes payable by them, to be made and delivered to the collector for each ward, township or district, and to issue their warrants with these duplicates to the respective collectors of county rates and levies, which warrants shall authorize and require them to demand and receive from every person in such duplicates named, the sum wherewith he stands charged. The act of 28th February, 1835, [P. L. 46,] makes it the duty of the commissioners, within three months from the delivery of the duplicate to the collector, to file a certificate under their hands and seal, in the office of the prothonotary of the court of common pleas of the county, stating the amount due and unpaid by such collector. The prothonotary is required to enter the same in his docket, and from the time of such entry the certificate shall have the same operation and effect as a judgment of the said court. Execution may be issued thereon in like manner as on judgments, for the amount remaining unpaid, at any time after the entry aforesaid.

§ 615. Since, under not dissimilar language, in respect to the report of county auditors, which from the time of filing is endowed by the act of 15th April, 1834, [P. L. 545,] with the effect of a judgment, it was decided that the report does not become a lien as against other lien creditors, until it is duly entered in the lien docket, the same may be necessary to make the commissioners' certificate a valid lien, as against creditors of the tax collector.

§ 616. In respect to the mode of enforcing the liability of a defaulting tax collector, the act of 15th April, 1834, is a substitute for the act of 11th April, 1799, [3 Sm. L. 392,] entitled "An act to raise and collect county rates and levies." The sixteenth section of this act requires the collectors of the several wards, townships and districts, within three months after receiving the corrected duplicates, subsequent to the appeal, to pay into the hands of the respective treasurers the whole amount of the tax charged and assessed in such duplicate, without further delay, except such sum as the commissioners may exonerate them from; and declares that for the payment of the balance remaining unpaid, all the estate, real and personal, of the delinquent collectors, shall be bound as security for the payment of such balance, at and from the expiration of the said three months. A transcript of this balance shall be then entered by the treasurer with the prothonotary, whose duty it shall be to file the same, which shall then operate, to all intents and purposes, as if judgment were then entered against them for such balance, in a court of record, provided that such balance shall not be a lien on such delinquent's property for a longer term than two years. The commissioners may issue their warrant to the sheriff or coroner of the county, requiring him to sell at public sale, the estate of the delinquent collector, after ten days' previous notice by advertisement; out of the proceeds of the sale, the balance due by the collector will be taken by the commissioners, and the overplus, if any, after all necessary charges are deducted, will be restored to the collector.

§ 617. Under this act of 1799, the balance found due by the collector became a lien on his personal, as well as upon his real estate, from the time of the filing of the transcript.[1] And, though the lien of the balance and of the transcript thereof, filed in the prothonotary's office, expired by the lapse of more than two years, the warrant of the commis-

---

[1] Commissioners v. Henry, 3 P. &. W. 26.

sioners, issued nearly four years after the filing of the transcript and seizure of the collector's lands thereunder, became
a new lien, which continued until the sale of the land. The
title of the vendee at this sale was superior to that of a purchaser at a subsequent sheriff's sale, on judgments recovered
between the date of the issue of the warrant and the sale
under it, which took place five months afterwards.[1] Though
the commissioners' warrant designates a day on which the
the sale shall take place, a sale on a day subsequent thereto
is good, the warrant naming no return day, and being, therefore, valid so long as the commissioners may choose, notwithstanding that a day was mentioned for its execution.[2]

§ 618. The act of 20th March, 1724–5, declared that "all
gifts, grants and sales, which should be made by any delinquent tax collector, of any of his estates, after the time at
which he ought to have paid the moneys arising from tax
assessments, should be deemed fraudulent, and should not
prevent or avoid the seizure and sale thereof for arrears of
taxes unpaid by him. Under this act, it was decided that
unpaid balances due by the collector, were a lien on his
lands, superior to a mortgage thereof made after the delinquency or default, and that when, on the failure of a collector
originally appointed to collect the taxes, another was appointed
in his stead, the estate of the latter, on his collecting these
taxes, became chargeable therewith, in the same manner as
if he had been the original collector.[3]

---

[1] Stauffer v. Commissioners, 1 W.
300.

[2] Schuylkill and Dauphin Improvement Co. v. McCreary, 58 Pa. St. 304.

Comp. Vankirk v. Clark, 16 Serg. &
R. 286.

[3] Warner v. Emory, 3 Y. 50.

CHAPTER XXIX.

LIEN OF GROUND-RENT LANDLORD.

§ 619. When the owner in fee of land grants the fee to another, but with a reservation to himself of a perpetual ground-rent, this rent is a rent-service,[1] to which, though nothing be said thereof in the deed, the right of distress is incident. The right thus reserved to the grantor is real estate, not in the land, but in the rent.[2] When the deed by which the rent is reserved likewise reserves to the grantor the right to distrain, and to re-enter on the land and hold it until all rent in arrear is paid, the rent in arrear has the properties of a lien on the land out of which it issues.[3] The right of re-entry is sometimes coupled with the right to forfeit the grant for non-payment of the rent.[4] A contract to

[1] Ingersoll v Sergeant, 1 Wh. 337; Wallace v Harmsted, 44 Pa. St. 492; Voeghtly v Pittsburg, etc, R. R. Co., 2 Grant 243, Cuthbert v. Kuhn, 3 Wh. 357; Miners' Bank v. Heilner, 47 Pa. St. 252. When the owner of the land in fee grants, not the land itself, but a rent out of it, and inserts a clause of distress in the deed, he grants a rent-charge. Distress is not incident to a rent-charge; the right thereto must be expressly granted. Such a rent is not apportionable.

[2] Workman v. Mifflin, 30 Pa. St. 362; Franciscus v. Reigart, 4 W 98; Voeghtly v. Pittsburg, etc., R. R. Co, 2 Grant 243, Hacker v. Cozens, 8 W. N. C 189; Cobb v. Biddle, 14 Pa. St. 444, Irwin v. Bank of the United States, 1 Pa. St. 349; Mitchell v. Steinmetz, 10 W. N. C. 43. In the

penultimate case, it was decided that both the rent and the land out of which it issues, may be separately taxed as real estate, and a treasurer's sale for taxes of the land would not discharge the rent.

[3] Bantleon v. Smith, 2 Binn. 146; Gordon v. Correy, 5 Binn. 552; Devine's Appeal, 30 Pa. St. 348; Sands v Smith, 3 W & S. 9; Walton v West, 4 Wh. 221; Workman v Mifflin, 30 Pa. St 362; Dougherty's Estate, 9 W. & S 189, Powell v. Whitaker, 88 Pa. St. 445. In Mather v. McMichael, 13 Pa. St. 301, and Hacker v. Cozens, 8 W. N. C 189, it does not appear whether the right of re-entry was reserved.

[4] Dougherty's Appeal, 9 W. & S. 189; Spangler's Appeal, 30 Pa. St. 277.

convey land subject to a ground-rent, not executed, cannot of course give rise to the landlord's lien for arrears of rent. A. contracted to convey land to B. and C., and others whom they might designate, for $29,700, payable either in cash within four years, or at the end of that time in ground-rents reserved, amounting to $1,782 per annum, and it was agreed that during these four years A. should have all the remedies of a ground-rent landlord for the recovery of the interest, including the right to re-enter on the premises. The interest of B. being sold by the sheriff before a conveyance of the legal title, it was held that A. had no lien for the annual interest unpaid.[1]

Relation of Lien.

§ 620. The lien of each unpaid installment of rent become due, relates not to the time it became payable, but to the date of the deed by which it was reserved, and prevails, therefore, over all conveyances of the land made, or liens thereon acquired, since that time.[2] The arrears of rent for the years 1834–1843, under a deed dated September 23d, 1806, though no judgments had been recovered for them, were preferred to judgments recovered against the ground-tenant February 14th, 1834, and subsequently, in distribution of the proceeds of a judicial sale of the land.[3] When the land is sold on a judgment recovered by the grantor, on the grantee's covenant to pay rent, this judgment must be paid from the proceeds of a sale thereon, in preference to an earlier judgment against the grantee, recovered by another creditor.[4] So, if the sale were on the judgment of the other creditor.[5] When land was conveyed May 2d, 1849, subject to a ground-rent, and three weeks afterwards the grantee mortgaged it, and in

[1] Moroney v. Copeland, 5 Wh. 407.

[2] Devine's Appeal, 30 Pa. St. 348; Fassitt v. Middleton, 5 Phila 196, 47 Pa. St. 214.

[3] Dougherty's Estate, 9 W. & S 189; Walton v. West, 4 Wh. 221; Mather v. McMichael, 13 Pa. St 301; Pancoast's Appeal, 8 W. & S. 381.

[4] Bantleon v. Smith, 2 Binn. 146; Commonwealth v. Lelar, 13 Pa. St. 22

[5] Gordon v. Correy, 5 Binn. 552.

1877 an action of covenant was begun for arrears of rent of a few years preceding, on which judgment was recovered, a sale under this judgment divested the mortgage.[1] When a part of the land out of which the rent issued was taken for a street, the ground-rent landlord was entitled to receive from the damages awarded, the rent in arrear when it was taken, though he did not obtain judgment on his covenant for the rent for several months afterwards, and notwithstanding an assignment by the ground-rent tenant of his claim for the damages, made six months before the judgment was recovered.[2] Judgments successively recovered for successive arrears of rent relate to the same date—that of the grant by which the rent was reserved.[3] The lien of the ground-rent is posterior to that of municipal claims and taxes in the city of Philadelphia, though they arise or are imposed subsequently to the deed which reserves the ground-rent.[4]

For How Much the Lien Exists.

§ 621. The cases already-cited, show that the lien exists for all arrears of rent, from the date of the grant by which it was reserved. As against other lien creditors of the grantee, however, the arrears of rent do not, it seems, bear interest when the landlord has neglected to make demand for the rent.[5] So, as against a purchaser who buys the land while there are arrears due.[6] As against the ground-tenant, arrears of rent would probably bear interest; at least if the

---

[1] Amanda Martin's Appeal, 9 W. N. C. 484.

[2] Powell v. Whitaker, 88 Pa. St. 445.

[3] Fassitt v. Middleton, 5 Phila. 196, 47 Pa. St. 214. One who has become bail for stay of execution of the first of these judgments, cannot share in the proceeds of a judicial sale of the ground-tenant's land until all the arrears of rent are paid, unless he has an assignment of the judgment whose stay he procured, with a waiver of the landlord's right of priority as to the other judgments and arrears.

[4] Mitchell v. Steinmetz, 10 W. N. C. 43.

[5] Dougherty's Estate, 9 W. & S. 189; Bantleon v. Smith, 2 Binn. 146; Makinson's Estate, 8 Phila. 381; McQuesney v. Hiester, 33 Pa. St. 435.

[6] McQuesney v. Hiester, 33 Pa. St. 435.

landlord enter under a clause of re-entry for arrears of rent, equity would not relieve the tenant until he paid interest on the arrears.[1]

Apportionment.

§ 622. Rent reserved by a deed which grants the fee in the land, is, as being a rent-service, apportionable. The grantor, therefore, can release a part of the land out of which the rent issues, without releasing the remainder for its proportional share.[2] But, if, by agreement between the purchasers of different parts of the land, in which the landlord acquiesces for more than twenty-one years, each purchaser obligates himself to pay a certain part of the rent, and, in fact, does pay it for that period of time, this agreement is not binding on a subsequent purchaser of the ground-rent, without notice of it.[3] That the ground-rent landlord has, under a judgment upon the covenant for rent in the deed, sold the land in four equal parts, and has since received payment from each of the purchasers of one-fourth of the rent, giving a receipt in full, is not evidence of apportionment as against a subsequent assignee of the ground-rent.[4]

The Lien not Impaired.

§ 623. The lien of arrears of rent upon the fee is not impaired by the existence of goods and chattels on the premises, sufficient to pay them, even though a distress has been made and then abandoned.[5] Taking a bond with warrant of attorney, and entering judgment thereon for arrears of rent,[6] or adverse recovery of judgment for arrears,[7] does not merge their lien in that of the judgment.

[1] McQuesney v. Hiester, 33 Pa. St. 435.

[2] Ingersoll v. Sergeant, 1 Wh. 337; Voeghtly v. Pittsburg, etc., R. R. Co., 2 Grant 243.

[3] Evans v. Martin, 8 W. N. C. 490.

[4] Quigley v. Molineaux, 10 W. N. C. 118.

[5] Howell v. Bateson, 9 W. N. C. 463.

[6] Gordon v. Correy, 5 Binn. 552.

[7] Bantleon v. Smith, 2 Binn. 146; Fassitt v. Middleton, 5 Phila. 96, 47 Pa. St. 214.

CHAPTER XXX.

LESSOR'S LIEN UPON THE LEASEHOLD.

§ 624. The right of the landlord secured by the acts of 21st March, 1772, and of June 16th, 1836, to take from the proceeds of an execution, rent in arrear not exceeding one year's, has reference only to sales in execution of chattels found on the demised premises.[1] When a lease for a term of years, reserving rent, also reserves to the lessor the right of re-entering upon the land, and receiving its profits for any arrears, and until they are paid, such right of re-entry is in effect a lien upon the leasehold interest. The right of re-entry may be accompanied with a reservation of a right of distress,[2] or of a right to forfeit or annul the lease for arrears.[3] When a sale of the leasehold takes place under an execution issued by any creditor of the lessee, the lessor's right of re-entry or of forfeiture for any arrears of rent then due is extinguished.[4] It follows that the landlord has a right to resort to the proceeds of the sale for such arrears. He has not been limited to one year's rent, but has taken out the rent due, of two years,[5] of three and one-half years,[6] of four years,[7] of nine years nine months,[8] and could take out rent

---

[1] Spangler's Appeal, 30 Pa. St. 277, n. (a.)

[2] Wood's Appeal, 30 Pa. St. 274.

[3] Spangler's Appeal, 30 Pa. St. 277, n. (a.); Dougherty's Estate, 9 W. & S. 189. In Miners' Bank v. Heilner, 47 Pa. St. 452, it is denied that a clause in a mining lease for thirteen years, providing that for default in payment of rent, the "lease shall be considered and held forfeited at the option" of the lessor, makes the rent

due a lien on the leasehold. But Judge Agnew's concurring opinion, p. 462, shows that in this very case, once before in the supreme court, a distribution to the lessor, as a lienor in virtue of this clause of forfeiture, had been affirmed.

[4] Wood's Appeal, 30 Pa. St. 274.

[5] Ibid.

[6] Powell v. Whitaker, 88 Pa St. 445.

[7] Ter Hoven v. Kerns, 2 Pa. St. 96.

[8] Dougherty's Estate, 9 W. & S. 189.

in arrear for an indefinite time. The limitation of the act of March 21st, 1772, [1 Sm. L. 370,] and of the eighty-third section of the act of 16th June, 1836, [P. L. 777,] does not apply to the sale of the leasehold itself.[1]

§ 625. The landlord's right to the proceeds of a sale in execution of the leasehold, under the clause of re-entry or of forfeiture, is superior to that of all other creditors of the lessee, including miners and laborers, under the act of April 2d, 1849, for labor performed on the demised premises.[2] A lease reserving a right to distrain for arrears of rent, but not a right to re-enter, does not create a lien on the leasehold in favor of the lessor. Hence, out of the proceeds of a sheriff's sale of the leasehold, under a mortgage thereon, the mortgagee will be entitled to payment.[3]

[1] Mather v. McMichael, 13 Pa. St. 301.

[2] Wood's Appeal, 30 Pa. St. 274, and cases already cited.

[3] Sands v. Smith, 3 W. & S 9. Hence the lessor could distrain on the chattels of the sheriff's vendee for rent due before the sale.

CHAPTER XXXI.

LIEN OF SURPLUS BONDS.

§ 626. By the act of 13th March, 1815, [6 Sm. L. 299,] it is made the duty of the treasurers of the several counties of the state to make public sale, at intervals of two years, of all unseated lands, or of such parts thereof, situate in the proper county, as will pay the arrearages of taxes due thereon, which shall have remained due and unpaid for the space of one year before, together with all costs necessarily accruing by reason of such delinquency, and to execute deeds therefor in fee-simple. The act of April 3d, 1804, [4 Sm. L. 201,] to which that of 1815 is a supplement, and the act of April 4, 1809, [5 Sm. L. 73,] make it the duty of the treasurer to take from the purchaser of the land thus sold, bonds, executed in his name, with warrants of attorney annexed, for any surplus of the purchase money that may remain after satisfying and paying the taxes and costs aforesaid, and to file them forthwith in the office of the prothonotary of the proper county. These bonds, thus filed, shall, from the date of the treasurer's deed, bind the lands by him sold, into whosesoever hands they may come, as effectually, and in like manner, as judgments; and actions may be begun on such bonds at any time within five years after such sale.[1] Their lien thus expires in five years.[2] Whatever defect of the bond is grave enough to make the treasurer's sale null will invalidate the bond itself as the basis of a lien. There would, in such case, be no title to be bound by it. A bond

---

[1] Section 4, act April 3d, 1804.

[2] Thudium v. Deardorff, 3 Pa. St. 90. But the bond may be sued more than five years after its filing, notwithstanding that its lien has expired.

is void which gives no description of the land to secure the payment of whose purchase money it was made.[1] One, however, which describes the land as a "tract of land situate in Rye township, in the county of Perry, containing twenty acres," is valid.[2] When the treasurer's deed described the land as situated in East Hanover township, Lebanon county, surveyed to A., containing four hundred and forty-one acres, and recited the sale as taking place August 18th, and the tax and the costs, as stated in the deed, left a balance of $3.19 of the purchase money, a surplus bond which described the land sold as "unseated land, sold as the property of A., dated August 12th, and for eighty-seven and one-half cents," was void, since it was impossible to identify the land on which it would become a lien.[3] A bond for six cents less than it ought to have been for, by mistake of the officer, is valid,[4] as is also one for twenty-five cents too much;[5] but one which is payable two years after date and does not contain a warrant of attorney to confess judgment, is void.[6]

§ 627. These bonds, together with their liens, inure to the benefit of those who were the owners of the land at the time of the treasurer's sale,[7] or of any person who has a lien, or any equitable interest therein. Such person may proceed to collect the amount of the bond, in the name of the treasurer, as fully as the owner of the land at the time of the sale might do. The money, however, when collected, must be paid into the court where the bond is filed, and distributed by its decree, in the same manner as moneys arising from a sheriff's sale of said land, would be.[8] Hence, when there was a mortgage on the land, at the time of the tax sale, the mortgagee was entitled to the proceeds of the surplus bond,

---

[1] Bartholomew v. Leech, 7 W. 472.

[2] Devor v. McClintock, 9 W. & S. 80.

[3] Rank v. Dauphin and Susquehanna Coal Co., 1 Pearson 453.

[4] Frick v. Sterrett, 4 W. & S. 269.

[5] Rank v. Dauphin, etc., Coal Co., 1 Pearson 453.

[6] Ibid.

[7] Section 4, act 3d April, 1804.

[8] Section 6, act of April 14th, 1840, [P. L. 351.]

in preference to a creditor who, having obtained a judgment against the former owner, subsequently to the tax sale, attached the bond in the hands of the obligee.[1]   Though the obligor in the surplus bond was, at the time of his purchase at the tax sale, the owner of a perpetual ground-rent issuing out of the premises, on which there were arrears at the time of the sale, he could not, in an action on the bond, set off such arrears, when the use-plaintiff was the assignee of the ground-tenant.[2]

[1] Kelso v. Kelly, 14 Pa. St. 204.   [2] Irish v. Johnston, 11 Pa. St. 483.

CHAPTER XXXII.

LIEN FOR PURCHASE MONEY.

§ 628. Liens on land may be created by the deed by which the title is conveyed. When the grant is made subject to the payment of a balance of purchase money, such balance becomes a charge on the land.[1] A deed conveying land to A., "to have and to hold the said land * * * to the said A., his heirs and assigns, subject to the payment of the said sum of $2,804.21, intended to be secured by mortgage, as aforesaid," and in fact secured by such mortgage, made that amount a lien.[2] Land was sold at public vendue, one of the written conditions of the sale, signed by the purchaser, being that one-half of the purchase money should be paid in four equal annual installments, and be a lien on the land. The deed granted the land "subject to the proviso or condition of sale that there shall be a lien on the land until the whole amount is paid" by the grantee or his heirs. The installments due were a lien on the premises.[3] In the *habendum* of the deed, the conveyance was described as "subject, nevertheless, to the reservation contained in a certain article of agreement made between the said H. S. and P. S., bearing date the 23d September, 1852, wherein is reserved, among other things, that the sum of $400 shall be paid by the said P. S. immediately after the decease of the said H. S. and S., his wife, to the heirs, or those legally entitled thereto, and also subject to a certain bond, duly executed, bearing even

---

[1] Episcopal Academy *v.* Frieze, 2 W. 16.

[2] Stewartson *v.* Watts, 8 W. 392. The lien of both the mortgage and the deed was divested by a sheriff's sale, on a judgment recovered against one who held the title by mesne conveyances from A.

[3] Barnitz *v.* Smith, 1 W. & S. 142.

date herewith, conditioned for the payment of the said $400 contained in the article of agreement, to be paid agreeably to said article of agreement." The $400 were charged on the land.[1]

§ 629. The heirs of P. B., deceased, conveyed land to J. S., "under and subject to the payment of £1,000, which the said J. S. obligated himself to pay at or immediately after the death of M. B., widow" of P. B., deceased, "to and among the heirs of P. B., deceased, in equal shares, with the annual legal interest of the said principal sum of £1,000, to be paid by the said J. S., his heirs, executors, administrators and assigns, unto the said M. B., yearly and every year on the first day April, during her natural life." This money was thus created a lien.[2] So was money payable on certain bonds, a lien upon land conveyed by A. to B., "subject, nevertheless, to the conditions and obligations contained in a certain article of agreement existing between the parties," one of which was the payment to various heirs of A. of these bonds, falling due in each succeeding year after A.'s death.[3] A father conveyed land to his son by a deed, the *habendum* of which was "to have and to hold the three pieces of land unto the said E. D., his heirs and assigns, * * * under and subject, nevertheless, to certain articles of agreement * * * bearing even date herewith, * * * reserving therein the payment of the interest of the principal sum of $1,000 yearly, during the joint lives of J. D. and C., his wife, or the survivor, and under and subject to the said principal sum of $1,000, upon the death of said J. D. and wife, to the persons in said agreement mentioned." This made the $1,000 a charge.[4] A conveyance to B. by A., "subject always to the right of the aforesaid M. W. in and

[1] Strauss' Appeal, 49 Pa. St. 353.
[2] Bury v. Sieber, 5 Pa. St. 431.
[3] Bear v. Whisler, 7 W. 144. Here there was a sheriff's sale of the premises, five years after A.'s death, but the lien of the deed was enforced by ejectment against the sheriff's vendee.
[4] Dewalt's Appeal, 20 Pa. St. 236.

to the same, * * * and also to pay in one year after her decease, the full sum of $500, lawful money, unto him the said " A., his heirs or assigns. The $500 were a lien.[1] When land of a decedent was sold by order of the orphans' court, the purchase money to remain charged on the premises during the life of his widow, the interest to be annually paid to her, and the deed to the purchaser was "subject, nevertheless, to the payment of the purchase money hereinbefore mentioned, with the annual interest thereon," such purchase money was a lien.[2] Land was devised, at a valuation to be made at the death of the testator's widow. Before her death the land was sold by the sheriff, his deed describing the devisee's interest sold, as subject to the valuation to be made. The vendee took the land, encumbered by the money to be ascertained by the subsequent valuation.[3] A. dying, his land was sold by the administrator to B., his widow, a part of the purchase money being paid by the widow's mother, C. This money had in part been borrowed by C. from D. Subsequently, B., by articles, agreed to sell the land to C., who was to pay B. $1,515 in cash, and $699 to the administrator, to complete the payment of the purchase money to him. Having paid B. $1,515 in pursuance of this arrangement, C. borrowed an additional sum from D., and therewith paid off the administrator, who thereupon delivered the deed

---

[1] Keech v. Speakman, 1 Cl. 72. A grantee of B. was obliged to pay interest on the $500, from the expiration of one year from the decease of M. W., although for four years no administrator of the estate of A., who had died before M. W., was appointed.

[2] Helfrich v. Weaver, 61 Pa. St. 385.

[3] Hart v. Homiller, 20 Pa. St. 248. In Pierce v Gardner, 83 Pa. St. 211, P. had a judgment v. S. and wife, for $881.31, but no mortgage for it. S.

and wife conveyed land bound by the judgment to D., the deed reciting that it was subject to a mortgage for $881.31. The lien of the judgment was not properly revived. D. gave a mortgage on the land, under which it was afterwards sold. It was decided that a sale on the judgment after that on the mortgage, conveyed no title, since, even if the judgment debt was made a lien by the deed to D., the prior sale on the mortgage divested it.

to B. B., on the same day, executed a deed to C., who now owed for money borrowed from D. and paid to the administrator, $1,378.09. This deed mentioned as the consideration $1,108.35. After the description of the land, it contained the clause, "The said real estate is conveyed subject to the payment of the sum of $1,378.09, being the balance of purchase money due, for which a judgment has been entered in the name of Samuel McClain. * * * Habendum, etc., * * * subject, nevertheless, to the payment of the·sum of $1,378.09, as aforesaid." The $1,378.09 were a charge in favor of Samuel McClain, who could enforce it by an action of ejectment and a conditional verdict therein.[1]

When the Lien Begins.

§ 630. The lien of the purchase money charged on the land by the deed of conveyance is superior to earlier liens upon the equitable title of the vendee, to complete which the deed is executed and delivered. When A. contracts to sell land to B., and, before the delivery of the deed, judgments are recovered against B., and, simultaneously with the delivery of the deed, which is subject to the unpaid purchase money, a judgment bond and mortgage for this purchase money are delivered by B. to A., this purchase money must be first paid from the proceeds of a sheriff's sale of the land on a judgment against B., although the mortgage was not recorded and the judgment for the purchase money was not entered until three months after their delivery.[2] *A fortiori* the lien of such a deed prevails over that of a judgment recovered against the grantee three weeks after its delivery.[3] It caused the divestiture of a mortgage executed six years subsequently by one to whom the grantee conveyed the premises, by a sheriff's sale on a judgment recovered against the mortgagor.[4] But, when the money is to be paid only at the

---

[1] Kensinger v. Smith, 94 Pa. St. 384.
[2] Episcopal Academy v. Frieze, 2 W. 16.
[3] Barnitz v. Smith, 1 W. & S. 142.
[4] Strauss' Appeal, 49 Pa. St. 353.

death of a widow, to whom, during her life, the interest thereon is annually payable, a judicial sale while she is living, on a judgment recovered against the grantee, will not divest a mortgage executed between the date of the grant and of the recovery of the judgment.[1] A charge by deed is valid against a subsequent purchaser,[2] and a sale on a judgment recovered after the purchase on a bond which accompanied the deed, as additional security for the money therein charged on the land, divests his title by relation to the deed.[3]

No Lien.

§ 631. In Pennsylvania there is no equitable lien for purchase money of lands. When the legal title has been conveyed, the grantor has no lien merely from the fact that the price stipulated for remains wholly or in part unpaid, although the parties against whom he desires to assert such a lien had notice of this fact at the time they acquired their respective interests or rights in or concerning the land. Before conveyance, a vendor has a lien by virtue of the legal title; after it, he has no lien except it be by judgment or mortgage, or by a charge in the deed of conveyance itself. This is the doctrine of all the cases on the subject.[4] When A. conveyed land to B., by deed, in consideration of $21,600, and on the same day one-half of the purchase money was paid, and for the remainder five bonds of equal sums, payable in successive years, were executed, and a receipt was at the same time given on the deed for the entire consideration, and the deed and title papers were delivered to B., who went into possession of the premises, A. was not permitted to share in the distribution of the proceeds of a sheriff's sale of the land under a judgment against B., in preference to judgment creditors of B., although they had had notice that the pur-

---

[1] Helfrich v. Weaver, 61 Pa. St. 385.

[2] Keech v. Speakman, 1 Cl. 72.

[3] Bury v. Sieber, 5 Pa. St. 431.

[4] Stephens' Exrs.' Appeal, 38 Pa. St. 9.

chase-money bonds were still unpaid.[1] When a lien for
purchase money is asserted, in virtue of the deed of conveyance, the intent to constitute it must be therein evidenced
by express and plain words; it cannot arise by implication.
A., to whom an estate for life or during widowhood was
devised, released this estate, by deed, to a remainderman
"for and in consideration of the payment to me yearly and
every year, during the continuance of my widowhood, of the
sum of $100, lawful money of the United States." This
did not make the $100 a lien, and A. could not recover that
annual sum from one who purchased the land at a sheriff's
sale, under a mortgage executed by the remainderman, subsequently to the release of her estate.[2]

---

[1] Kauffelt *v.* Bower, 7 Serg. & R. 64.
For approval of this case, see Bear
v. Whisler, 7 W. 144; Megargel *v.*
Saul, 3 Wh. 19; Hiester *v.* Green,
48 Pa. St. 96. In the matter of
Neagley & Perry's Estate, 2 Pearson
309.

[2] Hiester *v.* Green, 48 Pa. St. 96.
This case practically overrules Neas'
Appeal, 31 Pa. St. 293.

CHAPTER XXXIII.

LIENS ARISING FROM PARTITION OF LANDS.

Partition in the Common Pleas.

§ 632. The courts of common pleas have jurisdiction in all cases of partition of lands owned in joint-tenancy, coparcenary, or in common, and in partition of lands of a decedent this jurisdiction is concurrent with that of the orphans' courts.[1]

§ 633. When, under writ of partition from such court, the inquest shall be of opinion that the land cannot be divided without prejudice to or spoiling the whole, they shall make return to the court of that fact, together with a just valuation and appraisement thereof. The court, approving such valuation, may award the land to that co-owner, consenting to take it thereat, whose title is the oldest, or to such co-owner as shall offer in writing the highest price therefor above the valuation returned. The sheriff shall then execute a deed to this party for the land so taken, subject, nevertheless, to a lien in favor of the other co-owners, until payment be made to them of their respective shares of the valuation.[2]

§ 634. If no co-owner elect to take the land at the appraisement, or at some higher price, the sheriff shall sell it, executing a deed therefor to the purchaser on receiving the purchase money, or sufficient security therefor. The money or securities so taken shall be brought by him into court, and be distributed among the parties entitled to receive the same.[3]

[1] Section 1, act of 7th April, 1807, [4 Sm. L. 398;] Section 1, act of April 21st, 1846, [P. L. 426.]

[2] Section 2, act 11th April, 1799, [3 Sm. L. 387;] Section 14, act of May 5th, 1841, [P. L. 353;] Section 10, act 22d April, 1856, [P. L. 534.]

[3] Section 2, act 11th April, 1799, [3 Sm. L. 387.]

§ 635. When the land can be divided, the inquest have power to divide it into such number of purparts as shall seem most convenient and advantageous.[1] When they divide into purparts of unequal values, they shall value them respectively, charging them with such sums in favor of the co-tenants who do not take them, as shall represent the former shares of such co-tenants in the land.[2] At the return to the rule to accept or refuse to take at the valuation, the purparts shall be allotted to such co-owner as shall offer, in writing, the highest price above the valuation,[3] in which case a re-adjustment must be made by the court of the sums of money necessary to equalize the interests of the parties. The money which shall be finally determined by the court to be payable by the accepting party, shall be a lien on all the land so taken until paid.[4]

Voluntary Partition.

§ 636. Since the law will compel partition of an estate held in coparcenary, at the suit of one co-tenant, an agreement to make partition, even in parol, will, when effected in good faith, and fairly and equally, be binding on the co-owners, even on such of them as may be *femes covert* and minors.[5] When an agreement under seal, acknowledged and recorded, provides that the amount of the owelty shall be a lien on the respective purparts, such owelty will continue a lien as against judgments subsequently recovered.[6] So, when there was an agreement in writing for partition and valuation of

[1] Section 2, act 11th April, 1835, [P. L. 200.]

[2] Section 5, act of 7th April, 1807, [4 Sm L. 400]

[3] Section 10, act 22d April, 1856.

[4] Wetherill *v.* Warner, 6 Phila. 182. On a sale by the sheriff of a part of this land, on a judgment against the purchaser from the accepting co owner, the owelty must be paid from the proceeds. The later lien creditors or the *terre-tenant* would be sub-

rogated, as against the remaining lands taken by the co-owner.

[5] Calhoun *v.* Hays, 8 W. & S. 127. It will bind, if fairly made, a mortgagee of an undivided interest. The mortgage will be cast upon the purpart allotted to the mortgagor in severalty. Long's Appeal, 77 Pa. St. 151. Comp. Steel's Appeal, 86 Pa. St 222.

[6] Darlington's Appropriation, 13 Pa. St. 430.

an estate, but nothing was therein said concerning the owelty being and continuing a lien, the payment of the owelty was enforced as a lien against a sheriff's vendee of the land, who had notice at the sale that it was still unpaid, and who retained from his bid enough to pay it.[1]

[1] Long *v.* Long, 1 W. 265. The payment of the lien was enforced by debt against the party who accepted the purpart in partition, and the sheriff's vendee as *terre-tenant* In Dexter's Appeal, 2 W. N C. 621, it was decided that an agreement in writing. recorded in the clerk's office, by which a widow's dower is estimated at so much, and made a charge on the land, makes it a charge thereon, in whosesoever hands it may be; and from the proceeds of a judicial sale of the premises on a lien existing before the agreement was recorded, the capitalized value of the annuity thereby created, as well as the arrears due thereon, is payable from the proceeds.

CHAPTER XXXIV.

LIEN OF TAXES.

Personalty.

§ 637. Taxes, whether assessed on realty or on personalty, are not, by virtue of their assessment merely, a lien on the personal property of the person against whom they are assessed.[1] Nor do they become such by the delivery to the collector of his warrant for their collection. Annually to tie up the chattels of a county while the taxes are in course of collection, would be an insufferable annoyance. To enforce the payment of the tax, the power of distress is conferred on the officer, and a lien begins only when the distress is actually made.[2] On April 27th, 1833, the commissioners of Centre county made out the duplicate for county and state taxes for L. township, and delivered it to the collector. In this duplicate A. was taxed in a certain sum, which he neglected to pay. On July 31st, 1835, he made an assignment of his property for the benefit of creditors. The personalty thus assigned was not subject to distress for the tax.[3] Actual seizure under a collector's warrant, is necessary in order to acquire a lien on personalty for the tax.[4]

§ 638. The forty-sixth section of the act of 15th April, 1834, [P. L. 518,] declares that "the goods and chattels of any person occupying any real estate, shall be liable to distress and sale, for the non-payment of any taxes assessed upon such real estate, during his possession or occupancy, remaining unpaid, in like manner as if they were the goods

---

[1] Burd v. Ramsay, 9 Serg. & R. 109.
[2] Ibid.; Baskin v. Hummel, 5 W. 76; Parsons v. Allison, 5 W. 72;
Moore v. Marsh, 60 Pa. St. 46; Briggs' Appeal, 38 Leg. Int. 262.
[3] Parsons v. Allison, 5 W. 72.
[4] Moore v. Marsh, 60 Pa. St. 46.

and chattels of the owner of such real estate." Under this section only such chattels can be seized by the tax collector, under his warrant, as are the property of the occupier of the real estate on which the taxes are assessed. Hence, if, on a *fi. fa.* against the owner and occupier of real estate, chattels thereon are sold by the sheriff, they are not afterwards, and while in the process of removal by the sheriff's vendee, subject to seizure by the tax collector for taxes previously assessed on the real estate, and remaining unpaid at the time of the sheriff's sale.[1]

Tax on National Bank Shares.

§ 639. The several states of the Union are permitted, within certain limits, by the laws of the United States, to impose taxes on national banks. Beyond those limits their power of taxation does not extend.[2] By the acts of April 12th, 1867, [P. L. 74,] and of March 31st, 1870, [P. L. 42,] the shares of national banks located within this state are taxable for state purposes, at the rate of three mills per annum upon the assessed value thereof, and for school, municipal and other local purposes, at the rate that may be by law imposed on other moneyed capital in the hands of individual citizens within the state. If the bank elects to collect annually from its shareholders a tax of one per centum upon the par value of all the shares of stock, and pays the same into the state treasury on or before the twentieth day of January in every year, the shares of the bank,

---

[1] Moore v. Marsh, 60 Pa. St. 46.

[2] City of Pittsburg v. First National Bank of Pittsburg, 55 Pa. St. 45. A tax by the city of Pittsburg, on the business of a national bank, though under the authority of state law, was void. In County of Bucks v. Ely, 6 Phila. 414, it was decided that stock in a New Jersey national bank, held by a resident of Pennsylvania, cannot be taxed in this state. This is so, according to State Bank of Camden v. Pierce, 5 W. N. C. 344, though the New Jersey bank has an office in Philadelphia, where it receives deposits, which, at the close of each day, are carried to the bank in Camden. See, also, Commonwealth v. Manuf. and Mech. Bank, 2 Pearson 386; Commonwealth v. Girard National Bank, 6 Phila. 431, 1 Pearson 366.

and its capital and profits, shall be exempt from all other taxation under the laws of Pennsylvania.[1] A tax under this act on the par value of the shares, is a tax on the banking house, which, however it may be used, is a part of the capital of the bank.[2] The act of April 2d, 1868, [P. L. 55,] a supplement to that of April 12th, 1867, declares that the taxes assessed on national bank shares shall be a lien thereon, from the date of the levy of the tax, and that these shares, together with the accrued dividends, shall be subject to attachment or levy and sale for non-payment of the tax, as any other personal property. Taxes for the years 1870 and 1871, on national bank shares, continued to be a lien thereon, although a warrant for their collection did not issue until 1872. Any purchaser must see to it that no such tax remains unpaid.[3] The above laws are within the competence of the legislature of this state.[4]

Taxes on Real Estate.

§ 640. These are a lien on the real estate upon which they are assessed, only when they are made such by statute.[5] The act of 11th April, 1799, [3 Sm. L. 392,] which imposed a tax on seated lands in the state, provided, as methods for their collection, distress of chattels found thereon, or commitment of the body of the person who was liable for their payment. Having failed to declare the tax a lien on the land, and to designate a feasible method for the enforcement of such lien, the inference is irresistible that the act was not intended to create such a lien.[6] The act of 11th June, 1840,

---

[1] Section 4, act 31st March, 1870.

[2] Lackawanna County v. First Nat. Bank of Scranton, 94 Pa. St. 221.

[3] Jenkins v. London, 31 Leg. Int. 260.

[4] Hepburn v School Directors, 79 Pa. St. 159, 23 Wall 480; County of Lancaster v. Lancaster County National Bank, 7 W. N. C. 29; Allen v. County Commissioners, 5 W. N. C. 229.

[5] Burd v. Ramsay, 9 Serg. & R. 109;

Harrisburg v. Orth, 2 Pearson 340, 6 W. N. C. 121.

[6] Burd v. Ramsay, 9 Serg. & R. 109. For this reason, when land was sold in 1820, on a judgment recovered on a bond accompanying a mortgage, dated January 16th, 1812, the taxes of the years 1818 and 1819 were not paid out of the proceeds. The priority of the mortgage to the assessment of the tax is not adverted to.

[P. L. 612,] directed the commissioners of each county, annually, until the year 1846, inclusive, at the usual time for making county rates and levies, to add to the county rates and levies one mill on every dollar for the use of the commonwealth, upon all real estate, as well as personal, then taxable under existing laws for county purposes. It did not make such tax a lien on the real estate. Hence, when land situate in Philadelphia was sold under a mortgage, the tax was not paid out of the proceeds.[1]

§ 641. The act of February 3d, 1824, [8 Sm. L. 189,] provided that "all taxes, rates and levies which may hereafter be lawfully imposed or assessed, to be applied for any purposes,[2] either in the city or county of Philadelphia, on real estate situate in the said city or county of Philadelphia, shall be and they are hereby declared to be a lien on the said real estate, on which they may hereafter be imposed or assessed, together, also, with all additions to and charges on the said taxes, rates and levies which, by the provisions of this act, are directed to be made." Borough, city and county taxes on real estate have been made liens by sundry statutes, e. g., in Allegheny county, by act of April 5th, 1844, [P. L. 199;] in Chester county, by act of April 2d, 1868, [P. L. 595;] in Lycoming county, by act of April 4th, 1870, [P. L. 866;] in Allegheny City, by act of February 27th, 1860, [P. L. 85;] in Lancaster city, by act of March 15th, 1847, [P. L. 366;][3] in Harrisburg and Columbia, by act of April 10th, 1848, [P. L. 435;] in Titusville,[4] in cities of the third class, by the act of May 23d, 1874, [P. L. 235;]

---

[1] Parker's Appeal, 8 W. & S. 449. It was said that the act of February 3d, 1824, § 1, [8 Sm. L. 189,] did not apply to state taxes. The act of 16th April, 1845, [P. L. 495,] extended the provisions of the act of February 3d, 1824, to state taxes on real estate in the city and county of Philadelphia.

[2] Except state purposes. Parker's Appeal, 8 W. & S. 449.

[3] This act was ignored, in the decision of Gormley's Appeal, 27 Pa. St. 49.

[4] Appeal of Second National Bank of Titusville, 85 Pa. St. 528.

in the borough of York, by the act of March 15th, 1844, [P. L. 127.]

When the Lien Attaches.

§ 642. The act of 3d February, 1824, [8 Sm. L. 189,] does not in express terms declare the precise time when the lien of taxes shall attach. It is clear, however, that they become liens so soon as they are lawfully assessed or imposed.[1] The act of 16th April, 1845, [P. L. 488,] directed that no tax should continue a lien on real estate in the city or county of Philadelphia, longer than until the first day of July, in the year immediately succeeding that in which such tax is due and payable, unless the same should have been registered before that time in the office of the county commissioners of the said county, in a separate book to be kept for that purpose. If so registered, the lien was declared to continue for five years from the first day of January in the year next succeeding that in which such taxes were due, and no longer, unless a claim for the same should be filed in the office of the prothonotary of the proper county within the said term of five years. This implied that the lien of the tax began with its assessment.

§ 643. The consolidation act of February 2d, 1854, [P. L. 21,] dispensed with the necessity of the registration of taxes to preserve their lien, which was restored, however, by the second section of the act of April 21st, 1858, [P. L. 385,] which enacted that "in the month of January, annually, the receiver shall, in books to be called 'the register of unpaid taxes on real estate,' register all unpaid taxes (except occupation taxes) of the preceding year, and the said taxes are hereby declared to be a lien on all real estate, in accordance with the provisions of the act of February 3d, 1824." Since this act of 1858, as before, all taxes on real estate are a lien thereon, not simply from the time of their registration,

---

[1] Dungan's Appeal, 88 Pa. St. 414; Camac v. Beatty, 5 Phila. 129; Parker's Appeal, 8 Watts & S. 449.

but from the date of their assessment.[1] Hence, when a judicial sale of the land taxed takes place during the year of, but after the assessment of the tax, such tax is payable out of the proceeds as a lien.[2] The tax, however, becomes a lien only when the assessment is complete. Thus, when a sheriff's sale took place August 6th, 1860, it was said the taxes of that year were not yet a lien, because the rate per centum was still to be fixed, and appeals were to be yet held.[3]

Relation of the Tax Lien.

§ 644. The first section of the act of February 3d, 1824, [8 Sm. L. 189,] declares that the lien of all taxes, rates and levies imposed and assessed on real estate in the city and county of Philadelphia, shall have priority to, and shall be fully paid and satisfied before any recognizance, mortgage, judgment, debt, obligation or responsibility which the said estate may become charged with or liable to from and after the passing of this act. Under this provision, the lien of taxes, whensoever imposed, has precedence over other liens, whatever the date of their origin, if they have originated since the 3d February, 1824.[4] Accordingly, the city of Philadelphia tax for the year 1842 was a superior lien to a mortgage for purchase money, executed on the land in the year 1835,[5] and taxes for the years 1842–1845, inclusive, took precedence as liens, of a mortgage recorded in 1836,[6] and taxes assessed on land after the lien of a levy under a

---

[1] Camac v. Beatty, 5 Phila. 129; Dungan's Appeal, 88 Pa. St. 414; Smaltz v. Donohugh, 11 W. N. C. 219.

[2] Camac v. Beatty, 5 Phila. 129. In Dungan's Appeal, 88 Pa. St. 414, the real estate was levied on February 3d, 1877, and sold April 2d of the same year. It was said that the taxes of 1877 had attached as a lien, at the beginning of the year prior to the levy.

[3] Duffy v. Philadelphia, 42 Pa. St. 192.

[4] Gormley's Appeal, 27 Pa. St. 49, which decides that the lien of taxes, assessed on land subsequently to the mortgaging of it, does not take precedence of the mortgage, was decided in forgetfulness of the act of 3d February, 1824. See Philadelphia v. Cooke, 30 Pa. St. 56.

[5] Parker's Appeal, 8 W. & S. 449.

[6] Perry v. Brinton, 13 Pa. St. 302.

fi. fa. had attached, are preferred to such *fi. fa.*[1] Taxes are, by relation, prior to all ground-rents charged upon the premises by deeds, whether before or since the lien for taxes arises. Hence, when, there being unpaid taxes from 1869 to 1879, the owner of the land charged therewith granted, in 1874, a perpetual rent in fee of $100 annually, and the grantee of the ground-rent subsequently contracted to convey it to another, the latter could not be compelled to accept the grant thereof, since the land being subject to the taxes, whatever impaired the title to the land necessarily impaired the title to the rent. The tax lien may sweep away both the title to the land and that to the rent.[2]

§ 645. In order to preserve the lien of mortgages from being divested by judicial sales on account of the precedence of the lien of taxes and municipal levies, just considered, it was enacted, April 11th, 1835, that no lien created by the act of February 3d, 1824, should be construed to be such a lien as, by its priority to a mortgage, should prevent the latter's exemption from divestiture under the first section of the act of April 6th, 1830, [P. L. 293.] This act was followed by that of April 16th, 1845, [P. L. 488,] which declared that the lien of a mortgage on any real estate in the city and county of Philadelphia should not be affected in any way by any sale of the mortgaged premises under a subsequent judgment, (other than one entered upon a claim which was a lien

---

[1] Dungan's Appeal, 88 Pa. St. 414. Under the provision of the act of February 3d, 1824, a municipal charge for paving, assessed October 12th, 1829, was preferred to a mechanics' lien which began in the spring of 1829; Pennock v. Hoover, 5 R. 291 : and the lien for water pipe, laid January 4th, 1852, was superior to a mortgage executed in 1847. City of Philadelphia v. Cooke, 30 Pa. St. 56. After several mortgages to A., the land was mortgaged to B., who went into possession of it. During his possession taxes were assessed upon it. Subsequently the land was sold under the prior mortgages, A. becoming the purchaser, and from the proceeds the taxes assessed during B.'s possession were first paid. A. could recover the taxes from B personally. Shoemaker v. Commonwealth Bank, 11 W. N. C. 284

[2] Mitchell v. Steinmetz, 97 Pa. St. 251.

on the premises prior to the recording of the mortgage,) by reason of the prior lien of any tax charge or assessment whatsoever, but the same should continue as if such prior lien did not exist, where, by existing laws, the lien of such mortgage would otherwise continue, provided that the continuance of the lien of such mortgage should not prevent the discharge of such prior liens for taxes, charges or assessments by such sale, or the satisfaction thereof out of the proceeds of such sale. Under these acts, though a mortgage may not be divested by the lien of taxes which shall be assessed subsequently to the recording of the mortgage, the precedence of the lien of such taxes, accorded to them by the act of February 3d, 1824, is not impaired.[1]

§ 646. The taxes of the city and of the county of Allegheny upon lands situate therein, are made liens by the acts of April 5th, 1844, [P. L. 199,] and of February 27th, 1860, [P. L. 85,] and have priority to and must be fully paid before any other liens whatever. Hence, when land in the city of Allegheny was mortgaged July 22d, 1875, and was sold under the mortgage in 1878, the taxes thereon for the years 1876 and 1877 were paid from the proceeds in preference to it.[2]

§ 647. By the act of March 15th, 1847, [P. L. 366,] taxes of Lancaster city, and by the act of April 10th, 1848, [P. L. 435,] taxes of Harrisburg and Columbia, are declared to be liens on real estate on which they are assessed, and as such to have priority over any recognizance, mortgage, judgment, debt, obligation or responsibility with which the said real estate may become chargeable after the passage of these acts.[3] The act of February 28th, 1866, [P. L. 116,] makes taxes in the city of Titusville a lien on the real estate on which

---

[1] Perry v. Brinton, 13 Pa. St 202. Here the mortgage was recorded October 15th, 1836; the taxes were for the years 1842–5, inclusive.

[2] Germania Savings Bank's Appeal, 91 Pa. St. 345; Wallace's Estate, 59 Pa. St. 401.

[3] As to Harrisburg, see Harrisburg v. Orth, 2 Pearson 340.

they are assessed, until "fully paid and satisfied." This gives them priority to all other liens. Hence, the taxes of the years 1874 and 1875 were entitled to payment from the proceeds of a sheriff's sale of land in preference to an award of arbitrators dated May 21st, 1872.[1] Taxes, however, though made a lien, are posterior to other liens acquired before their assessment, unless some act of assembly secures them priority. Taxes for state, county and poor purposes in Crawford county are not made superior to liens earlier in origin, but rank according to the date of assessment.[2]

Duration of the Lien.

§ 648. The second section of the act of 21st April, 1858, [P. L. 385,] provides that the receiver of taxes of the city of Philadelphia shall, in the month of January annually, register all unpaid taxes of the preceding year, in a book to be called "the register of unpaid taxes on real estate." This seems to be a substitute for the registration in the office of the county commissioners of Philadelphia county, which had been required by the first part of the first section of the act of March 11th, 1846, [P. L. 114.] If the taxes are not registered in the January following the year in which they are assessed, they cease to be a lien. On A.'s land the taxes of the years 1875 and 1876, were assessed, but no claim therefor was filed until 13th December, 1877. The premises were mortgaged 17th July, 1877, and in 1879 an execution was levied on them on a judgment which had been rendered against the mortgagor before he had acquired the premises. The purchaser at this sale bought subject to the mortgage, the taxes being no lien.[3] The latter part of this section, which seems still to be in operation, directs that all taxes registered as aforesaid, shall cease to be liens after the

[1] Eaton's Appeal, 83 Pa. St. 152.
[2] Briggs' Appeal, 38 Leg. Int. 262. Land held by an assignee in trust for creditors, is liable to taxation.
[3] Smaltz v. Donohugh, 11 W. N. C. 219.

expiration of five years from the first day of January in the year succeeding that in which they became due, unless suit be brought to recover the same. From this it appears that the due registration of the taxes of Philadelphia will continue their lien for the period of five years from the first day of January in the year succeeding that in which they were assessed and became due.[1]

§ 649. In other cities and boroughs, different regulations exist with respect to the duration of the liens of taxes. Thus, in the borough of York,[2] the lien of taxes is limited absolutely to two years. An examination of the statutes pertaining to each municipality is necessary. The act of April 5th, 1844, [P. L. 199,] extends to Allegheny county and the municipalities therein, the provisions of the act of 3d February, 1824. Under this act, the lien of taxes was indefinite, though they were not registered in accordance with its direction. Hence taxes of the year 1852 were a lien in 1864, though unregistered.[3]

§ 650. To continue beyond five years from the 1st January next succeeding their assessment the lien of taxes in Philadephia, the first section of the act of March 11th, 1846, [P. L. 114,] requires that within that period "suit be brought to recover the same," and that such suit be "duly prosecuted to judgment." The second section of the act provides two methods for their recovery. When they exceed $100, a copy of the taxes in the "Register" may be filed in the office of the prothonotary of the district court of the city and county of Philadelphia, on which an action of debt may be brought, and a judgment may be recovered against the person whose duty it is to pay the tax; or a *sci. fa.* may issue upon such filed copy and be proceeded with as in the case of mechanics' claims. The fourth section of the act of 16th April, 1845, [P. L. 496,] provides that suit may be brought before any

---

[1] Duffy *v.* City of Philadelphia, 42 Pa. St. 192.

[2] Act of March 15th, 1844, [P. L. 127.]

[3] Wallace's Estate, 59 Pa. St. 401.

alderman or justice of the peace, or court of competent jurisdiction, against the person whose name is returned and registered in the register of unpaid taxes. After judgments have been recovered in any of these methods, the "lien of such judgments, and the transcripts filed of those recovered for taxes before magistrates, shall be and continue liens as in other judgments."[1]

§ 651. If the method adopted of continuing and enforcing the lien of the tax be that of a *scire facias*, it is necessary that, at whatever point of time within the period of five years (beginning with the 1st January next succeeding the assessment of the tax) such *sci. fa.* should issue, it should be so diligently proceeded in that a judgment may be recovered thereupon within five years from the date of its issue. Thus, a claim was filed for registered taxes in Philadelphia, on March 16th, 1871. On November 1st, 1871, a *sci. fa.* was issued thereon, and returned *nihil habet*. An *alias sci. fa.* issued November 17th, 1871, which was duly served. The defendant pleaded, a replication was filed, and the cause was put at issue. The trial took place, and the verdict was rendered in favor of the city on January 11th, 1877, more than five years after the issue of the *sci. fa.* Judgment on the verdict was properly arrested.[2]

§ 652. If, however, while the proceedings on the *sci. fa.* are pending, another *sci. fa.* " to revive and continue liens of claims " issues within five years of the filing of the claims, the lien will be continued, though judgment be not recovered on the original *sci. fa.* until more than five years have elapsed since its issue,[3] but such *sci. fa.* " to revive and continue the lien," issued pending proceedings on the original *sci. fa.*, after the expiration of five years from

<hr />

[1] Section 1, act of March 11th, 1846.

[2] City of Philadelphia *v.* Scott, 93 Pa. St. 25. The issue of a *sci. fa.* to "revive and continue lien " on October 31st, 1876, after the five years

from the filing of the claim had expired, did not preserve the lien.

[3] Ketcham *v.* Singerly, Leg. Int., 1877, p. 127.

the filing of the claims, will be ineffectual to preserve their lien, five years having elapsed from the issue of the original *sci. fa.* without judgment being obtained thereon.[1]

§ 653. The twenty-third section of the act of 22d April, 1846, [P. L. 486,] directs that when any person dies leaving real estate, which, by existing laws, is subject to tax for state or county purposes, such property, so long as it shall belong to the estate of such deceased person, may be taxed in the name of the decedent, or in the name of his administrator or executor, or heirs generally, and such tax shall remain a lien on the property taxed for the period of one year from the first day of June following the assessment of said tax. The expiration of this period of lien shall not prevent the collection of the tax within the time provided by existing laws in other cases.

Effect of Judicial Sale on Duration of Lien

§ 654. Though the general rule is, that a judicial sale of land divests all the liens that encumber it, provided they are of such a nature that their amount can be definitely ascertained, the lien of taxes of the city of Philadelphia is made an exception by the sixth section of the act of March 11th, 1846, [P. L. 115,] which declares, in respect to claims for taxes, municipal charges and assessments, in the city and county of Philadelphia, that "the lien of such claims shall not be divested by any judicial sale as respects so much thereof as the proceeds of such sale may be insufficient to discharge and pay." Under this provision, the lien of taxes which the proceeds of any judicial sale applicable thereto are insufficient to pay, will continue for so long a time as they would, under existing laws, if no such sale had taken place. Land in Philadelphia, on which registered city and state taxes for the years 1857, 1858 and 1859, were a lien,

---

[1] City of Philadelphia *v.* Scott, 93 Pa. St. 25. Here the claim was filed March 16th, 1871, and the second *sci. fa.* to revive and continue the lien issued October 31st, 1876.

was sold under a judgment, August 6th, 1860. The purchase money was exhausted in paying costs, and discharging the taxes of 1857, and a part of those of 1858. It was held that the land continued liable after the sheriff's sale, for the unpaid portion of the tax of 1858, and for the tax of 1859.[1] A sale took place under a mortgage, June 7th, 1879. Taxes of the years 1874–1878, amounting to $1,100, were unpaid. The proceeds of the sale were only $250. The taxes continued a lien.[2]

§ 655. If the city of Philadelphia has several liens for taxes of different years, the application of the proceeds of a judicial sale under a judgment for the taxes of the last year, to that judgment, will not disturb the lien of the taxes of the earlier years not satisfied from the proceeds. The liens of these taxes, whatever their ages, are of equal dignity. When, for taxes of 1862, a judgment was obtained by the city, under which the land was sold in 1868, and the proceeds of sale were exhausted in satisfying these taxes, the lien of the taxes of 1860 was not divested, and the title of a vendee at sheriff's sale in 1870, on a judgment for the taxes of 1860, prevailed over that of the sheriff's vendee at the sale of 1868.[3]

§ 656. When the proceeds of a judicial sale of land are sufficient to pay all the taxes then due, they are discharged, though the city neglect to insist on this application thereof. Taxes amounting to $25.10 were assessed in 1859 on a lot in Philadelphia, which was, under a judgment, sold in 1863 for $610. The purchase money was brought into court and distributed, but the city did not claim payment therefrom. In 1864, the city entered a lien for the taxes, and,

---

[1] Duffy v City of Philadelphia, 42 Pa. St. 192.

[2] Hogg v. Longstreth, 97 Pa. St. 255. The owner of land during these years, bought by him subject to a mortgage, was personally liable to the mortgagee for these taxes.

[3] Townsend v. Prowattain, 81½ Pa. St. 139.

under a judgment obtained thereon, the lot was sold. The purchaser acquired no title.[1] This principle obtains, though the sale is of only a portion of the land on which the tax was a lien. Taxes were assessed on a lot fronting on two parallel streets. This lot was divided into two lots, by a line parallel to the streets, and a house stood on each. Assessments for paving and water pipe were levied on one of these lots, and, on a judgment recovered thereon, it was sold, the proceeds being ample to pay both these assessments and the taxes. The city received only a portion of the taxes. The judgment for the taxes, on which a *levari facias* had issued, subsequently to the appropriation of the proceeds of sale, was opened and the *lev. facias* set aside.[2]

§ 657. Taxes on real estate in Harrisburg are made a lien thereon by the act of April 10th, 1848, which declares that this lien shall be fully paid and satisfied before any other lien. Land in this city was assessed with taxes for the year 1876, prior to the first day of May of that year. On that day it was mortgaged, and subsequently sold by the sheriff under a judgment later than the mortgage. The tax remained undivested, because the mortgage intervening was undivested.[3] But, under a similar act respecting Titusville, that of February 28th, 1866, [P. L. 116,] a sale on a judgment, the next lien to the taxes, discharges the lien of the taxes when the proceeds are sufficient to pay them. For so much of the taxes as the proceeds are insufficient to pay, the lien remains on the land.[4]

Proceedings on the Scire Facias.[5]

§ 658. Every essential requirement of the statutes which provide for the lien of taxes, and the enforcement thereof,

---

[1] Smith *v.* Simpson, 60 Pa. St. 168; Eaton's Appeal, 83 Pa. St. 152; City of Philadelphia *v.* Cooke, 30 Pa. St. 56; Harrisburg *v.* Orth, 2 Pearson 340.

[2] City *v.* McGonigle, 4 Phila. 351.
[3] Harrisburg *v.* Orth, 2 Pearson 340.
[4] Eaton's Appeal, 83 Pa. St 152.
[5] For more on this subject, see 2 Bright., Troub. & H. §§ 2016–2027.

must be strictly complied with. The act of 29th March, 1867, provides for the registering of the real estate in the name of the real owner, and requires that when such registry is made the claim for taxes shall be filed against the real owner by name, and the *sci. fa.* shall be served on him as a summons must be. Served otherwise, and no appearance of the defendant, a judgment by default for want of appearance, and a *levari facias* thereupon, will be set aside.[1] In the absence of any registry of real estate in the name of the real owner, the provisions of the act of 11th March, 1846, [P. L. 114,] apply. The *sci. fa.* must be served by posting a true and attested copy of the writ on a conspicuous part of the premises therein described, and by publishing a brief notice thereof in a daily newspaper in the county of Philadelphia, twice a week for two weeks before the return day. When the sheriff's return showed that he had made known, January 28th, by posting, etc., and the return day was the first Monday of February following, the service was fatally defective.[2] The act of 24th February, 1862, [P. L. 44,] does not apply to registered taxes. Hence, a claim for registered taxes will not be stricken off for failure to issue *sci. fa.* to the next return day, in accordance with the direction of that act.[3]

Interests Bound by the Lien.

§ 659. Taxes are a lien on the land and the titles of all persons whatsoever therein. If one has the legal, and another the equitable title, the taxes are payable out of the proceeds of a judicial sale of either title. Thus, taxes assessed on land in Philadelphia, after a contract to sell it had been made, and while the vendee was in possession, were paid out of the pro-

---

[1] City *v.* Kutz. 8 W. N. C. 502.

[2] O'Byrne *v.* Philadelphia, 93 Pa. St. 225. The sheriff's statement in his return that he has served the writ "agreeably to the act of assem-

bly," is immaterial. His explicit averments of what he did, must show service in consonance with the requirements of the statute.

[3] City *v.* Schellinger, 38 Leg. Int. 392.

ceeds of a sheriff's sale of his interest therein.[1] When A. contracted to convey land to B. and C., who were to pay for it in a stipulated time in cash, or were to accept deeds reserving to A. a ground-rent equal to the interest on the purchase money, and a sheriff's sale of B.'s interest under the contract took place, the taxes assessed during his occupancy of the land, subsequent to the execution of the contract, were paid out of the proceeds.[2] If, on a judgment against A., land held ostensibly by B., is sold, on the suspicion that B. holds it for A. in order to defraud A.'s creditors, taxes assessed on it while the title is in B.'s name, are payable out of the proceeds, although in fact B.'s title was good against that acquired by the purchaser at the sheriff's sale.[3]

What Does Not Discharge Lien.

§ 660. The act of February 3d, 1824, empowered all collectors of taxes to levy on goods and chattels which might be found on land on which taxes were assessed, and to sell the same, after ten days' notice of such sale. If, under this act, the collector, having distrained on sufficient goods found on the premises and liable for the tax, but belonging to a tenant of the owner of the premises, voluntarily abandoned them, the lien of the tax on the realty was not thereby impaired, as against other lien creditors.[4] The result is not different if the goods and chattels found on the premises belong to the owner of the land charged with the taxes. The refusal[5] or neglect[6] of the tax collector to levy on sufficient personal property found on the land, does not discharge it from the lien of the taxes, in favor of other creditors. If, however, a distress is made by the collector on chattels of the owner

[1] Vanarsdalen's Appeal, 3 W. N. C. 463.

[2] Moroney v. Copeland, 5 Wh. 407. B. was entitled to subrogation to the taxes so as to compel contribution from C.

[3] Dungan's Appeal, 88 Pa. St. 414.

The contrary was decided in Fisher v. Lyle, 8 Phila. 1.

[4] Parker's Appeal, 8 W. & S. 449.

[5] Germania Savings Bank's Appeal, 91 Pa. St. 345.

[6] Harrisburg v. Orth, 2 Pearson 340. Compare Cohen's Appeal, 10 W. N. C. 230.

found on the premises, sufficient to satisfy the tax, a reliuquishment of the distress will discharge the lien of the tax on the land, as to other lien creditors.[1] So, if the collector pay the tax, he discharges its lien. It cannot be kept alive for the purpose of securing re-imbursement to him, except as against the owner of the land himself.[2]

Seated and Unseated Land.

§ 661. The act of 11th April, 1799, [3 Sm. L. 392,] and its supplements, furnished as remedy for the collection of taxes on seated lands, the personal liability of the owner of the land at the time the taxes were imposed. No lien was created on the land, nor any recourse given against it. On the other hand, when the land was unseated, the assessment of the tax was made a charge on the land, and not on the person, and the only process to enforce its recovery was by a sale of the land itself.[3] When unseated land was taxed in 1805, 1806, 1807 and 1808, and became seated in 1809, and so continued until 1816, and when, under the act of 13th March, 1815, [6 Sm. L. 299,] requiring the treasurers of the several counties to sell on the second Monday of June, 1816. all unseated land for which taxes assessed should have remained due and unpaid for the space of one year, this tract was sold, the sale divested the title of the owner and conferred it upon the treasurer's purchaser.[4] In this case, the lien of the tax was four years old when the land was sold privately to A., and eleven years old when it was sold by the treasurer to B. A tax sale of unseated land divests a prior mortgage.[5] Though the unseated land is neither taxed nor sold in the name of the real owner, his title is in fact conveyed to the treasurer's vendee.[6]

[1] Parker's Appeal. 8 W. & S. 449; Harrisburg v. Orth, 2 Pearson 340.

[2] Parker's Appeal, 8 W. & S. 449.

[3] Robinson v. Williams, 6 W. 281; Fager v. Campbell, 5 W. 287; Strauch v. Shoemaker, 1 W. & S. 166.

[4] Robinson v. Williams, 6 W. 281.

[5] Fager v. Campbell, 5 W. 287.

[6] Strauch v. Shoemaker, 1 W. & S. 166. See Luffborough v. Parker, 16 Serg. & R. 351; McCord v. Bergantz, 7 W. 490; Morton v. Harris, 9 W. 323; Caul v. Spring, 2 W. 396.

§ 662. The thirty-seventh section of the act of 29th April, 1844, [P. L. 486,] provides that the county commissioners in each county shall furnish the state treasurer with a statement of the return made by the assessors of the value of all the property liable to state tax, in each county, distinguishing real from personal estate. The revenue commissioners must then determine the fair and just value of the property in the several counties. The county commissioners shall then assess and collect the state tax in their respective counties. The forty-first section adds that all real estate within this commonwealth, on which personal property cannot be found sufficient to pay taxes assessed thereon, and where the owner or owners thereof neglect or refuse to pay the said taxes for the space of two years, shall be returned to the county commissioners, and shall be sold as unseated lands now are sold in satisfaction of the taxes due by the owner or owners.[1] The collector must return all delinquent lands. When sold by the treasurer, the entire title passes to the purchaser. Taxes were assessed in 1878 against L., the owner of two improved lots in Pittston. In 1880 they were sold by the sheriff under a judgment, to C., and the taxes were not paid, as they had no right to be paid, from the proceeds. Subsequently, the lands were again sold for the taxes of 1878, by the treasurer of the county. This sale divested the title of the sheriff's vendee, notwithstanding that before the sheriff's sale there had been on the premises constantly sufficient personal property to pay all the taxes.[2]

---

[1] The owner has the right to redeem the lands for one year after receiving notice from the county treasurer that they have been sold.

[2] Cohen's Appeal, 10 W. N. C. 230.

CHAPTER XXXV.

MUNICIPAL LIENS.

Sources of Lien.

§ 663. In the city and county of Philadelphia, and of recent years in many other cities and boroughs of the state, numerous statutes have provided for the assessment of the costs of many kinds of municipal improvements upon lands contiguous to the site of such improvements, or abutting upon the streets and highways wherein such improvements are made. It were impracticable to enumerate these statutes, or to specify their several peculiarities. The improvements are of various classes, including opening and grading streets, paving cartways or roadways,[1] curbing and paving[2] or repairing and repaving sidewalks or footwalks,[3] laying down water pipes and gas pipes,[4] constructing culverts and sewers,[5]

---

[1] Pittsburg v. McKnight, 91 Pa. St 202; Pittsburg v. Walter, 69 Pa. St. 365; City v. Sanger, 8 W N C. 151; Olds v. Erie City, 79 Pa. St 380; Delaney v. Gault, 30 Pa. St. 63; McCausland v. Leuffer, 4 Wh. 175; Huidekoper v. Meadville, 83 Pa. St. 156.

[2] City of Philadelphia v. Lea, 9 Phila. 106; Act of April 18th, 1857, [P. L. 240;] Moroney v. Copeland, 5 Wh. 407; Appeal of First National Bank of Titusville, 85 Pa. St. 528; Pittsburg v. Cluley, 66 Pa. St. 449; Schenley v. Allegheny, 36 Pa. St. 29; Council v. Moyamensing, 2 Pa. St 224.

[3] Lea v. Philadelphia, 1 W. N. C. 189.

[4] Municipal Corporation's Act of May 23d, 1874; Allentown v. Hower,

9 W N. C. 198; City v. Greaves, 7 W. N. C. 487; City v. Cuthbert, 4 W. N. C. 263; Moroney v. Copeland, 5 Wh. 407; City v. McCalmont, 6 Phila. 543; Northern Liberties v. Swain, 13 Pa. St. 113; City v. Baird, 1 W. N. C. 126; Northern Liberties v. Coates' Heirs, 15 Pa. St 245; Britton v. City of Philadelphia, 32 Pa. St. 387; Act of February 2d, 1854, [P. L. 21;] Salter v. Reed, 15 Pa St 260; Philadelphia v. Cooke, 30 Pa. St 56; Pennell's Appeal, 2 Pa. St. 216; Act of April 16th, 1840, § 9; City v. Wood, 4 Phila. 156; District of Moyamensing v. Flanigan, 3 Phila. 458

[5] Coxe v. Philadelphia, 47 Pa. St. 9; Philadelphia v. Tryon, 35 Pa. St. 501; Philadelphia v. McNeeley, 7 W. N. C. 573; Kern v. Simmons, 7 W. N. C. 359; Lipps v. Philadelphia,

erecting bridges over streams which interrupt highways,[1] removal of nuisances,[2] cleansing docks.[3] Besides these liens, the act of 29th March, 1867, [P. L. 600,] requires the purchasers, devisees or allottees in partition of any real estate situate in the city of Philadelphia, to cause it to be registered, and for neglect thereof, after notice by public advertisement, subjects them to a fine of $5, and declares that should the neglect continue for six months, this fine and costs shall be a lien upon the real estate whose registration has been neglected, and that a claim therefor shall be filed and collected as municipal claims are by law collected. Among the municipalities, in regard to whose liens for improvement controversies have been had in the courts of the state, are the city of Philadelphia, with the incorporated districts of the county of Philadelphia, prior to the act of consolidation, Pittsburg, Lancaster, Harrisburg, Allegheny, Erie, Meadville, Titusville, York, McKeesport, and others. Since we cannot exhibit in detail the several provisions of the numerous laws and ordinances which give rise to municipal liens, we shall present a summary of the principles which are recognized in, and variously applied by them.

38 Pa. St 503; Philadelphia v. Greble, 38 Pa. St. 339; Wistar v. Philadelphia, 86 Pa. St. 215; Appeal of First National Bank of Titusville, 85 Pa. St. 528; Fifth Avenue Sewer, 4 Brewst 364; Commonwealth v. Woods, 44 Pa. St. 113; City v Scott, 8 W. N. C. 405; Stroud v. Philadelphia, 61 Pa. St. 255; Act concerning streets and sewers in Pittsburg, January 6th, 1864, [P. L. 1131.] It was decided in Philadelphia v. Greble, 38 Pa. St. 339; Lipps v. Philadelphia, 38 Pa. St. 503, and in Philadelphia v. Tryon, 35 Pa. St. 401, that the city of Philadelphia had, at the time these decisions were rendered, no authority to construct sewers in the limits of the old city, at the cost of the adjacent lots, but that it had such power within the limits of the former districts which had been incorporated into the city.

[1] Ballentine's Appeal, 5 W. N. C. 321; act of May 26th, 1871, [P. L. 1236.]

[2] Board of Health v. Gloria Dei, 23 Pa. St. 259; Kennedy v. Board of Health, 2 Pa. St. 366; Philadelphia v. Conrad, 1 W. N. C. 104; Broomall v. Chester, 1 W N. C. 228; Act of 22d March, 1869, [P. L. 482,] Act of 29th January, 1818; Act of April 7th, 1830, [P. L. 348.]

[3] Easby v. Philadelphia, 67 Pa. St. 337; City v. Edwards, 2 W. N. C. 182.

Liability of Lot for Work Done in Front of It.

§ 664. The simplest method of assessment is that which makes each property owner whose lot abuts on a street, liable for the actual cost of the improvement made before it. This method is pursued, occasionally, with respect to the grading and paving of streets, especially of footways. Notice is first given to the, owner to do the work himself, within a limited time. If he fails to comply with the requisition, the authorities of the city cause the work to be, done, and the expense of it becomes a lien upon his lot. The act of April 23d, 1829, [10 Sm. L. 403,] is an example of the application of this method to the paving and curbing of footways in private streets, courts and alleys.[1] The ordinances of the city councils may adopt the same system, an instance of which is that of 10th May, 1858, of the city of Philadelphia, with respect to the paving and curbing of footways in sundry streets. This ordinance required the owners of properties on these streets to pave and curb the footways before their respective properties within thirty days after notice, and authorized the commissioner of highways, in case of default, to employ persons to do the work at their cost.[2] Necessary repairing and repaving of footways fall under the same principle,[3] but, when a footway has been paved and curbed according to the style in vogue generally throughout the city, and at the expense of the lot owner, the city cannot, three years afterwards, and while the pavement and curbing are in good repair, change the alignment of the footway, considerably widening it, and require the putting in of a curbing much more costly than the former,

---

[1] See, also, act of 10th April, 1826, [9 Sm. L. 215,] in regard to paving footways in Philadelphia; the act of March 6th, 1820, [7 Sm. L. 260,] as to paving footways and gutters in Kensington; the act of 29th January, 1818, [7 Sm. L. 24,] in regard to the removal of nuisances in Philadelphia; the act of March 2d, 1859, [P. L. 96,] concerning Sunbury.

[2] City of Philadelphia v. Burgin, 50 Pa. St. 539. See, also, Ordinance of Philadelphia, May 3d, 1855; Watson v. Philadelphia, 93 Pa. St. 111.

[3] Lea v. Philadelphia, 1 W. N. C. 189.

by the owner. Such change, if made, must be paid for by the city itself.[1] The general borough act of 3d April, 1851, [P. L. 320,] confers on boroughs the authority to require and direct the grading, paving, curbing and guttering of the sidewalks by the owner of each lot of ground fronting thereon, and, on his default within the prescribed time, to collect by general regulation the costs of the work and material, together with twenty per cent. advance thereon, from said owner, as claims are by law recoverable under the provisions of the mechanics' lien laws.[2]

Notice Necessary.

§ 665. When this method of municipal improvement is adopted, either by statute or by ordinance, notice to the lot owners, and opportunity to themselves do the work, are essential to the validity of a lien for the work when subsequently done by the city.[3] When an ordinance of the city of Philadelphia, passed January 29th, 1870, directed the commissioners of highways to notify the owners of property on Nicetown lane, between certain points, to grade and pave the sidewalks in front of their several properties before the 1st day of April, 1870, but no notice was given until 1873 and 1874, no valid lien upon these properties was obtained by the city for the grading and paving before them.[4] Under an act of assembly which authorized councils to cause grading, paving and curbing "to be done on failure of the owner" of the several properties to do it within the time prescribed by the ordinance, it is necessary that notice of the ordinance should be given to the owner personally, and by publication thereof in a paper published in the borough.[5]

[1] Wistar v. Philadelphia, 80 Pa. St. 505.

[2] Borough of Mauch Chunk v. Shortz, 61 Pa. St. 399. But boroughs have no lien on adjacent lots, for the expense of constructing drains or sewers, though such construction be within the scope of their authority.

[3] City of Philadelphia v. Burgin, 50 Pa. St. 539.

[4] City v. Donath, 9 W. N. C. 415; City v. Lea, 9 Phila. 106.

[5] Wilvert v. Sunbury Borough, 81½ Pa. St. 57.

A general ordinance of Philadelphia, of May 3d, 1855, provided that when councils should order footways of a street to be paved, each owner should cause the same to be done before his lot in twenty days after being required thereto by the commissioner of highways. It directed that if the owner was unknown, the notice should be left upon the premises by the commissioner, who was, on default of the owner, to cause the footway to be graded, paved, curbed or repaired, as the case might be. The cost was to be charged upon the premises. A notice in writing, folded up and put under a stone on the premises, was not such as this ordinance required, and for paving done afterwards by the commissioner of highways, the city obtained no lien.[1]

Failure to Comply.

§ 666. If notice is duly given, the work must be at least commenced within the period limited. If not, the city may cause it to be done, and charge the expense of it as a lien on the abutting lots.[2] When a lot is bounded by three streets, and notice is given to its owner to pave the footway on each of these streets within twenty days, it is necessary that the paving should be begun on each of these streets within that time. Commencing work on one of the sidewalks within that time, will not preclude the city from obtaining a lien on the lot for paving the other sidewalks.[3] The owner of property may waive the notice provided for by statute or ordinance, and in such case his land will be liable for the costs of grading and paving, on his default.[4] If the owner of property, after notice to curb the footway in front thereof, contracts with A. (who had been selected by the district to

---

[1] Philadelphia v. Edwards, 78 Pa. St. 62. When the claim filed contains an averment that notice was given to the owner to pave the footwalk, it is *prima facie* evidence of that fact, under the act of 11th March, 1846, [P. L. 114;] Watson v. City of Philadelphia, 93 Pa. St. 111.

[2] Lea v. Philadelphia, 1 W. N. C. 189; Watson v. Philadelphia, 93 Pa. St. 111.

[3] City v. Lea, 9 Phila. 106.

[4] Philadelphia v. Burgin, 50 Pa. St. 539.

execute all necessary curbing within the district for such property owners as should make a contract with him to do it) to curb before his lot, and gives to A. his promissory note for the price, and A. files a mechanics' lien against the lot, on the ground that the curbing was the completion of a house which was in process of erection, but makes no charge against the commissioners of the district, the district has no lien for the curbing.[1]

Removal of Nuisances.

§ 667. As in the class of cases just referred to, the expense of paving and curbing is put upon the lots immediately before which they are done, on default of the owner thereof, after due notice, to cause them to be done himself, so, under the act of January 29th, 1818, [7 Sm. L. 5,] the act of 7th April, 1830, and several supplements, the board of health of Philadelphia was authorized to remove nuisances that might be found upon the premises of any person, after due notice to him and opportunity to remove the same, and to impose the cost of this removal, on his neglect, upon the premises from which the nuisance was abated. A certain lane, 15 feet wide and 146 feet long, which had been dedicated to public use for seventy years, led to grounds belonging to the church of Gloria Dei, in Philadelphia. In order to abate a nuisance on this lane, the board of health caused the footways to be paved, at the expense of the lots fronting thereon, and, having paved the cartway, filed a lien against the church. The lien was declared to be invalid, because the lane from which the nuisance had been removed was not the property of the church.[2] In the city of Chester, lands of A., which were lower than the adjoining lands, had been drained by a ravine, which conducted the water collecting thereon into the river Delaware. By the grading of a street which crossed this ravine, its channel was interrupted, and

---

[1] McCausland *v.* Leuffer, 4 Wh. 175.

[2] Board of Health *v.* Gloria Dei, 23 Pa. St. 259.

water began to stand in large quantities upon A.'s land
On his refusal to abate the nuisance, the city had a righ
under the act of 22d March, 1869, [P. L. 482,] to draw of
the water, to fill up these lands to grade, and to charg
thereupon the cost of this improvement.[1]

Proportional Assessment.

§ 668. A second principle, followed by sundry statutes, ha
been to group together several property owners, with respect
their vicinity with the site of the improvement contemplate
and to require them jointly to accomplish this improvemen
or on default within a certain time, to impose the cost of th
improvement, undertaken by the municipality, upon the
several properties in proportional shares. One of th
simplest applications of this method was that of the act of
May 13th, 1856, [P. L. 567,] and of the act of April 22d
1858, [P. L. 449,] which authorized the councils of Phila
delphia to provide by ordinance for the cleansing of th
docks on the Delaware and Schuylkill fronts of that city, t
require the owners of wharves and piers which surroun
these docks, to cleanse them, and, on their default after thirt
days' notice, to cause the cleansing to be done, and to appor
tion its cost among them in proportion to the extent of the
wharves, having the privilege of using such docks. Th
expenses thus apportioned were declared to be a lien upo
the several wharves. This power was transferred by the ac
of May 20th, 1864, [P. L. 906,] to the port wardens of th
city of Philadelphia. Under these statutes, the port warden
though not obliged to pass ordinances for the cleansing of
the docks, must give notice to the owners of wharves t
cleanse the same; otherwise no valid lien can be impose
thereon for the expenses incurred by the port wardens i
causing the docks to be cleansed.[2] And when the conten
of a large sewer, constructed by the city of Philadelphi

---

[1] Broomall v. City of Chester, 1 W.
N. C. 228.

[2] Easby v. Philadelphia, 67 Pa. St.

337. This provision concerning n
tice is, however, rendered practical
nugatory by the act of March 11t

empties into a dock, the wharves are not subject to a lien for the expense of cleansing it. The city must bear the expense itself.[1]

Assessment per Foot Front.

§ 669. When streets are to be graded, paved or curbed, sewers and culverts are to be constructed longitudinally therein, or gas and water pipes to be laid along them, for the supply of gas and water to the houses which face these streets, a favorite method has been to impose the cost of this improvement ratably upon the lots fronting on the streets in which these improvements have been made, according to the lengths of their respective fronts. Although, owing to the difference in the depth of the lots, and their different situations, the relative increase of their value occasioned by grading, paving or other work, will not be in exact ratio with the share of the expenses imposed upon them according to this method,[2] yet the departure from the strictly equitable distribution of the burdens is too slight to make the system liable to constitutional objections, and the constitutionality of such a plan of assessment has been frequently sustained.[3] Enumeration of the statutes which follow this method is inexpedient.[4] The acts of April 8th, 1864, [P. L. 324,][5] and of March 13th, 1866, [P. L. 354.] authorize the city of Philadelphia to construct culverts, and to assess the costs upon abutting properties, and make these assessments liens

1846, which directs that no plea averring want of notice to remove nuisances, shall be allowed in any action.

[1] City v. Edwards, 2 W. N. C. 182.

[2] Hammett v. Philadelphia, 65 Pa. St. 146.

[3] Ibid.; Extension of Hancock street, 18 Pa. St. 26 ; Wray v. Pittsburg, 46 Pa. St. 365; McMasters v. Commonwealth, 3 W. 292 ; Fenelon's Petition, 7 Pa. St. 173 ; Huidekoper v. Meadville, 83 Pa. St. 156 ; Stroud v. Philadelphia, 61 Pa. St. 255.

[4] Specimens are act of April 12th,

1828, [10 Sm. L. 157,] respecting the introduction of water into Moyamensing ; Act of 22d March, 1869, [P. L. 482,] in regard to sewers in Chester ; Act of April 6th, 1870, respecting Meadville ; Act of January 6th, 1864, respecting Pittsburg ; Acts of April 5th, 1849, [P. L. 341,] and April 8th, 1851, [P. L. 371,] respecting the city of Allegheny.

[5] This act does not require the consent of a majority of owners on a street, except for sewers and branch sewers. Slocum v. Philadelphia, 11 W. N. C. 167.

thereon,[1] and under the act of 9th March, 1826, [9 Sm. L. 53,] the district of Spring Garden had authority to introduce Schuylkill water into its streets, and to impose a lien on properties facing these streets, proportionately to their foot frontage, for the costs of the iron pipes.[2] Though the district of Moyamensing had no authority to contract debts, except for ordinary repairs and supplies, and for the payment of labor and salaries, and, by the act of consolidation, the city of Philadelphia succeeded to its powers subject to this limitation, a contract with one for the grading and paving of a street within the former limits of Moyamensing, he stipulating not to make any charge against the city, and to look solely to the lien upon the abutting properties, is within the authority of the city, and the costs of the grading and paving, duly assessed, will become a lien upon the assessed lots.[3] Under the act of 1st May, 1852, [P. L. 508,] conferring on the district of West Philadelphia the authority to introduce water·pipes into its streets and to assess the cost on the abutting lots, an assessment for the cost of laying·pipes in a certain street is valid, though the water-works in that district were not finished, and no water was introduced thereinto for twenty months after the filing of the lien.[4] And a valid lien for water pipes could be acquired under an ordinance which provided that no attachment to said pipes should be made for any other purpose than the extinguishment of fires, until the completion of certain projected water-works at Flat Rock, the use for putting out fires not being so foreign to the proprietors and occupants of the neighboring land that they may not justly be charged with the cost.[5]

Maximum Assessment.

§ 670. The principle of assessing the expense of certain

---

[1] Stroud v. Philadelphia, 61 Pa. St. 255. See, also, act of 20th April, 1869, [P. L. 1190;] Waln's Heirs v. City of Philadelphia, 11 W. N. C. 314.

[2] Pennell's Appeal, 2 Pa. St. 216.

[3] City v. Wood, 3 Phila. 145.

[4] Britton v. Philadelphia, 32 Pa. St. 387.

[5] City v. McCalmont, 6 Phila. 543.

public improvements upon properties abutting on the streets in which they are made, is sometimes subjected to a very important modification. Either by statute or by the ordinances of the municipality, a certain maximum assessment may be prescribed, and, in such a case, whatever the actual cost of the work may be, the municipality itself must bear all of it, that shall exceed the aggregate of the assessments imposed within this limitation. An illustration may be found in the eighth section of the act of April 21st, 1855, [P. L. 266,] wherein the legislature enacts that the charges in the city of Philadelphia " for culverts and pipes shall be at not exceeding the following rates per lineal foot, according to the fronts of the owners, to wit, for water pipes, seventy-five cents, making the usual allowance for corner lots; for culverts, seventy-five cents; and for street paving, one dollar per square yard; and all extra or further charges, and for intersections, shall be paid out of the general taxation."

Lots Must Front on Street.

§ 671. The plan of assessment now under consideration, requires the lots on which the assessments are made, to front upon and be conterminous with the street in which the improvement whose costs are assessed upon them, is taking place. Under the act of March 26th, 1851, [P. L. 252,] which required the district of Moyamensing to grade, curb and pave Gray's Ferry road, and to assess the expenses on the abutting properties, a lot separated from the road by the tracks of the Philadelphia, Wilmington and Baltimore railroad, forty-seven feet wide, could not be lawfully assessed for the costs notwithstanding that the strip of land on which the tracks of the railroad were, was likewise not assessable.[1] But when, long after a certain space in the middle of a street had been reserved for a market place, the city of Philadelphia caused it to be paved, the expense of the paving was

---

[1] Philadelphia v. Eastwick, 35 Pa. St. 75.

properly assessed upon the lots facing upon the street, though the intervals on both sides of this space, between it and the footwalks, had been already paved.[1]

Unilateral Assessment.

§ 672. Usually there are properties on both sides ʻof streets, and the equal charging of these opposite properties with the expenses of improvements in the intervening street, is contemplated by the statutes and ordinances on the subject of municipal liens. In the exceptional cases, however, in which over against a lot which is chargeable, there lies one which is for whatever reason exempt, the entire cost of the improvement will be cast on the property which is assessable. York street, Philadelphia, was one hundred feet wide. In its centre, running several squares, was a strip of ground twenty-two feet six inches in width, curbed on both sides, and designed for a market place, though actually used as such only for the length of about one square. For the entire expense of paving this street between this strip and the houses on one side of the street, the houses were chargeable.[2] Under the acts of April 5th, 1849, [P. L. 341,] April 8th, 1851, [P. L. 371,] and May 30th, 1852, [P. L. 204,] which confer on the city of Allegheny the power to open, grade and pave streets, and to assess the costs on properties abutting thereupon, in proportion to their respective frontages, if, on one side of a street thus paved, there is a common, the fee of which is in the city, the lots on the opposite side are assessable with the whole expense of paving the ̄street in front thereof; the city is not bound to bear any portion of the cost.[3] Such would be the case, also, where, on one side of a street, there is a cemetery, and the act of assembly which

---

[1] Slocum v. Philadelphia, 11 W. N. C. 167.

[2] Howell v. City of Philadelphia, 38 Pa. St. 471. The considerations leading to this decision were: 1st. The city had only an easement in the strip 2d. The contract for paving had stipulated that the city should not be at any expense for paving, except at the intersections.

[3] McGonigle v. City of Allegheny, 44 Pa. St. 118.

incorporates the cemetery company declares·that the tract of land used for the purposes of the cemetery "shall be exempt from taxation, excepting for state purposes." This would preclude any assessment for the expenses of constructing a sewer in the street, upon any of the lots in such cemetery.[1]

Remission for Intersections.

§ 673. It is quite usual for statutes or ordinances having respect to the improvements of streets, to except from the aggregate expense thereof which is to be assessed upon abutting properties, so much of such expense as arises from the work done and material consumed at the intersection of these streets with other streets. Thus, the act of February 2d, 1854, [P. L. 21,] by which the former city of Philadelphia and the outlying districts were united under one regime, directs that the city councils may by ordinance prescribe that paving of streets, except at the intersections thereof, and of footways, and laying of water pipes within the limits of the city, shall be done at the expense of the owners of the ground in front whereof such work shall be done, and liens may be filed by the said city for the same, as is now practiced and allowed by law.[2] Street A. has been for several years laid out on the city plans, and confirmed, but has not yet been opened, when, in street B., which crosses A. at right angles, water pipes are laid, and the intersection of the streets is paved, curbed and furnished with crossing stones. A lot fronting on B. street will not be chargeable with the costs of the pipes which lie across the intersection.[3] If street A. terminates in street B., which it meets at right

---

[1] Olive Cemetery v. Philadelphia, 93 Pa. St. 129. Yet, in Northern Liberties v. St. John's Church, 13 Pa. St. 104, it was held that a law exempting a church from taxation did not exempt it from municipal assessments.

[2] So, the act of April 12th, 1828, [10 Sm. L. 157,] for the introduction of water into Moyamensing; the act of March 27th, 1839, [P. L. 189,] in regard to water pipes in the district of Southwark, and many others.

[3] City v. Cuthbert, 4 W. N. C. 263.

angles, the cost of paving A. opposite the debouchure of B. street will not be cast on the lots fronting on A. street.[1] The act of the 30th March, 1866, [P. L. 354,] however, repeals all acts which limit the charges which may be made by the city of Philadelphia, for the construction of sewers, paving and laying water pipes, and gives councils full power to assess on abutting properties the cost of these improvements, even at intersections of streets.[2]

Sewers and Pipes at Intersections.

§ 674. Another concession is made not unfrequently to the owners of properties situated at the corners of streets, for the costs of sewers and water and gas pipes. Since such properties receive comparatively little benefit from the introduction of such improvements into one of the streets upon which they face, after they have been introduced into the other street, an allowance is often made from the amount of the costs of the improvement in one of the streets, which they would otherwise be expected to pay. Thus, the ordinance of the councils of Philadelphia of May 12th, 1866, provided that "on all corner lots an allowance shall be made of one-third the length of one of the fronts, such allowance to be always and only on the street or highway having the longest front. * * * And in case where a full block is unimproved, the depth of lot for computing the allowance shall be taken as half the length of the block; but in no case shall the allowance exceed fifty feet on a corner lot." Such allowances are *ex gratia*, and the reasonableness of the conditions upon which they are made cannot be assailed by property owners.[3] Under the ordinance just cited, the allowance can be claimed only when the sewer is constructed in the street the frontage on which exceeds that on the other street.[4]

---

[1] City v. Collom, 4 W. N. C. 160.

[2] Mooney v. Cottage Company, 9 Phila. 84.

[3] City v. Cottage Company, 9 Phila. 84.

[4] Ibid.

Power of Assessment Tolled.

§ 675. Though the councils of the city of Pittsburgh have the power, under certain statutes, to cause the grading and paving of streets to be done, without the co-operation of the abutting property owners, they may, nevertheless, invite these to grade the street under direction of the city regulator, and if these property owners do thus grade it, under the control of the city regulator, an ordinance passed two years afterwards, for the grading of a portion of this street, including the part thus already graded, will, as to this part, be inoperative and void. No valid lien can be acquired under it.[1] Indeed, it has been held that when Broad street, in the city of Philadelphia, had been recently paved, in the style and manner in which streets generally, in that city, were paved, and at the expense of the lot owners, an act of assembly which authorized the tearing up of this pavement for the purpose of putting down a much more costly one, in order to make the street a great public drive where fine equipages might disport themselves, and which imposed the cost of the repaving upon properties fronting on the streets, was unconstitutional.[2]

Improvements Conditioned on Consent of Owners.

§ 676. Since the improvements for which assessments may be constitutionally made upon properties in their vicinity, must be local in character, it is not unusual[3] for the co-operation of the owners of properties to be required by

[1] Pittsburgh v. Shaffer, 66 Pa. St. 454.

[2] Hammett v. Philadelphia, 65 Pa. St 146 It is said in this case, that the repairing of streets that have once been paved, and are still in a generally good condition, must be paid for out of the public coffers. But in Wistar v. Philadelphia, 80 Pa. St 505, it is conceded that a general power to pave implies a power to repair and repave when the condition of the cartway or footway requires it, and to assess the costs on the properties adjacent. See, also, Lea v. Philadelphia, 1 W. N. C. 189.

[3] Though by no means universal. The consent of property owners is not necessary, in order to make the cost of the construction of culverts in those parts of Philadelphia which formerly lay outside of the city limits, a lien on adjacent properties. City. v. Tryon, 35 Pa St. 401 ; Philadelphia v. McNeely, 7 W. N. C. 573. The commissioners of Spring Garden had authority, under the act of

statute as a condition precedent to the performance of the work of improvement. Sometimes the statutes that confer on the municipal authorities the power to institute such improvements, condition it upon the consent of the property owners to each particular improvement. This consent could rarely be expected to be universal. Either, therefore, the consent of a majority of the owners of property facing the street, or the part thereof on which the improvement is to be made,[1] or that of the owners of a majority of such properties, is sufficient.[2]

§ 677. When the statute limits a space of street, e. g., one square, within which, on the consent of the owners of properties therein, curbing, paving, etc., may be made at any one time, if, at any one time, the improvement is introduced into more than this space, e. g., two squares, the expense of such paving or curbing cannot be assessed upon these properties. Observance of the statutory limitation, even if it be in the form of a proviso, is essential to the preservation of the lien upon adjacent properties.[3] The city, in a proceeding to enforce the lien, must show affirmatively that the consent of the property owners, expressed in the prescribed mode, has been obtained,[4] unless, indeed, the act of assembly makes

12th March, 1830, to open Broad street 120 feet wide, and to cause it to be paved, without a prior application of the adjoining lot owners. Spring Garden v. Wistar, 18 Pa. St. 195. See, also, Philadelphia v. Wistar, 35 Pa. St. 427. The consent of lot owners in Philadelphia to the paving of the centre of the street, is not made necessary, by the act of 8th April, 1864. [P. L. 324.] Slocum v. Philadelphia, 11 W. N. C. 167.

[1] Specimens are the act of April 2d, 1868, [P. L. 610.] (Here, the phrase is, "the majority of the owners of property on both sides, and facing the streets.") Act of 16th May, 1857, [P. L. 541;] Act of March 19th, 1828, [10 Sm L 96;] Act of May 1st, 1861, [P L. 614;] Act of 16th March, 1819, [7 Sm. L. 177] The act of 8th April, 1864, [P. L. 324,] requires the consent in writing of a majority of the property owners to the construction of sewers and branch sewers. Slocum v. Philadelphia, 11 W. N. C. 167.

[2] Act of April 1st, 1868, [P. L. 567.] (The expression here is, " a majority in interest of the owners whose property is situated " in the streets to be paved.) Act of March 6th, 1820, [7 Sm. L. 260.]

[3] Kensington v. Keith, 2 Pa. St 218.

[4] Pittsburgh v. Walter, 69 Pa. St. 365. Here, the act forbade the grading or

the ordinance of councils, which directs the grading and paving to be done, itself conclusive evidence of the previous application of the necessary number of property owners.[1]

When Property Owners Must be Heard.

§ 678. Many acts of assembly confer on the municipal authorities the power, unconditioned by the previous consent of lot owners, to order streets to be graded, paved or curbed, etc., but require them, before exercising their discretion, to give an opportunity to the owners of property that may become chargeable with the costs, to represent their views with respect to the contemplated improvement. In such case, the action of councils is quasi-judicial in character, and it is a fundamental rule that all such proceedings, when they affect the rights or property of the citizen, are nugatory if unaccompanied by reasonable notice and opportunity for a hearing. Hence, when the act of assembly authorizing paving to be done, provided that no ordinance should be passed directing such paving to be done, "until —— days' notice of the improvement prayed for has been given in the official paper of the city," it was held that notice for at least two days must be given in such paper, and that a mere editorial publication of the general doings of the councils was not the notice required.[2]

Co-operation of Property Owners Invited.

§ 679. When the statutes bestow on the authorities of the municipality the absolute power to cause improvements to be made, and to charge their costs on the properties fronting on the streets in which they are made, the consent of the property own-

---

paving of streets, "unless upon the written application of the owners of a majority of the property." Comp. Olds v. Erie City, 79 Pa. St. 380.

[1] Olds v. Erie City, 79 Pa. St. 380. Here, the act directs that when an ordinance has passed, "the question whether a majority of persons holding property thereon have petitioned

therefor, shall cease and determine." Erie v. Bootz, 72 Pa. St. 196, decides that this clause is still a part of the law under the acts of April 10th, 1864, [P. L. 672,] and April 2d, 1868, [P. L. 610.]

[2] Olds v. Erie City, 79 Pa. St. 380. Comp. Erie v. Bootz, 72 Pa. St. 196.

ers is, of course, unnecessary.[1] The city councils may, however, self-limit the power of the city, and may require by ordinance that before any grading, paving or other improvement is undertaken on any street, or part of a street, the co-operation of the owners of property, in front of which this work is to be done, and upon which its cost will be assessed, shall be secured. (a) Councils may authorize the owners of property to make the contract with the paver. Thus, the resolution of March 9th, 1857, of the councils of Philadelphia, authorized the owners of property, or a majority thereof, fronting on Fifteenth street from Centre to Barclay, to pave the same, provided that the city should be at no expense therefor, except for the intersections, and that the contractors selected by these property owners should enter into an obligation to the city to keep the street in good repair for two years. Under this ordinance, a majority of the owners of property on Fifteenth street, between the designated cross streets, contracted with A. to do the paving under the direction of the chief commissioner of highways, and agreed to pay him for their respective fronts so much per yard. It was decided that all the properties fronting on the improvements were liable to a lien for their shares of the aggregate cost thereof, though the owners of some of them might not have participated in the making of the contract therefor.[2] (b) The

---

[1] This was the case under the act of March 12th, 1830, [P L. 427,] authorizing the paving of Broad street by the district of Spring Garden, "as soon as conveniently may be." Spring Garden v Wistar, 18 Pa. St. 195. See, also, act of April 6th, 1870, [P. L. 967,] respecting Meadville. Under the act of April 21st, 1855, [P. L. 266,] the authorities of the city of Philadelphia have power to construct sewers anywhere in the city without the previous petition of owners of property on the streets; that act changing the law as it had previously stood with regard to certain districts of the county of Philadelphia. Philadelphia v. Tryon, 35 Pa. St. 401. See, also, act of May 1st, 1861. [P. L. 614,] pertaining to the grading of streets in Erie.

[2] City of Philadelphia v. Wistar, 35 Pa. St. 427. In this case it is said that similar arrangements had long been made in Moyamensing and other districts of Philadelphia county. In Fell v Philadelphia, 81 Pa. St 58, a similar contract was made.

councils may require the consent of lot owners to the paving of the street on which their properties abut, as a condition precedent to the undertaking of the work. In such a case, the want of the consent of the lot holders will preclude the assessment of the expenses of the paving upon the lots, and the charging of them with the same.[1]

Selection of Paver by Lot Owners.

§ 680. The councils may require the selection of the paver by a majority of lot owners before the department of highways may enter into a contract with him. It is then necessary, in a proceeding to enforce the lien that may be asserted against any particular property, to show affirmatively that the paver who has done the work, was selected by a majority of the lot owners. The adoption of the work by the city, implied in its bringing suit for the use of the contractor, does not waive the need of this evidence.[2] If a majority of the lot owners sign a paper in favor of the award of the contract of paving to a particular person, the assent so expressed to his selection is revocable at any time until the contract is actually concluded,[3] though not afterwards,[4] and if enough names are withdrawn to reduce the number of property owners consenting, at the time of the award of the contract, to less than a majority of the whole number, the contract cannot support a lien on the adjacent properties for the costs of the paving.[3] A ratification by an ordinance of councils passed after the completion of the work of paving, under a contract which had been awarded without the consent of the majority of lot owners

[1] City v. Lea, 5 Phila. 77.

[2] Reilly v. Philadelphia, 60 Pa. St. 467; City v. Foulkrod, 1 W. N. C. 133. In Briggs v O'Rourke, 1 W. N. C. 325, a special injunction to restrain the paving of a certain street, and the filing of a lien against the properties thereon, on the ground that the paver had not been selected by a majority of the property owners on said street, was refused.

[3] City of Philadelphia v. Philadelphia and R. R. R. Co., 88 Pa St 314, 4 W. N. C. 226; Dickerson v. Peters, 71 Pa. St. 53; City v. Stewart, 1 W. N. C. 242.

[4] Long v. O'Rourke, 31 Leg. Int. 116, 6 Leg. Gaz. 118.

to the contractor, will confer validity upon the assessments of the expense thereof upon abutting properties.[1] When the consent of the necessary number of lot owners is alleged to have been given by their signatures to a certain paper, parol evidence by the contractor and certain property owners of this fact, is inadmissible, until the non-production of the paper is satisfactorily explained.[2] The selection, however, of a paver, prior to and with a view to induce, the passage of an ordinance authorizing the paving of a certain section of a street, will, if unrevoked, be sufficient to authorize the assessment of the costs of the work upon abutting properties, when the ordinance authorizing the work, and directing the commissioner of highways to enter into a contract with the selected paver, is duly passed immediately after the selection.[3] An ordinance required the selection of a paver by a majority of the owners of property upon Beckett, street, between Woodland street and Forty-third street. From a point on Beckett street, between these intersecting streets, to Forty-third street, extended a park, into which no street could be lawfully made. A paper was signed in favor of a certain paver by a majority of the lot owners on Beckett street, between Woodland street and the point at which Beckett street was intercepted by this park, who thus described themselves. The park belonged to a corporation, and, counting the corporation as one owner, the owners signing were in fact a majority of all the owners between the streets designated in the ordinance. It was held that the selection of the paver was valid.[4]

[1] City v. Hays, 93 Pa. St. 72.

[2] City v. Stewart, 1 W. N. C. 242. In this case, the originally selected contractor assigned the contract to another, but the validity of this assignment was, so far as the report of the case shows, not considered.

[3] Fell v. Philadelphia, 81 Pa. St. 58.

[4] Fell v. Philadelphia, 81 Pa. St. 58. If the highway department awards a contract to one who has not been selected as existing ordinances require, by a majority of the property owners, the councils may subsequently, by ordinance, ratify the contract and adopt the work done

Notice of Contractor's Application.

§ 681. Instead of the method of conceding the selection of the contractor to the owners of the properties which must bear the burden of the improvement, the city councils may, by ordinance, forbid the award of any contract for the paving of streets, by the highway department, unless the applicant for the contract shall give notice of his application in two daily newspapers having the largest circulation, by three consecutive insertions, at least two weeks prior to the making of such application. Such notice may be required to set forth the name of the contractor, the locality of the space intended to be paved, and the length in linear feet of such space, the name and residence of each person signing in favor of the applicant, and the number of feet owned or represented by each person so signing, fronting on the said street, and to add an invitation to the owners of properties on the street, to meet at the department of highways at a certain hour on a given day, to show cause why such contract should not be awarded to the applicant. Compliance with this ordinance will, in the absence of special plea or evidence to the contrary, be presumed,[1] but is essential to the validity of assessments for the cost of work done under such a contract. If, on trial of the *scire facias* on a lien filed for such assessments, the defendant having pleaded specially non-compliance on the part of the contractor with this ordinance, the plaintiff fails to give evidence of the compliance, the court will order a non-suit, notwithstanding that there is evidence of a written request for the appointment of the contractor, signed by a number of property owners, who are certified by the surveyor of the district, but, as it is alleged, mistakenly, to constitute a majority of the owners of property on the part of the

under it, and so make assessments therefor valid. City v. Hays, 93 Pa. St. 72. The councils of Philadelphia can award a contract without giving property owners an opportunity to select the paver. Dickinson v. Peters, 6 W. N. C. 458.

[1] Fell v. Philadelphia, 81 Pa. St. 58.

street which was paved.[1] Nor will the fact that the property owners knew the day on which the contract was to. be awarded, dispense with the necessity of publication thereof by the contractor, according to the ordinance.[2] The notice published must describe the kind of pavement the contract for the making of which is to be sought. But, if it describe the pavement as one of cobble-stones, and, at the time of the publication of the notice, the city ordinances required rubble-stones to be used for this purpose, the fact that, three days before the contract was awarded, a new ordinance was passed, authorizing the use of cobble-stones, will not validate that contract, since the kind of pavement advertised must be the kind of pavement actually laid.[3]

Competing Proposals.

§ 682. Sometimes, to secure the doing of the work at the lowest practicable cost, a general ordinance of the city may require the highway department, before entering into contracts, to advertise for proposals. In such case it is not necessary that the advertisement should take place after the passage of the special ordinance which commands the grading or paving to be done. The committee on streets may publish a notice inviting proposals, in order to ascertain the probable cost of the work, as a means of assisting the councils to decide whether it shall be undertaken. When, therefore, a notice asking for proposals was published August 7th, and the six succeeding days, and the proposals made in response thereto were opened May 13th, the ordinance directing the grading to be done, adopted August 16th, was valid, and, for the expense of the work done under the contract entered into

---

[1] Philadelphia v. Sanger, 5 W. N. C. 335.

[2] Ibid.

[3] Fell v. Philadelphia, 81 Pa. St. 58. The city may, by ordinance, ratify the contract and adopt the work done under it, though the contractor did not comply with the ordinance which required publication of his application, and after such ratification the assessments on adjacent properties will be valid. City v. Hays, 93 Pa. St. 72.

on the 20th of August, a lawful assessment and lien upon the abutting lots were made and obtained.[1]

Authentication of Contract.

§ 683. In order better to authenticate contracts, the act of 21st April, 1855, [P. L. 264,] required the approval of contracts for paving streets in the city of Philadelphia by the city solicitor. Under this act, the endorsement of the approval is unnecessary, and a certification of the bill of the contractor, by the surveyor and city solicitor, would imply, in an action in which the city is the legal plaintiff, a ratification by the proper authorities of the action of the highway department.[2]

Preconditions to Municipal Power to Assess Cost of Improvements.

§ 684. The power of the city, over grading, paving, etc., usually resides with the legislative branch of its government, and will be exercised by means of ordinance. If the legislature of the state has prescribed certain formalities, compliance with which is essential to the validity of any ordinance, an ordinance for the grading or paving of streets, in respect to which these formalities have been omitted, will be void. Thus, the act incorporating the city of Allegheny, makes all ordinances of its councils void, unless they shall be published in fifteen days after their passage in one or more newspapers of the city, and shall be recorded in the office of the recorder of deeds for Allegheny county. An ordinance for the paving of streets, passed June 25th, 1855, and not recorded until the 9th February, 1859, was of no effect, therefore, to support a lien upon properties abutting on the streets in which the paving was done. The act of 2d February, 1859, which declared that the omission to record the ordinance of June 25th, 1855, should not impair or affect contracts made in pursuance thereof, or assessments

---

[1] Darlington *v.* Commonwealth, 41 Pa. St. 68.   [2] Fell *v.* Philadelphia, 81 Pa. St. 58.

for the costs of the paving, provided that the ordinance was recorded within twenty days after the passage of the act, had the effect of. rehabilitating the ordinance, when it was recorded one week afterwards, and of validating the assessments for the expense of paving done under a contract entered into in pursuance thereof. The due publication of such a statute would be sufficient, though the ordinance itself did not contain any direction in respect to it.[1] When the statutory law does not require the recording of ordinances, recording is unnecessary to their validity.[2] The act of 3d April, 1867, authorizes the borough of McKeesport to require, by ordinance, the grading, paving or macadamizing of any street, lane or alley, or parts thereof, not less than one square, within such reasonable time as the council shall by ordinance direct. An ordinance requiring the grading and paving of a certain street, but which omitted to designate the time within which it must be done, was void, and assessments made for the costs of such grading, etc., upon adjoining property holders could not be enforced. The limitation in the contract of a time for the completion of the work, was not an adequate substitute.[3] A municipality having power to assess the costs of grading, paving, etc., on adjacent properties, may exercise it by means of a general ordinance prescribing the methods of procedure, followed by a special one which simply decrees the paving of the particular street.[4] The act of 20th April, 1869, [P. L. 1190,] authorizes the councils of Philadelphia to order the construction of branch sewers, whenever the same shall be approved by the board of surveys, and shall be, in the opinion of councils, required for the health, comfort and convenience of the inhabitants of the city. It is not neces-

[1] Schenley v. Commonwealth, 36 Pa. St. 29.

[2] Darlington v. Commonwealth, 41 Pa. St. 68.

[3] White v. Commonwealth, 37 Leg. Int. 354; Johnson v. Commonwealth, 37 Leg. Int. 354.

[4] Huidekoper v. Meadville, 83 Pa. St. 156.

sary, however, that an ordinance ordering the building of a sewer should declare that the construction of such sewer had the approval of the board of surveys, or was, in the opinion of the councils, necessary to the health of the inhabitants.[1]

Compliance with Ordinances.

§ 685. Since, when the power to pave streets is delegated to cities by the legislature, this power must be exerted by them by means of ordinances, authority to assess the expenses of such improvements on properties fronting on the streets must be found in such ordinances. They must be complied with by the executive departments of the city in the making of contracts, and by the contractor.[2] They will, however, receive a reasonable construction. ˉ An ordinance of the city of Pittsburgh, authorizing the paving of Centre avenue from Dinwiddie to Kirkpatrick streets, will, when it is ascertained that this avenue is already paved up to that side of Dinwiddie street which is farthest from Kirkpatrick street, be understood to warrant the paving of the avenue from the line at which the paving now ceases, to Kirkpatrick street. It could not have been the intention of the councils that the intersection of Centre avenue with Dinwiddie street should be left unpaved.[3] So, if an ordinance prescribes the grading of a certain street between designated points, and a contract therefor is entered into, and, owing to the fact that a part of the distance is, by a previous process

---

[1] Philadelphia v. McNeely, 7 W. N. C. 573. A party who actively procures work to be done by the city estops himself from denying the power of the city to do it, and to assess its cost on his property. Bidwell v. City of Pittsburg, 85 Pa. St. 412; McKnight v. City of Pittsburg, 91 Pa. St. 273.

[2] If the engineer disregards a grade of pavement prescribed by ordinance, the city may, by subsequent ordinance, ratify the work done, and thus make assessments therefor valid. McKnight v. City of Pittsburg, 91 Pa. St. 273. Substantial compliance with an ordinance requiring a sidewalk to be paved to the width of eight feet is sufficient to ground a valid assessment, the work being accepted by the city. Watson v. City of Philadelphia, 93 Pa. St. 111.

[3] Pittsburg v. Cluley, 74 Pa. St. 259.

of grading, at exactly the right level, the grading of the remainder of the distance will be a compliance with the spirit of the ordinance and contract made pursuant thereto.[1] If a short part of the distance whose paving is commanded by a city ordinance, be covered by a park, the penetration of which by any street is forbidden by law, the ordinance will be complied with by the paving of so much of the distance indicated in the ordinance as lies without the park.[2] After a contract has been awarded for the paving of a street, under an ordinance which required the bed to be made of sand and gravel, and water-stones to be used for the material of the paving, it is competent for the councils to authorize, by a new ordinance, the substitution of ashes for sand and gravel, and of rubble-stones for water-stones.[3] When a general ordinance requires streets forty feet in width to have a sidewalk of at least eight feet width, on each side, only such parts of a street of varying width as are forty feet wide, need have such sidewalks. The ordinance would not apply to the narrower parts of the street.[4] So, if, under a similar ordinance, owing to the angular character of a lot, or other cause, the pavement of a foot-way at one end is, excluding the curbing, only seven feet eight inches in width, but the city has accepted the pavement, and the contract and ordinance have been substantially complied with, in good faith, a lien for the expense of the pavement will be good.[5]

Contractual Exemption of City from Liability.

§ 686. In the city of Philadelphia, and in some other cities, the custom now obtains of requiring the contractor for the paving of footways and streets, to stipulate that the city shall not be liable for the expenses of the work, but that he will look solely to the lien which, by law, shall arise in favor

---

[1] Hutchinson v. Pittsburg, 72 Pa. St. 320.

[2] Fell v. Philadelphia, 81 Pa. St. 58.

[3] City of Philadelphia v. Arrott, 8 Phila. 41.

[4] Darlington v. Commonwealth, 41 Pa. St. 63.

[5] Watson v. Philadelphia, 8 W. N. C. 275.

of the city, upon the properties fronting upon the streets in which the improvement may take place. Though the effect of such an arrangement may be to defer the time of payment, or to increase the risks and trouble which the contractor may need to undergo, and thus to enhance the contract price of the work, it is fully within the power of councils to require such a stipulation, even when such power is not expressly conferred by statute. A similar stipulation that the city should not pay the contractor until it has first collected the assessments from the owners of the properties upon which they may be levied, is likewise valid. Property owners whose lots are charged with the expense of the improvement cannot complain of it.[1]

Mandatory and Directory Requirements.

§ 687. Not all the requirements of statutes, ordinances or contracts made in pursuance thereof, are of equal dignity, and while some must be strictly obeyed, in order that valid liens may arise for the expenses of the grading and paving of streets, or other improvements, others are merely directory, and compliance with them is not essential to the origin of lawful liens. An ordinance of the city of Philadelphia directs that when the district surveyor shall have measured that portion of the paving which is chargeable upon the property owners, upon the line of any street, and made out bills for the same, the chief commissioner of highways shall certify on these bills that the paving has been done in a workmanlike manner, and in conformity with the requirements of the ordinances, but it was decided that the omission of the commissioner to affix such certificate to the bills rendered, did not vitiate the lien of the assessments, he testifying at the trial of the *scire facias,* that he had supervised the work during its progress, and had inspected and approved it, when finished.[2] The act of May 16th, 1857,

---

[1] Schenley *v.* Commonwealth, 36 Pa. St. 29.

[2] Fell *v.* Philadelphia, 81 Pa. St. 58.

[P. L. 541,] authorized the collection by the city of Pittsburgh, of the value of all paving theretofore done, according
to an appraisement to be made, and assessed this valuation
on properties abutting on the streets paved, in proportion to
their foot frontage. It also provided that the assessments,
when made, should be a lien upon the properties on which
they were imposed, and required this lien to be filed within
twenty days in the office of the prothonotary of the district
court of Allegheny county. Under this law, an assessment
completed March 25th, 1858, was decided to be a lien,
though not filed until May 8th.[1] The act of June 6th,
1864, concerning paving, etc., in the city of Pittsburgh,
directs assessments of the costs thereof to be made, and
requires the city regulator to give notice of such assessments,
in order that the party interested may have opportunity to
correct any errors or mistakes. An omission to give such
notice is not fatal to the lien, but simply opens to the
defendant an opportunity to correct any errors or mistakes
which might have been corrected if the notice had been
given him.[2] When a contract stipulated that the paving
for which it provided, should not be done between the first
day of December and the first day of April, on account of
the injurious effects of frost, and the work was nevertheless
done, for the most part, between these dates, this departure
from the contract could not be taken advantage of by the
defendant, in the trial of the *scire facias*.[3] An ordinance of Sunbury directed the chief burgess, assisted by
the street commissioners, to cause pavements, footwalks,
grading and curbing to be made under the direction and
control of the borough regulators. This was sufficiently
complied with, when the chief burgess attended in person to the making of the crossings, and the committee on

[1] Magee v. Commonwealth, 46 Pa.
St. 358.

[2] Pittsburgh v. Coursin, 74 Pa. St. 400.

[3] Philadelphia v. Brooke, 81 Pa. St.
23.

pavements under his direction supervised the construction of the pavements, always conferring with the borough regulator.[1]

What Are Streets.

§ 688. The method of assessing the expenses of the grading and paving of streets, of the construction of culverts and sewers, or of the laying down of water and gas pipes therein, upon properties facing upon the streets in which these improvements are made, is one of very general application. It desiderates, however, that the street in which such work shall be done, shall be an open public highway. Though a street may have been laid out, it cannot be opened until damages occasioned to properties through which it may run, are ascertained and either paid or secured according to law. Until so opened, the cost of no construction in it can be lawfully imposed upon the properties which abut thereupon. Thus, though Pennsylvania avenue had been laid out for twenty years and across a certain lot, but no steps had been taken to open it, the cost of a culvert built along it, could not be assessed in part upon this lot.[2] When Ontario street, Philadelphia, was laid out, and viewers were appointed to assess the damages to the bisected lots, and the owner of one of these lots appealed from their report, wherein no damages were awarded him, the city could not, while the appeal was pending, and without giving security for the damages that might ultimately be assessed, lawfully open the street, and for the expense of building a culvert therein, no lien could be acquired against this lot.[3] Every directory provision of the law, however, with respect to the opening of streets, need not be complied with. The charter of the city of Allegheny requires notice of proceedings to open streets to be published in two newspapers of the city. When there was but one paper

---

[1] Wilvert *v* Sunbury Borough, 81½ Pa. St. 57.

[2] Coxe *v.* Philadelphia, 47 Pa. St. 9.

[3] Wistar *v.* Philadelphia, 71 Pa. St. 44.

published in the city, advertisement therein alone was sufficient, when personal notice was given to one of two co-tenants
through whose land the street was opened. Against this
land a valid lien could be obtained for the expense of grading
and paving.[1] Under the act of April 1st, 1870, [P. L.
751,] which empowers the city of Allegheny to lay out new
streets, lanes and alleys, and to widen, straighten and extend
old ones, charging the expense thereof on properties fronting
on such streets, etc., it cannot widen a chartered turnpike,
even with the consent of the company, without first con-
demning it for the purpose of taking it as a street.[2] And if,
in the grading of a certain street in that city, it becomes necessary to elevate it above the level of contiguous properties, and
a wall for the lateral support of the street thus elevated, is
built, but partly on these properties, without taking any steps
to secure the condemnation of the parts so taken, no portion of
the expense of the construction of this wall can be charged upon
lots abutting upon the street, if the wall will be rendered use-
less when such part of it as thus intrudes on private lands, is
taken down.[3] It has, however, been decided that into a public
road in the rural parts of Philadelphia, though a turnpike,
water pipes may be introduced by the city, under the act of
April 2d, 1854, even though no assessment of damages was
made in accordance with the ninth section of the act of
April 21st, 1855, [P. L. 264.] The cost of such water pipes
could be assessed upon properties facing upon the turnpike.[4]

---

[1] Darlington v. Commonwealth, 41
Pa. St. 68. [In this case, it was also
held that evidence was competent
that the defendant had made admis-
sions in deeds, that the street existed, for whose grading and paving
an assessment was made upon his
lot. It was also said that the omission to record the ordinance requiring the opening of a street did not
invalidate the ordinance, the law not
requiring such recording.]

[2] Breed v. Allegheny, 85 Pa. St.
214. Such want of power may be
taken advantage of, on a trial of the
scire facias. It is not waived by
omitting to appeal to the quarter
sessions from the report of the viewers, assessing damages upon the benefited lots. See, also, Wilson v. Allegheny, 79 Pa. St. 272.
[3] Western Penna. R. R. v. Allegheny, 92 Pa. St. 100.
[4] City v. McCalmont, 6 Phila. 543.

§ 689. It is competent for a city to adopt a street or road that has been dedicated to the public, though it be of unequal width, and whether it be straight or crooked, and to assess the expense of grading and paving it upon adjacent properties.[1] A street was opened through lands by a tenant, and the public had the constant use of it for the period of twenty-one years, when his term expired. The landlord, a married woman, instead of disowning what he had done, permitted the street to remain open and to be used by the public four or five years longer, when the city graded and paved it. Under a statute which authorized the grading and paving of permanent streets only, a valid lien was acquired for the expense thereof upon abutting properties.[2] The expense of grading no greater width of street, however, than had been dedicated, could be assessed on contiguous lots.[3] When water pipes were introduced by the city of Philadelphia into Fairmount place, which is private property, never having been dedicated to the public, no lien could be acquired by the city upon lots fronting thereon.[4] Under a power to lay out, open, grade, pave and macadamize any public street, the city of Erie can lay out, pave, etc., only a public highway on land, for travel on foot, on horseback or in carriages. The city constructed a pier parallel with the shore, twelve hundred feet out in the waters of the lake, reserving to itself a strip of land one hundred feet wide, covered to the depth of from seven to ten feet with water of the lake, and extending from the terminus of State street to the pier. On both sides of this strip it sold lots covered with water, and then constructed a dry causeway twenty feet wide in the centre of the strip, along its whole extent. It was held that no lien upon the adjacent water-covered lots

---

[1] Darlington v. Commonwealth, 41 Pa. St. 63.

[2] Schenley v. Commonwealth, 36 Pa. St. 29.

[3] Darlington v. Commonwealth, 41 Pa. St. 63.

[4] City v. Baird, 1 W. N. C. 126. The lien was, on rule, stricken from the record.

could arise for the expense of this construction.[1] The power
of paving sidewalks includes that of curbing them, if
such curbing is a usual and reasonable part of paving.[2]
But, omission to curb and gutter does not deprive the city of
the lien for the paving of the sidewalks, unless the result
thereof is that the paving is rendered worthless.[3] Curbing
may be necessary to preserve the pavements of the cartway,
and hence a lien may be obtained for it, together with the
paving of the cartway, under the act of January 6th, 1864,
[P. L. 1131,] which authorizes Pittsburgh to grade, pave and
set with curbstone the cartways of streets, though another act,
that of April 8th, 1857, [P. L. 240,] provides for the paving
of footwalks.[4] The ordinance of 8th June, 1870, of the city
of Philadelphia, prohibiting the department of highways
from entering into contracts for the repairing of any streets,
applies only to the cartways between the curbs, and not to
the sidewalks.[5]

Authority to Assess Conferred Ex Post Facto

§ 690. Not only may the municipality be empowered to
open, grade, pave and culvert streets, and to impose the costs
of the work on the properties which face upon them, but, in
at least one instance, the legislature has conferred on one city
the authority to appraise the paving, grading or preparation
for grading or paving already done, according to its actual
condition at the time of such appraisement, and has enacted
that the abutting properties shall be subject to a lien, in proportion to the number of feet front, for the total value thus
ascertained of the grading, paving and preparation for grading
and paving. Such a system of assessment is constitutional.[6]

When Frontage is not Measure of Benefits.

§ 691. The system of assessment of the costs of grading,

Reed v. Erie, 79 Pa. St. 346.

[2] Schenley v. Commonwealth, 36
Pa. St. 29. This is a question for the
jury.

[3] Wilvert v. Sunbury, 81½ Pa. St. 57.

[4] Pittsburgh v. Cluley, 66 Pa. St. 449.

[5] City v Lea, 9 Phila. 106.

[6] Act of May 16th, 1867, [P. L. 541,]
for Pittsburgh. Magee v. Commonwealth, 46 Pa. St. 358.

paving, etc., in streets, upon properties thereon, proportionately to their frontages, has been sanctioned as one which approximately distributes the burdens in accordance with the benefits received. Instead of the frontage rule, certain acts of assembly provide for an actual investigation of the benefits conferred in each particular case, and for the assessment of the costs of the improvement proportionately to the benefits thus found to exist. Thus the act of April 22d, 1858, [P. L. 471,] authorizes the councils of Pittsburgh to cause sewers to be made in any street, lane or alley, and to assess the costs upon properties benefited, the assessments to be made by at least three persons appointed by councils, and, when approved by councils, to be a lien upon the properties on which they may be levied. Under this act, property not situate in the alley in which a sewer is constructed may be assessed for its cost, and the assessment, when approved by councils, is conclusive.[1]

Indirect Cost of Improvements Assessed.

§ 692. The principle of assessment in proportion to specifically ascertained benefits, has been applied, not merely, as we have just seen, to the direct cost of the improvements in streets, but also to the indirect costs arising as damages for injury to properties, occasioned by the improvement. Thus, when, by the opening of any street, any properties through which it is conducted undergo damage, the amount of this damage is distributed upon properties found to be benefited by the opening, in proportion to the degrees of benefit experienced by them. The act of 6th January, 1864, [P. L. 1131,] concerning the opening, widening or lengthening of streets or alleys in the city of Pittsburgh, directs that viewers shall be appointed, who shall make a true and conscionable appraisement of damages, in excess of advantages, which the owners of any property may suffer by such improvements, and shall assess the same upon such other

[1] Commonwealth v. Woods, 44 Pa. St. 113.

properties as may be advantaged, in proportion to the benefits realized. The damages thus assessed may include the value of houses which have been compelled to be torn down on account of the grading.[1] This method of assessing damages is liable to variation in details. The entire damages may be imposed on the properties benefited, as in the act of April 21st, 1858, [P. L. 385,] in regard to the opening, widening and vacating of streets in Philadelphia;[2] or, some ratio of them may be borne by the municipality, and the residue only cast upon the benefited properties;[3] or, the law may give to the juries which are appointed to assess the damages the power to decide how much thereof shall be borne by the city and how much by properties benefited;[4] or, only so much of the damages may be imposed on benefited properties, proportionally to their respective benefits, as does not exceed the value of these benefits.[5]

§ 693. Under several acts, the properties found to be benefited, and upon which the damages may be assessed, may be in the vicinity of the street which has been opened, or in which the improvement of whatever kind has been made, though not situated on the street;[6] under others, only such properties as are on the line of the street which has been opened or improved are liable to assessments for damages.[7]

---

[1] Wray v. Pittsburgh, 46 Pa. St. 365.

[2] In Chestnut Avenue, 3 Phila. 265, it is said that an assessment which does not impose the whole amount of damages on properties benefited, is void. See, also, act of April 4th, 1831, [P. L 498;] April 7th, 1832, [P. L. 372;] April 6th, 1833, [P. L. 186;] April 6th, 1850, [P. L. 388;] Extension of Hancock Street, 18 Pa. St. 26.

[3] Act of April 1st, 1831, [P. L. 311,] concerning the opening of streets in Pittsburgh.

[4] Act of April 1st, 1864, [P. L. 206;] In re Mover Street, 6 Phila. 8.

[5] Act of April 6th, 1870, [P. L. 974,] respecting opening of streets in Meadville; Huidekoper's Appeal, 83 Pa. St. 167.

[6] Act of April 1st, 1864, [P. L. 206;] Act of 16th April, 1870, [P. L. 974;] Act of 6th April, 1850, [P. L. 388;] Extension of Hancock Street, 18 Pa. St. 26.

[7] Act of March 18th, 1869, [P. L. 395,] and April 10th, 1869, [P. L. 828,] with respect to the 22d ward of the city of Philadelphia. See Chestnut Avenue, 68 Pa. St. 81, 3 Phila. 265.

In the latter case, however, properties on parts of the street which have been already opened, may be assessed for the damages occasioned to properties by the opening and grading of the intermediate portion.[1] The act of April 6th, 1870, [P. L. 974,] respecting streets in Meadville, gives an appeal from the report of viewers appointed to assess the damages of opening streets on benefited properties, first, to the city councils, and, finally, to the court of quarter sessions of the county. The jurisdiction of this court, however, attaches only when there is an appeal, and then only in respect to the assessment upon the property of the appellant. This court has no power to increase the assessment upon any property whose owner has not appealed.[2] On an appeal to the court of quarter sessions, the benefit experienced by each property must be ascertained by a separate investigation, and only damages to the extent of the benefit thus ascertained may be assessed. Hence, when the aggregate of damages found by the viewers and on appeal, exceeds the aggregate of benefits ascertained, it is error in the court to assess the difference upon the properties benefited proportionately to the assessments already made on them, under the mistaken opinion that the entire damages must be distributed over the properties benefited, without respect to the measure of benefit received.[3] When the act of assembly requires the appointment of three freeholders to assess the damages and benefits, and allows an appeal to councils, who may either approve the report of the viewers, send it back, or quash it, and makes an approval by the councils final and conclusive, it is too late, after the approval of the viewers' report by councils, to object that one of the viewers was not a freeholder.[4] The damages and benefits are conclusively fixed by the assessment.[5] But, if the act of assembly requires notice

[1] Chestnut Avenue, 68 Pa. St. 81.

[2] Appeal of Luce Brothers, 83 Pa. St. 175.

[3] Huidekoper's Appeal, 83 Pa. St.

167; Appeal of Luce Brothers, 83 Pa. St. 175.

[4] Pittsburgh v. Cluley, 74 Pa. St. 262.

[5] Wray v. Pittsburgh, 46 Pa. St. 365.

of the making, of the assessments to be given to property owners, that they may have an opportunity to correct any errors, and such notice is not given, the assessments are not conclusive. Errors may be shown in them at the trial of the *scire facias.*[1]

Assessment on Rural Lands.

§ 694. The assessment on lands fronting upon streets, of the expense of grading, paving and curbing thereof, in proportion to their frontage, is appropriate in thickly populated districts, like cities and boroughs, where, by the application of such a method, the relative burdens imposed will not materially vary from the benefits conferred. In rural districts, however, it is inadmissible. The act of May 3d, 1870, [P. L. 1298,] appointed certain persons commissioners of Washington avenue, and constituted them a corporation. It enacted that the qualified voters within distances not exceeding one and a half miles from the road, on each side of it, should elect commissioners of this road to serve for one year. These commissioners were authorized to grade and macadamize the avenue, and to assess and collect a special tax on properties within varying distances from the road, at correspondingly varying rates per acre. These taxes, if not paid in ninety days, were declared to be liens on the lands on which they were assessed. The avenue was seven miles long and stretched through a purely rural country. It was determined that this law was unconstitutional.[2] By the act of 2d April, 1870, [P. L. 796,] a majority of property owners along Penn avenue, Pittsburgh, were empowered to elect commissioners to grade and pave it, assessing the total cost thereof upon the lands abutting upon it, through its entire length, according to the number of their feet front. This avenue extended for miles through partly urban, partly suburban and agricultural sections, penetrating cemeteries,

[1] Pittsburg *v.* Coursin, 74 Pa. St. 400.   [2] Washington Avenue, 69 Pa. St. 352.

farms, extensive suburban residences, villages and hamlets.
Under this law, declared unconstitutional, it was decided
that assessments even on a lot in one of the towns through
which the avenue ran, being its share of the entire expense,
as measured by the ratio of its number of feet front to the
entire length of the avenue, was void.[1]   One, however, who
petitioned for this improvement, and who was elected and
served as a commissioner, would be estopped from denying
the validity of the assessment on his lands.[2]   The act of
April 3d, 1873, [P. L. 504,] for opening, grading and paving Chestnut street, Philadelphia, between Forty-second and
Fifty-sixth streets, is, in so far as it provides for the assessment of the expenses thereof upon the agricultural lands
through which the street runs, unconstitutional,[3] as is likewise that for the grading of Market street, between Forty-
third and Sixty-third streets, for a similar reason.[4]   Upon
lands which are assessed as agricultural, the costs of curbing
and paving cannot be constitutionally assessed proportionately to their frontage.[5]   The cost of a water main, passing
in front of a tract of farm land, nine and one-half miles
from the centre of Philadelphia, intended to conduct water
to a distant part of the city, and furnishing no water supply
to this tract, cannot be constitutionally assessed upon it.[6]

Assessments for Bridge Construction.

§ 695. Since even the incidental costs of the opening and
grading of streets, occasioned by the necessity to indemnify
property owners for the damages caused by this improvement, may be assessed upon properties benefited thereby,
the legality of assessing the direct costs of the opening and
grading of streets upon properties benefited, even if not on

[1] Seeley v. Pittsburgh, 82 Pa. St. 360.
See, also, Kaiser v. Weise, 85 Pa. St.
366.

[2] Bidwell v. City of Pittsburgh, 85
Pa. St. 412.

[3] City v. Rule, 93 Pa. St. 15.

[4] Craig v. Philadelphia, 89 Pa. St.
265.

[5] City v. Lukens, 9 W. N. C. 348.

[6] Estate of John Crawford, 38 Leg.
Int. 420.

the line of such streets, cannot be questioned. A remarkable exception to the principle of this method of assessment has been, however, recognized. When the continuity of a-street is broken by an intersecting stream, and, under an act of assembly, a bridge is erected over this stream for the purpose of connecting the severed parts of the street, the assessment of the costs of such bridge upon properties in its vicinity, whether on the street or not, is unconstitutional. Such a bridge, it is said, serves an apparent and essential public purpose, and the costs of its erection could not be imposed on private shoulders. At any rate, assessments on individual property of the costs of such a construction, having so apparent a public use, could not be sustained, except by affirmative and distinct proof appearing of record of individual benefits conferred, and of their nature, amount and value. It is impossible to make a fair, equitable distribution of the costs of such a bridge on variously situated properties.[1]

Apportionment of the Lien.

§ 696. Under the acts 22d March, 1820, and of February 3d, 1824, it was not necessary to apportion a claim against two contiguous lots, on which were separate buildings belonging to the same owner.[2] When a claim was filed against a lot described as thirty-two feet in front, and running back eighty-two feet from street to street, the title of one who purchased this land at a judicial sale on the judgment recovered on this claim, was valid, notwithstanding that the lot was, in fact, divided into four lots, two fronting on

---

[1] Ballentine's Appeal, 85 Pa. St. 163. The bridge was constructed over Saw Mill Run, Pittsburgh, and the expenses, amounting to $12,-249.43, were assessed on a multitude of properties on eleven different streets, alleys and avenues. These lots were charged at different rates, according to the streets on which they faced, and on all but one of the streets the rates were uniform, irrespective of the distance from the bridge.

[2] Council v. Moyamensing, 2 Pa. St. 224.

each street.[1] When A. owned large tracts of land on both sides of B street, which land was subdivided into ten blocks by streets intersecting B street at right angles, a single claim might be filed under the acts of March 30th, 1852, [P. L. 204,] April 8th, 1851, [P. L. 372,] and April 5th, 1849, [P. L. 341,] which claim apportioned the assessment upon each of these blocks in the ratio of their feet front, and a separate *scire facias* properly issued on each several assessment thus apportioned on each block.[2] The act of January 6th, 1864, [P. L. 1131,] concerning grading and paving in the city of Pittsburgh, provides that after the expense of t'ie work has been assessed on the several properties abutting on the streets wherein it shall have been done, the city regulator shall give notice to the property owners in order that they may correct any errors or mistakes. Under this law, if A. owns several contiguous lots under different conveyances, the divisions between which are not patent to the eye, though they are shown by a private plan made by previous owners, but unknown to the city officers, he must have the assessment apportioned when notice is given him by the regulator to appear and attend to the correction of all errors. It is too late to take exception to the want of apportionment, on the trial of the *scire facias*.[3] Under certain acts of assembly,[4] liens could be imposed on properties abutting on streets in the district of Spring Garden, for the paving thereof, and for the introduction of water thereinto. On a street in such district was a property belonging to A., divided, however, into distinct lots, according to a plan. The expense of paving and water pipes was assessed in gross upon this property, without respect to its subdivision into lots. The several lots were liable for their shares in this gross assessment

---

[1] Delaney *v.* Gault, 30 Pa. St. 63.

[2] Schenley *v.* City of Allegheny, 36 Pa. St. 29. In City *v.* Cottage Company, 9 Phila. 84, it is said that a claim may be filed against an entire block for the costs of a culvert built in one of the streets.

[3] Hutchinson *v.* Pittsburgh, 72 Pa. St. 320.

[4] Act of March 9th, 1826, [9 Sm. L. 53.]

in proportion to their several frontages. Hence, when some of them were sold, but the district failed to demand any part of its assessment from their proceeds, and, subsequently, the remaining lots were sold, the district could take from the proceeds of each lot only its share of the original aggregate assessment. Each lot is liable for the cost of the curbing and paving, and water pipe placed before it, alone.[1] The act of March 22d, 1869, [P. L. 477,] provides that "where a claim has been filed against any lot or piece of ground, * * * and it shall appear * * * that said lot, in fact, consists of two or more lots belonging to different persons, the proper court shall permit the same to be so awarded and apportioned, that a due proportion thereof, and no more, shall be charged and recovered against the several lots included in the claim as originally filed." Under this act, the apportionment of the claim will be made, when a portion of the lot against which the claim was filed, has been sold since the filing thereof.[2]

What is Not the Subject of Lien.

§ 697. Land used for public purposes, cannot be charged with municipal liens.[3] If a street runs along the track of a railroad, no assessment for the cost of paving, grading, culverting, etc., can be levied upon the railroad, whether the company has merely an easement therein,[4] or is the owner of the fee.[5] When a street crosses a railroad nearly at right angles, by a bridge, the expense of paving the bridge cannot be assessed upon the railroad running under it.[6] Property of a railroad, however, such as a depot, which is not a part of its highway, does not enjoy exemption from

---

[1] Pennell's Appeal, 2 Pa. St. 216.

[2] City v. Penrose, 6 W. N C. 432.

[3] Yet, in Council v. Moyamensing, 2 Pa. St. 224, it appears that land belonging to " council," was charged with the costs of paving.

[4] City of Philadelphia v. Railroad Co., 33 Pa. St. 41. If the fee of the railroad is in another, a claim cannot be filed against him. Philadelphia v. Eastwick, 35 Pa. St. 75; Junction R. R. v. Philadelphia, 88 Pa. St. 424.

[5] Junction R. R. v. Philadelphia, 88 Pa. St. 424.

[6] Ibid.

municipal assessment.[1] When an act of assembly exempts land used for the purpose of a cemetery "from taxation, except for state purposes," it is not liable to assessments for a culvert constructed in the street on which the cemetery fronts.[2] Agricultural or rural land is not subject to assessment, at least on the plan of the per foot frontage, for grading, paving, culverting, etc., of avenues and streets.[3]

Interests Bound by the Lien.

§ 698. A lien for water pipes in the district of Kensington binds the whole interest in the land; not only the fee, but also a perpetual ground-rent reserved thereout by à former owner. A sheriff's sale on the judgment recovered on such lien divests the estate of the ground-landlord, as well as that of the ground-tenant.[4] When A. contracts to convey land to B. at a certain date, B. stipulating that either he will then pay the purchase money, or that the deed then to be executed shall reserve to A., as a perpetual ground-rent, a sum of money annually payable, equal to the interest on the purchase money, and B.'s interest in this tract, under the contract, is sold on a judgment recovered against him, a municipal lien for pipes, paving and curbing a footway is payable in full out of the proceeds.[5] If, on a judgment recovered against A., land in fact belonging to B., but supposed to be held by him for A. in a secret trust, is taken in execution and sold, municipal taxes and assessments which are liens on the land are payable out of the proceeds of the sale of this supposititious title.[6] If real estate is held by

[1] Western P. R. R. v. Allegheny, 92 Pa. St. 100; Philadelphia v. Philadelphia and Reading R. R., 88 Pa. St. 314.

[2] Olive Cemetery Co. v. Philadelphia, 93 Pa. St. 129. But, in Northern Liberties v. St John's Church, 13 Pa. St. 104, it was decided that an exemption of church property from taxation did not include an exemption from municipal assessments.

[3] Washington Avenue, 69 Pa. St. 352; Seeley v. Pittsburgh, 82 Pa. St. 360; Kaiser v. Weise, 85 Pa. St. 366; Bidwell v. Pittsburgh, 85 Pa. St. 412; City v. Rule, 93 Pa. St. 15; Craig v. Philadelphia, 89 Pa. St. 265; City v. Lukens, 9 W. N. C. 348.

[4] Salter v. Reed, 15 Pa. St. 260.

[5] Moroney v. Copeland, 5 Wh. 407; Vanarsdalen's Appeal, 3 W. N. C. 463.

[6] Dungan's Appeal, 88 Pa. St. 414.

two as tenants in common, and, on a judgment against one of them, his interest therein is sold, the municipal liens for paving, water pipe, etc., which are charged upon the land, are payable in full from the proceeds.[1]

For What the Lien Exists.

§ 699. In general, we have seen that the expenses incurred by opening, grading, paving, culverting, etc., streets, lanes, alleys, etc., may be assessed on properties benefited, proportionately to their benefits, and that a favorite method of ascertaining this is to divide the aggregate expense by the foot frontage. When the costs and expenses of improvements are assessed on properties, the value of the work done is immaterial, except as evidence of gross carelessness or fraud in the making or execution of the contract.[2] Fraud, affecting the interests of property owners, may be shown in defence against the assessment.[3] But, when a contractor, who has agreed to allow a drawback for dirt furnished by the city, causes a claim to be filed which ignores this drawback, notwithstanding that the city has furnished the dirt, this is not such evidence of fraud, as will vitiate the lien. The proper reduction may be made at the trial of the *scire facias*.[3] A stipulation in the contract, that the contractor is to look exclusively to the property owners for his compensation, does not impair the lien for the costs, though it may have the effect of increasing the contract price.[4] Under an ordinance which authorized the commissioner of highways to employ persons to pave footways, on default of the owners of properties after due notice, and to collect the costs from such owners, they may show the actual value of the work, for the purpose of reducing excessive

[1] Moroney v. Copeland, 5 Wh. 407. The defendant may be subrogated to the lien, to compel contribution by the co-tenant.

[2] Schenley v. Commonwealth, 36 Pa. St. 29; City v. Rule, 93 Pa. St. 15.

[3] Darlington v. Commonwealth, 41 Pa. St. 68.

[4] Schenley v. Commonwealth, 36 Pa. St. 29.

charges.[1] Under the act of April 1st, 1864, [P. L. 206,] which provides for the assessment of damages caused by the opening of streets upon properties benefited, only the damages, not legal expenses, (which would include counsel fees and costs,) can be thus assessed.[2] Under the the act of March 16th, 1819, [7 Sm. L. 177,] for the paving of streets in the Northern Liberties, which conferred the power to charge the cost of such work upon properties adjacent, the district could not by ordinance make a commission of ten per cent. on the costs, also a lien.[3] But the act of March 2d, 1859, [P. L. 96,] concerning Sunbury, makes the costs of paving footwalks, and twenty per cent. additional, a lien on abutting lots,[4] while that of January 6th, 1864, concerning Pittsburgh, provides that on default of the payment of the assessments for paving, after notice, the city solicitor shall file a claim for the amount of the assessments, with interest, and five per cent. additional as the solicitor's fee for collection.[5]

When the Lien Commences.

§ 700. Usually the municipal lien for the grading, paving, culverting, furnishing with water pipes and gas pipes, of streets, etc., begins with the commencement of the work. The act of April 16th, 1845, [P. L. 488,] declares that the assessments for work done or material furnished in the county of Philadelphia shall not be a lien on real estate " for more than six months from the time of doing such work, or unless a claim is filed therefor within that time." Sometimes the acts of assembly specially provide when the lien shall commence. The act of January 6th, 1864, [P. L. 1133,] relating to grading, regrading, paving, repaving, etc., in the streets of Pittsburgh, makes the assessments on abutting

---

[1] Philadelphia v. Burgin, 50 Pa. St. 539. Comp. City v. Rule, 93 Pa. St. 15; City v. Arrott, 8 Phila. 41.

[2] In re Moyer Street, 6 Phila. 81.

[3] Northern Liberties v. St. John's Church, 13 Pa. St. 104.

[4] Wilvert v. Sunbury Borough, 81½ Pa. St. 57.

[5] Pittsburgh v. Cluley, 66 Pa. St. 449.

properties liens 'thereupon "from the commencement of the improvements." It was, hence, decided that when A. sold a lot after the grading of the street on which it faced had been begun, but before the completion thereof, the assessment made on the lot subsequently to the sale was a lien on it at the time of the sale, and that A., as grantor, was liable to his grantee on his covenants of warranty.[1] The act of April 1st, 1864, [P. L. 206,] which provides for the opening of new streets in Philadelphia, the award of damages to property owners whose land may have been injured, and the assessment of all or a part of such damages on properties benefited, also enacts that if the assessments are not paid in thirty days after presentation of the bill to the owner, the city solicitor shall file a claim against his property without delay, in the proper court, which claim shall be a lien against the property. Under this act, the lien begins only with the filing of the claim. Hence, when a lot sold by the sheriff on a judgment recovered October 16th, 1877, is encumbered by a mortgage recorded September, 1875, the mortgage is not discharged, notwithstanding that an assessment of damages for the opening of the street on which the lot stood had been made in June, 1875, the solicitor not filing the claim until December, 1875, subsequently to the recording of the mortgage.[2]

Retroaction of the Lien.

§ 701. The act of 3d February, 1824, [8 Sm. L. 189,] declares that the lien of all taxes, rates and levies imposed in the city and county of Philadelphia "shall have priority to and be fully paid and satisfied before any recognizance, mortgage, judgment, debt, obligation or responsibility which the said real estate may become charged with or liable to, from and after the passing of this act." Under this provision, a 'lien for paving a street in the district of Kensington, the expense of which was assessed October 12th, 1829,

---

[1] Shaffer v. Green, 87 Pa. St. 370. Comp. Kaiser v. Weise, 85 Pa. St. 366; Pittsburgh v. Knowlson, 92 Pa. St. 116.

[2] Merriman v. Richardson, 5 W. N. C. 9.

was preferred, in the distribution of the proceeds of a sheriff's sale of the real estate, to mechanics' liens arising from work which commenced before the paving, and to a prior judgment.[1] Out of the proceeds of land sold by the administrator of its deceased owner, for the payment of his debts, a lien of the city of Philadelphia was paid before a judgment creditor whose judgment was older than the lien.[2] When land charged with a ground-rent, and with mortgages dated 1847, was sold May 3d, 1852, by the sheriff, under a judgment for arrears of the ground-rent, a claim of Kensington for pipes laid January 4th, 1852, was paid in preference to the mortgages.[3] The provisions of the act of 3d February, 1824, were, by the act of April 5th, 1844, [P. L. 199,] extended to the county of Allegheny.[4] So far, however, as the grading and paving of footwalks in the city of Pittsburgh are concerned, these are regulated by the act of April 18th, 1857, [P. L. 240,] and of April 22d, 1858, [P. L. 471.] These acts furnish an entire system, independent of that of February 3d, 1824, [8 Sm. L. 189,] and since they give to liens for curbing, grading and paving-sidewalks no retroactive operation, assessments for grading and paving done in 1857 will be postponed to a mortgage recorded July 27th, 1848, upon the same premises, in a distribution of the proceeds of the sheriff's sale thereof.[5]

§ 702. The act of January 6th, 1864, [P. L. 1131,] after providing for assessments for paving, etc., in the city of Pittsburgh, declares that they shall be liens upon the properties assessed, from the commencement of the improvements, and shall, if filed within six months after the completion of the improvements, continue liens for five years, and be revived by *scire facias* as other liens, and adds, "if, on any sheriff's sale or other judicial sale, enough be not realized to pay off the lien, it shall continue to be a lien until the whole amount,

---

[1] Pennock v. Hoover, 5 Rawle 291.
[2] Foy's Estate, 2 W. N. C. 188.
[3] Philadelphia v. Cooke, 30 Pa. St. 56.
[4] Wallace's Estate, 59 Pa. St. 401.
[5] Appeal of the City of Pittsburgh, 40 Pa. St. 455.

with the costs, be paid in full." This language confers upon such liens priority to all other liens, whatever their date of origin. Hence, the lien for paving and grading done in the latter half of 1869 and the beginning of 1870, must be paid from the proceeds of a sheriff's sale of the lot on which it was charged, in preference to a judgment recovered against its owner February 20th, 1868, and to mechanics' liens entered June 12th, 1868.[1]

§ 703. The act of April 1st, 1870, [P. L. 751,] respecting the opening, widening and extending of streets, lanes and alleys in the city of Allegheny, declares that the assessments of the expense thereof on properties benefited, shall be "first liens." thereupon, said liens to date from the commencement of the improvements, and shall continue first liens for five years, if filed within six months after the completion of the improvement. Under this provision, the lien will be a first lien only if filed in the time designated; if not, it will be a lien from the time of filing only.[2]

Duration of the Lien.

§ 704. Under the act of February 3d, 1824, the lien of municipal assessments, in the county of Philadelphia, was unlimited in duration. It was accordingly decided that a claim for curbing and paving done in 1831, was effectively filed February 15th, 1843;[3] another, for similar work done July 20th, 1828, was still a lien when filed March 19th, 1842, under the act of April 16th, 1840;[4] and a third, for water pipes laid October 29th, 1829, continued a lien until its filing, September 29th, 1845.[5] This act was extended to

---

[1] Pittsburgh's Appeal, 70 Pa. St. 142. And this priority of lien inures to the benefit of one who, after execution had issued on it, and the property was about to be sold, paid the city, at the solicitation of the defendant, and took an assignment of the lien. Hagemann's Appeal, 88 Pa. St. 21.

[2] Lofink v. City of Allegheny, 5 W. N. C. 46.

[3] Council v. Moyamensing, 2 Pa. St. 224. Comp. Thomas v. Northern Liberties, 13 Pa. St. 117.

[4] Pray v. Northern Liberties, 31 Pa. St. 69.

[5] Northern Liberties v. Swain, 13 Pa. St. 113.

Allegheny county by the act of April 5th, 1844, [P. L. 199,] and the lien of assessments in that county, in the absence of special conflicting statutes, continues indefinite in duration.[1]

§ 705. The act of 16th April, 1840, [P. L. 412,] which provides for the filing of municipal claims in Philadelphia, and for suit thereon, was designed to furnish a mode of enforcing these liens, not of limiting their continuance.[2] This act was followed by that of 16th April, 1845, [P. L. 488,] which enacts that no assessment for work done or material furnished after its passage, by or under the authority of the board of health, or of any municipal corporation, shall be a lien on real estate for more than six months[3] from the time of doing such work, unless a claim for the same shall be filed in the office of the prothonotary of the proper court within that time, nor shall the same continue a lien longer than five years from the time of filing the claim, unless revived by *scire facias* in the manner provided by law in the case of mechanics' claims.

§ 706. The acts of April 5th, 1849, [P. L. 341,] April 8th, 1851, [P. L. 372,] and March 30th, 1852, [P. L. 204,] in reference to the grading and paving of streets in the city of Allegheny, while providing for the filing of a claim, do so in order merely to enforce the lien, not as a means of continuing it. The lien continues indefinitely, and a claim may be filed at any time.[4] Such is the purpose of the filing of the claim under the act of May 16th, 1857, [P. L. 541,] which provides for the appraisement of the grading and paving of streets already done, and the assessment of the

---

[1] Wallace's Estate, 59 Pa. St 401.

[2] Council *v.* Moyamensing, 2 Pa. St. 224; Pray *v.* Northern Liberties, 31 Pa. St. 69.

[3] In Howell *v.* Philadelphia, 38 Pa. St. 471, the work of paving was done September 17th, 1858, and the claim was filed March 16th, 1859. If an affidavit of defence allege that the

work of paving had been completed more than six months before the filing of the claim, judgment will not be entered, for want of a sufficient affidavit of defence. City *v.* Wistar, 2 W. N. C. 370.

[4] Schenley *v.* Commonwealth, 36 Pa. St. 29.

valuation upon properties abutting on the streets in which it has been done in proportion to their frontages, and which, after declaring these assessments to be a lien, enacts that this "lien shall be filed by the city solicitor in the office of the prothonotary of the district court of Allegheny county," within twenty days after such assessments are made. The assessments are then made payable in five annual installments, and it is enacted that in case of default of payment of any of these installments for three months, a *scire facias* may issue. This requirement that the lien shall be filed in twenty days is directory, and the lien was not vitiated by failure to file it until the forty-fourth day.[1]

§ 707. Under acts which make assessments for municipal improvements liens, and declare that they shall continue to be such "until fully paid or satisfied," such assessments are liens of indefinite duration. Such are the acts of April 5th, 1849, [P. L. 341,] April 8th, 1851, [P. L. 372,] concerning Allegheny City,[2] and the act of February 28th, 1866, [P. L. 116,] which transforms Titusville into a city.[3]

§ 708. The act of April 1st, 1870, [P. L. 751,] concerning the assessment of damages on properties benefited by the opening of streets in the city of Allegheny, provides that the assessments "shall be first liens upon the properties assessed, said liens to date from commencement of the improvements for which they were made, and shall, if filed within six months after the completion of said improvements, continue first liens for five years, and be revived by *scire facias*, as other liens." Under this act, filing within six months is necessary only to preserve the first lien. A claim filed two years after the completion of the improvements, will support a *scire facias* and a judgment against the defendant.[4]

---

[1] Magee *v.* Commonwealth, 46 Pa. St. 358.

[2] Schenley *v.* Commonwealth, 36 Pa. St. 29; Allegheny City's Appeal, 41 Pa. St. 60.

[3] Eaton & Cole's Appeal, 83 Pa. St 152.

[4] Lofink *v.* City of Allegheny, 5 W N. C. 46.

§ 709. The act of January 6th, 1864, [P. L. 1131,] concerning streets and sewers in the city of Pittsburgh, directs that the assessments authorized by the act, shall be liens upon the properties assessed, from the commencement of the improvements for which they were made, and shall, "if filed within six months after the completion of said improvements, continue liens for five years," and shall be revived by *scire facias*, as other liens. Under this act, the claim must be filed within six months after the completion of the improvement, not of the approval of the work by the city engineer. Hence, when the contractor stopped paving on December 2d, 1874, and his work was approved the next day, a claim filed June 3d, 1875, was too late; the lien had expired.[1] When the last work was done by the contractor, in completion of his contract to pave a street, on September 5th, 1876, and he subsequently notified the city engineer, who, on inspecting the work, ordered a small amount of curbing to be reset, because it was out of line, and a certain portion of the pavement which had sunk to be brought up to grade, it was necessary to file any lien within six months of September 5th, 1876. Subsequent variations of the work to meet the judgment of the engineer, do not carry down the period of completion of the work to the time when these variations are made.[2]

Duration of Lien as Affected by Judicial Sales.

§ 710. Prior to the act of March 11th, 1846, [P. L. 115,] municipal liens were subject to the same rules, in respect to divestiture, as other liens. One of these rules is, that if a later lien is so fixed that it will not be divested by a judicial sale on a lien posterior to itself, all prior liens will be preserved from divestiture. Thus, a lien for water pipes, laid October 29th, 1829, in the district of Northern Liberties,

---

[1] Kaiser *v.* Weise, 85 Pa. St. 336; Pittsburgh *v.* Knowlson, 92 Pa. St. 116. In the former of these cases, the purchaser of land, who had given a mortgage for the purchase money, paid the assessments the 3d June, 1875. He was not permitted to set off the amount thus paid against the sum due on the mortgage. The payment was voluntary.

[2] Pittsburgh *v.* Knowlson, 92 Pa. St. 116.

began at that date. A mortgage was executed upon the land bound by this lien, June 10th, 1834. The act of April 11th, 1835, preserved the lien of a mortgage from divestiture by a sheriff's sale on a later lien, when the only lien preceding it was that of a municipal assessment. Hence when a sale took place of the aforesaid premises, in 1838 the municipal claim continued undivested.[1]

§ 711. The sixth section of the act of 11th March, 1846 [P. L. 115,] provides that judicial sales shall not divest municipal liens in the city and county of Philadelphia except to the extent to which the proceeds thereof, applicable to these liens, shall be sufficient to satisfy them.[2] One exception has, however, been judicially recognized. If the sale take place on the municipal lien itself, it is said the lien will be divested, whether the proceeds are or are not sufficient to satisfy it. Thus, when a claim for paving amounting to $12.84, was a lien on a certain lot, the proceeds of whose sheriff's sale, $75, were consumed in costs, and in the payment of registered taxes due the city, an *alias levari facias* was set aside, on the ground that the lien was extinct.[3] And when on such a lien, the lot bound by it is sold subject to a mortgage, and the proceeds are not enough to satisfy it, the purchaser at the sheriff's sale cannot, after paying and taking an assignment of it, be permitted to share, in virtue of it, in the proceeds of a second sheriff's sale of the lot, under the mortgage.[4]

§ 712. When, however, the municipality having two liens causes a sheriff's sale under one of them, the proceeds of which are insufficient to pay both, and are applied to the one under which the sale takes place, the other lien is not divested, except to the extent that the funds are applicable to it. On February 16th, 1869, the city of Philadelphia, to

---

[1] Northern Liberties *v.* Swain, 13 Pa. St. 113.

[2] Estate of John Crawford, 38 Leg. Int. 420.

[3] Moyamensing *v.* Shubert, 1 Phila 256.

[4] Brinton *v.* Perry, 1 Phila. 436.

the use of H., filed a claim amounting to $145.06, for paving, against a lot of ground, and on the 12th March, 1869, it filed another similar claim against the same lot, to the use of M., for $144.37. On this latter claim a judgment was recovered, and, under a *levari facias* thereon, the lot was sold for $70. The lien of the first claim was not disturbed, and, on a *scire facias* subsequently issued thereon, a judgment was recovered.[1]

§ 713. When the proceeds of a judicial sale are sufficient to pay the municipal lien, and are applicable thereto, the ordinary rules of divestiture are not affected by the act of March 11th, 1846. Thus, an orphans' court sale for the payment of debts of a decedent, will divest a municipal lien entered in the life-time of the decedent, but subsequently to the recovery of a judgment against him, when the proceeds are enough to pay the lien.[2] When a lot on which were arrears of ground-rent due, and a mortgage dated 1847, was sold on May 3d, 1852, for $3,250, and the proceeds were applied exclusively to the ground-rent arrears and the mortgage, the lien for pipes laid January 4th, 1852, in the district of Kensington, for $131, and, by the act of 3d February, 1824, made a first lien, was divested.[3]

§ 714. It is important to note that the fifth section of the act of April 16th, 1879, [P. L. 24,] provides that taxes, rates and levies, hereafter registered in cities of the first class, shall remain liens on the real estate against which

---

[1] Philadelphia *v.* Meager, 67 Pa. St. 345. City *v.* Lewis, 4 Phila. 135, is scarcely reconcilable with this. For paving done in 1850, a claim was filed on which a sale took place in March, 1856. The proceeds applicable to the lien were only one-third of its amount. A judgment entered by default in 1859, on a claim filed in October, 1858, for state and city taxes for the year 1854, was stricken off, on the ground that the sale in 1856 divested the lien of the taxes of 1854.

[2] Foy's Estate, 2 W. N. C. 188.

[3] Philadelphia *v.* Cooke, 30 Pa. St. 56; Myer *v.* Burns, 4 Phila. 314. Yet the court will not strike off a lien for the removal of nuisances on the ground that a sheriff's sale of the premises has divested it, the money being in court, awaiting distribution. City *v.* Conrad, 1 W. N. C. 104.

they are assessed until fully paid and satisfied, and shall not
be divested by any judicial sale upon any claim, except to
the extent to which distribution shall be made out of the
proceeds of such sale, on account of such taxes, rates and
levies.

§ 715. The acts of April 5th, 1849, [P. L. 341,] of April
8th, 1851, [P. L. 371,] and of 30th May, 1852, [P. L. 204,]
which declare that assessments for the paving of streets in
the city of Allegheny shall be and remain liens "until fully
paid and satisfied,'' does not continue them as liens after a
judicial sale, whose proceeds, applicable to them, are sufficient to satisfy them. Hence, when a lot against which
there was such a lien, was sold by order of the orphans' court
for the payment of the debts of its deceased owner, the proceeds were applied to it.[1]

The Claim.

§ 716. The act of 16th April, 1840, [P. L. 412,] first
made provision for the filing of claims for the purpose of
enforcing municipal assessments within the county of Philadelphia, and, as we have seen, the same was, by the act of
16th April, 1845, [P. L. 488,] made necessary to the continuance of the lien beyond the period of six months from
the doing of the work for which such assessments are made.
The tenth section of the former act requires that the claims
shall set forth " the name of the owner or reputed owner of
the premises against which their[2] claims are filed, and, as
nearly as may be, an accurate description of the real estate
against which the same is filed, and where the said real
estate is situate, which said claim shall be and remain a lien
against the estate, from the time when the debt was contracted." A *scire facias* may issue on this claim, which
shall be served and proceeded upon to judgment and execution, in the same manner as is now provided for by law, for

[1] Allegheny City's Appeal, 41 Pa.
St. 60.

[2] The incorporated districts within
the county of Philadelphia.

mechanics and materialmen, in the act of June 16th, 1836, entitled "An act relating to the lien of mechanics and others, upon buildings." The enumeration of the contents of the claim prescribed by the act of 16th April, 1840, is not exclusive of the necessity of all others.[1] The bill of particulars annexed, is a part of the claim,[2] and it is not necessary that the claim should refer to the acts of assembly which authorize the paving for which it is filed, and make the cost thereof a lien.[3] In Philadelphia the claim must be filed in the name of the city. The act of 13th May, 1856, [P. L. 570,] authorizes the councils of the city of Philadelphia to cleanse the docks of the Delaware and Schuylkill rivers, to apportion the expense of the same upon adjacent wharves, and to collect the assessments by filing liens. Though this power was transferred to the port wardens of Philadelphia, by the act of May 20th, 1864, [P. L. 906,] and the city solicitor was directed to file the lien, the claim properly purports to be that of the city of Philadelphia, and not of the port wardens.[4]

Averment of Time.

§ 717. The time when the work is done for which the lien is asserted, should be stated in the claim. To describe paving as done "within six months last past" is insufficient.[5] When the claim purports to be "for work done and material furnished," charged as follows, "1858, March 22d, to 16 feet of iron pipe, at 75 cents, laid on the north side of Jefferson street, in front of above property," the date is construed as that of the doing of the work.[6] Objection to a claim for

[1] Philadelphia v. Sutter, 30 Pa. St. 53.

[2] Kennedy v. Board of Health, 2 Pa. St. 366.

[3] Delaney v. Gault, 30 Pa. St. 63.

[4] Easby v. Philadelphia, 67 Pa. St. 337. The act of 11th March, 1846, [P. L. 114,] makes the claim *prima facie* evidence of all matters contained therein. Watson v. City of Philadel-

phia, 93 Pa. St. 111; Thomas v. Northern Liberties, 13 Pa. St. 117; City v. Burgin, 50 Pa. St. 539; Philadelphia v. Brooke, 81 Pa. St. 23; Philadelphia v. Esau, 32 Leg. Int. 239; Philadelphia v. Collom, 1 W. N. C. 525.

[5] Philadelphia v. Sutter, 30 Pa. St. 53.

[6] City v. Wood, 4 Phila. 156.

want of dates, must be taken by demurrer or motion to
strike off. It is waived by pleading to the *scire facias*.[1]

Claims for Removal of Nuisances

§ 718. Claims for the removal of nuisances are not regulated by the mechanics' lien act of 16th June, 1836, but by
the mechanics' lien law in operation before that date. Such
a claim, under the act of 29th January, 1818, [7 Sm. L. 24,]
and 7th April, 1830, [P. L. 348,] filed October 19th, 1841, need
no further specify the date of doing the work, than by stating
generally that it was done within six months preceding the
filing of the claim.[2] A claim filed by the board of health,
for removing a nuisance, "by filling a pond with dirt and
leveling the same, in doing which they, within six months
last past, incurred and paid" $526.50, sufficiently sets forth
the time.[3] So does one which states the expenses to have
been incurred by the plaintiff on the 30th June, 1849, for
causing certain filth to be carried off the premises, that date
being within six months previous to the filing of the claim.[4]

Kind of Work.

§ 719. A statement of the kind of work for which the lien
is asserted, should be made in the claim. It should appear
whether the work was grading or paving, and whether, if
paving, it was of a street or of a footwalk.[5] A claim for
"16 feet of conduit gas," under a law which gave the district
of Moyamensing the authority to assess the expense of gas
pipes on lots abutting on the streets into which they were
introduced, was fatally defective, and, at the instance of one
who purchased *bona fide* the lot against which it was filed,
after the filing thereof, a judgment subsequently recovered
on the claim, and the claim itself, were stricken off.[6]

[1] Howell *v.* Philadelphia, 38 Pa. St.
471.

[2] Kennedy *v.* Board of Health, 2
Pa. St. 366.

[3] Philadelphia *v.* Gratz Land Co.,
38 Pa. St. 359.

[4] Hubert *v.* Board of Health, 1
Phila. 280.

[5] Philadelphia *v.* Sutter, 30 Pa. St.
53

[6] Moyamensing *v.* Flanigan, 3
Phila. 458.

Description of Premises.

§ 720. Though the act of 16th April, 1840, requires the claim to give, "as nearly as may be, an accurate description of the real estate," certainty to a common intent is all that is necessary, and when the premises are described as containing forty-seven feet in front, when in fact they are only forty, the effect will be simply to reduce the amount of the claim proportionately, not to invalidate it altogether.[1] A claim describing property as six feet wider than it really is, will be amended on rule.[2]

Site of Improvement.

§ 721. When the claim describes the lot against which it is filed, as extending from one street to another, it must state distinctly on which of these streets the paving was done.[3] By mistake of the district surveyor, the claim purported to be against property situate on the east side of Germantown avenue, sixty-nine feet five inches south of Venango street, instead of south of Ontario street. There being no change of ownership since the filing of the lien, leave was given to amend, "saving all intermediate rights."[4]

Name of Owner.

§ 722. The name of the owner or reputed owner of the premises charged is required simply as an element in the description thereof. The name of the real owner need not appear in the claim. Hence, if the owner of an adjoining tract is, by mistake, given in the claim as the owner of the tract against which it is filed, the lien will not be vitiated, to such extent at least as to make void a sheriff's sale of the tract, on a judgment recovered on the claim.[5] A claim filed against "the heirs of John Coates, deceased, owner or reputed owner, or whoever may be the owner," is valid.[6] The act of

[1] Thomas v. Northern Liberties, 13 Pa. St. 117.

[2] City v. Uber, 1 W. N. C. 160.

[3] Philadelphia v. Sutter, 30 Pa. St. 53.

[4] City v. Wagner, 9 W. N. C. 511.

[5] Delaney v. Gault, 30 Pa. St. 63.

[6] Northern Liberties v. Coates' Heirs, 15 Pa. St. 245; Wistar v. Philadelphia, 86 Pa St. 215; City v. Cooke, 30 Pa. St. 56. See Northern Liberties v. Myers, 2 Parsons 239.

22d April, 1846, directs that property subject to taxation for state or county purposes, may, so long as it shall belong to the estate of such deceased person, be taxed in the name of the deceased owner, or in that of his executor or administrator, or his heirs generally, or in the name of one of them. All taxes thus assessed are declared to be legal. Under this act a claim may be filed against heirs generally.[1] The necessary constituents of the claim which must be filed for the liens of other municipalities than Philadelphia, must be ascertained by reference to the various laws which create such liens.

Under Act of 6th January, 1864.

§ 723. The act of January 6th, 1864, [P. L. 1131,] which empowers the councils of Pittsburgh to cause streets to be paved, directs that the costs shall be assessed upon the properties abutting upon them, in proportion to their frontages. When the amount for which each lot is liable shall be ascertained, it is made the duty of the city regulator to give notice to the owner thereof to pay it in thirty days. If payment is not made in that time, the assessments are to be handed to the city solicitor, with the plan and description of each lot, and he must file a claim. It follows that the claim thus prepared by the city solicitor need contain nothing more than the facts required by this act to be furnished to him. It need not indicate whether the paving and curbing were of the street or of the sidewalk, when in fact they were of the street, under the act of 1864, and not of the sidewalks, provision for which is made by a different act, that of April 18th, 1857, [P. L. 240.][2]

Under Act of 5th April, 1849

§ 724. The act of April 5th, 1849, [P. L. 341,] and that of April 8th, 1851, [P. L. 372,] authorize the councils of

---

[1] Wistar v. Philadelphia, 86 Pa. St. 215; Northern Liberties v. Coates' Heirs, 15 Pa. St. 245.

[2] Pittsburgh v. Cluley, 66 Pa. St. 449.

Allegheny City to grade and pave streets, and make the assessments upon abutting properties for the expense, a lien thereon. The act of 30th March, 1852, [P. L. 204,] prescribes a mode of enforcing the payment of these liens, minutely describing the form and contents of the claim to be filed. Hence, it is unnecessary that such claim should contain anything further, and, in particular, that it should allege that the work was done within six months before the filing thereof, or that it should distinguish between the grading and curbing of the cartway and of the footway. The requirement that the property charged with the assessment should be described with sufficient certainty to identify it, is met by setting forth the bounds of the property on three sides by well-known streets, and on the fourth side by a street not yet opened along the premises, but which, if extended from the point to which it is already opened, would constitute the boundary of the premises on the fourth side.[1]

Registration Under Act of 23d May, 1874.

§ 725. Under the municipal corporations act of May 23d, 1874, assessments may be made on properties upon streets into which water pipes are introduced, for the cost thereof, in proportion to the number of feet front. If not paid in a prescribed time these assessments are to be registered, but no particular form of registration is prescribed. It must, however, contain at least a brief description, including the location, of the property assessed, corresponding with that which the clerk of the department is required to make, giving the name of the owner or reputed owner, the amount of the assessment, its date, and what it is for. It need not conform strictly to all the requisites of a mechanics' lien. The name of the contractor or materialman need not be given, and a bill of particulars is unnecessary. Under this

---

[1] Schenley v. Commonwealth, 36 Pa. St. 29. The claim may, under these acts be filed at any time.

act, a registered claim, which did not give any description of the property upon which the lien existed, was properly stricken off.[1]

§ 726. The act of April 1st, 1870, [P. L. 751,] relative to streets in the city of Allegheny, provides that when the owner of a lot is unknown, the lien shall be filed against "unknown owner." Under this act, no inquiry can be made whether the owner was in fact unknown, in an ejectment between the purchaser at a sheriff's sale, under a judgment recovered on such a claim, and the former owner.[2]

The Scire Facias.

§ 727. The *scire facias* is a substitute for a declaration.[3] In form, it need not demand that cause shall be shown why execution should not be had, but it may summon the defendant to show cause why the lien should not be revived and continued.[4] When a single claim lawfully apportions itself upon ten distinct blocks of buildings, a *scire facias* properly issues against each.[5] Under the act of 16th April, 1845, [P. L. 488,] municipal liens in Philadelphia continue for only six months from the doing of the work, unless a claim is filed within six months thereafter. When such claim is filed, the lien is protracted for five years from the date of the filing, but no further, unless a *scire facias* issues within that time. A *scire facias* issued on January 10th, 1877, on a claim filed January 10th, 1872, is in time.[6] Under several acts pertaining to liens in other municipalities than Philadelphia, a *scire facias* is simply an instrument of enforcing, not of perpetuating, the lien, and it may issue at any time. The act of May 16th, 1857, [P. L. 541,] is an instance.[7] The act of 11th March, 1846, [P. L. 115,] provides that the

---

[1] Allentown *v.* Hower, 93 Pa. St. 332. Unless application is duly made to amend it.

[2] Emrick *v.* Dicken, 92 Pa. St. 78; White *v.* Ballantine, 38 Leg. Int. 356.

[3] City *v.* Scott, 8 W. N. C. 405.

[4] City *v.* Coulston, 8 W. N. C. 568.

[5] Schenley *v.* Commonwealth, 36 Pa. St. 29.

[6] City *v.* Scott, 8 W. N. C. 405.

[7] Magee *v* Commonwealth, 46 Pa. St. 358.

scire facias issued on municipal claims in the city of Philadelphia, shall be served "by posting a true and attested copy of the writ on a conspicuous part of the premises therein described, and by publishing a brief notice thereof in a daily newspaper in said county, twice a week for two weeks before the return day." Since the enforcement of a municipal lien is a proceeding *in rem*, every essential requisite of the act, in regard to the mode of service of the *scire facias*, must be complied with, and the sheriff's return must show such compliance by specific statement of what he did in making the service.[1] A return that a copy of the writ was posted "on the premises," instead of "on a conspicuous part" thereof, is insufficient.[1] If the return shows a posting of the copy of the writ within two weeks of the return day, the service is invalid.[2] So is it when the return fails to state explicitly that the advertisement twice a week for two weeks in a daily paper, took place before the return day of the writ.[1]

§ 728. The act of 29th March, 1867, [P. L. 600,] directs that when real estate in Philadelphia is registered in the name of the real owner, the *scire facias* must be served on him as in case of a summons. Under this act, a sheriff's return conformable to the act of 11th March, 1846, is vicious as respects property so registered, and a judgment taken by default, and a *levari facias* thereon, will be set aside.[3] A sheriff's sale on such a judgment will confer no title to the purchaser.[4] In other cases of irregularity of service of the *scire facias*, the title of the purchaser will not be impaired by this irregularity, but the defendant may, in an ejectment, avail himself of any substantial defence which he could have urged had due service of the *scire facias* been made.[5] The

---

[1] Wistar *v.* Philadelphia, 86 Pa. St. 215; Simons *v.* Kern, 92 Pa. St. 455.

[2] Wistar *v.* Philadelphia, 86 Pa. St. 215; City *v.* Olive Cemetery, 6 W. N. C. 238.

[3] City *v.* Katz, 8 W. N. C. 502.

[4] Simons *v.* Kern, 92 Pa. St. 455.

[5] Delaney *v.* Gault, 30 Pa. St. 63. Comp. Emrick *v.* Dicken, 92 Pa. St. 78, where a similar decision is made,

defectiveness of a sheriff's service of the writ, or of his return of such service, is waived, if the defendant appears and defends.[1]

Discharge of Lien.

§ 729. The act of 21st February, 1862, [P. L. 44,] provides that after a claim is filed in Philadelphia for a municipal assessment, the owner of the premises charged may give notice in writing to the counsel of record, or to the person, if any, to whose use the claim is filed; or, there being no such counsel or use-plaintiff, to the solicitor of the city, requiring him to issue a writ of *scire facias* to the next monthly return day, which shall be at least fifteen days from the date of said notice. If the writ shall not be issued, the court shall, on motion and due proof of such notice, strike the claim from the record. When a *sci. fa.* has issued in pursuance of such a notice, the plaintiff cannot suffer a voluntary non-suit if the defendant objects,[2] and if, the defendant not objecting, a voluntary non-suit is suffered, the lien is utterly gone.[3] The act just cited also provides that the person entitled to defend against a municipal claim may, at any time after the same is filed, pay the amount thereof, with interest and costs, into court, to abide the event of the proceedings thereon; thereupon the lien upon the land ceases, and must be stricken from the judgment index. If the plaintiff suffers a voluntary non-suit on the trial of the *sci. fa.*, issued in pursuance of notice to issue the same from the owner of the land, the lien is lost both on the land and on the money paid into court, which, on rule, will be returned to the defendant.[4]

---

in regard to defective service of the *scire facias*, under the act of May 20th, 1871, [P. L. 1034,] concerning Allegheny.

[1] City of Philadelphia *v.* Olive Cemetery, 6 W. N. C. 238. The return will not then be set aside.

[2] City *v.* Sanger, 8 W. N. C. 151.

[3] City of Philadelphia *v.* McGarry, 11 W. N. C. 168.

[4] *Ibid.*

CHAPTER XXXVI.

LIEN OF BAILEE.

Kinds of Bailment.

§ 730. Chattels are bailed for several purposes, of which it is material to notice here the following: (1) The modification of their physical qualities by the labor and skill of the bailee; (2) the change of their place; (3) their conservation at a given place, subject to the call of the owner. If the thing bailed for this last purpose be a living animal, there are, incident to its conservation, feeding, tending, etc. In bailments of all these kinds the bailee has a right to detain the thing bailed from its owner until he is compensated for his labor, his skill and his property consumed in executing the duties assumed by him towards it.

§ 731. Instances of the first class are when timber is delivered to another, that he may saw it into boards;[1] or tobacco, that he may manufacture it into cigars;[2] or lumber, to be made into doors;[3] or a horse to a farrier, to be shod;[4] or hides to a tanner, to be tanned into leather;[5] or a horse to a veterinary surgeon, to be cured of a disease,[6] or to be groomed.[7] The stereotyper has the right to detain the plates of a book which he has been employed to stereotype;[8] a jeweler, the gem he has engraved; a ship carpenter, the ship he has repaired; a tailor, the cloth he has made into clothes.[9]

[1] Pierce v. Sweet, 33 Pa. St. 151; Cross & Bro. v. Knickerbocker, 8 Phila. 496; Bean v. Bolton, 3 Phila. 87; Ritter v. Gates, 1 Am. L. Reg. 119.

[2] Matthias v. Sellers, 86 Pa. St. 486.

[3] McIntyre v. Carver, 2 W. & S. 392.

[4] Hoover v. Epler, 52 Pa. St. 522.

[5] Lee v. Gould, 47 Pa. St. 398.

[6] Rodgers v. Grothe, 58 Pa. St. 414; Cummings v. Gann, 52 Pa. St. 484.

[7] Hoover v. Epler, 52 Pa. St. 522.

[8] Moss v. Mogridge, 1 Phila. 121.

[9] Matthias v. Sellers, 86 Pa. St. 486, dicta.

§ 732. To the second class belongs the case of the common carrier, for the cost of transportation,[1] or of one who has been employed to float rafts of lumber down the Susquehanna.[2]

§ 733. To the third class belong deposits, as when goods are left with a warehouseman for safe keeping,[3] or when a horse is left with a veterinary surgeon, who feeds him,[4] or with a livery stable keeper,[5] or a groom,[6] or when cattle are put for agistment on the farm of another.[7]

§ 734. The bailee's lien is not confined, therefore, to cases where the bailee is compelled by law to receive the goods, and bestow any particular service upon them, e. g., a common carrier.[8] A bailment to which the right of detention until charges are paid is incident, is not inconsistent with a power in the bailee to sell the thing bailed. A. delivered tobacco to B. at specified prices, to be made into cigars of certain brands. Fixed prices, according to quality, were to be allowed B. for the manufacture, and advances were to be made to him for wages and for the internal revenue stamps. B. could sell at prices agreed upon, but, until sale, A. had the power to demand delivery to himself. Under this contract, and one year after it was entered upon, B. had ninety thousand cigars, valued at $2,820, in his possession. A.'s balance against B. was $2,585.40. If the cigars had been removed, A. would have been indebted to B. in $234.60, besides an item of $54.65. B. had a lien on the cigars for the money thus due him.[9]

§ 735. A lien similar to a bailee's lien exists in a few special cases, which may not be regarded as bailments. A.,

[1] Steinman v. Wilkins, 7 W. & S. 466; Lake Shore and M. S. Railway Co. v. Ellsey, 85 Pa. St. 283; Leonard's Exr. v. Winslow, 2 Grant 139.

[2] Davis v. Bigler, 62 Pa. St. 242.

[3] Steinman v. Wilkins, 7 W. & S. 466.

[4] Rodgers v. Grothe, 58 Pa. St. 414; Cummings v. Gann, 52 Pa. St. 484.

[5] Young v. Kimball, 23 Pa. St. 193; Buckner v. Croissant, 3 Phila. 219.

[6] Hoover v. Epler, 52 Pa. St 522.

[7] Magee v. Beirne, 39 Pa. St. 50.

[8] McIntyre v. Carver, 2 W. & S. 392; Matthias v. Sellers, 86 Pa. St. 486.

[9] Matthias v. Sellers, 86 Pa. St. 486.

at B.'s instance, takes out a policy of insurance on B.'s vessel, for B.'s benefit, paying the premium. He has a lien on the policy so long as he retains possession of it, and on the insurance money, in case the vessel is lost, which will be valid against an assignment of the policy by B. to others.[1]

Hotel Keepers.

§ 736. By the fourth section of the act of May 7th, 1855, [P. L. 479,] the proprietors of hotels, inns and boarding houses have a right to detain the goods and baggage of any sojourner or boarder, for the price of not more than two weeks' board. The first section of the act of April 7th, 1807, [4 Sm. L. 403,] gives to livery stable keepers and inn keepers a lien on every horse kept in their stables for the expense of their keep.

Consignee.

§ 737. When the owner of goods consigns them to another to sell on his account, the consignee has a right to detain them until his advances thereon, his charges of freight and storage therefor,[2] together with the commissions he would have been entitled to receive if a sale had been effected,[3] have been paid. But, when A. engages B. to procure a purchaser of iron, agreeing to pay B. a commission for this service and for collecting the price, but the iron is not to be shipped to B., and by him to the purchaser, but directly from A. to the purchaser, B. is not a factor or commission merchant, having either possession or a right of possession of the iron, and when he receives the proceeds of any part of the iron, he can not retain out of them (as against one to whom A. has assigned them with notice to B. before they came to B.'s hands) the commissions arising either from the other parts of the quantity sold, or from this particular installment.[4]

[1] Cranston v. Philadelphia Ins. Co., 5 Binn. 538.

[2] Macky v. Dillinger, 73 Pa. St. 85.

[3] Smedley v. Williams, 1 Parsons 359.

[4] Shoener v. Cabeen, 11 W. N. C. 222.

The Finder of Lost Articles.

§ 738. The finder of lost articles has no lien for expenses gratuitously incurred in taking care of them.[1] Hence, when a raft of lumber floating down the Susquehanna, without the knowledge of the owner, lodged on an island, the owner of the island had no lien upon it for his trouble and expense in securing it.[2] But, if the loser offers a reward to one finding and returning the lost article, as an inducement to vigilance and industry, the finder has a lien on the thing found until the reward is tendered to him.[3] The same is true, respecting property that has been stolen. One who finds it has a lien for the reward offered.[4]

Against Whom Valid.

§ 739. The lien is valid, not only against the owner by whom the bailment was made, but also against the owner's vendee who has no actual notice of the lien, the bailee not having parted with the possession of the thing,[5] and against a sheriff's vendee under an execution against the owner.[6]

When the Lien does not Arise.

§ 740. In the classes of bailments referred to above, the lien arises from the bailment itself. An express agreement that it shall exist is unnecessary.[7] An express agreement that it shall not exist, or any stipulation which is incompatible with it, will, however, preclude its existence.[8] A tanner, to whom hides were delivered to be tanned, agreed that, on completion of the process, they should be returned to the owner, and that he would await payment until the owner had succeeded in selling them. He had no right to detain the leather from the owner.[9] If a cigarmaker, to whom a tobacco merchant delivered tobacco to be made into

---

[1] Etter v. Edwards, 4 W. 63.

[2] Ibid.; Forster v. Juniata Bridge Co., 16 Pa. St. 393.

[3] Cummings v. Gann, 52 Pa. St. 484.

[4] Ibid.

[5] Swift v. Morrison, 2 W. N. C. 699.

[6] Pierce v. Sweet, 33 Pa. St. 151; Young v. Kimball, 23 Pa. St. 193.

[7] Pierce v. Sweet, 33 Pa. St. 151.

[8] Matthias v. Sellers, 86 Pa. St. 486.

[9] Lee v. Gould, 47 Pa. St. 398.

cigars, agreed that when the cigars were made the merchant should take them away, and that afterwards a settlement should be made between them, he had no lien on the cigars.[1] Nor had a sawyer, who agreed that he should be paid only after he had redelivered the lumber to the owner, and the latter had sold it.[2]

§ 741. When a livery stable keeper undertook to keep horses which were employed in carrying the mails, there was an implied agreement that the horses might be taken out from day to day for the performance of this service, but, on the return of the horses, the lien re-attached for all the charges incurred under the contract. A., a contractor for the carriage of the mails, sublet the contract to B., who made arrangement with the livery stable keeper for room for two teams, and for grain and hay, at a certain price per week. The two teams were kept in the stable for some time, when they were sold on execution against B. After this sale A. made a conditional purchase of one of the teams, for the purpose of carrying the mails under his original contract, and hired B. as his driver. The team was now occasionally kept at the livery stable. The stable keeper's lien re-attached for the charges of the keep of the team before the sale in execution, as well as afterwards.[3]

For Whom the Lien Does Not Exist.

§ 742. Since the right of detention, termed a lien, springs from the previous independent possession of the person in whose favor it arises, it can be predicated only of those who have such independent possession. The possession of goods of their employer by a mere servant, laborer or journeyman, is simply that of their employer, and, consequently, no lien can arise in their favor. They have no other security for their wages than the personal responsibility of their employer

[1] Matthias v. Sellers, 86 Pa. St. 486.

[2] Cross v. Knickerbocker, 8 Phila. 496.

[3] Young v. Kimball, 23 Pa. St. 193.

on the contract of hiring, unless they have expressly stipulated for it.[1] Hence, when A. agreed with the owner of a horse to take charge of it for six months for the compensation of $100, to tend it in the best manner, and to obey the owner's instructions, he had, as a mere servant, no lien on the horse for the wages;[2] nor had a laborer employed to dig ore a lien upon the ore.[3]

§ 743. An agreement for continued possession of and a lien upon timber, by one who was employed to cut it and haul it to a point convenient of access from a mill of the employer, gave him a lien on the timber there hauled and deposited, valid against a vendee of the employer, who had no actual notice of the lien.[4]

§ 744. When A., employed to do the carpenter work of a house, which was in course of erection, engaged B. to make thirty-four panel doors for it, and B., having a shop of his own, took there lumber belonging to the owner of the house, delivered to him by A., and there manufactured it into doors, the agreed compensation being fifty per cent. of the regular carpenter prices, B. was not a mere employe of A., and had a lien on the doors till he was paid.[5] So, when A., the owner of a saw mill, contracted with B. to take possession of it, make necessary repairs, and manufacture lumber for A. at $1.50 per thousand feet, retaining enough lumber in his possession to make him secure, B. had an independent possession of the lumber manufactured, and a lien on it.[6]

For What the Lien Exists.

§ 745. The lien upon the bailed property exists to secure the compensation of the bailee for service with respect to it, although the amount of compensation was fixed by an express agreement.[7] When service is performed by the bailee on

---

[1] McIntyre v. Carver, 2 W. & S. 392.
[2] Hoover v. Epler, 52 Pa. St. 522.
[3] Ritter v. Gates, 1 Am. L. Reg. 119.
[4] Swift v. Morrison, 2 W. N. C. 699.
[5] McIntyre v Carver, 2 W. & S. 392.
[6] Pierce v. Sweet, 33 Pa. St. 151.
[7] McIntyre v. Carver, 2 W. & S. 392;
Matthias v. Sellers, 86 Pa. St. 486.

distinct chattels under disconnected contracts, one of these chattels may not be detained by him to compel compensation for the service rendered to or about the other.[1] A carrier has no lien on commodities for freights become due on other commodities previously transported by him under independent contracts,[2] nor a warehouseman on certain goods for the storage of other goods under a separate contract.[3] But when a single contract contemplates service to be rendered to several articles, the lien exists upon every one of these articles for the entire compensation due under the contract. Thus, a warehouseman may surrender a part of a lot of goods stored in his warehouse at the same time by the same owner, and assert his lien for the storage of all, on the remainder.[4] Under a single contract to saw the timber cut from A.'s land, B. cut two hundred thousand feet of lumber, and delivered to A. all of it save sixty-eight thousand feet. He had a right to retain this until his charges for sawing the entire amount were paid.[5] When several horses of the same owner were kept at a livery stable under one arrangement, one of these horses could be detained for the keep of all or any under that arrangement.[6] Under a contract between A. and B. for the manufacture by B. of A.'s tobacco into cigars, at a certain rate of compensation, B. could deliver some of the cigars to A., and retain the remainder until all the compensation agreed upon was paid.[7]

§ 746. The principle here considered does not conflict with the rules in regard to appropriation of payments. Thus, when A. sawed shingles for B., under one contract, and under a distinct but synchronous contract sawed boards for B., and permitted the shingles to be withdrawn from his possession, the

[1] Pierce v. Sweet, 33 Pa. St. 151.

[2] Leonard's Exr. v. Winslow, 2 Grant 139.

[3] Steinman v. Wilkins, 7 W. & S. 466.

[4] Ibid.

[5] Cross v. Knickerbocker, 8 Phila. 496.

[6] Young v. Kimball, 23 Pa. St. 193.

[7] Matthias v. Sellers, 86 Pa. St. 486.

law, in the absence of an appropriation of payments by B.,
applied payments made by him to the shingles, so as to keep
alive A.'s claim for compensation for sawing the boards, upon
which he could assert a lien for it.[1]

By Whom the Bailment May be Made.

§ 747. The owner of the chattel may of course subject it
a lien by bailing it. But he may do this either directly or
through the agency of another. When he authorizes another
to make a bailment, the bailee has the same lien that would
have arisen had he himself made it. The owner of a lot of
ground on which, he was erecting a house, employed A. to
do the carpenter work for it. A. delivered to B. some of
the owner's lumber to be made into panel doors. B. had a
lien on the doors for his charges.[2] If a horse is left by its
owner with A. to take care of it, A. has the implied right to
employ a farrier to shoe it, and the farrier will have a lien
on the horse until his labor is paid for.[3]

§ 748. The real owner may be estopped from denying the
authority of one whom he permits to exercise apparent ownership, as against a bailee to whom the latter has delivered the
chattels. Thus, the owner of timber land contracted with
A. to cut and haul the timber to his mill, saw it, and pile it
beside a railroad, at a certain price per thousand feet. A.
employed B., who was ignorant that he was not the owner
of the lumber, to do the sawing. B. had a right to detain
the lumber from the real owner, as well as from A.[4]

§ 749. This is the principle of the factors' act of April 14th,
1834, [P. L. 375,] which provides that when any person
entrusted with merchandise with authority to sell or consign
the same, shall ship it to another person, such person shall
have a lien thereon, for any moneys advanced on the faith
of such consignment, provided he had no notice of the real

[1] Pierce v. Sweet, 33 Pa. St. 151.
[2] McIntyre v. Carver, 2 W. & S. 392.
[3] Hoover v. Epler, 52 Pa. St. 522.
[4] Cross v. Knickerbocker, 8 Phila. 496.

ownership, before making his advances. It also provides that if such merchandise is pledged by the person entrusted therewith as security for moneys advanced, the pledgee shall have the same right to retain possession as he would were the pledgeor the real owner.

§ 750. If a person entrusted with merchandise, with authority to sell, shall pledge it for a pre-existing debt, to one who is without notice of the real ownership, or if he shall pledge it for a new debt, to one who has such notice, in such case the pledgee acquires the rights of the pledgeor, and no more.[1] Hence, he cannot detain the goods until a loan made by him to the person entrusted with them, on a pledge of them by such person, (he having notice that such person was not the real owner,) is repaid.[1]

The Bailee's Right to Sell.

§ 751. At common law, the bailee's lien was, with an exception to be noticed below, a mere right of detention. He had no authority to sell the chattel for the purpose of realizing his demand.[2] Hence, a sawyer could not sell lumber on which he had a charge for sawing, notwithstanding a custom which was alleged to authorize such sale.[3] A veterinary surgeon could not sell a horse committed to his care, for the price of medicine, care and feed.[4]

§ 752. The act of December 14th, 1863, [P. L. 1864, p. 1127,] provides that in all cases where commission merchants, factors, common carriers or other persons have a lien on any goods, wares, merchandise or other property, on account of costs and expenses of carriage, storage or labor bestowed thereon, if the owner shall neglect to pay such costs and expenses for sixty days after demand made personally on such owner or consignee, such goods, etc., may be exposed to sale, or so much thereof as shall be necessary to discharge

---

[1] Mackey v. Dillinger, 73 Pa. St. 85.
[2] Rodgers v. Grothe, 58 Pa. St. 414.
[3] Bean v. Bolton, 3 Phila. 87.
[4] Rodgers v. Grothe, 58 Pa. St. 414.

the lien, together with the costs of sale and advertising. Notice of the sale must be published for three successive weeks in a newspaper in the county, and by six handbills put up in the most public and conspicuous places in the vicinity of the depot where the goods are. When such notice is impracticable, the judge of the court of common pleas of the city or county where the goods are, may make an order authorizing the sale of such goods, upon such terms as to notice as the nature of the case admits of. If the goods are perishable, they may be sold on the order of a justice of the peace. The surplus of the proceeds of sale, after paying the lien charges, the costs of the sale and advertising, shall be held subject to the order of the owner.[1]

§ 753. The act of April 7th, 1807, [4 Sm. L. 403,] conferring on all livery stable keepers and inn keepers a lien on every horse delivered to them to be kept in their stables, for the expense of such keep, empowers them, when such expenses amount to $30 and remain unpaid for fifteen days after demand made on the owner in person, or in case of his removal from the place where such inn or livery stable is kept, for ten days after notice of the amount due and demand of payment in writing left at his last place of abode, to sell the horses at public sale.

§ 754. The act of May 7th, 1855, [P. L. 480,] gives every proprietor of any hotel, inn or boarding house, the right to detain the goods and baggage of a sojourner or boarder for his debt for boarding or lodging for a period not greater than two weeks. Provision is also made for a sale thereof, on a warrant of an alderman or justice of the peace to a constable, to expose the same to public sale, after at least ten days' notice by notices put up in three or

---

[1] Under this act, a sale, though on account of irregularity it does not divest the title of the owner, will transfer to the vendee the right of detention until the bailee's charges are paid. Rodgers v. Grothe, 58 Pa. St. 414.

more public places in the ward of the city or borough, or in the township where such inn, hotel or boarding house is situate.

§ 755. A consignee has a right, after demand on the consignor for re-imbursement for all advances, and protection from all liability assumed by him, to sell the goods consigned, unless he has agreed to the contrary.[1] If, by agreement, the sale is to be made only on certain terms, the consignee has no authority to depart from them. Thus, when A., the consignor, informed B., the consignee, by letter, that he would send from New Orleans a cargo of molasses to Philadelphia, and requested B. to have it insured, and five days afterwards wrote again, desiring B., on the arrival of the cargo, if a fair profit could not be made, to put it in store, B. had no authority to sell it, except on the condition of making a fair profit, notwithstanding that he had gone to the expense of securing the insurance, and of paying freights and primage, and had accepted a draft for $1,975 on A.'s account.[2] After the goods have been received by a consignee, and advances made thereon by him, the consignor cannot impose any new terms on the consignee, who is simply bound to use due diligence and skill in selling the goods at the best rates the market affords, in the manner required by the established usages of trade.[3]

What Determines the Lien.

§ 756. The lien of the bailee is a right of detention. When, therefore, he voluntarily surrenders the property to which the lien attaches, to its owner, the lien ceases.[4] So was it, when a sawyer gave up to the owner of the lumber the shingles into which he had manufactured it,[5] or when

[1] Porter v. Patterson, 15 Pa. St. 229.
[2] Ibid.
[3] Smedley v. Williams, 1 Parsons 359.
[4] Pierce v. Sweet, 33 Pa. St. 151;

Rodgers v. Grothe, 58 Pa. St. 414; Swift v. Morrison, 2 W. N. C. 699.
[5] Pierce v. Sweet, 33 Pa. St. 151; Swift v. Morrison, 2 W. N. C. 699.

one who had received cattle for agistment, delivered them to their owner.[1] If A. pays the premium for a policy of insurance on B.'s vessel, and the policy is made out in B.'s name, A., by parting with the policy, loses his lien on it or on the money payable upon it.[2] A., owner of a saw mill and timber land, employed B. to cut the timber into logs, and deliver them on a creek near the mill, but on land of a stranger, the understanding being that the logs should remain there in the control of B. until his expenses were paid. The deposit of logs at the designated place was not such a delivery of them by B. as destroyed his lien, as against either A. or a vendee of A. without actual notice of B.'s right.[3]

757. If the bailee, either under the pretence of being its owner, or for the purpose of enforcing his lien, sells the bailed chattel or pledges it for his own debt, he puts an end to his possession and his lien.[4] Thus, when A., who was employed by B., to float lumber in rafts down the Susquehanna, sold them, as if they were his own, to C., it was not necessary that B., before bringing replevin to recover possession, should tender the amount due to A. for floating the lumber.[5] So, when a sawyer, after sawing the lumber of another, sends it to a distant market for sale, without notice to the owner, or demand for his charges, under a pretence that a custom of the trade authorizes such a step, neither the sawyer nor his vendee can detain the lumber for the charges. Such a custom is vicious.[6]

§ 758. The bailee has not, at common law, the right to transfer the thing bailed, together with his claim, to another. Such transfer could not convey to the transferee the lien of the bailee. Under the act of 14th December, 1863, [P. L.

---

[1] Magee v. Beirne, 39 Pa. St. 50.

[2] Cranston v. Philadelphia Ins. Co., 5 Binn. 538.

[3] Swift v. Morrison, 2 W. N. C. 699.

[4] Davis v. Bigler, 62 Pa. St. 242; Rodgers v. Grothe, 58 Pa. St. 414.

[5] Davis v. Bigler, 62 Pa. St. 242. Comp. Rodgers v. Grothe, 58 Pa. St. 414.

[6] Bean v. Bolton 3 Phila. 87.

1864, p. 1127,] however, which confers on bailees the right to sell, in a specified manner, the thing bailed, as a means of recovering their charges, the sale, though ineffectual to divest the title of the owner, on account of non-compliance with the statute, will transfer to the purchaser the original lien rights of the bailee.[1] If the bailee delivers possession of the thing to another for a purpose contemplated in the original bailment, his lien is not affected. Thus, when A., to whose care a horse had been put, delivers it to a farrier that it may be shod, he does not lose his lien, and, paying the farrier's charges, A. will be subrogated to his lien as such.[2] The transferee, asserting a lien for his own services, or for the services of the transferrer, must show that the transfer was consistent with the intention of the owner, in making the original bailment.[3]

§ 759. On a tender of the lawful charges of the bailee, or if the bailee prevent a tender by insisting that he holds the chattel for a demand for which he has no legal right to detain it, the lien ceases.[4] A railroad company, transporting stoves, determines its lien for freight by surrendering them to the consignee and accepting payment of the freight from him, although the consignor has instructed the company that they are not to be delivered till further orders, the consignee being ignorant, however, of such a restriction on the railroad's right of delivery.[5]

§ 760. An absolute release of his debt, by the bailee, would extinguish his lien; but a mere release from personal liability, reserving to the bailee his lien on the chattel bailed, has no such result.[6] That the bailee was indebted to the bailor when the former rendered his service, does not preclude his acquiring a lien on the chattel bailed, unless it was agreed

[1] Rodgers v. Grothe, 58 Pa. St. 414.
[2] Hoover v. Epler, 52 Pa. St. 522.
[3] Bean v. Bolton, 8 Phila. 87.
[4] Mackey v. Dellinger, 78 Pa. St. 85.
[5] Lake Shore, etc., R. R. Co. v. Ellsey, 85 Pa. St. 283.
[6] Pierce v. Sweet, 88 Pa. St. 151.

that the debt should be set off as a payment against the bailee's charges.[1]

§ 761. Since the bailee's lien continues until tender of his just charges, the owner cannot sustain replevin for the chattel bailed, without previously tendering these charges. Tender after the action begins is too late.[2] The same is true of the action of trover.[3]

---

[1] Moss v. Mogridge, 1 Phila. 121.

[2] McIntyre v. Carver, 2 W. & S. 392; Matthias v. Sellers, 86 Pa. St. 486. In Mackey v. Dellinger, 73 Pa. St. 85, A. had consigned goods to B., who made advance of $1,500 thereon, and then pledged them to C. for a loan of $3,700. In replevin by A. against C., C. could not set up B.'s right of detention against A. for B.'s advances, because C. had refused to deliver the goods except on condition that his loan to B. should be repaid. He had a right to insist on the payment of the $1,500 due from A. to B., and this he obtained by recoupment from the value of the goods. See, also, 38 Leg. Int. 240.

[3] Steinman v. Wilkins, 7 W. & S. 466. The jury cannot deduct the charges of the bailee, and find for the plaintiff the balance.

CHAPTER XXXVII.

LIEN OF CORPORATIONS ON CAPITAL STOCK.

Source of Lien.

§ 762. Corporations have no lien at common law upon shares of their capital stock, or dividends thereon, on account of debts due to them by the owners thereof. When such lien exists, it is by reason of some statutory provision, of some by-law of the corporation, enacted in conformity with law,[1] of some direction of its board of directors or of some usage,[2] subject to which the stockholder, it is to be presumed, contracted the debt. A by-law of an insurance company, that no stockholder who is indebted to the company, or in any way liable for the debt of another to it, shall, while so indebted or liable, be permitted to assign or transfer his stock, except by the special consent of the directors, confers on the company a lien on his stock and dividends for such debt or liability.[3] Under such a by-law, the company has a lien on the stock of A. for a debt to it of the firm of A., B. & Co.[4] A by-law, made after the death of a stockholder who is indebted to the corporation, cannot create a lien on his stock for his debt, as against his administrators or a purchaser from them.[5]

§ 763. By the ninth section of the act of April 7th, 1849, [P. L. 564,] which furnishes a method for the incorporation of various manufacturing companies, the corporation has a lien on stock for all arrears due thereon. The seventh

---

[1] Steamboat Dock Co. *v.* Herron's Adm., 52 Pa. St. 280; Geyer *v.* Ins. Co. 3 Pittsb. 41.

[2] Morgan *v.* Bank of North America, 8 Serg. & R. 73.

[3] Geyer *v.* Ins. Co., 3 Pittsb. 41.

[4] *Ibid.*; Mechanics' Bank *v.* Earp, 4 R. 384.

[5] Steamboat Dock Co. *v.* Herron's Adm., 52 Pa. St. 280.

section of the act of 29th April, 1874, [P. L. 75,] providing for the erection of a large variety of corporations, declares that no certificate of stock shall be transferred so long as the holder thereof is indebted to the company, unless the directors consent thereto. A similar provision exists in the seventh section of the general railroad law of February 19th, 1849, [P. L. 81.] Under this act, it has been decided that the corporation has a lien even for a debt not yet payable. Thus, when a stockholder has paid $5 per share on his stock, and future payments are to be made when calls shall be issued therefor by the directors, the stock is transferable only subject to such future calls as may be made.[1] The consent of directors to a transfer of stock, when the stockholder is indebted to the company, must be proved by a recorded resolution, unless the written minute of it has been lost.[2]

§ 764. By the tenth section of the act of 16th April, 1850, [P. L. 483,] it is declared that the stock of an incorporated bank shall be assignable and transferable on the books of the bank only, and no stockholder from whom a debt is actually due and unpaid is authorized to make a transfer thereof, or receive a dividend thereon,[3] until such debt is discharged or security is given for it, to the satisfaction of the directors.

For What the Lien Exists.

§ 765. Under the statute just cited, the bank has a lien on stock for unpaid stock subscriptions, or for any other indebtedness of the stockholder,[4] e. g., a note discounted by the bank, of which the stockholder is the maker,[5] or one of which he is

---

[1] Pittsburgh and Connelsville R. R. Co. v. Clarke, 29 Pa. St. 146.

[2] Ibid.

[3] A lien on the dividend is recognized in Klopp & Stump v. Lebanon Bank, 46 Pa. St. 88.

[4] Rogers v. Huntingdon Bank, 12 Serg. & R. 77.

[5] Waln's Assignees v. Bank of North America, 8 Serg. & R. 73; Kuhn v. Westmoreland Bank, 2 W. 136; Sewall v. Lancaster Bank, 17 Serg. & R. 283; Farmers' Bank v. Gilson, 6 Pa. St. 51; Presbyterian Church v. Carlisle Bank, 5 Pa. St. 345. Under a statute giving a lien

one of two joint payees and endorsers, the other endorsing for his accommodation. The lien of the bank arises at least as soon as the note is protested for non-payment.[1] A note drawn by A. and B. for the accommodation of C. and D., a firm, falls due on the third day of grace, and on that day, even before demand and protest, the lien of the bank, which discounted it, upon the stock held by C. and D., is complete.[2] When a stockholder deposited with a bank a draft on a house in Virginia, for collection, and the bank entered a credit therefor in his account, but subsequently, after several settlements of his deposit account, it learned that the draft had been dishonored, it had a lien on his stock for re-imbursement.[3]

Subject of Lien

§ 766. The lien is on all the stock of the debtor, how greatly soever its value may exceed the debt. The bank is not bound to appropriate so much of it as may be necessary to pay the debt, and discharge the remainder, at the request of the stockholder or of his assignee.[4] If a stockholder indebted to his bank, has also a deposit therein equal to the indebtedness, the bank is not bound to charge the debt against the deposit, and so cancel it. The deposit may be suffered to be withdrawn, and the bank may hold the stock for its security.[5]

Duration of Lien.

§ 767. The lien of the bank is extinguished by its permitting a transfer of the stock to be made upon its books.[6] But

when the stockholder was "indebted to the institution," the lien arose after the contract of indebtedness, and before the money became payable. Rogers v. Huntingdon Bank, 12 Serg. & R. 77 ; Grant v. Mechanics' Bank, 15 Serg. & R. 140.

[1] West Branch Bank v. Armstrong, 40 Pa. St. 278.

[2] Klopp v. Lebanon Bank, 46 Pa. St. 88, 39 Pa. St. 489.

[3] Mechanics' Bank v. Earp, 4 R. 383.

[4] Sewall v. Lancaster Bank, 17 Serg. & R. 283.

[5] Mechanics' Bank v. Earp, 4 R. 384.

[6] Sewall v. Lancaster Bank, 17 Serg. & R. 283.

the lapse of six years after any acknowledgment of the debt, though a bar to an action by the bank to recover it, does not interfere with its lien on the debtor's stock. The debt of the stockholder to a corporation was contracted January 4th, 1858. On a judgment against the debtor, another creditor attached the stock and sold it 23d July, 1859. In an action brought in 1867, by the purchaser, against the company for refusing to transfer the stock, its lien for the debt due it was a good defence.[1] The lien is a right of detention. To make it available for the actual recovery of the debt, the bank must get a judgment and then levy upon the stock in execution. The lien of the seizure in execution relates to the time when the debt matured.[2]

[1] Geyer v. Ins. Co., 3 Pittsb. 41.   [2] West Branch Bank v. Armstrong, 40 Pa. St. 278.

CHAPTER XXXVIII.

LIEN ON BANK DEPOSITS.

§ 768. A bank with which a customer has a deposit subject to check, may detain so much of it as may be necessary for the payment of any notes or bonds, already payable, on which he is liable to it.[1] But, until the notes or bonds are actually mature, the bank has no right to refuse to honor checks of the depositor, or (he becoming insolvent, and making an assignment in trust for the benefit of creditors,) of his assignee.[2] But, if the deposit account is made up of the proceeds of a note, discounted by the bank a short time before he becomes insolvent and makes an assignment for the benefit of creditors, it would seem that the bank could retain the money as against the assignee of the depositor, on a tender of the note and the discount. A., having had a deposit with a bank, in part consisting of the proceeds of a note discounted by it for him, five days before it matures obtains a discount of a renewal note for the same amount, and on the day of its maturity the old note is surrendered to him. On the next day A. makes an assignment for the benefit of creditors. The bank may, on tendering to A. the new note and the discount thereon,

---

[1] Reed v. Penrose's Adm., 36 Pa. St. 214, per Strong, J., p. 235; Assignee of Stewart v. National Security Bank, 6 W. N. C. 399.

[2] Dougherty Bros. & Co. v. Central National Bank, 93 Pa. St. 227. To the contrary is Assignee of Stewart v. National Security Bank, 6 W. N. C. 399. This last case decides that when, after the assignment, the assignor is permitted to carry on the business for the creditors, and to deposit moneys, the proceeds of the sale of assigned goods, and draw them out by his checks, though under the direction of the assignees, the bank has no right to detain any moneys thus deposited for debts of the assignor contracted before the assignment, though maturing afterwards. Comp. Sparhawk v. Drexel, 1 W. N. C. 560.

charge up the amount of the old note against the deposit.[1] If the bank receives a deposit in the name of A., it cannot refuse to honor A.'s checks upon it, on the ground that the money was in fact B.'s, and deposited by A. as B.'s agent, and that B. is a debtor to the bank and insolvent.[2] If, when the depositor dies, he is liable to the bank on debts which have not yet matured, the bank cannot retain the deposit from the administrator,[3] it not appearing that the deposit is the proceeds of the note discounted by the bank.[4]

§ 769. As a depositor, indebted to the bank on a matured note, can withdraw only so much of his deposit therefrom without its consent, as will leave enough to satisfy the debt, so the bank cannot refuse to apply the deposit to the debt when the depositor, by check, so directs it to be applied. A bank becoming insolvent, a citation was issued to it May 1st, 1877, to show cause why it should not make an assignment for the benefit of its creditors, and on May 7th a decree was entered that the assignment should be made. A depositor who was indebted to the bank, drew his check upon it, payable to the bank on account of his debt, on May 2d, 1877. The assignee could recover from him only the excess of his debt beyond the deposit thus appropriated by the check to its payment.[5]

---

[1] Dougherty Bros. & Co. v. Central National Bank, 93 Pa. St. 227.

[2] First National Bank v. Mason, 9 W. N. C. 265.

[3] Bosler's Adm. v. Exchange Bank, 4 Pa. St. 32; Appeal of Farmers' and Mechanics' Bank, 48 Pa. St. 57;

[4] Kensington Bank v. Shoemaker, 11 W. N. C. 215.

[5] Laubach v. Leibert, 87 Pa. St. 55.

CHAPTER XXXIX.

LIEN OF UNITED STATES ON DISTILLERY

§ 770. Section 3251 of the Revised Statutes of the United States, provides for the collection on all distilled spirits on which the tax prescribed by law has not been paid, a tax of seventy per cent. on each proof gallon, to be paid by the distiller, owner, or person having possession thereof, before removal from the distillery warehouse. The tax is declared to be a first lien on the spirits distilled, upon the distillery used for distilling the same, the stills, vessels, fixtures and tools therein, the lot or tract of land whereon the said distillery is situated, and on any building thereon, from the time the said spirits are in existence as such, until the said tax is paid. Under this act, when the fixtures of a distillery are levied on under an execution by a creditor of the distiller, the proceeds are payable to the United States, for the taxes upon the spirits distilled, in preference to the landlord's claim for rent due for the premises on which the distillery is situated.[1]

[1] Dungan's Appeal, 68 Pa. St. 204.

.

CHAPTER XL.

LIEN OF COLLATERAL INHERITANCE TAX.

§ 771. When, on the death of any person domiciled within this commonwealth,[1] or in another state, territory or country,[2] any real, personal or mixed estate, situate in this commonwealth,[3] of which he was seized or possessed, passes from him by operation of the intestate law, by will or by deed, grant, bargain and sale (intended to take effect in possession and enjoyment only at and after his death) to any person other than his father, mother, husband, wife, children and lineal descendants born in lawful wedlock,[4] or the wife or

---

[1] *In re* Short's Estate, 16 Pa. St. 63; Orcutt's Appeal, 97 Pa. St. 179.

[2] Section 11, act of 10th April, 1849, [P. L. 571;] Section 3, act of March 11th, 1850, [P. L. 170.]

[3] Real estate situate beyond the commonwealth is not subject to collateral inheritance tax. Commonwealth v. Coleman's Adm., 52 Pa. St. 468; Drayton's Appeal, 61 Pa. St. 172. Even personal estate in another state is liable to this tax, upon the excess of its value beyond the debts owing to the inhabitants of that state by the decedent. Commonwealth v. Coleman's Adm., 52 Pa. St. 468. When the resident of another state dies therein, having on deposit in this state United States bonds or other choses in action, these securities are not liable to a collateral inheritance tax. They have no *situs* within Pennsylvania. Orcutt's Appeal, 97 Pa. St 179. When a resident of this state died here, bonds

of the state of Kentucky belonging to him, cash on deposit in a bank in New York, and stock in foreign corporations, were subject to the collateral inheritance tax. *In re* Short's Estate, 16 Pa. St. 63. So was it with United States five-twenty bonds belonging to a resident of Pennsylvania at the time of his death therein. Strode v. Commonwealth, 52 Pa. St. 181. The tax attaches, not to the securities or other personal property specifically, but to their value, and only to so much of their value as remains for distribution to collateral beneficiaries after paying debts of the decedent, expenses of administration, and rightful claims of third parties. Orcutt's Appeal, 97 Pa. St. 179; Commonwealth's Appeal, 34 Pa. St. 204, Strode v. Commonwealth, 52 Pa. St 164.

[4] Section 1, act of 7th April, 1826, [9 Sm. L. 146.]

widow of his son,[1] or to any one in trust for such father, mother, husband, wife, children and lineal descendants, or widow of a son,[2] such estate is subject to a tax or duty for the use of the commonwealth, at the rate of five per cent. of the clear value thereof, unless it be valued at less than $250, in which case it is not liable to such tax.[3]

§ 772. When an estate, real or personal, passes by will to a father, mother or other person, (to whom an estate devolving is not liable to the tax,) for life only, and the remainder to collateral heirs liable for the tax, such estate must be appraised immediately after the death of the testator. The value of the life-estate must be deducted from that of the entire estate, and the remainder will be subject to the collateral inheritance tax aforesaid.[4]

§ 773. In all cases of devise, descent or bequest in remainder, to collateral relatives or strangers, liable to the collateral inheritance tax, the devisee, heir or legatee may elect to await his coming into actual possession of the estate or property, and may, in order to obtain this privilege, give security to the register of wills of the proper county for the payment thereof, together with six per cent. interest per annum.[5]

§ 774. The collateral inheritance tax on real estate remains a lien thereon until, together with lawful interest, it be paid. But no such tax is a lien on any other property or estate than that which is chargeable therewith.[6]

§ 775. When any legacy is charged on land, the heir or

[1] Section 11, act of April 10th, 1849, [P. L. 571.]

[2] Section 1, act April 7th, 1826; Section 11, act of 10th April, 1849.

[3] Section 1, act 7th April, 1826; Section 14, act 22d April, 1846, [P. L. 489.]

[4] Section 11, act of 10th April, 1849, [P. L. 571.]

[5] Section 1, act 11th March, 1850, [P. L. 170.] See, also, act 4th May, 1855, [P. L. 425,] and Wharton's Estate, 10 W. N. C. 105.

[6] Section 1, act 11th March, 1850, [P. L. 170.] But all personalty, in whatever form, is treated as a unit as respects the collateral inheritance tax. *In re* Short's Estate, 16 Pa. St. 63.

devisee, before paying the same, must deduct the collateral inheritance tax to which it may be subject. This tax on the legacy is a charge on the land until it be paid, and the payment thereof may be enforced by the orphans' court, as may that of the legacy itself.[1]

§ 776. It is the duty of the register of wills to enter in a book the appraisement of all property subject to the collateral inheritance tax. This tax is a lien on the property chargeable therewith, until settled and satisfied. After remaining due and unpaid for one year, the register may file a copy of the claim in the proper prothonotary's office and proceed to recover the same in the name of the commonwealth, by *scire facias,* according to the provisions of the act of March 11th, 1846, entitled "An act relating to registered taxes and municipal claims in the county of Philadelphia," and any supplements thereto, against the owner or owners of such real estate for the time being. The lien of such tax will not be lost by failure to file or sue the same, within the period of twenty years after it is assessed.[2] If not sued for within that time it ceases to be a lien as against purchasers of the real estate chargeable therewith.[3]

---

[1] Section 62, act of 24th February, 1834, [P. L. 84.]

[2] Section 15 act of 10th April, 1849,

[P. L. 571; Section 3, act of May 4th, 1855, [P. L. 425.]

[3] Section 3, act of May 4th, 1855, [P. L. 425.]

CHAPTER XLI.

§ 777. The act of 29th September, 1787, [2 Sm. L. 425,] provides for escheat to the commonwealth of Pennsylvania, of all estates of persons dying intestate without heirs or any known kindred. An inquest is directed to be impaneled by the sheriff or coroner of the county in which the intestate died, and in which was situate his real or personal property, which inquest must decide whether an escheat has occurred of any goods, chattels, effects, claims, or demands (in the county in which they are impaneled, and also in any other county of the state,) of the person whose death shall have been notified to the executive or auditor-general.

§ 778. In case of escheat, the jury may summon before them, any person holding any goods, chattels or effects, or the evidences of any claims or demands of any such decedent. The inquisition thus taken shall be certified and transmitted by the deputy escheator, as soon as conveniently may be after the holding of such inquisition, into the office of the prothonotary of the court of common pleas of the proper county.[1]

§ 779. A copy of the award of such jury, if they find an escheat to have occurred, shall be filed by the proper officers, in the office of the prothonotary of the counties in which, by their verdict, escheated property shall have been found to be, and, from the date of filing such award in each county, the same shall be deemed and held in law to be a lien on the real estate in said county of each and every person in whose

---

[1] Section 1, act of April 2d, 1821, [7 Sm. L. 457.]

2x

hands any part or portion of such estates may be found to
be.[2] Under this last provision it is indispensable that the
inquisition filed ascertain that an escheat has occurred. The
omission of that fact is fatal to the lien. It must also find
that the decedent died intestate and without heirs or any
known kindred. An inquisition defective in these respects
is a nullity, for the purpose of lien, as against judgments,
mortgages and other liens.[3]

[2] Act of 19th March, 1823, [8 Sm.　　　[3] Ramsey's Appeal, 2 W. 228.
L. 100.]

CHAPTER XLII.

SUBROGATION TO LIENS.

Subrogation of Joint Principal Defendants Against Each Other.

§ 780. If two co-tenants mortgage a tract of land for purchase money, and one of them takes up the bonds secured by the mortgage, these bonds become extinguished as to one-half, but as to the other half they are payable from the one-half of the proceeds of a sheriff's sale of the tract, that represents the interest of the other co-tenant.[1] If one of these co-tenants pays off the entire mortgage in installments, he is entitled, on making the last payment, to take an assignment of it, and, obtaining judgment on it, to levy on the interest of the co-tenant for one-half of the mortgage debt, as against a subsequent judgment creditor of the co-tenant.[2] When A. and B. have an equitable title to land, under articles of sale to them, as tenants in common, and taxes are imposed and assessments for iron pipes, paving and curbing are made thereon, and, on judgment against B., his interest is sold, and these taxes and assessments are paid in full from the proceeds, B. is entitled to subrogation to their lien, so as to enforce contribution from A.[3] When A. obtained judg-

---

[1] Watson's Appeal, 90 Pa. St. 426.

[2] Duncan v. Drury, 9 Pa. St. 332.

[3] Moroney v. Copeland, 5 Wh. 407. Yet, in Mehaffy v Share, 2 P. & W. 361, where four persons bought land in common, giving a joint bond for the purchase money, it is intimated that one paying more than his share could not be subrogated to the bond, or the judgment on it. Especially is this the case, according to Greiner's Estate, 2 W. 414, when the joint debtor in a bond, of which he has paid less than his share, has died. The co-debtor who has paid more than his share, cannot claim as a specialty creditor, on the bond, against the decedent's estate.

ment against B., C. and D., joint debtors, B., paying the whole, was subrogated to it to the extent of one-third.[1]

Subrogation of Partners against Copartners.

§ 781. In general, one partner who pays a debt of the firm, cannot be subrogated to the joint judgment as against other creditors or partners. A. and B. were partners for the purpose of buying, killing and salting hogs, and conveying the pork to Baltimore for sale. On a note drawn by A. and endorsed by B. and C., $1,500 were borrowed by A., who immediately gave $850 to B.; the remaining $650 were lent to C., who was to repay it to the bank that had discounted the note. C. gave to B. $363 of it. The bank obtained a judgment against A. and another against B. B.'s property being sold on another judgment, the bank's judgment was paid from the proceeds. B. had no right to revive the bank's judgment against A. to his own use, so long as the partnership account was unsettled, and it did not clearly appear that A. was indebted to B.[2] When, however, one or more partners, for sufficient consideration, make certain joint debts their own exclusively, the remaining partner assumes the relation of a surety to the debt, and, on paying it, is entitled to subrogation to it against the copartners who had undertaken to save him harmless from it. The firm of A., B. & C. being indebted, C. retires, A. and B. undertaking to pay all the firm debts. Subsequently, a judgment is recovered against A., B. & C. for one of these debts; C., paying it, takes an assignment thereof. Subsequently, B.'s property

[1] Springer's Adm. v. Springer, 43 Pa. St. 518. Lowrie, C. J., remarks that the record did not show that the defendants were not all sureties; it did not also show that they were not all principals.

[2] Baily v. Brownfield, 20 Pa. St. 41. In Singizer's Appeal, 28 Pa. St. 524, A. and B. were equal partners. A. dying, his administrator paid $709.85 more of firm debts than he collected firm assets. B., after collecting some firm assets, made an assignment for the benefit of creditors. A.'s administrator was not permitted to receive anything out of the proceeds of B.'s separate property, for the payments on account of firm debts which he had made.

being sold on a later judgment against him, C. was permitted to first take from the proceeds the amount of the judgment to which he had been substituted by assignment.[1]

§ 782. When a settlement of partnership equities is effected, the right of subrogation of one partner to claims against the partnership, for the purpose of compelling contribution from the copartners, revives. Thus, A. and B., partners, assigned their firm assets for the benefit of creditors of the firm; the surplus, if any there should be, to be distributed equally to A. and B. On the same day, A. assigned all his individual property for the payment of his creditors, equally and ratably, among whom the partnership creditors claimed and received a dividend thereout. A.'s assignee was properly subrogated to the partnership claims paid by him against the surplus of the firm assets, remaining after the discharge of all firm debts, to the extent of B.'s share of the partnership debts paid by him, although the joint deed of assignment had directed any surplus remaining to B. to be paid to C., his creditor.[2]

Subrogation of Creditors of Partner Against Copartners.

§ 783. Since a partner cannot, in general, be subrogated to the judgment or other lien against the firm, merely because he has paid it, neither can the creditor of such partner. A. and B. were partners, and insolvent, against

---

[1] Scott's Appeal, 88 Pa. St. 173. In Frow, Jacobs & Co.'s Estate, 73 Pa. St. 459, A., B., C. and D, having been in partnership, A. withdrew, the other partners assuming to pay all the firm debts. Subsequently A. was compelled to pay certain of these debts, when B. and C. made an assignment of all their estate for the benefit of the creditors of the firm of B., C. and D. A. was subrogated to the claims he had paid, and was entitled to payment from the proceeds of the assigned estate. In Clark, Reeves & Co. v. Martin, 6 W. N. C. 30, a judgment having been recovered against A. and B., as partners, and A. having agreed with B to pay it, an attachment execution issued by C., (to whom, as his trustee, A. had the judgment assigned, on paying it,) and levied on debts due to B., was set aside.

[2] In re Assignees of Swayne, 1 Cl. 457.

whom C. had a judgment. D. had two later mortgages of
A.'s land. Under an execution on C.'s judgment the mortgaged land was levied on. The partnership accounts being
unsettled, D. could not, on tendering to C. the amount of
his judgment, compel him to assign it; it could not be
known but that A. was in equity bound to pay the whole of
C.'s judgment.[1] Against A. and B. as partners, C. recovered
a judgment. D. then recovered a lien against B. alone, by
filing the transcript of a balance found due by him in the
orphans' court, on a guardianship account. B.'s property
being sold on execution, under C.'s judgment, D. was refused
subrogation to it, for the purpose of enforcing payment of
it from A.'s real estate, since it did not clearly appear that
on settlement of the partnership account, A. would have
been in equity bound to pay any portion of C.'s judgment.[2]

Subrogation of Firm Against its Members.

§ 784. As one partner cannot be subrogated to a partnership claim, so as to be let in upon the property of another
partner, so the firm, or creditors of the firm claiming through
them, cannot be subrogated to a judgment which had been
recovered against two of the members of the firm when
they owned the land, prior to the formation of the partnership, for the purpose of enforcing payment from the individual property of these partners, their reciprocal equities
not having been previously determined. A., B. and C.,
a partnership, obtained from A. and B., real estate, which
they used for a planing mill. Upon it a new mill was
erected, whence mechanics' liens arose. A. and B. also
owned individual property. On a sale of the planing mill,

---

[1] Fessler v. Hickernell, 82 Pa. St.
150. In Pierce v. Yost & Campbell,
1 W. N. C. 472, the common pleas
refused to subrogate one partner
who, after dissolution of the firm,
paid a judgment against it, saying

the remedy was a suit for contribution.

[2] Sterling v. Brightbill, 5 W. 229.
An alienee of A.'s land resisted the
request for subrogation. See Neff v.
Miller, 8 Pa. St. 347, for a recognition of this case.

and the absorption of its proceeds by judgments against A. and B. prior in origin to the partnership, the mechanics' lien creditors could not be subrogated to these judgments in order to enforce them against individual property of A. or B., against the objection of individual judgment creditors of A. and of B.[1]

Subrogation of Surety to the Creditor's Joint Lien Against Principal.

§ 785. When a judgment or other claim is against two or more, one of whom is a mere surety, the latter, on paying the security, is entitled to the use of it. A. obtains judgment against B. and C.; C. being surety. On paying it, C. may issue an execution in the name of the plaintiff and levy on B.'s property.[2] A. and his wife execute a mortgage on the wife's lands, the proceeds of which are to be partly applied to the extinction of a prior mortgage thereon, and the residue of which is given to A. The wife, therefore, as to the residue, is a surety for A. Dying, the wife devised the land to C., subject to A.'s curtesy. The mortgage thus became a lien on the estate of A., who was, as to a part of it, a principal, and on the remainder in fee. The land being sold under the mortgage, the devisee was subrogated to the decedent's rights, as surety, against A. Hence, the proceeds of the sale, after paying the mortgage, being $12,000, and the value of the curtesy one-third of this sum, while the sum loaned to the husband at the execution of the mortgage was $4,221, the entire $12,000 was payable to the devisee, as against assignees for the benefit of creditors, to whom A. had assigned his estate four years before' the death of his wife.[3] If, while a judgment against a principal and a surety is a lien on land of the former, a third person purchases the land, he thereby extinguishes the judgment,

---

[1] Knouf's Appeal, 91 Pa. St. 78. That a partnership account between A. and B. is unsettled, will prevent B.'s subrogation to a judgment recovered against A., for which he made himself liable as surety. Baily v. Brownfield, 20 Pa. St. 41.

[2] Duffield v. Cooper, 87 Pa. St. 443.

[3] Platt's Estate, 2 W. N. C. 468.

as to the surety, to the extent of the value of the land. If the purchaser subsequently takes an assignment of the judgment, he cannot revive it against the surety.[1] The surety, on paying the judgment, may revive it in the name of the plaintiff against the property of the principal.[2] If, after judgment is recovered against A. and B., B. being a surety, A. gives B. a consideration to become principal, e. g., pays him the amount of the judgment, on his undertaking to pay the creditor, B., of course, will have no right of subrogation to the judgment against A.[3] A. gave bond to the state as an auctioneer, with B. and C. as sureties. Two days after, B. and C. entered into partnership with A., for the prosecution of the business of auctioneers, and judgment was recovered on the bond for duties unpaid. In settlement of the accounts, B. and C. agreed to pay the judgment. B. and C. then assigning for creditors, their assignee paid the judgment, taking an assignment of it, and issued an execution, which was levied on the property of A. Since the judgment had been paid, the assignee and the sheriff were trespassers.[4] The right of the surety to subrogation is limited to the excess of the indebtedness of the principal to him on all accounts at the time the subrogation is sought. If the former is indebted to the principal, though in a distinct account, to an amount equal to what he has paid for the principal, he has no right of subrogation.[5] The right of a surety to subrogation against the principal does not depend on an assignment of the security by the creditor.[6] The act of 22d April,

---

[1] Wright v. Knepper, 1 Pa. St. 361.

[2] Cochran v. Shields, 2 Grant 437; Zerns v. Watson, 11 Pa. St. 260. If the creditor releases property of the principal debtor sufficient to pay the debt, this will be a defence for the surety, in a sci. fa. to revive the judgment. Holt v. Bodey, 18 Pa. St. 207.

[3] Cowden's Estate, 1 Pa. St. 267. Hence, if time is given to A. after this arrangement between him and B., B. will not be discharged.

[4] Kuhn v. North, 10 Serg. & R 399.

[5] Neff v. Miller, 8 Pa. St. 347; Coates' Appeal, 7 W. & S. 99.

[6] Duffield v. Cooper, 87 Pa. St. 443. The assignment here was by an attorney of the creditor, who was not shown to have authority to make it.

1856, [P. L. 534,] in regard to the real estate of several persons, subject to a common encumbrance, does not apply to subrogation of a surety to the securities of the creditor.[1]

Surety's Subrogation to Creditor's Several Lien Against Principal.

§ 786. When the surety for a debt pays it, he is entitled to any judgment or other security for the same debt, possessed by the creditor against the principal. After a bank lends money to A. on a note drawn by him and endorsed for his accommodation by B. and C., it recovers judgment against A. B. paying one-half of it, the judgment recovered against A. was, with the consent' of the bank, marked to his use, in order that he might enforce re-imbursement.[2] A bank discounted a note drawn by A. and endorsed for his accommodation by B. A. failing to pay, a judgment was recovered against him. The bank had also already recovered a judgment against him for an earlier debt, which had not been duly revived, but the later judgment was a lien on A.'s land when it was sold by the sheriff. After prior lien creditors were satisfied from the proceeds, the bank was compelled to apply the residuum to the judgment on the note, in exoneration of B., rather than to the judgment whose lien it had permitted to expire.[3] When A. and B. mortgage in a single deed, lands belonging to them severally, for A.'s debt, and B. is compelled to pay this debt, or any part of it, he is entitled to subrogation to the mortgage as against A.'s lands, which have been sold to C., C. having undertaken to pay A.'s debt, but failed to do so.[4] One who becomes bail in error for both defendants in an action of ejectment, may, after the judgment is affirmed, pay the costs and, taking an assignment of the judgment, issue an execution to recover the same, even though one of the defendants asserts that she had no interest in the ejectment.[5]

[1] Duffield v Cooper, 87 Pa. St. 443.
[2] Burns v. Huntingdon Bank, 1 P. & W. 395.
[3] Westmoreland Bank v. Rainey, 1 W. 26.
[4] Sheidle v. Weishee, 16 Pa. St. 134.
[5] Bank v. Harper, 8 Pa. St. 249.

But, when the surety is probably indebted on other accounts, to the principal, he will not be entitled to subrogation. A. makes a note which B. endorses for his accommodation. A. and B. are in partnership in a business to which the note has no relation, and it appears that B. has received considerable moneys on account of the partnership, for which he has not accounted. On paying the note, B. will not be subrogated to the judgment recovered against A., by the payee.[1]

Surety's Subrogation Against Principal Transferred to his Creditors.

§ 787. When a judgment is recovered against the principal and surety, and then another against the surety, the plaintiff in the latter may be subrogated to the joint judgment, after it has been paid by the surety, or out of the surety's land, for the purpose of enforcing it against the principal. This right can not be disturbed by the surety, after the judgment has been recovered against him for his individual debt. A. obtained judgment against K. and L., L. being surety; then B. obtained one against L.; afterwards C., who had endorsed a note for L., was compelled to pay it; L.'s real estate was then sold by the sheriff, and A.'s judgment was paid, and only a part of B.'s. A. assigned his judgment to B., and L. a few days afterwards assigned his right of subrogation to C. B.'s right to use the judgment prevailed over C.'s.[2] If the record fails to show that

---

[1] Baily v. Brownfield, 20 Pa. St. 41.

[2] Huston's Appeal, 69 Pa. St. 485. This case is inconsistent with Bank v. German, 3 Pa. St. 300. A. got a judgment against D. as maker, and another against E. as accommodation endorser of a note. Then B. obtained a judgment against E., and subsequently C. obtained one against him. E.'s estate being sold, its proceeds were absorbed in paying A's judgment. A. then assigned his judgment against D. to E., and E. to C. It was decided that C.'s right of subrogation was superior to B.'s. See remarks on this case in Neff v. Miller, 8 Pa. St. 347, where the claim to subrogation of the creditor whose lien on the surety's lands immediately followed that against the principal and surety, was resisted by later creditors of the surety who had attached his claim against the principal arising from the appropriation of his estate to the payment of the principal's debt.

the surety in a joint judgment is such, until a sheriff's sale of the principal's estate, out of whose proceeds the surety's creditors seek payment by subrogation, the right of subrogation cannot be asserted against creditors of the principal who have recovered judgments since the joint judgment against the principal and surety, which remain unpaid at the time of the sheriff's sale.[1] If, owing to the surety's indebtedness on distinct accounts to the principal, he is not entitled to subrogation to the joint judgment, for the purpose of enforcing it against his principal, his lien creditors are not entitled to this subrogation. B., who had bought land from A. on a promise to pay a certain judgment against A., which he failed to keep, became, with A., co-defendant in a smaller judgment, as A.'s surety, in favor of C. A. then recovered a judgment against him for another debt, under which his land was sold. Later lien creditors of B. could not insist that the money taken out of the proceeds for C.'s judgment, should be deducted from A.'s judgment, since B. was indebted to A. to a much larger extent.[2]

Surety's Subrogation Against Principal Transferred to his Surety.

§ 788. When a surety in one judgment is at the same time principal in another, and he pays the judgment in which he is surety, the surety in the other judgment, on paying it, is subrogated to the first judgment. A. obtained a judgment against X. and Y., in which Y. was surety. B. also obtained one against Y. and Z., in which Z. was surety. Y.'s land being sold in execution, A.'s judgment was paid from its proceeds. Z. then paid B.'s judgment, taking an assignment of it. He was entitled to subrogation to A.'s judgment,

---

[1] Indiana County Deposit Bank's Appeal, 9 W. N. C. 270.

[2] Coates' Appeal, 7 W. & S. 99. Here the subrogation was designed to be enforced, not against A.'s property judicially sold, but against his claim from a fund produced by sale of B.'s property.

for the purpose of enforcing it against X., there being no
evidence that he had been indemnified by Y., his principal.[1]

**Surety's Subrogation Affected by Subsequent Liens Against
Principal.**

§ 789. The surety may be subrogated to the joint judgment
against himself and the principal, on paying it, although, since
this judgment was recovered and before the payment thereof,
another creditor of the principal has recovered a judgment
against him. A. sold land to B., giving a bond, with C.
and D. as sureties, conditioned that certain encumbrances
thereon should not be pressed faster than the installments
of the purchase money were to be paid. Being, however,
pressed faster, D. paid them off, partly in cash, partly by
joining with C. in confessing a judgment to one of the
encumbrancers, which C. agreed to pay. C. failing to keep
his promise, D. paid the judgment, after other judgments
had been recovered against C. On a sale under one of these
judgments, D. was entitled to subrogation to the judgment
he had paid.[2] If record notice is not given, however, of the
relation of suretyship of the defendant in the joint judgment
who has paid it, until the sheriff's sale of the principal's
estate, against whose proceeds the right of subrogation is
asserted, this right will be denied, as against creditors of the
principal having liens on the property at the time of its sale.
After C. recovered judgment against E. and F., F. being
surety, D. also recovered one against E. Execution then
issuing on C.'s judgment, F. paid it to the sheriff, who
returned "money made." Nearly two years afterwards, E.'s
land was sold on D.'s judgment. After the sale and before
distribution of the proceeds, F. asked to be subrogated to A.'s
judgment, but his request was denied.[3] After judgments

[1] Neff v. Miller, 8 Pa. St. 347. Here
later judgment creditors of Y. had
attached his claim against X.

[2] Fleming v. Beaver, 2 Rawle 128.
In Bear v. Patterson, 3 W. & S. 233,
Kennedy, J., suggests that the right
of subrogation would depend on the
surety's having paid the judgment,
before other liens had been acquired
on the principal's property.

[3] Douglass' Appeal, 48 Pa. St. 223.

had been recovered against A. and B. severally, one was obtained against them jointly, B. being merely a surety, though the record did not show this. Judgments were then recovered severally against A. and against B. B.'s property was sold by the sheriff, and a part of A.'s at the same time. From the proceeds of B.'s, the judgments down to and including the joint judgment were paid in full, and from the proceeds of A.'s, the judgments against him, prior to the joint judgment against A. and B., were paid, and the fund exhausted. A sale of the remainder of A.'s property then took place, and, though the record did not show that B. had been a mere surety, his judgment creditors applied for subrogation to the joint judgment against A. and B. It was denied them.[1]

§ 790. Even if the fact that one of the parties is a surety appears on the record, before the sale of the principal's land, yet, as against subsequent creditors of the principal, the right of subrogation may be lost, if a considerable time elapses before the record is made to disclose this fact, after the surety has paid the judgment. A judgment was recovered against A., as maker, and B., as endorser of a note, 30th November, 1820; to April Term, 1827, a *fi. fa.* issued, and was levied on A.'s land, whereupon A. paid the judgment; and, on 17th November, 1828, at which time other judgments had been recovered against B., he obtained an order of the common pleas that the judgment against B. should be revived to his use, B., as he alleged, being the real principal. B.'s land was then sold, and, in distribution of the proceeds, A.'s claim to take out the amount of the judgment which he had paid was denied, because of his delay in disclosing on the record that he was a surety.[2] A judgment was recovered

[1] Indiana County Deposit Bank's Appeal, 9 W. N. C. 270.

[2] Goswiler's Estate, 3 P. & W. 200. A judgment was obtained against A., B. and C., C. being surety. C. paid the judgment, and more than six years afterwards brought *assumpsit* against B. to recover what he had

against A. and B., B. being surety, but not so appearing on the record. Then a judgment was recovered against A., and, subsequently, another against A. and B. On this last, B.'s property was sold, and, from the proceeds, the first judgment was paid in full, but satisfaction was not marked on the record, and the residue was applied to the third judgment. A. having made an assignment for the benefit of creditors, the assignee sold his real estate under an order of the common pleas so as to divest liens. The first judgment was (about a month before the appointment of an auditor to distribute the fund raised by the assignee's sale, and nearly a year after its payment out of B.'s property,) assigned to B., who claimed its amount from the fund. His subrogation was refused because of his failure to have the judgment marked to his use shortly after it was paid out of his property.[1]

Subrogation of Surety as Against Sureties Subsequently Intervening.

§ 791. When, after one has become surety for a debtor, another accedes to the obligation for the purpose of giving time or other favor to the principal debtor, but in such

---

paid for him The action was held barred by the statute of limitations. He then sought subrogation to the judgment, but this was denied also, for the same reason. Fink v. Mehaffy, 8 W. 384. Co-sureties on a sheriff's bond could not, after the statutory period of five years for bringing actions on such bonds against the sureties, be substituted to an action brought by a creditor who had been injured, against a surety therein, to recover contribution from him. Bank of Penna. v. Potius, 10 W. 148. In an action for a distributive share of a decedent's estate, it was shown in set-off that the plaintiff had become bound, as principal, with A. as surety. in a certain bond, and that the plaintiff as principal, and the decedent as surety, had become bound to A. to save him harmless. The decedent had paid the bond apparently thirty years before. The set-off was not permitted; the decedent had done nothing in six years, such as taking an assignment of the bond, or bringing suit on it, to indicate his purpose to seek subrogation. On the contrary, the bond had been destroyed by the erasure of the name and seal of the surety, and the seal of the decedent was torn off. Rittenhouse v. Levering, 6 W. & S. 190.

[1] Gring's Appeal, 89 Pa. St. 336.

a way as not to extinguish the surety's debt to the creditor, the surety may, if compelled to pay the debt, be subrogated to the securities against the accessory debtor. A note drawn by B. and payable to C., is endorsed for B.'s accommodation to A. Separate judgments were subsequently obtained by A. against B. and C. Execution issued on the judgment against B., when, to induce A. to stay it, D. gave him a note for the amount. After the stay had expired, B. having failed to pay the note, A. sued D., and obtained judgment. C. then paid the original note, and was subrogated to the judgment against D.[1] Judgment was obtained by A. on a note, against B., its maker, and another against C. and D., the accommodation endorsers. Then E. and F. became absolute bail in the judgment against B., to obtain stay of execution for one year from the return day of the writ. The debt not being paid, the recognizance of bail was sued out, and judgment obtained thereon. C. paying one-half of the debt, was subrogated to the judgment against E. and F. on the recognizance.[2] If a judgment is recovered against A. and B., the record showing that B. is surety, and subsequently, at A.'s instance, and without communicating with B., C. becomes bail for stay generally, A. giving him a judgment and assigning him stock as collateral security, and a judgment is then obtained on the recognizance against C., B., if compelled to pay the judgment against A. and himself, will, on distribution of the proceeds of C.'s land, be subrogated to the judgment against him on the recognizance.[3] For a debt due C. by A., A. delivered to him a note drawn by himself, and endorsed for his accommodation by B. C. endorsed the note to D., who, it not being paid at maturity, obtained separate judgments against A., B. and C. E. became bail for stay of execution, at the request of each

[1] Potts v. Nathans, 1 W. & S. 155.
[2] Burns v. Huntingdon Bank, 1 P. & W. 395.
[3] Schnitzel's Appeal, 49 Pa. St. 23, 5 Phila. 441.

defendant for himself alone. C. then paying the note, was subrogated to D.'s right of action on the recognizance against E., as the bail for stay for A.[1]

§ 792. When A. endorsed notes for B.'s accommodation, which were discounted by a bank, and subsequently B.'s wife mortgaged her real estate to the bank to secure those notes, though, so far as appears, no stipulation was made for forbearance, A. had a right that the mortgage should be enforced, and its proceeds applied to the payment of the notes.[2] A landlord having, on expiration of the lease, recovered a judgment against the tenant before two justices, A. entered into recognizance for the removal of the cause on *certiorari* to the common pleas, conditioned to pay any rent that might accrue until the final decision of the *certiorari*, and all costs. The judgment of the common pleas affirmed that of the justices, when a writ of error was taken to the supreme court, B. becoming bail therefor. The proceedings below being affirmed, and the landlord placed in possession of the premises by a *habere facias possessionem*, A. was liable to him on his recognizance for rent down to his obtaining possession, but A. was entitled to subrogation to the landlord's action against the bail in error, for rent accruing after the suing out of the writ of error, and for costs incurred in the supreme court.[3] A. and B. were partners in an iron furnace. A. died, and his administrator continued the business for the benefit of the estate. B. then sold his interest to C., who undertook to save B. harmless from all debts. Subsequently A.'s administrator filed a bill in equity for settlement of the partnership affairs and for an injunction and receiver. C. induced him to waive his prayer for an

---

[1] Shaw v. McClellan, 1 Cl. 384. If E. had become bail for stay for A., at C.'s request, C. would have had no action against him, but that E. became bail for stay for C., at C.'s request, did not deprive C. of the right of action against him as bail for A.

[2] Woods v. People's National Bank of Pittsburgh, 83 Pa. St. 57.

[3] Clapp v. Senneff, 7 Phila. 214.

injunction, by giving him a bond signed by himself, D. and E., conditioned to pay all sums to A.'s administrator that should be ascertained to be due. A decree was ultimately rendered in favor of A.'s administrator for $4,000 against B. and C. D., one of the sureties, paid one-half, and B. was compelled by execution to pay the other half. B. was entitled to subrogation to the bond of C., D., and E., in order to compel E., the other surety, to re-imburse him. D. and E. were sureties primarily liable, while B., by his contract with C., was secondarily liable.[1]

Subrogation of Sureties Secondarily Liable Against Other Sureties.

§ 793. A person acceding to a debt subsequently to its inception, *e. g.*, a bail for stay of execution, may become, as respects the original surety, primarily liable for the debt. It is also possible for one, either at the time that another person becomes a surety, or subsequently, to make himself a party in such way as to be liable only as the surety of the other parties to the debt. In such case, he will be entitled, on paying the debt, to be subrogated to the judgment or other lien against the other parties, whether they be principal or sureties. A subsequent endorser is a surety to all the preceding endorsers and the maker, though the preceding endorsements are for accommodation of the maker. Hence, if the later endorser pays the judgment recovered against him and all the preceding endorsers, he may be subrogated to it, to enforce repayment in full from the anterior endorsers.[2] For the rent of premises leased by A. to B., C. and D. became sureties. B. subsequently assigned his lease to E. He failing to pay the rent, the sureties paid the arrears and got control of the premises. They then procured an assignment by E. to F., on H.'s becoming surety to the lessor for the rent that might become due. F. failing to

---

[1] McCormick's Adm. v. Irwin, 35 Pa. St. 111.

[2] Lloyd v. Barr, 11 Pa. St. 41.

pay the rent, C. was compelled to pay it. C. was entitled to subrogation to A.'s rights on H.'s contract of suretyship, since, as between C. and D. and H., the primary duty of paying A. rested on H.[1] The sureties in a replevin bond, entered into by an assignee for the benefit of creditors, in a replevin of goods belonging to the assigned estate, which have been distrained for rent that has fallen due to the assignor's landlord, do not assume such a relation to the sureties on the assignee's bond for the faithful discharge of his duties, that the latter, on paying money for the assignee's waste of the estate, a part of which is applied to the rent, will be subrogated to the landlord's rights, so as to enforce payment of the sum applied to the rent, from the sureties in the replevin bond. Their obligation is to the landlord alone, and as soon as his rent is paid, though after the action of replevin has been commenced, their liability is extinguished. To subrogate the assignee's sureties to the replevin bond, would make the bail in the latter bond bear a part of the losses occasioned by the assignee's waste, a liability foreign to that which they assumed.[2]

Subrogation of Primarily Liable Sureties.

§ 794. One person may, as we have seen, become, though a surety, primarily liable as to another surety, by becoming bail for stay, or by inducing the other to become surety on a promise of indemnity, or otherwise. A special bail for stay of execution is entitled to subrogation to the judgment against the principal, to enforce re-imbursement from him, if no other lien creditors are injured.[3] If, execution issuing against B., on A.'s judgment, D., in order to save B.'s property, gives a note to A., which he accepts in payment, and D.

---

[1] Bender v. George, 92 Pa. St. 36.

[2] Keely v. Cassidy, 93 Pa. St. 318. What would have been the effect of the entry into the replevin bond, with knowledge that the rent had not been paid, and for the purpose of aiding the assignee to misappropriate the goods distrained, is not considered. Comp. Wagner v. Elliott, 10 W. N. C. 8.

[3] Armstrong's Appeal, 5 W. & S. 352.

is obliged to pay it, he is entitled to subrogation to A.'s judgment, as against one who had obtained a later judgment, but before D. executed the note, though at the time the note was given to A., nothing was said of an assignment of the judgment.[1] Yet, when several judgments were recovered against A., and, on a later one, execution issued, and B., becoming bail for stay, subsequently paid the debt, he was not subrogated to the judgment in the distribution of the proceeds of A.'s land, as against judgments recovered later than the one paid by him.[2] A bail for stay of execution on a judgment recovered for arrears of ground-rent reserved in a deed conveying the fee, is not entitled to subrogation to the judgment, on paying it, as against a later claim for rent under the same deed, with respect to the proceeds of the land charged with the rent.[3] When no other judgments are recovered against the defendant until the expiration of the stay, the bail, three years after such expiration buying the judgment, was entitled to payment of it out of the proceeds of the principal's lands, in preference to liens acquired before his purchase of the judgment. These later lien creditors, not obtaining their liens until expiration of the stay, could not have been injured by it.[4] A bail for stay of execution as to the principal debtor, may not, on paying the debt, be subrogated against an original surety. Hence, when a judgment was recovered against A. and B., B. being surety on a note, and bail for stay was entered for A., a subsequent release of B. by an assignee of the judgment,

---

[1] Cottrell's Appeal, 23 Pa. St. 294, cited in Mosier's Appeal, 56 Pa. St. 76.

[2] Armstrong's Appeal, 5 W. & S. 352. The bail for stay became such, apparently, after the later judgment had been recovered. To the same effect is Lathrop's Appeal, 1 Pa. St. 512, though it does not appear whether the bail for stay became such after the later judgment was recovered. He paid the debt after the later judgment was recovered. See, also, McCurdy v. Conner, 31 Leg. Int. 373; Titzel v. Smeigh, 2 Leg. Chron. 271.

[3] Fassitt v. Middleton, 47 Pa. St. 214.

[4] Hartman's Appeal, 6 Pa. St. 76.

was no defence in an action on the recognizance of bail.[1]
When, judgment being recovered against A., B. becomes
special bail for stay of execution, and A. subsequently makes
an assignment for the benefit of creditors, B., after paying
the judgment, will be subrogated to it, and will be paid from
the proceeds of the assigned real estate, in preference to
general creditors.[2]

§ 795. Desiring a loan from C., A. induces B. to join him
in a bond to C., by executing an indemnifying bond jointly
with D. to B. D. is subsequently compelled to pay the
bond to B. This subrogates him to C.'s bond against A.
and B., for the purpose of compelling re-imbursement from
A.[3] When, at the request of a surety whom the principal
has indemnified by a mortgage, another person pays the
debt on a promise of assignment of the mortgage, the mortgagor cannot assert that such payment was an extinguishment of the mortgage. The assignee may enforce it to compel
re-imbursement.[4] When one accedes to a debt as a surety,
in such a way as to extinguish the liability of the original
surety, and without any understanding with him, he is not
subrogated to the security by which the original surety was
indemnified. A. was endorser for B., who confessed to him
a judgment to indemnify him against liability. Two months
later the note matured, and a new note, endorsed by C. on
B.'s promise that A. would assign the judgment, (of which
promise A. had no knowledge,) was accepted by the creditor
in payment of the old note. D. then obtained a judgment
against B. Two months afterwards A. assigned his judgment to C. B.'s property being sold, D.'s judgment took
the proceeds in the distribution, A.'s judgment having been
paid by the novation of the debt.[5]

---

[1] Keller v. Roop, 2 W. N. C. 207.

[2] Brewer's Appeal, 7 Pa. St. 333.
It matters not that the bail for stay
is also the assignee for the benefit
of creditors.

[3] Rittenhouse v. Levering, 6 W. &
S. 190.

[4] Brien v. Smith, 9 W. & S. 78.

[5] Webster's Appeal, 86 Pa. St. 409

Subrogation of Surety Against Co-Surety of Equal Degree.

§ 796. When one of two or more sureties, who are liable for the debt in equal degree, *inter se*, pays the debt, he is entitled to contribution from the others, and, as a means to effect this, he will be subrogated to the creditor's securities. A judgment note was executed by A., as principal, and B. and C. as sureties. B. having paid a part of the note, could enter judgment in the name of the payee, to his use, against the three makers, and levy in execution on the property of C., so as to compel him to re-imburse one-half of the amount paid by B.[1] A. obtained judgment against B. and C., as sureties for D. D. assigned a mortgage to B. to indemnify him against this liability, and a portion of A.'s debt was paid by B. out of the proceeds of it. Then, on execution against C., the residue of the debt was made. C. was entitled to subrogation to A.'s judgment, for the purpose of compelling B. to repay him one-half of the amount paid from his property.[2] On a note drawn by A., and jointly endorsed for his accommodation by B., C. and D., judgment was obtained against the endorsers, which B. and C. paid in equal parts. C. was subrogated by order of the court, on his petition, to the judgment, in order to oblige D. to pay to him one-sixth of the judgment.[3] A bank discounted for A. a note drawn by him to the order of B. and C., and endorsed by these for his accommodation. This note was duly protested at maturity for non-payment. B. had stock in the bank, upon which it had a lien for this debt. Then, D. obtained judgment against B., on which the stock of B. was levied and sold to D. The bank then obtained a judgment for the note against A. and B., and, nearly a year after, another against B. and C., as co-endorsers. C., paying the note, took an assignment of the judgments, and levied on

[1] Wright *v.* Grover, etc., Co., 82 Pa. St. 80.

[2] Moore *v.* Bray, 10 Pa. St. 519.

[3] Croft *v.* Moore, 9 W. 451. Here A., C. and F. were in partnership, and the proceeds of the note were used by A. in paying the stock he had subscribed to the partnership.

B.'s stock and the dividends due thereon, and they were sold to C. C.'s title to the stock was superior to D.'s, who bought subject to the bank's lien, which, with the assignment of the judgments, passed to C.[1] A. and B. were sureties for C.; A. died and C. became insolvent, and the two estates were insufficient to repay one-half of the debt to B. after he had paid the whole of it. B. was subrogated to the debt as against the estate of A., and a dividend was allowed him on the footing of the entire debt, and not merely of one-half of it.[2]

§ 797. A. selling land to D., on which were liens, entered into a bond with B. and C. as sureties, to indemnify D. against them. E., one of these lien creditors, being about to proceed against the land, C. paid one-half of E.'s judgment in cash, and as to the other half, which it was B.'s duty to pay, entered into a judgment with B. and E. to F., as collateral security for a judgment already obtained by F., a creditor of E., against E. C. being obliged to pay this judgment to F., was subrogated to it, for the purpose of enforcing the repayment of it, in full, from B.[3] When, of three defendants in a judgment, A., B. and C., it is uncertain whether A. and B. are principals, or A. alone, C., on paying the judgment, will be subrogated to it only for the purpose of enforcing payment of one-half of it from the land of B. An admission in writing made by B. when C. paid the last of several installments of the judgment, that he was a co-principal, while it would be sufficient to justify subrogating C. to the whole of the judgment as against B. himself, cannot have such result as against B.'s lien creditors. Hence, when B. was indebted to A., and on that account signed A.'s bond, on which judgment was obtained, but it did not appear that the understanding between A. and B. was that B.'s indebtedness

[1] West Branch Bank v. Armstrong, 40 Pa. St. 278. Thompson, J., remarks that joint endorsers, even for accommodation, have no rights of subrogation. This can scarcely be deemed authoritative, and is inconsistent with Agnew v. Bell, 4 W. 31.

[2] Hess' Estate, 69 Pa. St. 272.

[3] Fleming v. Beaver, 2 Rawle 128.

should be extinguished by his going on the bond and assuming a co-principal's place, (so that he might have been a mere surety,) C., who was an undoubted surety and had paid the whole debt, could claim out of the proceeds of B.'s estate only as if he and B. had been co-sureties, *i. e.*, one-half of the amount paid by him.[1] The lien creditors of a surety whose property has been sold and applied to the debt for which he was surety, are entitled to subrogation, through him, to the judgment of the creditor, to compel payment of their liens, from the estate of the co-surety, to the extent to which he is liable to contribute to the surety.[2]

Surety's Subrogation to Collateral Securities of Co-Surety.

§ 798. When a security is placed by the principal[3] in the hands of a surety, to indemnify him from his liabilities for the principal, the co-surety, though not intended to be protected by the security, has a right to share *pro rata* in the proceeds. If it is converted into money, which is applied to the debt, the surety to whom it was given will be liable to the co-surety for one-half of any residuum of the debt which the latter may be compelled to pay to the creditor. The security may be assigned to the surety either at the time he becomes such,[4] or long after the origin of the debt,[5] and it may have been secondarily designed to protect other creditors than the surety, if its primary intent was to indemnify him, and it was in fact applied to this purpose.[5] A. obtained a judgment against B., C. and D., (C. and D. being sureties,) on a note, and B., after the note was made, but shortly before the judgment was recovered, assigned to C. a mortgage on D.'s lands, principally to secure C. from his liability to A., but

[1] Himes *v.* Keller, 3 W. & S. 401.
[2] Moore *v.* Bray, 10 Pa. St. 519.
[3] Remarks in Agnew *v.* Bell, 4 W. 31, seem to justify this limitation of the principle. If a stranger to the debt undertakes, by giving A. a security to indemnify him for becoming co-surety, to assist in discharging A.'s duty as such, the surety could scarcely insist on being relieved in equal degree.
[4] Agnew *v.* Bell, 4 W. 31
[5] Moore *v.* Bray, 10 Pa. St. 519.

secondarily as a means of repaying debts owing to B.'s mother and sisters. The proceeds of this mortgage were all applied to the payment, in part, of A.'s judgment. C. remained liable, on D.'s paying the residuum of the debt out of his estate, to re-imburse him one-half of the amount thus paid.[1] A note of which A. was maker, and B. and C. endorsers for his accommodation, was discounted. At the same time A. confessed a judgment to B. to indemnify him from the liability. Subsequently, the note not being paid, B. issued execution on the judgment, and the proceeds of a sale thereunder were applied to the note, leaving a residue, less than one-half of it, which C. was compelled to pay. C. could oblige B. to repay him one-half of this residue.[2]

Subrogation of Surety to Collateral Securities of the Creditor.

§ 799. If the principal debtor gives securities to the creditor, the surety, on paying the debt, is entitled to the control of these securities. A. made a note payable to B., which B. endorsed to C., for A.'s accommodation. A. at the same time executed a mortgage to C., to secure the note. B. ultimately paid the note, but nothing was then said of an assignment of the mortgage. More than two months afterwards the mortgage was assigned to B. by C., on which judgment was obtained to the use of B., and the premises were sold. The sheriff's vendee's title was good against a previous mortgagee who had not recorded his mortgage.[3] A. and B., a firm, being about to obtain discounts from C., A. executes to C., a mortgage. This not being sufficient, A.'s mother, D., likewise mortgages her land to secure discounts not exceeding $25,000. Notes to the amount of $20,000 were discounted. A. then paid $10,000 to C., who satisfied the mortgage. In a *sci. fa.* on D.'s mortgage, it was held that the excess in value of the premises mortgaged by A.,

[1] Moore *v.* Bray, 10 Pa. St. 519.
[2] Agnew *v.* Bell, 4 W. 31.
[3] Gossin *v.* Brown, 11 Pa. St. 527.

over $10,000, must be deducted from the amount which otherwise might be recoverable on D.'s mortgage, D.'s right of subrogation having been to this extent defeated.[1]   A bank has a lien on the stock of its debtor.   Hence, when one of two joint accommodation endorsers of a note discounted by the bank, was a stockholder in it, and the bank acquired a lien on his stock, on due protest of the note for non-payment, and, a judgment being recovered against the endorsers, the other one paid it in full, taking an assignment of it, he was also subrogated to the lien on the stock. The purchaser of this stock at a prior sale in execution by a creditor, other than the bank, acquired title subject to this lien.[2]   When A. made a note payable to B., for B.'s accommodation, and B. got it discounted by a bank in which he was a stockholder, B. became a debtor to the bank thereon, on the last day of grace.   An assignment of the stock by B. on that day, of which the bank had no notice until the following day, was subject to its lien, and A., on subsequently paying the note, was entitled by subrogation, to the stock, although he had not notified the bank that he expected it to hold the stock for his security.[3]   A., who has mortgaged his land, induces B. to pay the mortgagee one-third of the mortgage, and take an assignment of that proportion thereof.   A.'s wife mortgages her land to indemnify B., and A. also assigns to B. a policy of insurance on a mill.   The mill burning down, more than the amount of the mortgage assigned to B. was paid to him on the

[1] Wharton v. Duncan, 83 Pa. St. 40. In Eberly v. Rice, 20 Pa. St. 297, A. had borrowed $1,000 from B., and executed a mortgage and judgment bond to secure its repayment.   Execution on the judgment being issued, A.'s mother gave a judgment bond for the amount of the debt, to procure a stay of proceedings.   It was said, in a *sci. fa.* to revive the judgment, that an impairment of the value of A.'s mortage, by causing the premises to be sold at a sacrifice, would *pro tanto* discharge the judgment against A.'s mother.

[2] West Branch Bank v. Armstrong, 40 Pa. St. 278.

[3] Klopp v. Lebanon Bank, 46 Pa. St. 88.

assigned policy. This was a complete defence to a *sci. fa.* on the mortgage against A.'s wife, she being entitled to an application to the mortgage debt, of the proceeds of the policy.[1]

§ 800. A., intending to lend money to B, induces C. to join him as surety in a note on which he borrows it from D. He then lends it and a small sum in addition to B., who executes a mortgage to A. to secure the repayment of the loan. C., being compelled to pay the note, was entitled, without assignment, to subrogation to the mortgage, and could enforce it to the extent not only of the money lent by A. to B., but also of the reasonable expense of collecting the mortgage.[2] A. and B. as principals, and C. as surety, make certain bonds payable to D. Subsequently, A. and B. dissolving partnership relations, A. undertakes to pay these bonds, and confesses a judgment to B. to secure their payment. C., however, was compelled to pay them by suit. B. then paid C. over one-half of the debt, and gave a bond to secure $825, the residue, payable at a future time. The giving of time thus, destroyed C.'s subrogation to B.'s judgment against A. B., however, or his assignees of the judgment against A., could demand payment thereof from the proceeds of A.'s real estate.[3] A., as trustee for B., bought a tract of land for B., and executed a mortgage on it for purchase money. The vendor afterwards wishing his money, A. procured it on a promissory note, assigning the mortgage to the bank. On his paying the note, he was subrogated to the mortgage.[4] A bank discounted notes drawn by A., and endorsed by B. for

---

[1] Buckley *v.* Garrett, 47 Pa. St. 280.
[2] Knox *v.* Moatz, 15 Pa. St. 74.
[3] Cornwell's Appeal, 7 W. & S. 305. Had C. not given time to B., he would, says Kennedy, J., have been subrogated to A.'s judgment to B., in preference to those to whom B. had assigned it prior to A.'s default,

for the sole consideration that they agreed to indemnify B. from all loss or damage on account of the bonds made by A.; B. and C. to D., as fully as the judgment itself would have indemnified him.
[4] Kinley *v.* Hill, 4 W. & S 426.

his accommodation. Subsequently, the wife of A. executed a mortgage to secure these discounts. The bank brought suit on the mortgage and realized enough to pay the notes, but applied the proceeds to other indebtedness of A. B. had a right that the proceeds should be used to extinguish the notes of which he was accommodation endorser.[1] When, after A. leased land to B., C. being B.'s surety for the rent, B. assigned the term to D., at C.'s instance, on E.'s becoming surety for rent subsequently accruing, C. was entitled to the security of E.'s guarantee, and a release of it by A. would have discharged C.[2] A surety in a judgment is entitled to his creditor's right of subrogation to an earlier judgment, for the purpose of enforcing payment out of other property of the principal, upon which the later judgment was no lien;[3] but this subrogation cannot be extended to the bond given by the claimant of goods levied upon under an earlier judgment, which, pending the interpleader, has been paid out of the real estate on which the later judgment, paid by the surety who seeks subrogation, was a lien. The sureties in the claimant's bond are answerable only to the plaintiff in the execution.[3]

Creditor's Subrogation to Surety's Securities.

§ 801. The principle is well settled that where a surety, or a person standing in the position of a surety for the payment of a debt, receives security for his indemnity, the creditor is entitled to it, though he may have had no knowledge of it, and have given no credit in reliance upon it.[4] A. and B., originally joint principal debtors to D., with C. as their surety, arrange between themselves that A. shall pay the debt, and A. confesses judgment to B. to indemnify him from liability. This judgment inures to the use of the creditor.[5]

---

[1] Woods v. People's National Bank of Pittsburgh, 83 Pa. St. 57.

[2] Bender v. George, 92 Pa. St. 36.

[3] Wagner v. Elliott, 10 W. N. C. 8.

[4] Rice's Appeal, 79 Pa. St. 168; Kramer's Appeal, 37 Pa. St. 71; Bender v. George, 92 Pa. St. 36.

[5] Cornwell's Appeal, 7 W. & S. 305.

A. is induced to go on the bond of B. as assignee for the benefit of creditors of M., by a bond executed by B., C. and D., to indemnify him. After judgment is recovered against A. for B.'s default, A. can sustain an action on the bond of indemnity, and the judgment recovered will be used in such way that the money obtained thereunder shall be applied to the plaintiff in the judgment on the assignee's bond against A.[1] When bills of exchange are accepted by A. for the accommodation of the drawer, and the latter then executes a judgment note, as security for the amount for which A. has thus become liable, it being understood that the drawer is to deliver certain goods to A. sufficient in value to liquidate his liabilities, (but the drawer does not comply with this promise,) the holders of the acceptances have a right to share *pro rata* in the proceeds of the judgment entered on the note, and this right cannot be disturbed by A.'s assignment to them of different parts of the judgment.[2] An iron and railroad company executed a mortgage to secure certain bonds, some of which it delivered to A. as indemnity for liabilities to be assumed by him for it. A., in pursuance of his agreement, obtained moneys from B. for the company, and B. recovered a judgment against A. therefor. In distribution of the proceeds of the mortgaged property, B. was entitled to a dividend on the bonds pledged to A., though his loan to A. had not been on their credit, nor on the credit of the company, and notwithstanding claims of the company growing out of other matters, which would have defeated A.'s demand for such dividend

---

[1] Carman *v.* Noble, 9 Pa. St. 366. Hence, it matters not that A. has not paid the judgment against him, before suing B., C. and D.

[2] Kramer's Appeal, 37 Pa. St. 71. That a holder of one of these acceptances has other securities for his debt, does not change the application of the principle mentioned in the text, except that his ratable share in the proceeds of the judgment will be retained in court until he has realized his other securities. In Moorehead *v.* Duncan, 82 Pa. St. 488, a judgment to indemnify a surety on a note, was treated as the property of the bank which discounted it, in a distribution of the principal debtor's estate.

on his own account.[1] After A. leases land to B., C. becoming surety for the rent, B. assigns the term to D., who fails to pay the rent. C. gets control of the premises, and procures D. to assign to E., on F.'s becoming surety for the subsequently accruing rent. A. was entitled to this guarantee, though he did not know of its existence till some time after D.'s assignment to E. and the execution of the guarantee.[2] If, on dissolution of a partnership, one partner binds himself, for a valuable consideration, to pay the firm debts, he assumes to the other partner the relation of principal to surety. If he enters into a bond, with a surety, for the faithful discharge of his undertaking, the creditors of the firm may enforce the bond, and the judgment recovered thereon, to the extent of their several debts.[3] If a judgment confessed by a principal to indemnify a surety, is sold by the latter to one who has no knowledge of the creditor's equity, the assignee of the judgment will be entitled to it, as against the creditor.[4]

Subrogation of Quasi-Sureties.

§ 802. Analogous to the relation of a surety is that of an executor who pays debts of the decedent in excess of the funds coming from the estate of the latter into his hands. He is subrogated to the rights of the creditors whose debts he thus pays, against the decedent's estate.[5] Since, however, a creditor whose debt belongs to a deferred class cannot claim payment from the estate, until debts of the preferred classes are all paid, the executor, on paying simple contract debts, could not be re-imbursed from the funds in his hands until specialty creditors had been paid in full.[5] An administrator, who pays debts of the decedent in excess of the personal property, may be subrogated to the debts thus paid against the realty sold under an order of the orphans' court, the sale

---

[1] Rice's Appeal, 79 Pa. St. 168.
[2] Bender v. George, 92 Pa. St. 36.
[3] Kerr v. Hawthorne, 4 Y. 170.

[4] Appeal of Mifflin County National Bank, 38 Leg. Int. 349.
[5] Greiner's Estate, 2 W. 414.

taking place within five years from the intestate's death, or
within any longer period thereafter, during which the debts
paid by him have preserved their lien by proper revival.[1]
This subrogation may likewise be enforced against the proceeds of the realty sold in partition in the orphans' court.[2]
When a recognizance is entered into by an heir, (who accepts
land in proceedings in partition,) for the shares of the other
heirs, and these shares are advanced by their guardians, on
their arrival at majority the guardians may enforce the
recognizance for their own re-imbursement, although other
creditors of the heir have recovered judgments since the
giving of the recognizance.[3] When, after an assignment for
the benefit of creditors by A. to B., A., as B.'s agent,
exchanges a portion of the property so assigned, or its substitute, for real estate, on which there are liens which the
grantee must discharge, and, A. dying, his administrator
receives the conveyance in trust for B., paying from the personal assets the liens, he, as representative of the estate, is
entitled to subrogation to the liens as against the title of B.,
the assignee. A. assigned his property for the benefit of
creditors, to B., who then re-assigned a portion, A. executing mortgages thereon. These mortgages were entrusted
to A., who sold them to C., partly for cash, and partly for
real estate, on which were ground-rent arrears, taxes, etc.,
which A. was to pay. A. dying, his administrator completed
the contract by paying these arrears, taxes, etc., and taking a
deed. The land so acquired was held in trust for B., as assignee.
The administrator was subrogated to the ground-rent arrears,

---

[1] Demmy's Appeal, 43 Pa. St. 155.
In Blank's Appeal, 3 Grant 192, the
administrator's right of subrogation
is denied in form, but conceded in
substance. It is said he must settle
an account showing that he has paid
out for debts more than he has received, and then he may recover the

excess out of the personal or real
assets of the decedent.

[2] Wallace's Appeal, 5 Pa. St. 103;
McCurdy's Appeal, 5 W. & S. 397.
The same limitation affects the lien
of the debts after the administrator
has, by paying them, become subrogated to them, as before.

[3] Kelchner v. Forney, 29 Pa. St. 47.

taxes, etc., which he had paid, as against the proceeds of the real estate sold by order of the orphans' court for the payment of debts, the balance going to B., the assignee.[1] Since the personal estate of a decedent is, as respects the realty, primarily liable for his debts, the real estate is related to the personalty, as a surety to a principal. Hence, if the real estate is sold for debts, and, subsequently, personal estate is discovered, the heirs will be subrogated to the claims of creditors satisfied out of the land. Instead, therefore, of allotting to the widow one-third of this personalty, absolutely, she may receive only the interest thereon during her life.[2] When A. devises certain land for the payment of debts, and other tracts specifically to certain persons, and the husband of one of these, in order to save her land from sale on execution for one of A.'s debts, pays it, he may compel re-imbursement from the proceeds of the land which was appropriated by the will to the payment of debts.[3]

§ 803. If the owner of a ground-rent assigns it, guaranteeing its payment until buildings shall be erected on the land out of which it issues, and, on default of the owner of the land, pays installments of the rent to his assignee, he is subrogated to the rights of the assignee.[4] The late bankrupt law of the United States directed that if one having a lien on the property of the bankrupt desired to prove his whole claim against the estate in the hands of the assignee, he should release or convey his lien to the assignee. Hence, a judgment creditor (whose judgment was recovered before the committing of the act of bankruptcy,) claiming on his entire debt against the estate in the assignee's hands, the assignee was subrogated to the judgment, as against later judgment creditors having a lien on the property.[5] A later of several judgment creditors, compelled, in order to prevent a sacrifice of the property at an impending judicial sale, to pay the

---

[1] Robb's Appeal, 41 Pa. St. 45.
[2] Phipps v. Phipps, 3 Cl. 275.
[3] Wilkins' Estate, 9 W. 132.

[4] Elkinton v. Newman, 20 Pa. St. 281.
[5] Wallace v. Conrad, 7 Phila. 114.

judgment on which the sale was about to take place, will be subrogated to it, although the plaintiff therein refuses to assign it, but causes it to be marked satisfied, there being no judgments recovered, while the judgment appears so satisfied. Several judgments were recovered against A. and B., tenants in common of land, B. being surety in all of them. An execution issuing on an earlier judgment, the court, at B.'s instance, ordered A.'s undivided interest to be first sold. C., a later judgment creditor, believing this method of sale would sacrifice his interests, paid the execution, and, the plaintiff refusing to assign it, the sheriff returned " money paid in full of debt, interest and costs." The judgment was marked "satisfied." On the petition of C., the entry of satisfaction was erased, and the judgment ordered to stand to his use, there being no judgments or other liens obtained before the erasure.[1] It is the duty of the owner of land to pay all taxes assessed upon it during his ownership. If A., to whom the land has been mortgaged by a prior owner, (subject to which mortgage the present owner bought the premises,) is compelled to pay the taxes so assessed, after having become the purchaser under a judgment recovered on his mortgage, he will have a right of action against the defaulting owner, for the taxes so paid;[2] hence, he ought to be subrogated to the city's and state's claim for taxes, in distributing the proceeds of the defaulting owner's estate, assigned for the benefit of creditors.[3]

Creditor with Narrower Lien Subrogated to Broader Lien.

§ 804. When a creditor has a lien on several distinct funds belonging to his debtor, and another creditor has a

---

[1] Mosier's Appeal, 56 Pa. St. 76.

[2] Hogg v. Longstreth, 10 W. N. C. 95. A later mortgagee in possession is, as to an earlier mortgagee, bound to pay the taxes accruing during his possession. Shoemaker v. Commonwealth Bank, 11 W. N. C. 284.

[3] But subrogation was refused in Assigned Estate of Morris, 8 W. N. C. 178, though the assignor whose estate was being distributed, and who had neglected to pay the taxes, was himself the mortgagor, and the proceeds of a sheriff's sale of the premises were largely diverted to the taxes, from the mortgage debt.

lien on only some of these same funds of the same debtor, the narrower lien creditor has a right that the broader lien creditor shall either have recourse to the fund charged by his own lien alone, for the purpose of realizing his debt, or that, if he resorts to the fund common to both liens, and consumes it, he shall permit the narrower lien creditor to use the broader security for the satisfaction of the restricted lien out of the fund which it cannot reach.[1] After a judgment, and then a mortgage, had become a lien on tract m, the judgment by revival became a lien, also, on tract n, which had been purchased between the date of the original judgment and that of the mortgage. The debtor then purchased tract o, and afterwards another judgment was recovered against him, becoming a lien on the three tracts. These tracts were all sold in execution. The proceeds of o were applied to the second judgment, which was the only lien upon it. The first judgment being the first lien on m, and the only one on n, the proceeds of n were applied to it, and the residuum was paid from m. The remainder of the proceeds of m was paid to the mortgagee.[2] When, after liens on several tracts had been recovered, the debtor executed a mortgage on one of them only, the mortgagee was entitled, on a sheriff's sale of the mortgaged premises and the application of its proceeds to the earlier liens, to use these liens as against the fund produced by the sale of the other tracts, by the administrator of the deceased debtor, for the payment of debts.[3] After the mortgaging of a lot, one hundred feet in front, mechanics' liens were acquired on a part of it,

---

[1] Delaware, etc., Canal Co's Appeal, 38 Pa. St. 512; Horning's Exr.'s Appeal, 90 Pa. St. 388.

[2] Hastings' Case, 10 W. 303. Thus the same result was reached as if the mortgagee had been subrogated to the judgment as against tract n.

[3] Ramsey's Appeal, 2 W. 229. If a mortgagee pays an execution levied on the premises under a judgment earlier than the mortgage, and embracing other property in its lien, he is entitled to the use of the judgment to compel re-imbursement from the other property. Gratz v. Farmers' Bank, 5 W. 99.

thirty feet in front, by the erection of a building thereon. The mechanics' lien creditors had a right to be subrogated to the mortgage, if the latter was paid out of the proceeds of the part on which the building stood. A release by the mortgagee of the residue of the lot, after notice from the lien creditors of their equities, would preclude him from asserting his mortgage against them.[1] A. having mortgaged to B. several tracts of land, and subsequently one of them to C., and C. having then made an assignment of his estate for the benefit of creditors, the assignee could not excuse himself for a surrender of the mortgage, on the ground that the premises were already covered to their full value by the earlier mortgage, the other lands embraced in this mortgage being ample to pay it. He could have been subrogated to it as against these other lands.[2] When a bank recovers a judgment against A. for a debt for which it has a lien on his stock, and a subsequent lien is obtained on his land, the judgment may be paid from the proceeds of the land sold in execution, but the subsequent lien creditor will then be subrogated to the bank's lien on the stock.[3]

§ 805. The equity of the restricted lien creditor is complete the instant his lien attaches. Hence, judgments or other liens subsequently recovered on the property not embraced within his lien, cannot interfere with the assertion of this equity against such property. A. owned several tracts of land, on which judgments recovered against him became a lien. He then mortgaged some of these tracts,

[1] McIlvain v. Mutual Ins. Co., 93 Pa. St. 30. Without notice from the mechanics' lien creditors of their equities, the mortgagee could release parts of the premises with impunity. In Wilbur's Appeal, 10 W. N. C. 133, A. mortgaged land to B., and subsequently a part thereof to C., and then conveyed the doubly mortgaged lots, subject to both mortgages, to D. B. released all except the part conveyed to D. from his mortgage, having received no notice from C. of his mortgage. B. was entitled to payment of his mortgage from the proceeds of D.'s land.

[2] McLellan's Appeal, 76 Pa. St. 235.

[3] Ramsey's Appeal, 2 W. 228.

and afterwards other judgments were recovered and bound all the tracts. All the mortgaged tracts were sold on execution under the first judgments and the mortgage, and all the remaining tracts were sold under the later judgments. The mortgagee not being paid in full from the mortgaged premises, was subrogated to the earlier judgments, as against the other tracts, despite the subsequent judgments, which were the second lien on them.[1] A. owning lots *b* and *c*, a judgment was recovered against him. He then mortgaged *b*, and subsequently, *c*. Finally, another judgment was obtained against him. The lots were both sold by the sheriff, *b* for $950, and *c* for $270. After dividing the costs equally between the funds, the first judgment was thrown on the proceeds of *c*, so that the proceeds of *b* might be applied to the mortgage thereon.[2] After a mortgage and a judgment had become a lien on certain land, a mortgage was executed on the undivided seven-eighteenths thereof, and other judgments then became liens on the whole. The land being sold in execution, the proceeds, after satisfying the first mortgage and judgment, were applicable to the mortgage, to the extent of seven-eighteenths of the entire fund, that being the proportion of the land which the fund represented, on which the mortgage was a lien. The first judgment and mortgage could not be cast on that part of the fund which represented the value of the premises covered by the second mortgage, for the purpose of admitting the later judgment creditors upon the remaining eleven-eighteenths.[3]

§ 806. A creditor of A. and B., as individuals, whose judgment is subsequent to one against A., B. and C., as a

---

[1] Delaware, etc., Canal Co.'s Appeal, 38 Pa. St. 512. Before the first installment fell due on the mortgage, the mortgagee paid $7,375 to the mortgagor for lumber, for a right of way for a railroad, for teaming and other services. The lumber was cut from the mortgaged land, in possession of which the mortgagor continued. These circumstances were held not to disturb the right of subrogation of the mortgagee.

[3] Devor's Appeal, 13 Pa. St. 413.

partnership, which binds both their firm and their individual property, will be subrogated to this earlier judgment, for the purpose of enforcing it, to the extent of his debt, out of partnership property, when it has been levied from the individual property of A., although other judgments have been recovered against the partnership since the judgment against A. and B. And a creditor who has obtained a second judgment against A. and B. before other judgments have been recovered against the firm, will be subrogated after the first lien creditor of A. and B., to the first judgment against the partnership.[1]

§ 807. When the later lien has been acquired on a part of the estate which is bound by the earlier lien, the equity of the second lien creditor to the use of the first lien cannot be affected by a subsequent sale of a part of the premises embraced within the first, but not embraced within the second lien, or by the acquisition of liens on the part so sold, by creditors of the vendee. After a judgment had become a lien on several tracts of land owned by A., he mortgaged one of them. The mortgaged premises were then sold by the sheriff, and the proceeds permitted by the judgment creditor to be applied to the mortgage. After the mortgage was executed, but before the sale thereunder, A. sold one of his remaining tracts to B., who, several months afterwards, gave a mortgage for the entire purchase money. Some of the mortgage bonds were assigned to *bona fide* purchasers. This land being subsequently sold on a judgment obtained on one of these bonds, A.'s first judgment creditor was permitted to take the proceeds. In having allowed A.'s mortgagee to take the proceeds of the first sale, he had simply given effect to the mortgagee's right of subrogation.[2]

[1] Lathrop's Appeal, 1 Pa. St. 512.

[2] Horning's Exr.'s Appeal, 90 Pa. St. 388. Even if the mortgagee had had no right of subrogation, the first lien creditor would have been in no default, unless the later lien creditor of B. had given notice to him to take the proceeds from the first judicial sale.

Different Funds in Two Counties.

§ 808. The right of a later creditor with a lien on one fund to be subrogated to the earlier creditor's lien on two funds, when the earlier creditor shall have consumed the fund on which the later creditor had the lien, exists when the two funds are in different counties. A. obtained by devise lands in Northumberland and in Lycoming counties, charged with a debt of the devisor, and with legacies. He mortgaged part of the Northumberland land to B., and C. then obtained a judgment against him in the same county, which was subsequently transferred to Lycoming, after D. had obtained a judgment against A. in the latter county. Subsequently, several liens were obtained in both counties, at different dates. The lands in both counties being sold, and their proceeds brought into court for simultaneous distribution, the funds were marshalled so that the debt and legacies (an earlier lien to B.'s mortgage) should be paid in full out of the funds arising from land not embraced within the mortgage, lying in Lycoming county, although the creditors with the first lien on lands in this county, after that of the decedent's debt and of the legacies, were interested in a different method of distribution.[1] A. had land in Philadelphia and Chester counties; B. had a first lien on both; C. then obtained one on the Philadelphia property, and, subsequently, D. received a mortgage on the Chester land. Finally, E. obtained, by judgment, a lien in both counties. On this judgment, the Philadelphia property was sold, but the proceeds were still undistributed when, under B.'s judgment, the Chester land was sold. B. was paid from the proceeds. In neglecting to claim from the fund in Philadelphia, he was giving effect to C.'s equity, which was superior to D.'s, whose mortgage was later in date than C.'s lien.[2] If, however, the creditor enti-

---

[1] Cowden's Estate, 1 Pa. St. 267.

[2] McDevitt's Appeal, 70 Pa. St. 373. McGinnis' Appeal, 16 Pa. St. 445, is scarcely consistent. A. had lands in Cumberland and Franklin counties. B. obtained judgments in

tled to subrogation fails to warn the earlier lien creditor to do nothing to impair this equity, the latter may deal with his first lien, so as to give advantage to still later judgment creditors. A. having lands in two counties, B. recovered a lien for a debt in both; C. then obtained one in one of the counties, and, subsequently, D. obtained one in both. C., not warning B. of his right of subrogation, B. agreed with D. to permit D.'s judgment in the county in which C. had no lien, to be preferred to his own to the extent of $800. B. had a right to first take $800 from the proceeds of the fund on which C. had a lien, the land in the other county having been already sold, and its proceeds consumed in paying $800 to D., and the residue to B.[1]

§ 809. If the creditor who has a first lien on one fund, acquires a lien for the same debt on a second fund, but only after another creditor has acquired a lien on the first fund, the second creditor has no equity which will compel the first creditor to resort to the fund on which he has last obtained a lien, especially as against other creditors subsequently obtaining liens on the second fund. Consequently, the first lien creditor may release his lien upon the second fund for the benefit of the creditors having subsequent liens thereupon. A. had land in Perry and in Philadelphia county. He mortgaged the Perry land to B., to whom he at the same time executed a bond with warrant of attorney. He then mortgaged the same land to C. Sixteen months afterwards B. entered a judgment in Philadelphia county, on his warrant

---

Franklin and transferred them to Cumberland. C. then obtained a judgment in Franklin, 2d April, 1849, and on 5th April, 1849, D. obtained one in Cumberland. On 9th April, 1849, two judgments were recovered in Franklin. A.'s land in Cumberland was then sold by the sheriff, and the proceeds were applied to B.'s judgments, and the residue to D.'s. A.'s property in Franklin was then sold, and D. was denied subrogation for the unpaid balance of his judgment, not only against C., but also against the judgments recovered in Franklin county later than his own.

[1] Quakertown Building Ass. v. Sorver, 11 Phila. 532.

of attorney, and subsequently other liens were acquired on the property in that county. B. then released his judgment in that county. His right to take from the proceeds of the land in Perry county, the full amount of his mortgage, at the expense of C., was not thereby impaired.[1]

When Funds Do Not Belong to the Common Debtor.

§ 810. If one creditor has a lien for his debt on two funds, belonging to different persons, and another creditor has a lien on the property of one of these persons only, no right of subrogation in general inheres in the latter, as against the property of the person who is not his debtor. If A. has a judgment against B., and another against C. as a surety for B., for the same debt, and D. has a subsequent mortgage on B.'s property, and, an execution being levied under A.'s judgment on the mortgaged premises, D. buys the judgment, he acquires only the rights of A. as against C., and if the proceeds of the mortgaged premises are enough to pay the judgment, C. has a right to the satisfaction of the one against him. D. cannot enforce it by subrogation.[2]

Later Creditor Subrogated to Earlier as to One Fund.

§ 811. When an earlier lien creditor has made himself liable to a later lien creditor, for the common debtor's debt, the later creditor will be subrogated to the lien of the earlier creditor, the fund being insufficient to pay both, and the earlier creditor being insolvent. The earlier creditor may make himself liable to the later, either by being a co-defendant or by separately guaranteeing the debt. Against A., several judgments were recovered, on a later of which, an execution was issued and levied on personal property of A. B., who intended to buy this property, promised to guarantee the payment of the debt if the execution was released, and it was then released by its owner C. Subsequently, the earlier judgments were assigned to B. A.'s real estate being

---

[1] Miller v. Jacobs, 3 W. 477.　　[2] Gratz v. Farmers' Bank, 5 W. 99.

afterwards sold on execution, and B. being insolvent, the proceeds applicable to his judgment were paid to C., whose debt he had promised to pay.[1] B. obtained judgment against A. to secure the payment of debts, and also to indemnify B. for liabilities assumed for A. to C., and others. C. then obtained a judgment against A. and B. on one of these liabilities. B. issued execution, which was levied on A.'s personal property, and C. then issued execution levied on the same property. B. being insolvent, he was not entitled to take the proceeds until C. was fully satisfied.[2] A. obtains a judgment against B. and C., co-principals. On the same day, C. obtains a judgment against B. B.'s property being sold by the sheriff, C. was not permitted to take anything from the proceeds until A.'s judgment was fully paid.[3] Against B., A. obtained a judgment. Then C. recovered one against both A. and B. as partners, and finally D. recovered one against them as partners. A. and B., becoming insolvent, assigned their joint effects for the benefit of their creditors. Subsequently, E. obtained a judgment against A. and B., to whom, as collateral security for a pre-existing debt, A. assigned his judgment against B. In a distribution of the proceeds of a sheriff's sale of the separate estate of B., A.'s judgment assigned to E. could not be paid in preference to C.'s and

---

[1] Himes v. Barnitz, 8 W. 39. The assignee from B. takes the judgment subject to C.'s equity, especially if he has notice of B.'s agreement to pay C.'s judgment. In Moore's Appeal, 7 W. & S. 298, A. executed a mortgage to B. Then C. obtained a judgment against A., and on the same day B. guaranteed its payment. Subsequently B. assigned $1,000 of the mortgage to D. In distributing the proceeds of A.'s property, it was decided that D. should receive his $2,450 in preference to C., although B., his assignor, was insolvent; the case being distinguished from Himes v. Barnitz, in that the promise of guarantee was made after the mortgage to B. was executed, while in Himes v. Barnitz the promise to pay the later judgment was made before B. became owner of the earlier judgment.

[2] Worrall's Appeal, 41 Pa. St. 524, 4 Phila. 253.

[3] Vierheller's Appeal, 24 Pa. St. 105.

D.'s.[1]   C. obtained a judgment against F., son of A., and then D. obtained one against A. and B., B. being surety. On an execution on C.'s judgment, A. and B. gave a bond to C. for the debt, but the property was sold at $750 to B., who paid nothing for it, except the sheriff's costs. C., two days after, entered judgment on the bond against A. and B. D. then issued execution on his judgment, and personal property of B. was sold, the proceeds paying D.'s judgment in full, and C.'s judgment (on which, also, an execution had issued,) in part. Then A.'s real estate was sold on a judgment older than any above referred to, and the balance of the proceeds, after paying it, were paid, not to B., who was insolvent, (by subrogation to D.'s judgment, which B.'s personal property had been sold to pay,) but to C., in whose judgment B. was a co-defendant.[2]

Subrogation of Vendor against Terre-Tenant.

§ 812. If the *terre-tenant*, on purchasing land bound by a lien, assumes the duty of paying it, in whole or part, as a discharge *pro tanto* of the purchase money, the vendor, if he subsequently pays the lien, may be subrogated to it, to compel performance of the vendee's duty. The vendee may assume this duty, either by express agreement or by the fact that he purchases the land at a sheriff's sale. After mortgaging land, A. conveyed it to B., who agreed to pay the mortgage debt as a part of the price he was to pay for it. A judgment was afterwards recovered against B. B. failing to pay the mortgage, A. took an assignment of it to a trustee, and caused the land to be sold under it. The trustee was

---

[1] Datesman's Appeal, 77 Pa. St. 243. In Hancock's Appeal, 34 Pa. St. 155, a mortgagee assigned one of the bonds, guaranteeing its payment, and subsequently assigned the other bonds. The later assignees were not postponed to the earlier, but all shared ratably in the proceeds of the mortgaged premises.

[2] Erb's Appeal, 2 P. & W. 296. In C.'s judgment, B. was the principal debtor, since she had obtained the personal property of F. at sheriff's sale at a nominal price, in consideration of her entering into this obligation.

entitled to receive the amount of the mortgage debt from the proceeds, notwithstanding the objection of the judgment creditor of B., whose equity could rise no higher than his debtor's.[1] After mortgaging two distinct tracts of land for $6,000 and interest, A. sold one of them to B., who agreed to apply $4,000 of the purchase money and interest to the satisfaction *pro tanto* of the mortgage. His remaining tract being seized in execution, and its proceeds applied to the discharge of the mortgage in full, A. had a right to enforce the mortgage against B.'s tract, to compel the repayment of the $4,000 and interest.[2] A., on whose land three judgments are liens, sells it to B., who retains purchase money enough to pay them. B. then mortgages it to C., and afterwards reconveys a small part of it to A., released from the lien of C.'s mortgage. A. erects a building on this reconveyed part, and then assigns for the benefit of creditors. On a sale of B.'s land under the mortgage, C. had no right of subrogation to the judgments, which were paid from the proceeds, and which B. had assumed to pay, as against the fund made by the assignee's sale of A.'s building.[3] After A. executed a bond and mortgage of land, a judgment was recovered against him for another debt, on which the land was sold by the sheriff to C., subject to the mortgage. On paying the mortgage, A. had a right to the use of it, to compel re-imbursement from the land sold to C.[4]

§ 813. The vendor's right of subrogation against the vendee may pass to the surety in the debt which the vendee has undertaken to pay, in discharge of the purchase money. A. and his wife, owning distinct tracts of land, mortgaged them jointly for a debt of A.'s. Subsequently, they con-

---

[1] Morris *v.* Oakford, 9 Pa. St. 498.

[2] Shepherd's Appeal, 2 Grant 402. Hence, the mortgagee releasing B., on payment of $4,000, *without* interest, he could not enforce the pay-ment of the interest out of the land remaining to A.

[3] Blank *v.* Eichelberger, 6 W. N. C. 25.

[4] Hansell *v.* Lutz, 20 Pa. St. 284. C. is not personally liable.

veyed A.'s tract to B., who promised to pay the mortgage on account of the purchase money. B. paying only the principal of the mortgage, and not the accumulated interest, the mortgagee recovered judgment on the mortgage, and sold the tract belonging to A.'s wife. She was entitled to subrogation to the mortgage, in order to extort from B.'s land re-imbursement of the money thus made out of her tract.[1]

Subrogation of Vendor's Creditors Against His Vendee.

§ 814. If, after several liens are acquired, of which an earlier binds two tracts, and a later only one, the debtor sells the tract which is not covered by the later lien for a full consideration, the equity of the vendee over-rides that of the later lien creditor to compel the earlier lien creditor to resort to the land sold, or to permit him, on paying the earlier lien, to use it against the land which has been sold. The right of subrogation of the later lien creditor is extinguished by the superior right of the vendee. Two mortgages, four judgments, and then a mortgage became, successively, liens on A.'s land. A. then acquired more land, and one of the judgments became by revival a lien on it. A. then sold this last acquired tract to B., who was ignorant of the lien of the judgment, and paid a full price. A.'s other lands being sold, and the proceeds consumed by the first mortgages and judgments, the owner of the last mortgage had no right to subrogation to the judgment which was a lien also on B.'s tract.[2]

§ 815. If the vendee's equity is superior to that of a later of several lien creditors, all of whose liens existed at the time of his purchase, *multo fortiori* will it prevail over the right of one who acquires his lien after the purchase, to subrogation to the lien which existed on the land at the time of its alienation by the debtor. Against A., who owned three

[1] Sheidle *v.* Weishee, 16 Pa. St. 134.   [2] Hoff's Appeal, 84 Pa. St. 40.

tracts, B. obtained a judgment. A. then sold one tract to C., who paid a part of the purchase money, and, for the remainder, gave a note promising to pay to the order of A., "on account of the lien on his property in favor of" B., $300. After this sale, other judgments were recovered against A. The two tracts remaining to A. were then sold, and the proceeds applied to B.'s judgment. The creditors with judgments obtained after the sale to C., could not be subrogated against C.'s tract, even to the extent of the unpaid purchase money.[1] While A. owned tracts m, n, and o, B. recovered a judgment against him. He then sold m to E., who gave judgment notes for $2,000 of the purchase money. Judgments were entered thereon and were assigned 18th and 19th February, 1857, to H. C. recovered a second judgment against A. 5th January, 1857. Then, under B.'s judgment, tracts n and o were sold. C. then filed a bill in equity, asking to be subrogated to B.'s judgment, so as to get the purchase money due from E. His prayer was denied.[2]

§ 816. After the first of two judgments has been paid out of the debtor's land, it may be enforced by a later judgment creditor by subrogation thereto against land sold by the debtor, though the later judgment was recovered after the sale, if the purchaser has made this land, in equity, liable to the later judgment creditor. Thus, when, after A. and B. had recovered successive judgments against C., C. negotiated with D. to sell to the latter a part of the land bound by them, and D. induced A. to extinguish his judgment, and, after the conveyance should be effected, to enter another for

[1] Ebenhardt's Appeal, 8 W. & S. 327. See Dunn v. Olney, 14 Pa. St. 223.

[2] Lloyd v. Galbraith, 32 Pa. St. 103. In Consor's Appeal, 11 W. N. C. 220, B. obtained judgment against A., who then sold to E. Subsequently C. and D. obtained judgments against A. On a sheriff's sale of A.'s remaining land, and payment thereout of B.'s judgment, D. was not entitled to subrogation to B.'s judgment, for the purpose of compelling the application of the purchase money yet due A. by E., to his debt. He must proceed by attachment.

the same amount, on a promise to "make it the same as if it were the first lien" on C.'s other land, A., after satisfying the first judgment, and taking another from C., subsequently to the delivery of C.'s deed to D., and after the remaining land of C. was sold in execution, and its proceeds consumed in paying B.'s judgment, (now become the first lien thereon,) was entitled to the use of B.'s judgment, so as to compel compliance on D.'s part, with his agreement, by sale of his land.[1] As we have seen, however, the mere fact that the vendee is indebted on bonds or notes for the purchase money, does not make his land liable to be taken in execution under an earlier judgment after it has been paid out of the debtor's remaining land, for the benefit of a later lien creditor, whose lien did not embrace the land sold, whether such lien was recovered before or after the sale to the vendee.[2] Of this protection of the purchaser, his creditors, though their liens were later in origin than the judgments against the vendor claiming subrogation, may avail themselves,[3] as may also an assignee of the judgments which the vendee has given to the vendor for the unpaid purchase money,[4] and the promise of the vendee to pay the purchase money to the vendor's order, on account of A.'s lien on his property, will not give subsequent creditors a right of subrogation to A.'s lien.[5]

§ 817. The protection accorded to a purchaser of land against the subrogation of creditors having no liens thereon, to liens that did cover his purchase, after they have been satisfied out of the debtor's remaining estate, does not extend

---

[1] Dunn v. Olney, 14 Pa. St. 219. That A. bought the property of C. that was sold by the sheriff, and afterwards sold it at an advance, cannot impair his right of subrogation. B.'s judgment in this case was revived by *sci. fa.* to A.'s use, against C. and the *terre-tenant.*

[2] Lloyd v. Galbraith, 32 Pa. St. 103; Ebenhardt's Appeal, 8 W. & S. 327; Bruner's Appeal, 7 W. & S. 269.

[3] Ebenhardt's Appeal, 8 W. & S. 327.

[4] Lloyd v. Galbraith, 32 Pa. St. 103.

[5] Ebenhardt's Appeal, 8 W. & S. 327.

to purchasers *mala fide*, with a view to defraud creditors.
After a judgment had become a lien on several tracts
belonging to A., one of which was also mortgaged for the
same debt, A. made a conveyance of parts of his land not
mortgaged, for the purpose of defrauding other creditors.
These creditors, on recovering judgments, may buy in the
earlier judgment and the mortgage, and, issuing execution
thereon, may levy on the lands sold, and, applying the
proceeds to this judgment, may reserve the mortgaged land
for execution on their own judgments.[1]

Subrogation of Terre-Tenant Against Vendor

§ 818. When the owner of land bound by liens sells it to
another, whom it is his duty to indemnify against the lien,
the vendee, on paying it, or on the sale of his land under
execution, is entitled to subrogation to the lien, for the purpose of enforcing indemnity from the defendant's other
property. The vendor assumes the duty of indemnifying
against judgments against himself when he receives the full
price of the land from the vendee.[2] If the vendee sells the
land to another, his right of subrogation passes to the latter,
who, on paying the lien and taking an assignment of it, may
enforce it against other land of the original vendor.[3] The
subrogation of a vendee against other lands of the vendor,
may be effected, notwithstanding other liens have been
acquired since the purchase, whether after[4] or before[5] the
vendee has paid the prior lien. A., having mortgaged land
to B., sold a part of it to C., who, having no knowledge of
the existence of the mortgage, paid the full consideration.
C. subsequently paid the debt to B., taking an assignment
of the mortgage. Judgments were then recovered against
A., and the remainder of his land, encumbered by the mort-

---

[1] Harrison *v.* Waln, 9 Serg. & R.
318.

[2] *In re* McGill, 6 Pa. St 504.

[3] Bruner's Appeal, 7 W. & S 269.

[4] Fluck *v.* Replogle, 13 Pa. St. 405.

[5] Bruner's Appeal, 7 W. & S. 269;
Ziegler *v.* Long, 2 W. 205.

gage, was sold thereunder by the sheriff. C. could enforce the payment of the mortgage, which this sale did not divest, from the land so sold.[1] A. sold land to B., taking a mortgage for the purchase money. B. then sold three undivided fourth parts to C., D. and E., by parol. A. being about to sell the land under his mortgage, E. paid it, taking an assignment thereof. E. was entitled to revive the judgment sur mortgage.[2] A., a vendee under articles, owing a part of the purchase money, contracted to convey an undivided one-half of the premises, after erecting a house thereon, to B. From the house thus erected, but which was not completed, mechanics' liens arose. Prior to executing the conveyance and finishing the house, the land was judicially sold. B. had a right that the costs of sale and the liens should be paid out of A.'s one-half of the proceeds, and was entitled to receive the other half, less the amount due by him on his contract, abated proportionately to the cost of completing the building.[3] A. and B., co-tenants of land, mortgage it for $8,000, and subsequently make partition thereof, and, by agreement, A.'s part is to be held liable for $5,000 and B.'s for $3,000 of the mortgage. On execution against B., a part of his purpart was subsequently sold to A., and then, on another execution, the remainder was sold to C. These sales were subject to the mortgage, which was the first lien. Finally these parts of B.'s purpart were sold under the mortgage, and the entire mortgage debt made therefrom. C. was entitled to subrogation to the mortgage to compel A. to pay, first, the $5,000, his share of the mortgage, according to the agree-

---

[1] Fluck v. Replogle, 13 Pa. St. 405. Ejectment was brought against the sheriff's vendee.

[2] Champlin v. Williams, 9 Pa. St. 341. It is not said for how much the judgment would be revived. B.'s fourth would be liable for the whole mortgage, but C.'s and D.'s each for only one-third of what B.'s failed to realize.

[3] Barnes' Appeal, 46 Pa. St. 350. The amount which B. owed on the contract was payable to creditors of A., who had liens on his interest remaining after his contract with B.

ment made in partitioning the land; secondly, such part of the $3,000 as was represented by the ratio of the value of the part of B.'s purpart which A. had purchased at the sheriff's sale, to that of the entire purpart. Purchasers of B.'s land, at sheriff's sale, must pay the $3,000 in proportion to the value of their respective tracts.[1] From the *terre-tenant's* equity of subrogation flows his right that the remaining lands of his vendor shall be first sold in enforcement of the lien,[2] and from the same equity it follows that if the remaining lands are first sold, creditors having subsequent liens against the grantor, or a grantee or devisee of the remaining lands, cannot be subrogated to the lien which has been realized out of them.[3]

§ 819. If the purchaser of land which is encumbered retains sufficient of the purchase money to re-imburse him for payment of the lien, he has no equity of subrogation, nor is an equity created by the fact that the vendor has assigned a part of the purchase money unpaid, since the vendee has the same defences against the assignee as against the vendor. Creditors of the vendor getting liens after the sale, can insist that the prior lien, subject to which the vendee bought, shall be paid by him, or out of his land, to the extent of the retained purchase money.[4] The same result happens if the purchase is made expressly subject to the lien, the vendee obligating himself to pay it as a part of the purchase money. If such is the contract, the vendee cannot, by taking an assignment of the judgment against the vendor, recovered

---

[1] Carpenter *v.* Koons, 20 Pa. St. 225. This was *assumpsit* by C. for contribution.

[2] McCormick's Appeal, 57 Pa. St. 54.

[3] In the matter of Jones' Petition, 2 Pearson 129.

[4] *In re* McGill, 6 Pa. St. 504. Comp. Lloyd *v.* Galbraith, 32 Pa. St. 103; Bruner's Appeal, 7 W. & S. 269;

Ebenhardt's Appeal, 8 W. & S. 327. In this last case, it is said that the mere fact that purchase money is still due, does not take away the vendee's equity that the prior lien shall be paid out of the other lands of the vendor; it must have been agreed that the retained purchase money should be applied to the lien.

before his purchase, enforce it as against judgments acquired after the purchase,[1] and a mortgagee, by releasing parts of the land remaining in the possession of the mortgagor, does not diminish his right to make his entire debt from the land sold.[2] A purchaser at sheriff's sale, subject to a mortgage or other lien, holds the land liable to the duty of paying its proportional part of the lien which encumbered it jointly with other tracts, or of paying the whole lien, if it was the only property bound by it.[3] Hence, if such purchaser pays the mortgage and takes an assignment of it, he cannot claim repayment from the former owner of the land, or his assignee for the benefit of creditors;[4] nor can he cause judgment to be entered on the accompanying bond, in another county, and levy on the property of the mortgagor therein.[5] When the purchaser of land subject to a mortgage, is the wife of one against whom are judgments, she is not entitled to an assignment of the mortgage, on tendering payment, for the mere purpose of enforcing it against the land, in case it should be sold on those judgments on the hypothesis that her apparent title was in fraud of the judgment creditors of her husband. She can have no equity against what she alleges to be her own property.[6]

Subrogation of Terre-Tenant Against Terre-Tenant.

§ 820. When a part of the land bound by a lien is sold to

---

[1] Zeigler v. Long, 2 W. 205. If the executor sells land, subject to a mortgage executed by the decedent, the mortgagee will be directed by the orphans' court to levy on the land, before claiming from the assets of the decedent. Gould's Estate, 6 W. N. C. 562.

[2] Wilbur's Appeal, 10 W. N. C. 133.

[3] Carpenter v. Koons, 20 Pa. St. 222; Cooley's Appeal, 1 Grant 401; Hansell v. Lutz, 20 Pa. St. 284; Wallace v. Blair, 1 Grant 75; Colton v. Colton, 3 Phila. 24. If the mortga-

gor's assignee for the benefit of creditors, who is also owner of a judgment immediately following the mortgage, purchases the premises under his own sale, subject to the mortgage, he cannot, on paying the latter, be subrogated thereto as against the personal fund. Sheffy's Appeal, 97 Pa. St. 317.

[4] Carpenter v. Koons, 20 Pa. St. 222.

[5] Dollar Savings Bank v. Burns, 87 Pa. St. 491.

[6] Insurance Co. v. Roberts, 6 Phila. 516.

3A

A., and, subsequently, B. purchases another part, having
either actual knowledge of A.'s prior purchase or the constructive knowledge implied in A.'s recording his deed within
six months of its execution, B. is, as to A., primarily liable
to pay the encumbrance, unless A. has agreed himself to pay
it, or some part thereof. Hence, if B.'s land should be taken
in execution, and the proceeds applied to the lien, he would
have no subrogation against A.'s land.[1] On twenty-seven
acres of A.'s land was a mortgage, when he made another on
ten of the same acres. He then sold three acres, not embraced in the second mortgage, to B., for a full consideration,
giving a general warranty. The remaining twenty-four
acres were then sold to C.; expressly subject to the first mortgage. C.'s title was subsequently sold by the sheriff, subject
to the two mortgages, to D. Under the second mortgage,
the ten acres were then sold to E., subject to the first mortgage, which likewise bound the remaining seventeen acres.
The ten acres were then released from this mortgage. The
fourteen acres owned by D. were, as respects the three acres
first sold, primarily liable for the mortgage.[2] If the land
first sold should, after a sale of another part of the premises
bound by the same mortgage, be levied on and sold thereunder, the first vendee would be entitled to subrogation thereto, to compel re-imbursement from the second
vendee. Though A., the first vendee, had bought his tract
at $5 per acre, paying for only eleven acres and one hundred
and eighteen perches, the surveyor having, by mistake, found

---

[1] Nailer *v.* Stanley, 10 Serg. & R.
450. If A. conveys land to B., by
deed of general warranty, and subsequently dies, devising other tracts
to C., the devised tracts are primarily liable, as between B and C., for
the mortgage debt. If, the *bona fides*
of the conveyance to B. being denied, the land so conveyed is sold
as the property of the residuary devisee, C., and from the proceeds C.'s

creditors receive a dividend, they cannot be subrogated to the mortgage
against the land in the hands of B.,
who, besides being A.'s grantee, has
also bought it at the judicial sale of it
as C.'s. Jones' Petition, 2 Pearson 128.

[2] Mevey's Appeal, 4 Pa. St. 80. It
is not said what the equities were
between the fourteen acres of D. and
the ten of E., which the mortgagee
had released.

the contents to be so much, whereas, the tract, which was conveyed by metes and bounds, contained twenty-six acres, this mistake could not be indirectly rectified by selling A.'s land first, after the statute of limitations had barred an action for the value of the fourteen acres unpaid for.[1]

§ 821. The lien creditor cannot disturb the equities of successive purchasers by any act done by him with knowledge of the facts out of which they spring. Hence, if, after A., whose lands are bound by B.'s judgment, sells one tract, B., in order to facilitate a sale of the remaining tract to C., releases it from the lien of the judgment, and this latter tract is ample for the payment of the judgment, C. cannot, on taking an assignment of the judgment, enforce it by execution against the tract first sold.[2] Lots *l*, *m* and *n*, subject each to a ground-rent, were conveyed to A., who, having mortgaged them by a single deed to B., conveyed them to C. C. then sold *n* to D.; two months later, *m* to E., and more than a year afterward, *l* to F. Three days after the sale to F., the mortgagee, knowing of the sale of *m* to E., released *n* and *l* from the mortgage, expressly reserving its lien on *m*. Lot *l* was worth enough to satisfy the mortgage. E., eighteen years after his purchase, executed a mortgage to G. On a sheriff's sale of *m*, under a judgment recovered for arrears of ground-rent, twelve years after the execution of G.'s mortgage, both mortgages were divested, and it was held that the release of B.'s mortgage, as to lot *l*, extinguished it as to *m*, and it could, therefore, take none of the proceeds.[3]

§ 822. When a part of the lands bound by a common encumbrance, is sold subject to the duty of paying a proportional part thereof, other purchasers, whether simultaneous or subsequent, will be entitled to subrogation to the lien to

---

[1] Paxton *v.* Harrier, 11 Pa. St. 312. Culp *v.* Fisher, 1 W. 494, holds the principle that land first sold is liable for the whole mortgage, although a part afterwards sold was released by the mortgagee.

[2] Lowry *v.* McKinney, 68 Pa. St. 294.

[3] Amanda Martin's Appeal, 9 W. N. C. 484.

compel performance of this duty. When land bound by a judgment is sold at the same time to A. and B., in undivided halves, and a judgment is afterwards recovered against B., under which his one-half is sold, and the proceeds are exhausted in the payment in full of the first judgment, the creditor of B. is entitled to subrogation to the first judgment, so as to compel payment of one-half of it by A.[1] If A., owning unimproved land, mortgages it, and subsequently dividing it into four lots of equal size and value, sells them simultaneously to four persons, who erect improvements of different values, and, on a subsequent sale under the mortgage, the lots bring different prices, owing to the difference in the values of the improvements, each lot must contribute one-fourth of the amount due on the mortgage, and no more. An excess beyond this must be returned to the owner of each lot.[2]

§ 823. A sheriff's sale of a part of land bound by an encumbrance, which is not thereby divested, makes the land sold liable for its proportional share of the debt, even as to later purchasers of the remaining parts. The latter, if compelled to pay the whole encumbrance, would be subrogated to it to compel contribution. A., owning land subject to a mortgage of $3,000, one of the two tracts composing it was sold in execution to B., and afterwards the other tract was sold by the sheriff to C., the mortgage continuing undivested. The mortgage being paid by C., or out of C.'s tract, C. may, by substitution to it, compel B.'s tract to contribute such part of the money made out of C.'s land, as corresponds with the ratio of the value of B.'s tract to the whole mortgaged premises.[3] A., owning three lots, mortgages e and f to B., then all three to C., and finally lot g to D. Lots e and f were sold by the sheriff to X., subject to the

[1] Gearhart v. Jordan, 11 Pa. St. 325.   222; Wager v. Chew, 15 Pa. St. 323;
[2] Leech v. Bonsall, 10 Phila. 384.   Mevey's Appeal, 4 Pa. St. 80.
[3] Carpenter v. Koons, 20 Pa. St.

mortgages. On subsequently purchasing the first and second mortgages, X. could enforce the mortgage on the three lots, against lot *g* for a proportional part of the mortgage debt.[1] When a tract of land situate partly in Northumberland and partly in Columbia county, was mortgaged, and, on a judgment subsequently recovered in Northumberland, for another debt, the part of the premises in that county was sold, the sheriff's vendee, paying off the mortgage and taking an assignment of it, could enforce payment from the land in Columbia of its proportional part only of the mortgage debt.[2] If A. and B. purchase lands subject to a lien, as tenants in common, but for partnership uses, and, on settlement of the partnership business, it appears that A. is indebted to B. to an amount equal to one-half of the lien on their undivided interests, A., on paying the lien, would not be entitled to subrogation to it as against B.'s undivided one-half.[3]

No Subrogation.

§ 824. A mere volunteer, it is said, is not, on paying a debt, entitled to subrogation to the securities of the creditor,[4] but it is hardly practicable to define the term "volunteer" in this regard.[5] A purchaser of a debt is a mere volunteer, in one sense, yet he is subrogated to all the securities of his creditors. Thus, a purchaser of a debt of its stockholder to a bank, has a right to the bank's lien on the debtor's stock.[6] A creditor of a vendee under articles, whose judgment is a first lien on the equitable title, is entitled, on purchasing the vendor's claim for unpaid purchase money, to a judgment in ejectment recovered by him against the vendee to compel

---

[1] Colton *v.* Colton, 3 Phila. 24.

[2] Fisher *v.* Clyde, 1 W. & S. 544.

[3] Gearhart *v.* Jordan, 11 Pa. St. 325.

[4] Keely *v.* Cassidy, 93 Pa. St. 318; Hoover *v.* Epler, 52 Pa. St. 524;

Mosier's Appeal, 56 Pa. St. 81; Wallace's Estate, 56 Pa. St. 406; Webster's Appeal, 86 Pa. St. 409.

[5] Keely *v.* Cassidy, 93 Pa. St. 318.

[6] West Branch Bank *v.* Armstrong, 40 Pa. St. 278.

the payment thereof.[1] An oral agreement that one who pays for the mortgagor parts of the debt, shall be repaid out of the mortgage, to which the mortgagee verbally assents, constitutes an assignment of the mortgage *pro tanto*, and if the party paying afterwards becomes assignee for the benefit of creditors of the mortgagor, he is entitled to repayment as a mortgage creditor.[2] If an assignee for the benefit of creditors pays from his own moneys a judgment under which execution has been levied on the assigned real estate, he is subrogated to the judgment, as against the proceeds of the land when sold by himself.[3] If a mortgagor procures a transfer of the mortgage to a trustee, for himself, by executing to the mortgagee another mortgage on different premises, and then, the next day, induces another creditor to release to him stocks held as collateral security, by causing the trustee to assign the first mortgage, the creditor thus purchasing the mortgage, may enforce it against a mortgage subsequent in date, but already existing when the assignment was made.[4] That a principal debtor says to the surety and to the bank which has discounted his note, that a legacy, when received by him, shall be paid upon the note, does not constitute an assignment of the legacy, and a subsequent assignment by the debtor in trust for the benefit of his creditors will carry the legacy.[5] The same is true when the debtor draws a check on a deposit in a bank, which is not presented until he makes an assignment for creditors. The bank must pay the deposit to the assignee for creditors.[6]

§ 825. A tax collector who pays the taxes from his own funds, is a mere volunteer, and not entitled to subrogation to

---

[1] Foster *v.* Fox, 4 W. & S. 92.

[2] Brice's Appeal, 9 W. N. C. 227. When a stranger to the debt pays all or a part of it, he becomes, in the absence of evidence to the contrary, a purchaser of the debt and its securities.

[3] Leonard's Appeal, 37 Leg. Int. 324.

[4] Appeal of Workmen's etc., Ass., 6 W. N. C. 141.

[5] Wylie's Appeal, 92 Pa. St. 196.

[6] Bank *v.* Gish, Assignee, 72 Pa. St. 13.

the tax lien.[1] When, in extinguishment of an old note, which had been discounted by a bank, a new note endorsed by a different surety is accepted by the bank, the endorser on the new note, as a volunteer, cannot be subrogated to a judgment which had been taken by the former endorser from the principal, as indemnity for his liability. Failing to take an assignment of this judgment for three months after the novation, within which time other judgments are entered against the principal, the new endorser will be postponed to them, in the distribution of the proceeds of a judicial sale of the principal's estate.[2] If a part of land charged with a widow's statutory dower is sold in parcels, the vendees undertaking to pay the dower, the vendor cannot be subrogated to the widow's right of distress, so as to compel the vendees to contribute the share of the dower they have assumed to pay, but which the vendor was compelled to pay on their default.[3] A. mortgaged a tract of land to B., and then conveyed it, in 1852, subject to the mortgage, to C. C. leased a part of it to D. Taxes were assessed on it for the years 1853 and 1854. The personal property of D. on the premises was seized for the taxes, when D. paid them. Subsequently judgment was obtained on the mortgage, and the land was sold thereunder. Though the taxes were a first lien by law, D. was not subrogated to them, as against the proceeds of the sale, for the reason that this would have made the mortgagee pay what C. ought to have paid.[4] There can be no subrogation of a surety to the creditor's claim until

[1] Wallace's Estate, 59 Pa. St. 501.

[2] Webster's Appeal, 86 Pa. St. 409. One employed to take charge of a horse, is not a volunteer in buying the feed and procuring other necessaries for it, and on paying for these things, will be subrogated to the claims of the parties who furnished the feed, of the farrier, and others. Hoover v. Epler, 52 Pa. St. 522.

[3] Shouffler v. Coover, 1 W. & S. 400.

[4] Gormley's Appeal, 27 Pa. St. 49; City of Philadelphia v. Cooke, 30 Pa. St. 56. Comp. Hogg v. Longstreth, 10 W. N. C. 95; Assigned Estate of Morris, 8 W. N. C. 178; Shoemaker v. Commonwealth Bank, 11 W. N. C. 284.

it is fully paid,[1] unless the creditor consent.[2]   Giving a note
to the creditor must have been in payment, else the giver of
the note will not be subrogated.[3]   When the debtor himself,
or one who purchases his property subject to the duty of
paying a mortgage made by him, pays such mortgage, it is
extinguished, and, though a later lien creditor, this purchaser
has no right of subrogation to the mortgage as against other
property of the debtor.[4]

[1] Hoover v. Epler, 52 Pa. St. 522;
Kyner v. Kyner, 6 W. 221; Cottrell's Appeal, 23 Pa. St. 294; Bank
of Penna. v. Potius, 10 W. 148; Klopp
v. Lebanon Bank, 46 Pa. St. 88; Delaware, etc., Canal Co.'s Appeal, 38
Pa. St. 512.

[2] Burns v. Huntingdon Bank, 1 P.
& W. 395.

[3] Hoover v. Epler, 52 Pa. St. 522.

[4] Sheffy's Appeal, 97 Pa. St. 317.
Here, the mortgagor's assignee for
the benefit of creditors, who owned
a judgment against the mortgagor
subsequent to the mortgage, bought
the premises subject to the mortgage,
and, on paying it, claimed to be subrogated to it, as judgment creditor,
against the personal fund.

CHAPTER XLIII.

DIVESTITURE OF LIENS.

Sales Which Discharge Liens.

§ 826. By ordinary sheriffs' sales in execution, liens are discharged,[1] unless the sale is used not for the purpose of obtaining payment of the debt, but simply to change the form of security. Thus, when a judgment creditor caused the land of his debtor to be sold in execution, and bought it himself, under an agreement with the debtor to reconvey on payment of his judgment, a mortgage which had been executed subsequently to the judgment was not divested.[2] When land is appropriated under the power of eminent domain for canals, streets, etc., liens are divested from the part so appropriated. Damages awarded under the act of March 8th, 1815, incorporating a lock navigation company, were applied to legacies charged on the land taken,[3] and to a mortgage upon it.[4] Liens on land taken for Fairmount Park,[5] or for Broad street,[6] or other streets,[7] received the damages awarded.

§ 827. Sales by the orphans' court for the payment of debts, divest municipal liens[8] and liens for taxes,[9] judgments

---

[1] Beekman's Appeal, 38 Pa. St. 385.

[2] Good v. Schoener, 10 Leg Int. 151.

[3] Workman v. Mifflin, 30 Pa. St. 362; Reese v. Addams, 16 Serg. & R. 40.

[4] Schuylkill Nav. Co. v. Thoburn, 7 Serg. & R. 411; Penna. R. R. Co. v. Jones, 50 Pa. St. 417.

[5] Mackinson's Estate, 8 Phila. 381.

[6] Philadelphia v. Dyer, 41 Pa. St. 463.

[7] Cresson's Claim, 3 Cl. 107. In matter of Noble Street, 1 Ash. 276; Powell v. Whitaker, 88 Pa. St. 445; Workman v. Mifflin, 30 Pa. St. 362.

[8] Foy's Estate, 2 W. N. C. 188.

[9] Wallace's Estate, 59 Pa. St. 401.

against the decedent,[1] legacies,[2] recognizances of the accepting heirs, at whose death,[3] or at the death of whose alienee[4] the sale takes place, and mortgages.[5] A sale under the act of 18th April, 1853, [P. L. 503,] "relating to the sale and conveyance of real estate," will divest debts of the decedent, as well those not of record as mortgages,[6] and the lien of an attachment in execution.[7] A sale in partition in the district court or common pleas[8] divested a mortgage on an undivided interest.[9] Sales in the orphans' court in partition divest liens,[10] e. g., a judgment on an undivided one-half,[11] a mortgage by the sole heir, (the sale taking place on the petition of the widow for the assignment of her dower,) and the lien of taxes and judgments against the heir,[12] and debts of a decedent.[13] Under the forty-second section of the act of 24th February, 1834, [P. L. 81,] a sale in partition in the orphans' court will not discharge the lien of the decedent's debts, if made within two years of his death. Hence, when, within two years of A.'s death, his land was sold in partition and bought by B., a co-tenant, and, subsequently, under judgment against B., the whole interest was sold, A.'s creditors were entitled to one-half of the proceeds.[14]

§ 828. An orphans' court sale for the payment of a legacy charged on land, will divest all the legacies.[15] A sale of

[1] Billmeyer v. Slifer, 2 Pittsb. 539; Moliere's Lessee v. Noe, 4 Dall. 451; Hillbish's Appeal, 89 Pa. St. 490.

[2] McLanahan v. Wyant, 1 P. & W. 96.

[3] Gilmore v. Commonwealth, 17 Serg. & R. 276; Hillbish's Appeal, 89 Pa. St. 190.

[4] Crawford v. Crawford, 2 W. 339.

[5] Bowers v. Oyster, 3 P. & W. 239; Cadmus v. Jackson, 52 Pa. St. 295; Moore v. Shultz, 13 Pa. St. 98.

[6] Jermon v. Lyon, 81 Pa. St. 107.

[7] Neely v. Grantham, 58 Pa. St. 433. See Helfrich v. Weaver, 61 Pa. St. 385.

[8] Baird v. Corwin, 17 Pa. St. 462.

[9] Girard Life Ins. Co. v. Farmers', etc, Bank, 57 Pa. St. 388; Wright v. Vickers' Adm., 81 Pa. St. 122.

[10] Commonwealth v. Pool, 6 W. 32; Browne v. Browne, 1 P. A Browne's Rep. 97; Bank v. Stauffer, 10 Pa. St. 398.

[11] Appeal of John Withers, 14 Serg. & R. 185.

[12] Steel's Appeal, 86 Pa. St. 222

[13] Wallace's Appeal, 5 Pa. St. 103.

[14] Wilson's Appeal, 45 Pa. St. 435.

[15] Solliday v. Gruver, 7 Pa. St. 452.

partnership real estate by a receiver appointed by a court of equity, divests the liens upon it.[1] The sale of an assignee in trust for the benefit of creditors, under the act of February 17th, 1876, divests liens.[2] A treasurer's sale of unseated land for taxes, divests a mortgage.[3] A sale by order of the common pleas, of an habitual drunkard's land, by his committee, divests liens.[4] A sale by an executor or testamentary trustee, under a direction in a will to sell and apply the proceeds to debts, which are not specified, divests the lien of these debts.[5]

Principles.

§ 829. With few exceptions, which have been introduced by statute or by judicial decision, a sale on any lien divests all others, whether anterior or posterior to that on which the sale takes place.[6] The lien of mortgages and of municipal claims and taxes, has been preserved by statute from divestiture by sales on subsequent liens, under certain conditions and limitations, but when the sale takes place on a prior lien, mortgages are not exempted from discharge.[7] Liens prior to that on which the sale takes place are not divested, (1) when they are created by last wills and testaments, as

---

[1] Foster v. Barnes, 2 W. N. C. 700.

[2] Herbst & Buehler's Appeal, 90 Pa. St 353; Tomlinson's Appeal, 90 Pa. St. 224; Carver's Appeal, 89 Pa. St. 276; White v. Crawford, 84 Pa. St. 433; Strickler's Estate, 2 Pearson 307.

[3] Fager v. Campbell, 5 W. 287; Kelso v. Kelly, 14 Pa. St. 204.

[4] Malone's Appeal, 79 Pa. St. 481.

[5] Grant v. Hook, 13 Serg. & R. 259; Cadbury v. Duval, 10 Pa. St. 265. The purchaser is not bound to see to the application of the purchase money.

[6] Willard v. Norris, 2 Rawle 56; Presbyterian Congregation v. Wallace, 3 Rawle 109; Keen v. Swaine, 3 Y. 561; Helmbold v. Man, 4 Wh. 410; Willard v. Morris, 1 P. & W. 480; Modes' Appeal, 6 W. & S. 281; Stewartson v. Watts, 8 W. 392; Hoover v. Shields, 2 W. & S. 135; Miller v. Musselman, 6 Wh. 354; Stackpole v. Glassford, 16 Pa. St. 163; Roberts v. Williams, 5 Wh. 170; McLaughlin v. McLaughlin, 85 Pa. St. 317; Girard Life Ins. Co. v. Farmers', etc., Bank, 57 Pa. St 388.

[7] Municipal liens and taxes are made a first lien; they are also preserved from divestiture by any sale, except to the extent to which they may be satisfied from the proceeds of such sale.

permanent provisions for wives and children; (2) when,
from their nature, they cannot be readily valued; (3) when
it is plain, from the agreement of the parties,· that they were
intended to run with the land.[1]   A. confesses judgment in
the penal sum of $2,600, conditioned to support his mother
and pay her annually $25 during her life.   On the second
of two later judgments, his land was sold.   The lien of the
$2,600 was not discharged.[2]   A mortgage to secure an
annuity,[3] though the annuity was secured likewise by a
recognizance, was not discharged by a sale on a later judgment, though this judgment was for owelty due the heirs.[4]
So, a mortgage to indemnify a surety against a liability not
yet determined, is not divested by a sale on a subsequent
judgment.[5]   A duty imposed upon a devisee to maintain two
daughters of the devisor during their lives, is not discharged
by a sale of the devised land under a judgment against the
devisee.   The sheriff's vendee purchases subject thereto.[6]
Arrears due on an annuity will be discharged, though the
annuity itself is not, by a sale on a later lien,[7] and so will
arrears due on dower, secured by recognizance or otherwise.[8]
Yet, when a first mortgage is payable in installments, some
of which only are due when the sale takes place on a later
lien, they are not payable from the proceeds.[9]

Intervention of Fixed Lien.

§ 830. When, either by virtue of some statute or of
the character of the lien, it is not divested by a sale on a
later lien, this fixed lien will save from divestiture all liens

---

[1] Helfrich v. Weaver, 61 Pa. St.
385 ; Cowden's Estate, 1 Pa. St. 267 ;
Heist v. Baker, 49 Pa. St. 9 ; Hiester
v. Green, 48 Pa. St. 102.

[2] Rutty's Appeal, 84 Pa. St. 61.

[3] Knaub v. Esseck, 2 W. 282.

[4] Mentzer v. Menor, 8 W. 296.

[5] Miller v. Musselman, 6 Wh. 354,
provided the mortgage discloses on
its face its character.

[6] Ripple v. Ripple, 1 Rawle 386.

[7] Fickes v. Ersick, 2 Rawle 166.

[8] Lauman's Appeal, 8 Pa. St. 473 ;
Dickinson v. Beyer, 87 Pa. St. 274 ;
Shertzer's Exr. v. Herr, 19 Pa. St. 34 ;
Zeigler's Appeal, 35 Pa. St. 173 ; Da-
vison's Appeal, 38 Leg. Int. 294 ;
First National Bank v. Cockley, 2
Pearson 122.

[9] Field v. Oberteuffer, 2 Phila. 271.

which precede it.[1] A sale on a judgment against a devisee, of the devised land, did not divest a judgment recovered against the devisor in his life-time, because of a testamentary charge on the land for the widow's maintenance, which could not be discharged by such a sale;[2] nor does a sale on a judgment against an heir who has accepted lands in partition, charged with the widow's dower, divest a judgment recovered against the administrator for a debt of the decedent.[3] Arrears of a widow's dower are not divested by a sale on a judgment against the accepting heir, when a mortgage, the first lien, intervenes, since the mortgage is not divested;[4] so, if the sale is on a mortgage following the first mortgage.[5] Arrears due on a perpetual ground-rent are not divested by a sale on a judgment following a first mortgage, executed by the ground-rent tenant.[6] A sale on a judgment against an heir, of land bound by the dower of the widow of his ancestor, does not discharge a legacy charged on the land by one who owned it before this ancestor.[7] So, when municipal liens for water pipes, etc., were made a lien, and accorded precedence to mortgages, but not so as to cause the mortgage to be divested by a sale on a later lien, the fixity of the mortgage preserved the lien of the municipal assessment, until statutory provisions to the contrary.[8]

§ 831. When the lien, *e. g.*, a mortgage, preceding that on which the sale was effected, is preserved from discharge merely by an agreement of the parties to the sale, and not by law, it will not protect the prior lien from divestiture. Hence, this prior lien, *e. g.*, a legacy, must be paid from the proceeds of the sale.[9]

[1] Fisher's Appeal, 33 Pa. St. 294; Helfrich *v.* Weaver, 61 Pa. St. 385.

[2] Mix *v.* Ackla, 7 W. 316.

[3] Swar's Appeal, 1 Pa. St. 92.

[4] Wertz's Appeal, 65 Pa. St. 306.

[5] Schall's Appeal, 40 Pa. St. 170; Helfrich *v.* Weaver, 61 Pa. St. 385.

[6] Devine's Appeal, 30 Pa. St. 348.

[7] Lauman's Appeal, 8 Pa. St. 473.

[8] Northern Liberties *v.* Swain, 13 Pa. St. 113.

[9] Tower's Appropriation, 9 W. & S. 103.

§ 832. A sale on a judgment or other lien against a fractional interest in land, will divest prior liens against the entire estate.[1] The sale of the interest of A., under articles of agreement to convey land to A. and B., in common, divests municipal liens which encumber the land.[2] If a judgment binds the lot of a decedent, an orphans' court sale may be made of an undivided half or third, or of any other fraction, and the judgment thus discharged from the part sold, must receive the proceeds.[3]

Fixed Liens Divested.

§ 833. To the rule that a sale on an earlier lien divests all later ones, liens of the class called "fixed" are no exceptions. By a sale on such a lien, a charge in favor of a widow for life[4] will be divested. A sale on a judgment,[5] or on a mortgage,[6] will divest a subsequent mortgage. A sale on a judgment recovered for arrears of ground-rent, will divest a mortgage executed by the ground-tenant, before the judgment was recovered.[7] But, if land is deeded to McHugh, and then a judgment is recovered against him as McCue, a sale on this judgment will not divest a mortgage subsequently executed in the name of McHugh, the mortgagee having no actual notice that the judgment was against his mortgagor.[8] If two mortgages are executed and recorded the same day to secure the purchase money due on two successive contracts of sale, a sheriff's sale on that which secures the purchase money of the earlier contract, will divest the other.[9] A sale on a judgment recovered for a part of a debt secured by a mortgage, divests that mortgage, and, therefore, all mortgages

[1] Hildebrand v. Wertz, 1 L. Bar, 22d January, 1870.

[2] Moroney v. Copeland, 5 Wh. 407.

[3] Billmeyer v. Slifer, 2 Pittsb. 539.

[4] Mix v. Ackla, 7 W. 316.

[5] Lindle v. Neville, 13 Serg. & R. 227; McDevitt & Hays' Appeal, 70 Pa. St. 373; Dexter's Appeal, 2 W. N. C. 621.

[6] Selden's Appeal, 74 Pa. St. 323; Appeal of Workmen's, etc., Ass., 6 Pa. St. 141. In re Bastian, 90 Pa. St. 474.

[7] Amanda Martin's Appeal, 9 W. N. C. 484.

[8] McCue v. McCue, 4 Phila. 295.

[9] Appeal of Williamsport National Bank, 91 Pa. St. 163.

and other liens succeeding it, though prior to the judgment.[1] A sale on a mortgage after the mortgagor's death, divests the lien of a judgment recovered against an heir, as, also, the title of a sheriff's vendee under such judgment.[2] So, if the sale is on a judgment against the decedent.[3] The surplus, after satisfying this judgment, will be divided among the heirs, but the share of the heir who is the defendant, will be appropriated to his judgment creditor.

Contracts of Sale.

§ 834. Two cases deserve a special notice: when there have been contracts of sale, and when there have been conveyances fraudulent as to creditors. Under articles of agreement for the sale of land, the vendee has the equitable, and the vendor the legal title, until the execution of the deed. A sheriff's sale under judgments against the vendee, or other liens upon his equitable title, does not divest the title of the vendor, nor the liens which bind it.[4] If the vendee himself contracts to sell the land, before acquiring the legal title, a sale of the second vendee's interest on a judgment against him, will not divest a judgment in favor of the first vendee for a part of the purchase money.[5] *Multo fortiori* will a judgment for the unpaid purchase money due the holder of the legal title, not be divested by a judicial sale of the equitable title.[6] A sale after the conveyance of the legal title, upon a judgment recovered against the vendee before it, will not divest a mortgage for the purchase money, executed simultaneously with the conveyance.[7] If, however, the sale takes place upon the lien reserved for purchase money, (the vendor still retaining the

[1] Clarke *v.* Stanley, 10 Pa. St. 472.
[2] Estate of Elizabeth Jacoby, 9 Phila. 311.
[3] McCormick *v.* Sullenberger, 2 Pearson 346.
[4] Creigh *v.* Shatto, 9 W. & S. 82; Auwerter *v.* Mathiot, 9 Serg. & R. 397; Moroney *v.* Copeland, 5 Wh. 407. An orphans' court sale has the same result. Diehl's Appeal, 33 Pa. St. 406.
[5] Vierheller's Appeal, 24 Pa. St. 105.
[6] Canon *v.* Campbell, 34 Pa. St. 309.
[7] Cake's Appeal, 23 Pa. St. 186; Parke *v.* Neeley, 90 Pa. St. 52.

legal title,) the entire title, legal and equitable, is sold, and the judgment or mortgage for the purchase money would be payable from the proceeds.[1]

§ 835. A sheriff's sale on a judgment or other lien against the vendor, originating after the execution of the contract of sale, does not divest the interest of the vendee, or any encumbrances upon that interest.[2] It divests the interest of the vendor, which is simply a right to receive the unpaid purchase money, and all judgments which were recovered against him after the contract was made.[3] It will not discharge judgments against the vendor before the contract was entered into, and the sheriff's vendee will take the land subject to them.[4] A sale of the estate of the vendor, under a judgment recovered against him,[5] or a mortgage executed by him,[6] before the contract of sale, will divest judgments recovered against him between the time the contract is entered into and the execution of the deed of conveyance. The liens existing before the contract must be paid in full; those originating afterwards will be paid only to the extent to which there may be a surplus of money still due from the vendee to the vendor, after paying the pre-existing liens. The rest belongs to the vendee, or to the liens which encumber his title at the time of sale,[7] and which are also divested.[8] When A. conveys land to B., taking a judgment for the purchase money, and B. holds it for a firm, consisting of himself and C. and D., and this firm put up valuable improvements upon it, C. and D. hold the relation towards B. of vendees under articles, bound to pay him two-thirds of

---

[1] Canon v. Campbell, 34 Pa. St. 309; Vierheller's Appeal, 24 Pa. St. 105; Hersey v. Turbett, 27 Pa. St. 418; Love v. Jones, 4 W. 465; Horbach v. Riley, 7 Pa. St. 81; Ziegler's Appeal, 69 Pa. St. 471.

[2] Vierheller's Appeal, 24 Pa. St. 105; McMullen v. Wenner, 16 Serg. & R. 18.

[3] Stewart v. Coder, 11 Pa. St. 90.

[4] Patterson's Estate, 25 Pa. St. 71

[5] Siter, James & Co.'s Appeal, 26 Pa. St. 178.

[6] Fasholt v. Reed, 16 Serg. & R. 266; Thompson v. Adams, 55 Pa. St. 479.

[7] Siter, James & Co.'s Appeal, 26 Pa. St. 178.

[8] Thompson v. Adams, 55 Pa. St. 479; Mellon's Appeal, 32 Pa. St. 121.

the judgment which he is personally liable to pay. A sale of C.'s and D.'s interests in this land under judgments against them, will transfer to the sheriff's vendee this duty. B. dying, an orphans' court sale of the land will discharge the lien of the judgment, and will convey to the administrator's vendee the right to receive two-thirds of the judgment and the duty to execute a conveyance for the undivided two-thirds to the sheriff's vendee, on his tendering that amount, the purchaser at the orphans' court sale having notice of the equity of the purchaser at the sheriff's sale.[1]

Fraudulent Conveyance.

§ 836. When, after judgments have been recovered, the defendant alienes his land, for the purpose, as is suspected, of defrauding his creditors, and other judgments are then recovered against him, a sale on any of these later liens is simply a means of vesting in the vendee "the right which the creditors have to avoid the conveyance, and, therefore, it does not affect prior liens,"[2] and to such liens the proceeds of the sheriff's sale are not applicable.[3] Against A., who had conveyed to his son, in 1842, a lot of ground, judgments were recovered in February and in March, 1855. A sale of this lot taking place on the later of these judgments, arrears of ground-rent, subject to which A. had owned the land, and taxes, were not permitted to share in the proceeds.[4] So, when

---

[1] Billmeyer v. Slifer, 2 Pittsb. 539.

[2] Fisher's Appeal, 33 Pa. St. 294. A., four years before his death, procured land to be conveyed to his wife, paying the purchase money. B., to whom A. was then indebted, and to whom three years later A. became additionally indebted, obtained a judgment after A.'s death against his administrator for both debts, and a sheriff's sale of the land took place thereon. The product of the sale was payable to B. and not to A.'s administrator.

A. had no title to the land, except as to B. or creditors similarly situated. The wife, by paying that part of the judgment which represented the debt contracted after the conveyance to her, might have saved the land, but a sale taking place on the entire judgment, as to a portion of which her title was void, the sheriff's sale divested her title. Ecker v. Lafferty, 3 Pittsb. 500.

[3] Byrod's Appeal, 31 Pa. St. 241; Dungan's Appeal, 88 Pa. St. 414.

[4] Fisher's Appeal, 33 Pa. St. 294.

3B

A. procures, with his own money, a conveyance to be made
to B. of land for A.'s own use, and this land is then sold on
judgments recovered against A., since the conveyance to B.,
taxes, which are a lien on the land, irrespective of the person in whom is the title, are not payable from the purchase
money.[1]   Difficult, however, to reconcile with this last case,
is a late decision: A. conveyed land to C. at B.'s direction,
for whom C. was to hold the legal title, and who was to erect
improvements and sell the land, paying A. its price, together
with advances to be made, and retaining for himself the
profit.   The project miscarrying, C., with the consent of A.
and B., conveyed the land to D., who had no notice of B.'s
equitable interest.   On a judgment against B., before the
commencement of his equity in the land, the land was sold
after the sale of it to D.   The taxes for the year of the sheriff's sale, being a first lien, were paid out of the proceeds.[2]
D. having a judgment against A., the latter bought land and
caused the title to be conveyed to B., for his use, for the purpose of defrauding D.   C., lending money to A., and knowing that B. was a trustee for A., took a mortgage from A. to
secure the loan.   D. then revived his judgment, so as to make
it a lien on A.'s title.   Judgment was then entered against
B., on a bond executed by him at A.'s direction, for another
of A.'s debts.   On the judgment upon a bond which accompanied C.'s mortgage, the land was sold.   The proceeds were
applied, first to C.'s mortgage, then to D.'s judgment.   Since
the mortgage bound A.'s actual title, that title was sold under
it as well as B.'s, and liens on A.'s title, in their order, were
entitled to the product of the sale.[3]

§ 837.   A sheriff's sale may be made the instrument for
defrauding creditors of the defendant.   When, after such a
sale, judgments are recovered against him, and a second sheriff's sale is effected on them, the proceeds must be applied

[1] Fisher v. Lyle, 8 Phila. 1.   [3] Stiles v. Bradford, 4 Rawle 393.
[2] Dungan's Appeal, 88 Pa. St. 414.

exclusively to these judgments, not to earlier judgments, which the proceeds of the fraudulent sale did not satisfy.[1]

§ 838. The judgments recovered against the fraudulent grantor after his conveyance, are liens in the order of their recovery, and in this order must be paid from the proceeds of the sale made upon any of them.[2] It is error to apply the money to a later judgment, because it is the instrument of the sale.[3] A. conveyed land to a trustee for the sole and separate use of his wife, in payment of a debt due her. Subsequently a judgment was recovered against him; a mortgage was then made of this land by A. and his wife, and another judgment was recovered against him. A sale under this last judgment divested the mortgage from the supposed interest which A. had, and which was sold, and it was, therefore, entitled to the proceeds in preference to the subsequent judgment.[4]

§ 839. If, for any reason, successive judicial sales of A.'s interest in the same land take place, all the liens which are payable out of the proceeds of the first sale, are utterly divested, and cannot claim against the proceeds of the second sale. The *testatum* executions, or other liens which are acquired against A. after the first sale, are exclusively entitled, in their order, to be paid from the proceeds of the second sale. While A. owned three tracts, several judgments were obtained against him, under one of which, these tracts were sold by the sheriff to B. Some time afterwards, two *testatum* executions were issued, and became liens on any interest of A. in land, and other judgments were recovered against him. A.'s interest in the same three

---

[1] Beekman's Appeal, 38 Pa. St. 385. If the purchaser at the second sale should recover in ejectment against the purchaser at the first sale, alleged to be fraudulent, "he would seem to re-instate the prior unsatisfied liens," says Lowrie, C. J.

[2] Fisher's Appeal, 33 Pa. St. 294; Hoffman's Appeal, 44 Pa. St. 95; Beekman's Appeal, 38 Pa. St. 385; Wiehl v. Ditsche, 34 Leg. Int. 338.

[3] Hoffman's Appeal, 44 Pa. St. 95.

[4] Boyle v. Abercrombie, 5 Rawle 144.

tracts was again sold under one of the *testatum* executions. The proceeds were exclusively applicable to the *testatum fi. fas.*, and to the other liens obtained since the first sheriff's sale.[1]

Mortgages.

§ 840. Till the year 1830, mortgages were precisely like judgments or other liens, with respect to divestiture by judicial sale. A sale on an earlier, a simultaneous or a posterior lien, discharged them from the land.[2] The act of 6th April, 1830, [P. L. 293,] prevented such discharge by sale on a later lien by virtue of any writ of *vend. ex.*[3] or *levari facias* on a judgment sur mortgage, provided the mortgages were preceded by no other liens save other mortgages, ground-rents, and the purchase money due the commonwealth. The act of April 11th, 1835, [P. L. 190,] and of 16th April, 1845, [P. L. 488,] add to the liens whose anteriority to the mortgage does not cause its discharge by a sale on a subsequent lien, the lien of municipal assessments and taxes, under the act of 3d February, 1824, but provides that if the judgment (later than the mortgage) on which the sale takes place, is for a municipal assessment or tax which was a lien before the recording of the mortgage, the mortgage will be divested. The act of 23d March, 1867, [P. L. 44,] saves from divestiture by any judicial sale what-

---

[1] Abbott *v.* Remington, 4 Phila. 34. On what hypothesis the second sheriff's sale was made was not made known to the auditor and court. This case is affirmed in Beekman's Appeal, 38 Pa. St. 385.

[2] Presbyterian Congregation *v.* Wallace, 3 R. 109; Mode's Appeal, 6 W. & S 280. There is one exception. When the mortgage is to the state, it is not divested by a sale on any other lien than itself. Thus, a mortgage to the trustees of the loan office of Pennsylvania was not di-

vested by two successive sales on later judgments; Febiger *v.* Craighead, 2 Y. 42, 4 Dall. 151. And a mortgage to the state for the purchase money of land was not divested by a judicial sale of the premises on another lien, and was not, therefore, entitled to the proceeds. Duncan *v.* Rieff, 3 P. & W. 368. Comp. Connelly *v.* Withers, 9 L Bar 117.

[3] The act of 16th April, 1845, [P. L. 488,] extends the provision to a sale by virtue of any writ of execution.

ever, whether in virtue of the order or decree of the orphans' court,[1] or of any writ of execution, or otherwise, any mortgage that is preceded by no other liens except other mortgages, ground-rents, purchase money due the state, taxes, charges, assessments and municipal claims, whose lien, though afterwards accruing,[2] has, by law, priority given it.[3] The act of 10th March, 1870, [P. L. 37,] repealed that of 23d March, 1867, as to all the state except Philadelphia and the counties of Perry and Venango. The rest of the state thus fell under the operation of the act of April 6th, 1830. The act of 1867 was restored, as to Allegheny and Berks counties, by the act of 9th April, 1872, [P. L. 1103.][4]

§ 841. Under these acts, the mortgage which the sale will not divest must be earlier than any lien which such sale will divest. Hence, if a mortgage is recorded the same day that a judgment is recovered, since a sale on a later lien discharges the judgment, so will it the mortgage.[5] A sale on such simultaneous judgment itself would also divest the mortgage.[6] A sale on one of two contemporaneous mortgages, of equal lien, discharges both. And two

---

[1] Penn Square Ass.' Appeal, 81½ Pa. St. 330. The mortgagee may agree that an orphans' court sale shall divest his first mortgage, which, in that case, will be entitled to the proceeds. McClure's Appeal, 37 Leg..Int. 308.

[2] City of Harrisburg v. Orth, 6 W. N. C. 121, 2 Pearson 340.

[3] Mortgages on unseated lands, and sales of the same for taxes, are not included within the operation of this act.

[4] A first mortgage means one before which there is no other lien. Green's Appeal, 10 W. N. C. 73, and a second mortgage is one imme-

diately following a first mortgage. Rice's Appeal, 79 Pa. St. 168. In determining whether a mortgage is divested, reference must be had to the liens existing at the date of the judicial sale. If a former lien has been satisfied before the sale, it is, of course, no longer a lien. Clarke v. Stanley, 10 Pa. St. 472. The record at the time of sale is the sole evidence of the liens then existing. Magaw v. Garrett, 25 Pa. St. 319; Coyne v. Souther, 61 Pa. St. 455; Norris v. Brady, 4 Phila. 287.

[5] Magaw v. Garrett, 25 Pa. St. 319; Bratton's Appeal, 8 Pa. St. 164.

[6] Bratton's Appeal, 8 Pa. St. 164.

mortgages executed on the same day, for parts of the purchase money due on the same contract of sale, if recorded
within sixty days of their dates, though on different days,
are contemporaneous in this sense.[1] A mortgage purporting
to be for purchase money, and recorded sixty-two days after
its date, may be shown by parol to have been delivered within
the sixty days preceding its recording, and so not to have
been divested by a sale on a later lien, notwithstanding
mechanics' liens binding the equitable title of the mortgagor
from a time anterior to the execution of the mortgage. That
the acknowledgment was within that time, that it was taken
by an alderman who was also a subscribing witness, that the
conveyance of the land whose purchase money was secured
by the mortgage was within that time, are circumstances
that should put the sheriff's vendee upon inquiry.[2] If two
mortgages represent the purchase money due on two successive
contracts of sale, they are, though executed simultaneously and
recorded within sixty days, not equal liens. That which secures
the money due on the first contract, is a superior lien to the
other. A sale on the latter will not divest the former. A.
contracted to sell a house to B., and B. the same house to C.
B. directed A. to make the deed directly to C., and C. to
execute two mortgages to A., one for the purchase money due
by B., and the other for the balance of the purchase money
due by C. on his contract with B. The latter, A. instantly
assigned to B. The former was the first lien, and was not
discharged by a sale on the latter. A sale on the former
would discharge the latter.[3] If A. conveys land to B.,
and on the same day B. executes two mortgages to A.,
respectively for $200 and $1,000, not purporting to be for
purchase money, the consideration mentioned in the deed
being $600 only, and the $200 mortgage is recorded a day

---

[1] Dungan v. American Life Ins.
Co., 52 Pa. St. 253. See Pease v.
Hoag, 11 Phila. 549.

[2] Parke v. Neeley, 90 Pa. St. 52.

[3] Dungan v. American Life Ins.
Co., 52 Pa. St. 253.

later than the other, a sale on it will not divest the other.[1]
A sale on a judgment recovered against a vendee under
articles, between their date and that of the execution of the
deed, will not divest a mortgage for the purchase money,
made and recorded simultaneously with the deed.[2] A. sold
land to B., and B. to C., A. making a deed directly to C., who
executed on the same day two mortgages, one to A. for the
purchase money due him by B., and another to B. for the
purchase money due him by C., less the amount of the
mortgage to A. The execution and recording of the two
mortgages on the same day, affected with notice of their
relative positions a purchaser of the mortgage to B. B.'s
mortgage was postponed to A.'s and divested by a sale on A.'s.[3]

Anteriority of Judgments, Legacies, Mechanics' Liens.

§ 842. A sale on a lien later than a mortgage, divests it,
if judgments precede it, whether these judgments have been
recovered against the mortgagor, or against a prior owner of
the mortgaged land.[4] So, if a legacy charged on the land,
and payable at a determinate epoch, precedes the mortgage,[5]
though the same will also charged an annuity on the land,
which is not discharged by the sale.[6] So, if a mechanics'
lien precedes the mortgage. If on its face it be valid and
relates to an earlier date than that of the recording of the
mortgage, this mortgage will be divested by a sale on a later
mortgage, though the work done was in fact (but this did
not appear by the record,) partly under one and partly under
a later disconnected process of construction, and though the
claim was filed more than six months after the close of the first
process of construction, and the second process of construction did not begin until after the recording of the mortgage.[7]

[1] Norris v. Brady, 4 Phila. 287.

[2] Cake's Appeal, 23 Pa. St. 186;
Eckert v. Lewis, 4 Phila. 422

[3] Appeals of Williamsport National Bank, 91 Pa. St. 163.

[4] Byers v. Hoch, 11 Pa. St. 258.

[5] Helfrich v. Weaver, 61 Pa. St.
385; Towers' Appropriation, 9 W. &
S. 103; Woods v. White, 10 W. N. C.
19

[6] Cowden's Estate, 1 Pa. St. 267.

[7] Harper's Appeal, 4 W. N. C. 49.

If, however, the mechanics' lien be void on its face, its ante-riority to the mortgage will not cause the discharge of the latter: *e. g.*, when the claim is apportioned against several distinct blocks of houses, separated by streets, a sheriff's sale under the mortgage divests the title of the vendee under a prior sale upon a judgment later than the mortgage.[1] If, after a mortgage is recorded, a mechanics' claim is filed, which does not state when the building began, but which is accompanied by a bill of particulars, showing work done before the mortgage, but not excluding the supposition that it might have been done in the shop in anticipation of the actual commencement of work on the ground, a sheriff's sale on a later judgment will not divest this mortgage, whatever information the purchaser at the sale may have had as to the beginning of the process of erection, and although this erection may have begun before the recording of the mortgage.[2]

Anteriority of Ground-Rent, Widow's Dower, Etc.

§ 843. When the deed by which the mortgagor acquired the land, charges it with the payment of a determinate sum of money at a certain time, a sale on a judgment later than the mortgage, will divest it; so, if the money be payable on A.'s death, and A. be dead when the sale takes place. If A. be still living, neither the mortgage nor the charge by deed is divested.[3] A sale on a judgment later than a mort-gage, of land charged with a perpetual ground-rent, does not divest the mortgage, though there are arrears of ground-rent due at the time of sale.[4] So, a sale of a coal lease on a *fi. fa.* subsequent to a mortgage of the leasehold, does not discharge the mortgage, though, under the reservation in the lease of a right of re-entry, the lessor has a lien upon the leasehold for arrears of rent, and these are paid out of the proceeds of the sale.[5]

[1] Goepp *v.* Gartiser, 35 Pa. St 130.
[2] Reading *v.* Hopson, 90 Pa St. 494.
[3] Strauss' Appeal, 49 Pa. St. 353.
[4] Devine's Appeal, 30 Pa. St. 348.
[5] Miners' Bank of Pottsville *v.* Heilner, 47 Pa. St. 452.

§ 844. A widow's third, charged on land, does not cause a mortgage executed by the heir, devisee or purchaser in partition, to be divested by a sale on a later lien during her life-time,[1] even if there are arrears of dower due at the sale.[2] When land subject to a widow's third, is, by order of the orphans' court after the decease of the accepting heir, sold, and a part of the purchase money is charged upon it, until the death of his widow, to whom the annual interest is to be paid, and the purchaser subsequently executes a mortgage thereof, this mortgage is not divested by a sale on a *testatum fi. fa.*, though there are arrears due to both widows, who are alive at the time of sale.[3]

Anteriority of Municipal and Tax Liens

§ 845. The priority of municipal claims and taxes created by the act of 3d February, 1824, liens superior to a mortgage, will not cause its divestiture by a sale on a later lien,[4] unless the sale takes place on a judgment recovered on a claim for an assessment, or tax actually imposed before the recording of the mortgage. A sale on a judgment for a tax assessed after such recording, will not divest the mortgage.[5] Under the act of 23d March, 1867, section three, [P. L. 44,] a sale on a judgment[6] or a mortgage,[7] which follows a mortgage, will not discharge the latter, though taxes assessed prior to the execution of it are a lien at the time of sale. Under the act of April 1st, 1864, [P. L. 206,] an award of a road jury is not a lien on the land, until a claim is filed therefor by the city solicitor. Mortgages are not divested by a sale on a later judgment, though before their execution

---

[1] Zeigler's Appeal, 35 Pa St. 173.

[2] Schall's Appeal, 40 Pa. St. 170; Wertz's Appeal, 65 Pa. St. 306. Contra, Kurtz's Appeal, 26 Pa. St. 465.

[3] Helfrich v. Weaver, 61 Pa. St. 385

[4] Act of 11th April, 1835, § 2, [P. L.

190;] Act of 16th April, 1845, § 4, [P. L. 488.]

[5] Perry v. Brinton, 13 Pa. St. 202; Cadmus v. Jackson, 52 Pa. St. 295.

[6] City of Harrisburg v. Orth, 6 W. N C. 121.

[7] Lea v. Brown, 9 W. N. C. 418.

an award had been made and confirmed by the court of quarter sessions, the claim not being filed till afterwards.[1]

When Mortgage Precedes all Other Liens.

§ 846. When a mortgage is neither preceded by, nor simultaneous with any other lien, a sale on a later lien cannot divest it, though the mortgage was executed before the act of April 6th, 1830, the sale taking place after the passage of that law.[2]　The excess of proceeds, after paying the subsequent liens, must be given to the defendant,[3] and if the mortgagee is the purchaser, he cannot decline to pay the amount of his bid by giving credit for it upon his mortgage. His mortgage is not discharged.[4]　Nor is it when one of two joint mortgagees becomes the purchaser at the sheriff's sale, under a later judgment.[5]　Though A. and B., co-tenants, execute a joint mortgage of their land, and, subsequently making partition thereof, agree that A.'s purpart shall be charged with five-eighths, and B.'s with three-eighths of the mortgage, a sale of B.'s purpart under a subsequent judgment against him, does not discharge the mortgage.[6] A sale on a second mortgage does not divest the first mortgage.[7]　A sale of the undivided two-ninths of land acquired by inheritance, on judgments against the heir, does not disturb a mortgage put upon the entire estate by the ancestor.[8] A mortgage executed at the time of a conveyance of land for the purchase money, is not discharged by a sale on a judgment recovered against the vendee under articles previously, but after the contract of sale had been made.[9]

Mortgage: Sale on Earlier Lien.

§ 847. A sale on any lien, though it be of such a class that its priority to a mortgage would not have caused

[1] Merriman v. Richardson, 5 W. N. C. 9.

[2] Garro v. Thompson, 7 W. 416.

[3] Street v. Sprout, 5 W. 272; Garro v. Thompson, 7 W. 416.

[4] Crawford v. Boyer, 14 Pa. St. 380.

[5] Wallace v. Blair, 1 Grant 75.

[6] Carpenter v. Koons, 20 Pa. St. 222.

[7] Mevey's Appeal, 4 Pa. St. 80.

[8] Estate of Elizabeth Jacoby, 9 Phila. 311.

[9] Cake's Appeal, 23 Pa. St. 186

the divestiture of the latter, by a sale on a later lien, will divest all succeeding liens, and, therefore, all subsequent mortgages. Hence, if a sale is made on a judgment based on a municipal lien, which is in fact older than the mortgage, the mortgage will be discharged,[1] provided the claim was duly registered before the recording of the mortgage; otherwise the mortgage will not be discharged.[2] A mortgage executed in 1849, of land on which is a perpetual ground-rent, is divested by a sale on a judgment recovered in an action of covenant for arrears of ground-rent begun in 1877.[3]

Mortgage: Sale on Later Lien for Same Debt.

§ 848. A sale on a later judgment, recovered for the mortgage debt,[4] or for any part of it,[5] such as arrears of interest,[6] though other parts of the mortgage debt are not due,[7] divests the mortgage. Hence, a *sci. fa.* cannot be subsequently sustained on the mortgage.[8] If, after the execution of bonds and a mortgage to secure them, the mortgagor makes a promissory note for the amount of one of them and the accrued interest, to one to whom it has been assigned, a sale on the judgment subsequently obtained on this note, divests the entire mortgage, and the proceeds of the sale are payable to the various assignees of the bonds, in preference to later lien creditors, although there was nothing on the record to

---

[1] Northern Liberties v. Swain, 13 Pa. St. 113; Perry v. Brinton, 13 Pa. St. 202.

[2] Act of 23d January, 1849, [P. L. 686,] applicable to Philadelphia.

[3] Amanda Martin's Appeal, 9 W. N. C. 484. But see Schoening v. Speck, 8 W. N. C. 44.

[4] McCall v. Lenox, 9 Serg. & R. 302; Berger v. Heister, 6 Wh. 210; Cronister v. Weise, 8 W. 215; Pierce v. Potter, 7 W. 475; Horning's Exr.'s Appeal, 90 Pa. St. 388; Blocker v. Blocker, 11 Leg. Int. 64; Bratton's Appeal, 8 Pa. St. 164; Bradley v.

Chester Valley R. R. Co., 36 Pa. St. 141.

[5] Dougherty & Potts' Appeal, 1 W. N C 593; Larimer's Appeal, 22 Pa. St. 41.

[6] Clarke v. Stanley, 10 Pa. St. 472; West Branch Bank v. Chester, 11 Pa. St. 282; Mendenhall v West Chester, etc., R. R. Co., 36 Pa. St. 145; Hartz v. Wood, 8 Pa. St. 471.

[7] McGrew v. McLanahan, 1 P. & W. 44; Larimer's Appeal, 22 Pa. St. 41.

[8] Berger v. Heister, 6 Wh. 210.

show the identity of the debt represented by the note, and that secured by the mortgage.[1] A sale on a transcript of a judgment of a justice of the peace, for interest due on a bond secured by a mortgage, divests it.[2] The mortgage may secure a previous debt, for which the subsequent judgment is rendered; a sale on this judgment will discharge the mortgage.[3] If there are two executions in the sheriff's hands at the same time, one on a judgment on a bond secured by a mortgage, the other on a judgment for a distinct debt, the mortgage creditor may preserve the lien of his mortgage by staying his writ, and at the sale giving notice thereof, and that the purchaser will buy subject to the mortgage.[4] If a mortgage is taken for one part of the purchase money of land, and a judgment note for the balance, a sale on the judgment entered on such note, will not affect the mortgage. They are not for the same debt.[5] When a mortgage secures several bonds, assigned to different persons, the proceeds of the land must be divided *pro rata* between them,[6] although the mortgage has been expressly assigned to one of these persons only, and the others, at the time of the assignment to them of other bonds, had no knowledge of the existence of the mortgage.[7]

§ 849. If, subsequently to a first mortgage, a judgment for the same debt has been recovered, but the sheriff's sale takes place on some other lien, whether between the mortgage and the judgment,[8] or after both,[9] the lien of the mortgage is not divested; the proceeds of the sale are not applicable to it, or

---

[1] Bittinger's Appeal, 6 W. N. C. 231.

[2] Hartz v. Wood, 8 Pa. St. 471.

[3] Ridgway v. Longaker, 18 Pa. St. 215.

[4] Shryock v. Jones, 22 Pa. St 303.

[5] Cummings' Appeal, 23 Pa. St. 509.

[6] Donley v. Hays, 17 Serg. & R.

400; West Branch Bank v. Chester, 11 Pa. St 282; Mendenhall v. West Chester, etc., R. R. Co., 36 Pa. St. 145.

[7] Betz v. Heebner, 1 P. & W. 280.

[8] Kuhn's Appeal, 2 Pa. St. 264.

[9] Commonwealth v. Wilson, 34 Pa. St. 63; Cross v. Stahlman, 43 Pa. St. 129.

to the judgment. This principle is affirmed by the fifth section of the act of April 16th, 1845, [P. L. 488.]

Mortgages: Orphans' Court Sale.

§ 850. Except in those counties in which the act of 23d March, 1867, [P. L. 44,] operates, an orphans' court sale of a decedent's lands for his debts not of record, under the act of 18th April, 1853, will divest a mortgage executed by him prior to his death, and a first lien.[1] A first mortgage put on the land by A., and subject to which he sells to B., is discharged by an orphans' court sale of it for B.'s debts.[2] Where the act of 1867 operates, such sales are like sales in execution, and do not discharge first mortgages.[3]

Mortgages: Partition.

§ 851. The right of a co-tenant to divest the title of his co-owner, when needful to effect partition, is in the nature of a prior lien to any encumbrance which a co-tenant may put upon his undivided interest. Notwithstanding the acts of April 6th, 1830, and March 23d, 1867, a sale in partition will divest a mortgage created by a co-tenant. A mortgage on an undivided third was discharged by sale in partition in the district court.[4] After such sale, a *sci. fa.* on such mortgage cannot be sustained,[5] nor an ejectment,[6] and a sale on the mortgage will be void. If, on petition of the widow of a decedent, for the setting apart of her dower, a sale is made of the land, a mortgage previously put on it by the sole heir will be divested.[7]

---

[1] Jermon v. Lyon, 81 Pa. St. 107; Blank's Appeal, 3 Grant 192. In the former of these cases, the mortgage was preserved by an agreement between the heirs, the vendee and the mortgagee.

[2] Cadmus v. Jackson, 52 Pa. St. 295; Moore v. Schultz, 13 Pa. St. 98; Ross' Estate, 9 Pa. St. 17.

[3] Bloomer's Estate, 2 W. N. C. 68; Grice's Estate, 2 W. N. C. 211.

[4] Girard Life Ins. Co. v. Farmers' and Mechanics' Bank, 57 Pa. St. 388

[5] Wright v. Vickers' Adm., 81 Pa. St. 122. A sale on the mortgage divests the owelty. McCandless' Appeal, 10 W. N. C. 563.

[6] Baird v. Corwin, 17 Pa. St. 462. Here the mortgagee received the proceeds of the sale of the two-fifths bound by his mortgage. The whole mortgage debt was discharged, though only partially paid.

[7] Steel's Appeal, 86 Pa. St. 222.

If the partition is effected by a physical division of the land into purparts of equal value, one of which is allotted to each of the co-tenants, the mortgage is translated from the undivided interest in the whole of the original tract, to the entire interest in the part of it thus allotted to the mortgagor.[1] If the purparts are unequal, and the one assigned to the mortgagor must be charged with owelty, in order to equalize the co-tenants, this owelty is a charge upon the entire interest in the purpart, and prior in rank to the mortgage. From the proceeds of its judicial sale the owelty must be first paid.[2]

Effect of Agreements on Discharge of Mortgage.

§ 852. An orphans' court sale of a decedent's lands, which would otherwise divest a mortgage imposed on them by him, will not have that effect if the purchaser, the heirs and the mortgagee agree, and the deed is expressly subject to the mortgage.[3] The lien of the mortgage may be continued if the condition of sale, (in writing signed by the purchaser,) the sheriff's return and deed show that such was the understanding at the sale.[4] Nor, is it necessary that the sheriff's deed manifest this understanding, when in fact the purchaser and the mortgagee both believed, at the sale, that the mortgage would not be discharged by it, and the price bid was correspondingly less than it would otherwise have been.[5] The understanding at the sale, that a mortgage will not be discharged, may be produced by an announcement by the sheriff,[6] or his crier,[7] to that effect, though neither the levy nor the return of sale, nor the sheriff's deed, is expressly subject to the mortgage. Whispers among bystanders at the sheriff's sale that the mortgage will not be divested, will not preserve it, the sheriff not so declaring, and the record of the sale not

---

[1] Wright v. Vickers' Adm., 81 Pa. St. 122.

[2] Appeal of McCandless' Exr., 10 W. N. C. 563.

[3] Jermon v. Lyon, 81 Pa. St. 107.

[4] Schall's Appeal, 40 Pa. St. 170.

[5] Zeigler's Appeal, 35 Pa. St. 173.

[6] Stackpole v. Glassford, 16 Pa. St. 163.

[7] Towers' Appropriation, 9 W. & S. 103; Towers v. Tuscarora Academy, 8 Pa. St. 297.

so showing.[1] Yet, when, just after the act of April 6th, 1830, had been passed, a sale took place, the bystanders at which had no knowledge of the passage of the act, a sale on a later lien divested a first mortgage, such being the general understanding.[2] The understanding at the sale which will preserve a lien that would otherwise be divested, should appear from the conditions of the sale; loose declarations made at the time of sale, or notice given that there are subsisting liens, are not sufficient.[3] All the parties to the purchase, all the lien creditors, must consent, and even then the encumbrance will not be saved from discharge as to a purchaser from the sheriff's vendee with notice, the record not showing that the sheriff's sale was subject to the mortgage.[4]

§ 853. If the sheriff's purchaser does not pay the amount of the mortgage from his bid, the mortgagee consenting, for his accommodation, that it shall remain on the land, this agreement, though binding on the mortgagee, is not valid as to one who purchases the land from him without notice of it.[5] Though a purchaser at sheriff's sale admits in court that he bought subject to a mortgage, and paid a correspondingly less price for the land, and that he signed a condition of sale of this character, a subsequent sheriff's sale under this mortgage, though valid against the purchaser, would not be valid against his lien creditors, to whom, to the exclusion of the mortgagee, the proceeds must be paid.[6] When a sale took place on the second of two mortgages, the mortgagee becoming the purchaser, and, in ignorance that there was a judgment before both mortgages, notice was read that the first mortgage would not be divested, and the price paid was less than what would have been paid by the amount of the first mortgage, a *sci. fa.* subsequently sued out on this first mortgage

---

[1] Fickes *v.* Ersick, 2 R. 165.

[2] Shultze *v.* Diehl, 2 P. & W. 273.

[3] Barnet *v.* Washabough, 16 Serg. & R. 410.

[4] Loomis' Appeal, 22 Pa. St. 312.

[5] Roberts *v.* Williams, 5 Wh. 170.

[6] Mode's Appeal, 6 W. & S. 280.

was sustained against the sheriff's vendee.[1]   A mortgage for purchase money, not recorded for three years, nor until judgments had been recovered against the mortgagor, was preserved from divestiture by a sale on one of these judgments, when notice was given by the mortgagee, at the sale, that the mortgage would not be discharged, the price paid was correspondingly less, and the purchaser subsequently admitted that he had bought subject to the mortgage, and the judgment creditors made no objection. A *sci. fa.* was subsequently sustained against a *terre-tenant* who had bought from the purchaser at sheriff's sale, paying less than the price of the land, by the amount of the mortgage.[2]   And ejectment was sustained on a mortgage, after a sheriff's sale under an earlier lien, the sheriff stating that the sale would be subject to the mortgage for about $600, and the purchaser paying $160 only for the land, which was worth $1,200.[3]   There being two mortgages on land, which was subsequently aliened to one who became also owner of the first mortgage, the land was next sold to A., who agreed to take subject to this first mortgage.   At a sheriff's sale under the second mortgage, the second mortgagee became the purchaser, but, in written conditions signed by himself, agreed to buy subject to whatever might be due in law on the first mortgage.   The first mortgage was held to be not divested.[4]

Legacies.

§ 854. Legacies charged on land are discharged by a sale on a judgment against the devisee of the land,[5] or against the accepting heir.[6]   When land is devised to four sons, and

---

[1] Ashmead *v.* McCarthur, 67 Pa. St. 326.

[2] Crooks *v.* Douglass, 56 Pa. St. 51.

[3] Muse *v.* Letterman, 13 Serg. & R. 167.

[4] Helmbold *v.* Man, 4 Wh. 410.

[5] Cowden's Estate, 1 Pa. St. 267; Donaldson *v.* West Branch Bank, 1 Pa. St. 286; Bank *v.* Donaldson, 7

W. & S. 407; Barnet *v.* Washabaugh, 16 Serg. & R. 410; Hanna's Appeal, 31 Pa. St. 53; Drake *v.* Brown, 68 Pa. St. 223; Towers *v.* Tuscarora Academy, 8 Pa. St. 297; Towers' Appropriation, 9 W. & S. 103.

[6] Nichols *v.* Postlethwaite, 2 Dall. 131; Jane Gallagher's Appeal, 48 Pa. St. 121.

a certain sum is charged on it in favor of the testator's daughters, a sale of the share of one of the sons, on a judgment against him, divests from it the legacy.[1] If the legacy is partly payable in money, and partly in "horses, cattle, sheep or other stock at fair prices," the whole legacy is payable from the proceeds of the land on which it is charged, sold on a judgment against the devisee for his debt.[2] A legacy payable in equal annual installments in ten years, is divested by a sale after the ten years, and after the death of the devisee, on a judgment recovered against him in his life-time.[3] Nor is it necessary that the legacy should be already payable when the judicial sale takes place. Thus, when the testator directed the payment of a legacy of £200, in installments of $100 every fifth year, and only one installment had become due when the sale took place on a judgment against the devisee, the entire legacy was divested from the land in the hands of the sheriff's vendee.[4] If the future time at which a legacy is payable is uncertain, a judicial sale of the land before the arrival of that time, will not divest it, e. g., when the legacy is to be paid alternatively, on the attainment of majority by, or on the marriage of, the legatee.[5] A legacy of $2,000 charged on land, to be paid to the legatee between the ages of twenty-one and twenty-five years, was not divested by a sale on a judgment against the devisee before the legatee reached the age of twenty-one.[6] When a devise of land, to take effect after the termination of a life-estate, is made, subject to a valuation to be made at the life-tenant's death, a sheriff's sale of the land during her life, on a judgment against the devisee of the fee, does not discharge the money payable accord-

[1] Lapsley v. Lapsley, 9 Pa. St. 130; Loomis' Appeal, 22 Pa. St. 312; Barnet v. Washabaugh, 16 Serg. & R. 410.

[2] Jane Gallagher's Appeal, 48 Pa. St. 121.

[3] Riley's Appeal, 34 Pa. St. 291.

[4] Hellman v. Hellman, 4 Rawle 439; Lobach's Case, 6 W. 167; Loomis' Appeal, 22 Pa. St. 312.

[5] Cowden's Estate, 1 Pa. St. 267.

[6] Dewart's Appeal, 43 Pa. St. 325.

ing to the valuation to be subsequently made.[1] A devise was made subject to the payment of $3,000 in four equal annual installments, after the decease of the widow. A sale by order of the orphans' court, during her life, for legacies presently payable, did not divest the $3,000.[2] In his lifetime, A. conveyed land to B. and his children, for their lives; he also, by his will, devised the same in fee to B.'s children, as tenants in common, subject to the payment of $2,500. A sheriff's sale of the interest of these grantees in the deed, before they had elected to take under the will, did not divest the $2,500, which continued a charge on the land, the sheriff's vendee subsequently electing to take under the will.[3] An orphans' court sale for the payment of debts of the devisee, on his death,[4] or for the payment of the legacies under the fifty-ninth section of the act of February 24th, 1832, [P. L. 84,] divests legacies. When land was devised to three persons as tenants in common, charged with legacies, and it was subsequently divided among them, by partition in the common pleas, each purpart remained charged with only one-third of the legacies.[5]

§ 855. When, between the legacies and the later lien on which the sale takes place, there is a lien which is not divestible by the sale, the legacies cannot be divested. Thus, when the devisee of lands charged with legacies died, and one of his heirs accepted them in partition, charged with his widow's dower, a sale on a judgment against the heir did not divest the legacies.[6] When land is devised to A., who is also

---

[1] Hart v. Homiller, 20 Pa. St. 248, 23 Pa. St. 39. Here the interest of the defendant was described in the writ and in the sheriff's deed as subject to the valuation. The price paid was $100; the valuation afterwards made was $2,250.

[2] Solliday v. Gruver, 7 Pa. St. 452.

[3] Newman's Appeal, 35 Pa. St. 339.

The right of election passed to the sheriff's vendee.

[4] McLanahan v. Wyant, 1 P. & W. 96.

[5] McLanahan v. Wyant, 2 P. & W. 279.

[6] Lauman's Appeal, 8 Pa. St. 473. Yet, arrears due to the widow of the devisor, and to the widow of the

made executor of the devisor's will, which charges a legacy on it, and A. then sells it to B., subject to the legacy, the latter is discharged by a sale on the mortgage which B. executes for the purchase money, although A. becomes the purchaser.[1]

Annuities.

§ 856. When a will charges an annuity on land, a sale of it on a judgment against the devisee, during the life of the annuitant, divests the arrears due at the time of the sale, but not installments becoming due afterwards.[2] The annuitant obtained two judgments for arrears due her for successive periods of time, on the second of which the land charged with the annuity was sold. From the proceeds, not only the two judgments, but the arrears become due between the time when the second action was brought and the sale, were payable.[3] The devisee of land charged with an annuity in favor of the widow of the devisor, died, and his land was sold in partition, subject to the dower of his own widow. The arrears due both widows at the time of a sale on a judgment against the purchaser in partition, were payable from the proceeds, but the annuity and the dower remained undivested.[4] A sale by order of the orphans' court, during the life of the annuitant, for legacies presently payable, will not divest the annuity charged by the same will upon the land.[5] When the annuity is secured by a mortgage, (the first lien,) a sale on a judgment later than the mortgage does not divest

---

devisee, were both paid from the proceeds. In Towers' Appropriation, 9 W. & S. 103, the legacies were followed by a mortgage made by the devisee, and though, by agreement, the mortgage was not divested by a sale on a later judgment, the legacies were divested.

[1] Woods v. White, 10 W. N. C. 19.

[2] Reed v. Reed, 1 W. & S. 235;

Cowden's Estate, 1 Pa. St. 267; Hart v. Homiller, 20 Pa. St. 248.

[3] Mohler's Appeal, 5 Pa. St. 418. The widow having assigned one of these judgments without guarantee, the proceeds were payable *pro rata* to her and her assignee on the entire amount of arrears due.

[4] Lauman's Appeal, 8 Pa. St. 473.

[5] Solliday v. Gruver, 7 Pa. St. 452.

it as respects installments falling due afterwards.[1] A sale on a judgment recovered against the devisor in his life-time, divests an annuity charged by his will on the land, in favor of his widow.[2]

The Principal of a Widow's Dower.

§ 857. When, in proceedings in partition, or for the assignment of a widow's dower, a principal sum is charged on land, the interest of which is to be paid annually to her, she has an estate in the nature of a rent-charge.[3] A judicial sale of the land out of which the dower issues, on a lien later in origin than the decease of her husband, and during her life-time, will not divest this estate.[4] Thus is it when the sale is on a mortgage, the first lien after the dower,[5] (though it divests the arrears of a dower,[6]) or when the sale is on a judgment succeeding such a mortgage,[7] or on a judgment next succeeding the dower, though there are arrears due,[8] or on a second mortgage, another mortgage being the sole lien between it and the dower, on which dower are arrears due.[9] When an heir, who has accepted the land of his deceased father, subject to the widow's dower, dies, and this land is sold under an order of the orphans' court for the payment of debts, the widow still living, such sale does not divest the principal of the widow's dower.[10]

---

[1] Knaub v. Esseck, 2 W. 282.

[2] Mix v. Acla. 7 W 316.

[3] Gourley v. Kinley, 66 Pa. St. 270; Schall's Appeal, 40 Pa. St. 170.

[4] Fisher v. Kean, 1 W. 259; Mentzer v. Menor, 8 W. 296.

[5] Zeigler's Appeal, 35 Pa. St. 173; Davison's Appeal, 38 Leg. Int. 294; White v. Williams, 3 Phila. 460.

[6] Zeigler's Appeal, 35 Pa. St. 173; Plumer's Appeal, 11 W. N C. 144.

[7] Kurtz's Appeal, 26 Pa. St. 465. The proceeds here were applied to the mortgage, on the theory that the mortgage was divested. In this respect. this case is inconsistent with Zeigler's Appeal, 35 Pa. St. 173; Schall's Appeal, 40 Pa. St. 170; Wertz's Appeal, 65 Pa. St. 306.

[8] Lauman's Appeal, 8 Pa. St. 473; Baily v. Commonwealth, 41 Pa. St. 473; Kline v. Bowman, 19 Pa. St. 24; Schertzer's Exr. v. Herr, 19 Pa. St. 34; Wynn v. Brooke, 5 Rawle 106.

[9] Schall's Appeal, 40 Pa. St. 170.

[10] Vandever v Baker, 13 Pa. St 121. Here the dower was secured by mortgage.

§ 858. A sale on a mortgage given by an accepting heir, in partition, to secure the owelty of other heirs, will not, during the widow's life, divest her dower. Hence, at her death, the sheriff's vendee cannot interpose this sale as a defence against the suit of the other heirs for their shares in the principal of the dower.[1] When a recognizance is given by an heir, who accepts lands in partition, to secure the interests of his co-heirs and the widow's third, and judgment is recovered thereon during the widow's life, at the suit of one of the heirs, and the land is sold, the principal of the dower, though there are arrears due, is not divested. At her death, the same heir may bring another action on the recognizance to charge the land with his share of the principal.[2] That the widow has remarried, and her husband has become *terre-tenant* of the land charged with her dower, will not cause a sale of it, on a judgment recovered against him, to divest the dower, she living.[3] An allotment of A.'s land, at his death, in proceedings in partition in the common pleas, to one of his heirs, does not divest a dower which encumbered it in A's life-time.[4] When land is encumbered by the dowers of the widows of two successive owners, neither these dowers, though there are arrears due on each, nor an immediately succeeding mortgage, is divested by a sale on a lien later than the mortgage.[5] A sale on a lien prior to the date őf origin of the widow's dower, will divest it.[6]

§ 859. If the interest of a decedent in land is an equitable one under articles of sale, and, in proceedings in partition, this interest is allotted to an heir, and subsequently, on payment of the unpaid purchase money, the deed containing no reference to the inchoate title of the ancestor, or to the

[1] Medlar *v.* Aulenbach, 2 P. & W. 355.

[2] Mentzer *v.* Menor, 8 W. 296. So, when a recognizance secures the widow's one-third alone. Connelly *v.* Withers, 9 L. Bar. 117.

[3] First Nat. Bank *v.* Cockley, 2 Pearson 122, 2 Leg. Opin. 208.

[4] Seaton *v* Barry, 4 W. & S. 183.

[5] Helfrich *v.* Weaver, 61 Pa. St. 385.

[6] Fisher *v.* Kean, 1 W. 259.

proceedings in partition, is made directly to the heir, and if, afterwards, judgments are recovered against the heir, under which the land is sold, the purchaser having no actual notice of the widow's dower, this dower is divested from the land, though the widow be still living.[1] When land encumbered with a widow's dower is sold on a judgment later than the dower, and she dies between the levy of the execution and the sale, the principal of that dower is divested by the sale, and must be paid from the proceeds;[2] *a fortiori* when her death occurs before the recovery of the judgment on which the sale is effected.[3]

Annual Arrears of Dower.

§ 860. Installments of dower due the widow are divested by a judicial sale on a lien arising subsequently to the origin of the dower, provided there is no intermediate lien which, under existing laws, would not be divested. When, following the dower, are several judgments, a sale on one divests arrears.[4] So does a sale on a mortgage, the first lien after the dower.[5] When a *sci. fa.* was sued out on a recognizance given to secure the owelty of heirs and the widow's dower, before the widow's death, and a judgment was recovered, and the land subject thereto was sold by the sheriff, arrears of dower for six years were payable from the proceeds to the widow, though she had become the wife of the owner of the land. This made

---

[1] Dickinson *v.* Beyer, 87 Pa. St. 274. Comp Hibberd *v.* Bovier, 1 Grant 266, where it is said that a mortgage to secure maintenance for A and his wife for life would be divested by a sheriff's sale to a purchaser having neither constructive nor actual notice of its existence.

[2] Riddle & Pennock's Appeal, 37 Pa. St. 177; Bailey *v.* Commonwealth, 41 Pa. St. 473.

[3] Hillbish's Appeal, 89 Pa. St. 490. Here the partition took place in 1837; widow died in 1858; judgment against the accepting heir in 1862,

who died in 1870, and his land was sold by his administrator for payment of debts.

[4] Lauman's Appeal, 8 Pa. St. 473; Dickinson *v.* Beyer, 87 Pa. St. 274; Schertzer's Exr. *v.* Herr, 19 Pa. St. 34.

[5] Zeigler's Appeal, 35 Pa. St. 173; Plumer's Appeal, 11 W. N. C. 144; Davison's Appeal, 38 Leg. Int. 294. Here the widow was remarried at the time of the sale. As to estoppel of the purchaser from alleging divestiture of arrears, see Plumer's Appeal, *supra*.

no presumption of payment.[1] A sale on the second of two
mortgages, which are the first liens succeeding the dower,[2] or
on a judgment immediately succeeding the first mortgage,[3]
will not divest the intervening mortgage, nor, consequently,
the arrears of dower, whether these arrears fell due before or
after the execution of the intervening mortgage.

Arrears of Rent on a Lease.

§ 861. The reservation in a lease of a right of re-entry
and of forfeiture for non-payment of rent, constitutes the
equivalent of a lien upon the leasehold, but a sheriff's sale
of the leasehold, under an execution against the lessee, divests
it, so far as arrears of rent due at the time of the sale are
concerned. Such arrears are payable from the proceeds of
the sale in preference to the *fi. fa*, or the wages of labor due
under the act of 1849.[4] When a mortgage of the leasehold
intervened between the date of the lease and the execution,
the arrears were paid, though the mortgage was not divested.[5]

Arrears of Ground-Rent.

§ 862. When, after an estate in a rent for life or in fee,
issuing out of certain land, has been created by reservation
in a deed which conveys the land itself, liens arise against
the land, a judicial sale on any of such liens will divest the
arrears on the ground-rent, due or becoming due down to
the acknowledgment of the sheriff's deed.[6] The sheriff's
vendee is not liable for rent that accrues between the date of
the sale and of the acknowledgment of his deed.[7] Yet,

[1] First Nat. Bank *v.* Cockley, 2
Pearson 122, 2 Leg. Opin. 208

[2] Schall's Appeal, 40 Pa. St 170.

[3] Wertz's Appeal, 65 Pa. St. 306

[4] Wood's Appeal, 30 Pa. St. 274;
Spangler's Appeal, 30 Pa. St. 277,
note.

[5] Miner's Bank *v.* Heilner, 47 Pa.
St. 452. The history of the case (p.
454) shows this. See, also, Judge
Agnew's opinion, p. 462. This is in-

consistent with the principle of
Wertz's Appeal, 65 Pa. St 306; Devine's Appeal, 30 Pa. St. 348.

[6] Mather *v.* McMichael, 13 Pa. St.
301; Dougherty's Estate, 9 W. & S.
189; Pancoast's Appeal, 8 W. & S.
381; Ter Hoven *v.* Kerns, 2 Pa. St.
96; Watson *v.* Bradley, 1 Phila. 177.

[7] Thomas *v.* Connell, 5 Pa. St. 13.
This was a case stated in covenant,
the question being whether the pur-

when a sale of the land took place September 23d, 1835, and, on return of the writ, a motion was made to set the sale aside, and, on April 26th, 1836, the court confirmed the sale, it was determined that a six months' installment of rent falling due in the interim, was not payable from the proceeds. "The date of the sale," said Sergeant, J., "is the point of time to which all the lien debts are to be computed."[1] A sale on a judgment recovered for arrears of ground-rent, after other judgments against the ground-tenant, will divest all arrears.[2] If a first mortgage intervene between the deed which reserves the ground-rent and the lien on which the sheriff's sale takes place, the arrears of ground-rent then due will not be divested, because the mortgage will not be.[3] When there are two ground-rents reserved to successive owners, and a mortgage is executed subsequently to the creation of the later of them, a sale on this mortgage does not divest the arrears due on the first of these ground-rents: the land continues liable for them.[4]

Debts of a Decedent.

§ 863. Prior to the act of 1832, in regard to the estates of decedents, a sheriff's sale on liens obtained upon lands in the ownership of heirs, divested the debts of the ancestor. A. died, and his estate devolved on B., C. and D., by inheritance. Their interests being sold on a judgment against

chaser at the sheriff's sale was personally liable for rent falling due between the day of sale and the date of the sheriff's deed.

[1] Walton v. West, 4 Wh. 221. Cited approvingly, Bachdell's Appeal, 56 Pa. St. 386.

[2] Bantleon v. Smith, 2 Binn. 146; Potts v. Rhodes, cited 2 Binn. 148. So, when the judgment for arrears, on which the sale takes place, is preceded only by a judgment for the prior arrears. Fassitt v. Middleton, 47 Pa. St. 214.

[3] Field v. Oberteuffer, 2 Phila. 271; Devine's Appeal, 30 Pa. St. 348. Here the mortgage was executed when there were no arrears of ground-rent.

[4] Hacker v. Cozens, 8 W. N. C. 189. Lauman's Appeal, 8 Pa. St. 473, is inconsistent with this. So is Miners' Bank v. Heilner, 47 Pa. St. 454, 462, where, though a mortgage on a leasehold was not divested by a sale on a later lien, arrears of rent due on the lease, which reserved a right of re-entry, were paid from the proceeds.

them, the debts of A., unpaid at the sale, were paid from the proceeds, although the sale took place long before the lien of these debts, for which no action had been brought, would have expired.[1] When land is devised to A., charged with the payment of the testator's debts, and, on a judgment against A., is sold, these debts (they having been reduced to judgment) will continue to bind the land. If the sheriff's vendee permits land devised to others to be sold for these debts, and becomes the purchaser, he will be a mere trustee for the other devisees, of the land so purchased.[2] If land is devised to A., without charge of debts upon it, but subject to the widow's maintenance or dower, as she shall prefer, a sale on a judgment against A. will not divest a judgment recovered against the testator in his life-time. The indivestible charge in favor of the widow, prevents the discharge of the earlier encumbrance.[3] For the same reason the debt of the ancestor, for which a judgment has been recovered against his administrator, is not divested when, in proceedings in partition, the land was charged with the widow's dower, and afterwards, but·before the judgment against the administrator, a judgment was obtained against the accepting heir for his own debt, on which the land was sold.[4]

§ 864. Since the act of 1832, a sale of inherited land on a judgment against the heir, does not divest the ancestor's debts. A subsequent sale, therefore, of the same land, under an order of the orphans' court for the payment of the ancestor's debts, will convey the better title. The legislation since 1832, has designed to commit the administration of decedents' estates exclusively to the orphans' court.[5] Yet, when judgments were recovered against three devisees, and

---

[1] Milliken v. Kendig, 2 P. & W. 477; Luce v. Snively, 4 W. 396; Custer v. Detterer, 3 W. & S. 28.

[2] Parr v. Bouzer, 16 Pa. St. 309.

[3] Mix v. Acla, 7 W. 316.

[4] Swar's Appeal, 1 Pa. St. 92.

[5] Horner v. Hasbrouck, 41 Pa. St. 169. Here the purchaser under the execution had notice of the debts of the decedent.

the devised land was sold, debts of the testator, and the expenses of the administration of his estate, were paid from the proceeds, to the detriment of legatees.[1]

§ 865. An orphans' court sale for the payment of a decedent's debts discharges them, including judgments recovered against him in his life-time, though, by the misconduct of the administrator, the proceeds are not actually paid to the creditors.[2] A sheriff's sale of decedent's lands, on a judgment against him, discharges the lien of all his debts, and they must be paid from the proceeds in preference to the debts of the devisee.[3] A sale in partition in the orphans' court discharges the debts of the decedent, and the administrator who has advanced them from his own funds is subrogated to them as against the proceeds.[4] First mortgages, created by a decedent, are saved from divestiture by an orphans' court sale in partition, or for the payment of his debts, by the act of 23d March, 1867, [P. L. 44,] supplemented by the acts of March 10th, 1870, [P. L. 37,] of 24th April, 1869, [P. L. 1213,] of 28th June, 1871, [P. L. 1379,] and of 9th April, 1872, [P. L. 1103,] in the city of Philadelphia, and the counties of Allegheny, Perry, Berks and Venango. Where these statutes do not operate, mortgages of a decedent are, like all his other debts, divested by orphans' court sales for payment of his debts,[5] and a mortgage given by a former owner of the land is, for this purpose, regarded as

---

[1] Hanna's Appeal, 31 Pa. St. 53. And in Cowden's Estate, 1 Pa. St. 267, the property of a devisee charged with his ancestor's debts was sold by the sheriff in 1844, on a judgment against the devisee, and these debts were paid from the proceeds.

[2] Moliere's Lessee v. Noe, 4 Dall. 451.

[3] Evans v. Duncan, 4 W. 24. But, after paying the liens on record before the decedent's death, the surplus must be paid to the executor or administrator, he giving adequate security. Creditors who have obtained judgment against the personal representative, even though it is highly probable there are no other creditors, are not entitled to receive the proceeds directly. Willing v. Yohe, 1 Phila. 223.

[4] Wallace's Appeal, 5 Pa. St. 103.

[5] Moore v. Shultz, 13 Pa. St. 98.

a debt of the decedent.[1] When these statutes do apply, the first mortgage of a decedent will not be divested by an orphans' court sale for the payment of his debts. Hence, if such mortgage, or other undivestible lien, is the only debt of such decedent, the orphans' court cannot properly grant an order for the sale of his land.[2]

§ 866. When inherited lands are conveyed by the heir to A., on whose death they are sold by the order of the orphans' court for A.'s debts, a judgment recovered against the administrator of the heir's ancestor is divested, and cannot, therefore, be subsequently revived by *sci. fa.* against the land.[3] So, when A., accepting land of his deceased father in partition, entered into a recognizance for the owelty of other heirs, and died, devising the land to B., from whom it passed successively to C. and D., and, D. dying, his administrator sold under the order of the orphans' court for D.'s debts, the lien of the recognizance was divested.[4] When a power is given by testament to the executor to sell the decedent's lands, and from the proceeds to pay his debts generally, and to educate his minor children, and a debt due by his son to A., for the purchase money of a tract of land which the son holds in trust for the decedent, is specified as one of decedent's debts, a sale under the power discharges the land of the lien of all debts not of record in the decedent's life-time, without the purchaser's seeing to the proper application to them of the

---

[1] Cadmus v. Jackson, 52 Pa. St. 295; Moore v. Shultz, 13 Pa. St. 98.

[2] Grice's Estate, 2 W N. C. 211. That a bond accompanies the mortgage makes no difference; neither bond nor mortgage can be paid from the proceeds of an orphans' court sale for debts. Bloomer's Estate, 2 W. N. C. 68.

[3] Custer v. Detterer, 3 W. & S. 28.

[4] Crawford v. Crawford, 2 W. 339. Not reconcilable with these cases is Stallman's Estate, 6 Phila 389, where it was decided that when A., one of whose debts was in judgment, died, devising an undivided half of a tract of land to B., who sold it to C., the owner of the other undivided half, and C. died, and this land was sold for his debts by order of the orphans' court, such sale did not divest the debts of A. from what had been his undivided one-half.

purchase money.[1] So, when, after specifically devising certain lands, the testator directs three trustees to sell the remainder, if necessary, for the payment of "any of his debts," the person to whom they sell will not be bound to see that general debts, even those for which judgments have been recovered in due time against the executor, shall be paid by the trustees from the proceeds; yet, he will take the land discharged of the lien of all debts not of record in the lifetime of the testator.[2]

Municipal Liens and Taxes.

§ 867. Such liens are subject to the general rule, that a judicial sale divests all liens,[3] except so far as the application of this rule has been modified by statute or construction. By construction the principle has been introduced that when, between the lien on which the sale takes place and the earlier municipal lien or tax, an undivestible lien, such as a mortgage, intervenes, the municipal lien or tax is not divested. This is true, whether the municipal improvements were made or taxes assessed before the mortgage;[4] or, originating subsequently, became a superior lien to the mortgage, by reason of some statute.[5] Since, by the act of April 11th, 1835, a mortgage is preserved from divestiture, though a municipal lien have precedence of it, it was decided that on a sale on a lien later than such a mortgage, the municipal lien was not divested, because the mortgage was not.[6] As to Philadelphia, this result was modified by the act of 16th April, 1845, [P. L. 488,] which declares

---

[1] Grant v. Hook, 13 Serg. & R. 259.

[2] Cadbury v. Duval, 10 Pa. St. 265. See Spear v. Hannum, 1 Y. 380, 2 Dall. 291.

[3] Eaton's Appeal, 83 Pa. St. 152; Pittsburgh's Appeal, 70 Pa. St. 142.

[4] Northern Liberties v. Swain, 13 Pa. St. 113; City of Harrisburg v. Orth, 2 Pearson 340.

[5] The acts of 3d February, 1824, and of 27th March, 1824, make it a first lien. A provision that the lien of taxes, etc., shall continue until fully paid and satisfied, makes them a first lien. Pittsburgh's Appeal, 70 Pa. St. 142; Eaton's Appeal, 83 Pa. St. 152.

[6] Northern Liberties v. Swain, 13 Pa. St. 113; Harrisburg v. Orth, 2 Pearson 340.

that the intervention of an undivested mortgage, shall not prevent the divestiture of municipal liens or taxes, unless the sale is on a judgment recovered to enforce a lien in fact existing before the execution of the mortgage.[1] Following this act is that of March 11th, 1846, [P. L. 115,] which saves from divestiture municipal liens and taxes, only so far as the proceeds of the sale lawfully applicable thereto, shall be sufficient to satisfy them. If sufficient to satisfy them, they are divested, though the proceeds be not in fact applied to them.[2]

§ 868. The sale which effects this divestiture may be an orphans' court sale for the payment of a decedent's debts,[3] or in partition, on the petition of the widow,[4] or a sale on a judgment.[5] It may be the sale of an equitable title under articles of agreement for the sale of the land,[6] or the sale of the interest of one of several co-tenants,[7] or the sale of the estate of a partnership in land,[8] or the sale of a supposed title of A. in lands held in the name of B., though B.'s title is in fact *bona fide* and valid against all the world.[9] When, after A.'s equitable title in land situate in · Philadelphia, of which B. holds the legal title, is extinguished by B.'s conveyance to C., at A.'s direction, (C. having no knowledge of A.'s equity,) taxes are assessed, which become a first lien on the land, and a levy and sale in execution of A.'s title then takes place, on a judgment recovered before the origin of his equity, and, therefore, not a lien on it, the lien of the

[1] Northern Liberties *v.* Swain, 13 Pa. St. 113; Janney *v.* Harlan, 3 Cl. 230.

[2] City of Philadelphia *v.* Cooke, 30 Pa. St. 56; Myer *v.* Burns, 4 Phila. 314; Smith *v.* Simpson, 60 Pa. St. 168; City *v.* McGonigle, 4 Phila. 351.

[3] Foy's Estate, 11 Phila. 106, 2 W. N. C. 188; Wallace's Estate, 59 Pa. St. 401.

[4] Steel's Appeal, 86 Pa. St. 222.

[5] Commissioners of Spring Garden's Appeal, 8 W. & S. 444

[6] Moroney *v.* Copeland, 5 Wh. 407; Vanarsdalen's Appeal, 3 W. N. C. 463.

[7] Moroney *v.* Copeland, 5 Wh. 407.

[8] Vanarsdalen's Appeal, 3 W. N. C. 463.

[9] Fisher *v.* Lyle, 8 Phila. 1.

taxes assessed subsequently to C.'s purchase, is divested, the proceeds being sufficient to satisfy them.[1] When an estate in remainder in land is sold under a personal judgment against the remainderman, the lien of taxes assessed against the life-tenant is not divested.[2]

§ 869. Under the act of April 5th, 1849, regarding Allegheny City, assessments for the grading and paving of streets are made liens till fully paid. The act of February 3d, 1824, was extended to Allegheny county by the act of April 5th, 1844. Under these acts, an orphans' court sale divests claims for grading and paving, when the proceeds of the sale are sufficient to pay them.[3]

§ 870. If the sale takes place on the lien itself, it will be divested, though the proceeds are insufficient to satisfy the claim, and are applied to another lien of the municipality.[4] If a sale takes place on a municipal claim, subject to a mortgage, the vendee cannot afterwards, when the same lot is sold under the mortgage, claim a part of the proceeds by virtue of an assignment of so much of the municipal claim on which the lot had been sold to him, as was not paid by the proceeds.[5] If there are two liens belonging to the same municipality, a sale on one does not divest the other, unless the proceeds are sufficient to satisfy both.[6]

---

[1] Dungan's Appeal, 88 Pa. St. 414.

[2] Philadelphia v. Hepburn, 36 Leg. Int. 105.

[3] Allegheny City's Appeal, 41 Pa. St. 60.

[4] Philadelphia v. Meager, 67 Pa. St. 345; Moyamensing v. Shubert, 1 Phila. 256.

[5] Brinton v. Perry, 1 Phila. 436. An extinction of the lien, however, is not an extinction of the debt. City of Philadelphia v. Cooke, 30 Pa. St. 56.

[6] Philadelphia v. Meager, 67 Pa. St. 345. In City v. Lewis, 4 Phila. 135, a lien was filed, on which judgment was recovered January 20th, 1855, and the property was sold for one-third this judgment. Meantime, taxes were assessed for the year 1854, for less than the proceeds of this sale, a lien for them was filed in 1858, a judgment obtained in 1859. This judgment, and a lev. fa., were subsequently set aside by the court, on the ground that the proceeds of the first sheriff's sale would have satisfied the taxes, and ought to have been applied to them.

§ 871. Under a statute providing that a judicial sale shall discharge taxes or municipal liens only to the extent to which the proceeds of the sale are sufficient to satisfy them, the sheriff's vendee takes the land encumbered with the residuum of the lien, after proper application to it of the purchase money.[1] So was it with registered taxes of the city of Philadelphia for the years 1857, 1858 and 1859, when the sale, which took place in 1860, produced enough to pay those of 1857 and a part of those of 1858 only.[2] Taxes, rates and levies in Titusville, though a lien till fully paid, are discharged by a judicial sale, to the extent to which the money produced at the sale is sufficient to satisfy them.[3] So are the municipal liens of the city of Pittsburgh, under the act of January 6th, 1864, [P. L. 1131,] which contains a similar provision.[4] Taxes for city and county in Allegheny City were divested by a sale on a mortgage executed before they were assessed.[5] If taxes are assessed before the sheriff's sale, they must be paid from the proceeds.[6] The proceeds of land sold on petition of the widow of a decedent, in assignment of her dower in the orphans' court, were applied to taxes assessed for the two years preceding the sale.[7]

Mechanics' Liens.

§ 872. If, on one of several claims growing out of the same process of erection of a building, a sheriff's sale takes

[1] Townsend v. Prowattain, 31 Leg. Int. 28. On a second sheriff's sale the remainder of the lien is payable. If the proceeds of the first sheriff's sale are enough to satisfy the municipal lien, a subsequent sale on the lien is not valid, unless these proceeds were consumed in paying liens prior to the municipal lien; and the purchaser at the second sheriff's sale must show this. Smith v. Simpson, 60 Pa. St. 168.

[2] Duffy v. Philadelphia, 42 Pa. St. 192.

[3] Eaton's Appeal, 83 Pa. St. 152; Appeal of Second National Bank of Titusville, 85 Pa. St. 528.

[4] Pittsburgh's Appeal, 70 Pa. St. 142. Comp. Spring Garden's Appeal, 8 W. & S. 444.

[5] Germania Savings Bank's Appeal, 91 Pa. St. 345.

[6] Camac v. Beatty, 5 Phila. 129.

[7] Steel's Appeal, 86 Pa. St. 222.

place, the lien of all the other mechanics' claims, originating
in the same way, is necessarily divested,[1] and a *sci. fa.* cannot
be subsequently supported on them;[2] but the costs already
accrued on a *sci fa.*, though no judgment has been rendered,
are payable from the proceeds.[3] For the erection of a
barn, begun November 6th, 1824, there were claims for ·
carpenters' and masons' work, filed April 2d, 1825, for work
done respectively on November 16th, and December 23d,
1824. On judgments recovered on other debts on March
23d and 25th, 1825, a sale took place of the whole farm.
The mechanics' liens binding the barn only, were divested,
and a first lien on its proceeds.[4] A sale on a judgment[5] or
on a mortgage,[6] (although whether its lien is anterior or posterior to the mechanics' liens is, at the time of sale, doubtful,[6])
divests these liens. *A fortiori*, when the sale is on a mortgage earlier than the commencement of the improvements;
a claim filed after such sale, for materials furnished before
it, will be stricken off.[7] A sale on a judgment for arrears of
ground-rent, will divest mechanics' liens arising from the
erection of a building by the ground-tenant.[8]

Judgments.

§ 873. A judgment, the first lien, immediately followed by
a mortgage, is divested by a sale under the mortgage.[9] So
is a judgment against A., who afterwards alienes his land to
B., by a sale on judgments subsequently recovered against
B.[10] A sale on a judgment against the owner of an undivided

[1] Barnes' Appeal, 46 Pa. St. 350.
[2] Anshutz v. McClelland, 5 W. 487;
Matlack v. Deal, 1 M. 254; Johns v.
Bolton, 12 Pa. St. 339.
[3] McLaughlin v. Smith, 2 Wh. 122.
[4] Werth v. Werth, 2 Rawle 151.
[5] Diller v. Burger, 68 Pa. St. 432;
Fordham's Appeal, 78 Pa. St. 120;
Pennock v. Hoover, 5 Rawle 291;
Buckley's Appeal, 48 Pa. St. 491;

Perigo v. Vanhorn, 2 M. 359; Den-
kel's Estate, 1 Pearson 213.
[6] Parish's Appeal, 83 Pa. St. 111.
[7] Eldridge v. Madden, 7 W. N. C.
226.
[8] Fox v. Ketterlinus, 10 W. N. C.
506.
[9] Horning's Exr.'s Appeal, 90 Pa.
St. 388.
[10] Commonwealth v. Alexander, 14
Serg. & R. 257

fractional interest in land divests from it a judgment against a former owner which bound the entire land, prior to its division among co-tenants.[1] Judgments against a tenant in common are, on partition of the land in the orphans' court, and allotment thereof to another co-tenant, payable out of the owelty due the defendant; their lien is merged in that of the owelty. When this is paid, the lien of the judgment is extinct.[2] Prior to the act of 1848, the husband had a life-estate in the lands of his wife. A.'s wife, being a widow of a former husband, a judgment against A. became a lien on his life-estate in his wife's life-estate in the land of her deceased first husband. This land was sold in partition, and a month afterwards the interest of A. therein was sold on the judgment obtained against him. The vendee was entitled to the annual payments secured to the widow, in the proceedings in partition. The sale in partition merged the lien of the husband's judgment into the rent which represented the dower.[3] A judgment against an accepting heir or his alienee, was divested by a sale in partition, on petition of the widow, there being one heir only.[4] If, in partition, there is an allotment of distinct but equally valuable parts of the land in severalty to the different co-owners, the lien of a judgment against one of them is concentrated upon the part allotted to him, and discharged from the purparts of the others.[5] A sale under a judgment, not itself a lien, divests all prior judgments.[6]

§ 874. Land was taken by a railroad under the act of 1849, and damages were assessed, and a judgment entered therefor in favor of the owner. The forty-third section of this act, which declares that such damages shall forever remain a lien

[1] Hildebrand v. Wertz, 1 L. Bar, 22d January, 1870.

[2] Diermond v. Robinson, 2 Y. 324.

[3] Bachman v. Chrisman, 23 Pa. St. 162.

[4] Steel's Appeal, 86 Pa. St. 222.

[5] Bavington v. Clarke, 2 P. & W. 115. Comp. McCandless' Appeal, 10 W. N. C. 563.

[6] Kelhoffer v. Herman, 6 Phila. 308; Kerr's Appeal, 92 Pa. St. 236.

on the road, prevented the divestiture of the judgment by a sale on a mortgage of all the road, rights, franchises, etc., of the company, which took place before the commencement of the steps to obtain an assessment of damages.[1] The same result happens if the judgment for damages is obtained before the sale.[1]

§ 875. A judgment obtained for a debt which is likewise secured by a mortgage, is not divested when the mortgage itself would not be. A sale on a second judgment succeeding a first mortgage, did not divest the intermediate judgment for a part of the mortgage debt, the other part being not yet due.[2] When the sale took place on a judgment immediately following a first mortgage, a succeeding judgment on a bond for which the mortgage was collateral security, was not divested.[3] But, when A. sold land to B. for $2,400, taking a mortgage for $1,900, and a judgment note for $500, on which judgment was entered the day following the recording of the mortgage, which was the first lien, a sale on a later judgment divested the judgment for $500; it was not a part of the mortgage debt.[4]

Recognizances in Orphans' Court.

§ 876. A sale on a judgment recovered against a decedent in his life-time, of land taken by an heir in partition, will divest the recognizance of the heir, though the debt represented by it be not extinguished;[5] so, if the sale is on a judgment obtained against the administrator of the decedent for a debt of the latter.[6] An orphans' court sale, for the payment of his debts, of the lands of the heir, accepted by him in partition of his ancestor's estate, divests the recognizance entered into by him to secure the owelty

---

[1] Western Penna. R. R. Co. v. Johnston, 59 Pa. St. 290.

[2] Commonwealth v. Wilson, 34 Pa. St. 63.

[3] Kuhn's Appeal, 2 Pa. St. 264; Cross v. Stahlman, 43 Pa. St. 132; Shryock v. Jones, 22 Pa. St. 303.

[4] Cummings' Appeal, 23 Pa. St. 509.

[5] Commonwealth v. McIntyre, 8 Pa. St. 295.

[6] Commonwealth v. Hantz, 2 P. & W. 333.

of his co-heirs.[1] If the heir has conveyed the land accepted by him in partition, to another, a sale by the orphans' court for the payment of the debts of the alienee, discharges the recognizance;[2] the same result follows on an orphans' court sale for debts, of the interest of one to whom the heir has devised the land. A sheriff's sale on a judgment against the accepting heir, discharges his recognizance from the land sold,[3] except so much of it as secures the widow's dower, she living at the time of the sale.[4] When, at an administrator's sale under the order of the orphans' court, for the payment of the decedent's debts, the purchaser gives a recognizance to secure the purchase money, and subsequently, he dying, an orphans' court sale of the land takes place for the payment of his debts, such sale divests the lien of the recognizance.[5]

Sheriffs' Recognizances.

§ 877. A sale on judgments against A., recovered after he has become surety in a sheriff's recognizance, does not divest the lien of the recognizance, since the amount ultimately payable on the recognizance is uncertain.[6] The same principle applies as to the sheriff's own land; a sale on judgments against him subsequent to his recognizance, leaves it still binding the land. Hence, a surety who had paid for his defaults, was prevented from claiming re-imbursement from the proceeds.[7] A sale on an earlier lien than the recognizance will divest it. Hence, if, after sale on a mortgage executed by a sheriff before he became such, a *sci. fa.* is sued out on his recognizance, and the vendee under the

---

[1] Gilmore *v.* Commonwealth, 17 Serg. & R. 276. Here the land was bought at the orphans' court sale by a surety in the recognizance. Hillbish's Appeal, 89 Pa. St. 490.

[2] Crawford *v.* Crawford, 2 W. 339.

[3] Kelchner *v.* Forney, 29. Pa. St. 47; Hartman's Appeal, 21 Pa. St. 488.

[4] Baily *v.* Commonwealth, 41 Pa. St. 473; Connelly *v.* Withers, 9 L. Bar 117.

[5] Ramsey's Appeal, 4 W. 71.

[6] McKensey's Appropriation, 3 Pa. St. 156.

[7] Hoffman's Estate, 2 Pearson 157

mortgage is cited as *terre-tenant*, judgment must be given for the *terre-tenant*.[1] A sale of the sheriff's land under a judgment recovered on his recognizance, against him and his sureties, divests it from that land. If the price brought at the sale is not less than the penalty of the recognizance, the lands of the sureties are discharged.[2]

Lien by Deed.

§ 878. When a charge is made in a deed by which land is conveyed, to be paid on the death of A. and B., a sheriff's sale of the land on a later judgment, A. and B. being both dead, will divest it; if made before their death, the charge would not be divested.[3] When A., by deed, conveyed land to B., charged with $1,000, the interest of which was to be paid annually to A. during his life, and, at his death, the principal sum to C., a sheriff's sale of the land on a judgment against B., during A.'s life-time, did not divest the $1,000 charge;[4] nor did a sale, during the life of B., of land charged with the payment of a sum of money to A., after B.'s death, divest it.[5] When a deed recited that the conveyance was subject to the payment of a certain mortgage for purchase money, of the same date, and such mortgage was in fact made, and the grantee subsequently conveyed to another, against whom a judgment was recovered, a sale on this judgment divested the lien of the deed and of the mortgage.[6] A., against whom was a judgment for $881.31, conveyed his land, bound by its lien, to B., the deed containing the clause "this deed is made subject to a mortgage against the above-described premises held by C., balance due $881.31." No mortgage in fact existed, and the lien of the judgment was not revived. A sale on a mortgage executed by B. to D., divested the lien

---

[1] Spang *v.* Commonwealth, 12 Pa. St. 358.

[2] Commonwealth *v.* Montgomery 31 Pa. St. 519.

[3] Strauss' Appeal, 49 Pa. St. 353.

[4] Dewalt's Appeal, 20 Pa. St. 236; Heist *v.* Baker, 49 Pa. St. 9.

[5] Bear *v.* Whisler, 7 W. 145.

[6] Stewartson *v.* Watts, 8 W. 392.

of the deed, and no action could be sustained against the sheriff's vendee by A.'s judgment creditor.[1] A father, by writing, "bargained and sold" to his son, a tract of land, the articles at their close saying it was mutually understood and agreed that the son was to support his father and mother during their lives, and that, at the decease of both, the land should be the property of the son. A sheriff's sale on a judgment against the son during the life of the mother, but after the death of the father, did not divest the duty of support of the mother from the land.[2]

[1] Pierce v. Gardner, 83 Pa. St. 211.   [2] Loudermilch v. Loudermilch, 2 Pearson 134.

TABLE OF CASES CITED.

A.

B.

C.

E.

F.

I.

J.

PAGE

N.

P.

Q.

R.

T.

W.

GENERAL INDEX.

GENERAL INDEX.

ATTACHMENT IN EXECUTION—Continued.

ATTACHMENT, ACT OF 17th MARCH, 1869 .... § 460

BAILEE'S LIEN—Continued.

BANK DEPOSITS, LIEN ON

CAPITAL STOCK, LIEN ON

COLLATERAL INHERITANCE TAX, LIEN OF

COUNTY AUDITORS' REPORT, LIEN OF

DEBTS DUE THE STATE, LIEN OF................§ 612

DECEDENTS' DEBTS, LIEN OF....................§ 488

DECEDENTS' DEBTS—Continued.

EXECUTIONS—Continued.

EXECUTIONS—Continued.

EXECUTIONS—Continued.

EXECUTIONS—Continued.

EXECUTIONS—Continued.

FOREIGN ATTACHMENT, LIEN OF .... § 407

ACTS OF ASSEMBLY.

JUDGMENTS—Continued.

JUDGMENTS—Continued.

JUDGMENTS—Continued.

JUDGMENTS—Continued.

JUDGMENTS—Continued.

JUDGMENTS—Continued.

JUDGMENTS—Continued

JUDGMENTS—Continued.

JUSTICES' DOMESTIC ATTACHMENT .... § 455

JUSTICES' EXECUTION ATTACHMENT .... § 402

JUSTICES' FOREIGN ATTACHMENT .... § 450

LANDLORD'S LIEN ON GOODS, &c.—Continued.

MECHANICS' LIENS ....§ 1

MECHANICS' LIENS—Continued.

MECHANICS' LIENS—Continued.

MECHANIC'S LIENS—Continued.

MECHANIC'S LIENS—Continued

MECHANIC'S LIENS—Continued.

MECHANIC'S LIENS—Continued.

MECHANIC'S LIENS—Continued.

MECHANIC'S LIENS—Continued.

MECHANIC'S LIENS—Continued.

MORTGAGES, LIEN OF ....§ 76

MORTGAGES—Continued.

MORTGAGES—Continued.

MORTGAGES—Continued.

MORTGAGES—Continued.

MORTGAGES—Continued.

MORTGAGES—Continued.

MORTGAGES—Continued.

MORTGAGES—Continued.

MUNICIPAL LIENS—Continued.

MUNICIPAL LIENS—Continued.

MUNICIPAL LIENS—Continued.

PARTITION, LIENS ARISING FROM .... § 632

PURCHASE MONEY, LIEN OF .... § 628

RECOGNIZANCE IN ORPHANS' COURT .... § 554

RECOGNIZANCE IN ORPHANS' COURT—Continued.

RECOGNIZANCE OF SHERIFFS AND CORONERS, § 574

SUBROGATION TO LIENS—Continued.

SURPLUS BONDS, LIEN OF............................§ 626

TAXES, LIEN OF ....§ 637

TAXES—Continued.

TAX COLLECTORS' ARREARS, LIEN OF ....§ 614

TESTAMENTARY LIENS ....§ 533

WAGES—Continued.